Ephemeral City: *Cite* Looks at Houston

Ephemeral
City

Cite Looks at Houston

Edited by **Barrie Scardino**, **William F. Stern**, and **Bruce C. Webb**

Foreword by Peter G. Rowe

 University of Texas Press, Austin

This publication was made possible through the cooperation and support of the Rice Design Alliance.

It was also prepared with support from

Anchorage Foundation of Texas
Houston Endowment Inc.
Barbara J. Amelio
Alfred Glassell III and Marli Andrade
Lynn and Bill Herbert
Louisa Stude Sarofim
Mr. and Mrs. Wallace S. Wilson

First edition, 2003

Requests for permission to reproduce material from this work should be sent to Permissions, University of Texas Press, Box 7819, Austin, TX 78713-7819.

♾ The paper used in this book meets the minimum requirements of ANSI/NISO Z39.48-1992 (R1997) (Permanence of Paper).

Library of Congress Cataloging-in-Publication Data

Ephemeral city : *Cite* looks at Houston / edited by Barrie Scardino, William F. Stern, and Bruce C. Webb ; foreword by Peter G. Rowe. —lst ed.
p.   cm.
Includes bibliographical references and index.
ISBN 0-292-70187-X (cloth : alk. paper)
1. Architecture —Texas —Houston —20th Century.   2. Urban beautification —Texas —Houston.   3. City planning —Texas —Houston   4. Houston (Texas) —Buildings, structures, etc.   I. Scardino, Barrie, 1945 – II. Stern, William F.   III. Webb, Bruce, 1941 – IV. *Cite* (Houston, Tex.)
NA735.H68E64   2003
711'.4'09764235 —d c21
2003007216

Contents

Foreword

Common and not-so-common depictions of Houston, Texas, suggest a sprawling city that is difficult to define concisely, wears many labels, is at odds with urban development practices in most other parts of the United States, is risk-taking almost to the point of possessing a "cowboy mentality," and is hot, humid, flat, and wedded to oil interests. The tenor and tone of much of this excellent anthology of articles from the magazine *Cite*, especially with regard to "the idea of the city" and "places in the city," also describe Houston, variously, as being built largely by private interests, as an exercise in light-handed planning with a paucity of development restrictions, and as an inchoate community with little public space and suburban neighborhoods as pass-through settlements. Indeed, for many who live there or have lived there for any length of time, it is difficult to argue with these perceptions, in spite of the comfort and local familiarity also experienced there by a great many. As an ephemeral city, the title of this volume suggests, Houston often appears enigmatic and meta-morphosing, a city "slipstreaming through space in pursuit of a million individual dreams and destinations" as it "melts, flows, and congeals in new configurations," as Bruce Webb notes in his introduction.

Houston is, however, largely a late-20th-century city about which it might also be ventured that time and space have come together in ways — coincident with this epoch — that are both unusual and inherently dis-ruptive to more conventional notions of place and its role in identity con-struction. If one turns the question of ephemerality around and asks what it is about the city that is somehow less changing and more permanent, several aspects present themselves as emphatically as the ephemera.

First, Houston is relatively low-lying, climatologically challenged, and flood-prone. Second, Houston remains a metropolis of expanding freeways and roadway networks, seemingly in search of fictionless horizontal mobility and unfettered land development. Third, Houston is a major nexus, if not the major nexus, for the servicing, processing, and flow of petrochemical materials and associated capital that form its lifeblood and that of a significant portion of the nation's industrial complex downstream. Either singly or in combination, all three phenomena — or permanences — can involve and have involved substantial temporal displacements of space. They have been and remain rather constantly de-territorializing in their effects on Houston's spatial terrain and, as such, may be seen as a sort of firmament from which arise the more ostensible ephemera — or less long-lasting traces of particular forms of building and settlement described in this volume.

To be sure, floods come and go, resulting in destruction, urban modification, and reconstruction. Gradients of transportation accessibility change focus, producing further locational advantages for some and relative disadvantages for others. Material and capital flows rise and fall and, with them, the vicissitudes of daily life for many and the temporal opportunities to adorn the city with symbols of individual and collective aspiration. Indeed, it is this ever-present and unvarnished capacity for destabilization and shape-shifting that makes Houston unique. Rather than place being fundamental to individual and shared identity, it would seem that registrations of space-time dynamics and the prospect of change and of getting ahead in the world are more determining for Houstonians, imbuing their city with a rest-lessness, temporary familiarity, espousal of individuality, and lack of concern for preservation, as well as much else among the paraphernalia of traditional city-building.

Probably because of this firmament, which can result in a persuasive anything-seems-possible attitude, Houston has also been graced by many remarkable works of architecture from an unusually large group of dis-tinguished and renowned architects. As early as 1976, Ada Louise Huxtable of the *New York Times* commented on the unprecedented wave of contemporary buildings — many of them exemplary — and for some well-known architects like

Philip Johnson, Houston has been an arena of rather constant production, in his case dating from the Menil House in 1950, followed by additions to the University of St. Thomas campus, the Pennzoil Tower, the Transco Tower, and the University of Houston's College of Architecture.

Certainly, Houston has served as something of a mecca for bold and new forms of commercial architecture. The city has also been the scene of its own interesting and evolving production of domestic architecture, including townhouses from the late 1970s and 1980s, single-family houses of distinction, and, more recently, extensive inner-city renewal close to downtown. In addition to Johnson and Kevin Roche, other enduring and internationally known architects who have added, over time, to the "Houston Collection"—because, in a sense, that is how it might be regarded—include Mies van der Rohe, Renzo Piano, Rafael Moneo, Skidmore Owings & Merrill in several incarnations, Ulrich Franzen, Cesar Pelli, Ricardo Bofil, and I. M. Pei, not to mention local heroes like William Caudill, Anderson Todd, Hugo Neuhaus, and Howard Barnstone.

Clearly, decisions about what to include and, by the same token, what to exclude, in an anthology that spans 20 years of *Cite* magazine's vibrant and timely publication are difficult. Nonetheless, the editors of *Ephemeral City* in their selection have rendered verbal and illustrated portraits of Houston's urbanism and architecture that admirably cut across time and the historical circumstances of the contemporary city while extending particular attention to episodes of development and architectural production that have stamped Houston's landscape as distinctive, if at other times elusive. Also, by being a nonlinear or otherwise not overly interrelated collection of portraits, the selection stays true to the central purpose of *Cite*, which is to exert influence by filling the void in architectural criticism and commentary in the local press, rather than by treating Houston as an object of theoretical and, one would suspect, arcane speculation. Wittingly or not, this volume also serves another function, and that is to provide a well-referenced archive of cases and commentary of value to scholars of the contemporary American city, away from the well-trodden domain of the East and West coasts. On all counts, *Ephemeral City* is a welcome contribution.

Peter G. Rowe
Dean, Faculty of Design
Harvard University

Preface

For the past 20 years, *Cite* has been an unofficial chronicler of Houston's architecture and its iconoclastic urban culture. This volume brings together articles from that oeuvre that we believe form a portrait of a dynamic city — and one that is frequently misunderstood.

Houston's emergence as an important American city is a relatively recent development. Growth and a pervasive sense of newness during the last quarter of the 20th century became hallmarks of the city. In 1984 an American Institute of Architects urban design assistance team visited the city and noted with astonishment that between 1974 and 1981 the city produced enough new jobs to attract nearly 50,000 new residents, and, over that same period, per capita income jumped 108 percent. From 1975 to 1985, office space increased by 100 million square feet in more than 1,000 new buildings. "Houston," the AIA report concluded, "was viewed across the country as something of an economic miracle." By the time *Cite* published its first issue in 1982, Houston was approaching 600 square miles in area; border to border it stretched 25 miles.

By sponsoring *Cite*, the Rice Design Alliance (RDA) gave voice to critical observation of Houston during this remarkably dynamic period in its history. *Cite* became part of the broad spectrum of programs of RDA, a nonprofit organization dedicated to the advancement of architecture, urban design, and environmental quality, particularly in the Houston area. David Crane, then dean of architecture at Rice University, founded RDA in 1972 to address Houston's lack of civic interest in planning and urban design. Hardly anyone was discussing publicly what was being built, what ought to be built, or what the city as a whole should be. Crane rounded up other academics and architects, and his fledgling group began to sponsor public forums and lectures. They addressed big issues such as land use, mass transit, preservation, zoning, air quality, and flood control.

RDA's activities have grown in the past 30 years to include public lecture series featuring architects and critics from around the world; architectural tours both in and outside of Houston; public forums on significant civic issues; design charettes and competitions; architectural and photographic exhibitions; and a grants program to encourage speculative projects and research on Houston.

Cite was a natural outgrowth of RDA. Its first editorial committee consisted mainly of RDA members from the city's two universities; although they had little publishing experience, they held a belief that Houston was a worthwhile subject for critical discussion. Not only did the local press fail to cover architecture and planning, the national press misunderstood Houston, finding it at best an anomaly and at worst an example of the City Bad, a place away from which urban progress would be measured. Indeed, "Houstonization" was coined as a pejorative term for uncontrolled, speculative sprawl.

Houston was, in fact, a wild, confusing place. It was (and remains) the only large American city without zoning, and, as British critic Reyner Banham observed, it had a reputation as a place where "property wheels and deals with fewer restrictions than anywhere else in the Anglo Saxon world." As a result, an extraordinarily high level of building activity brought noted architects (usually from out of town) to try new ideas, which in turn helped to focus more attention on the city.

To the founders of *Cite*, Houston was neither good nor bad, but it was fascinatingly young, loose, misbehaving, audacious, and unique. Unlike older, well-established cities, it was still in the process of forming, still seeking what kind of city it would become. Giving the new publication an appropriate name was not easy. The founders felt that "The Architecture and Design Review of Houston" alone seemed irredeemably dull. "Sprawl" was rejected because it seemed ubiquitous for all Sun Belt cities. "Radar," an imperfect acronym for Rice Design Alliance Architecture Review, finally lost out to *Cite* (pronounced "sight"), a name rife with homonyms and ripe for puns. Columns and departments abound: CiteLines, CiteSeeing, Big Cité Beat, CiteSurvey, HindCite, UnCitely, Re:Cite, Out of Cite, and Over-Cite.

The first issue of the magazine, published in August 1982, featured a photograph of a City of Houston manhole lid on its cover, and the lead article, "Trading Toilets: The Subterranean Zoning of Houston," described how the limitation of sewage capacity inside Loop 610 was stifling inner-loop development and encouraging suburban sprawl. The issue set the editorial pattern that *Cite* would follow in future issues with articles on architecture, planning, the urban environment, the city's past, building preservation, and reviews of books and exhibitions.

Cite was sustained by an enthusiastic corps of writers who were also willing to edit and rewrite copy. Mostly *Cite*'s writers demonstrated a tough-love approach, delivering commanding articles and critical commentary on architecture, preservation, and city planning, and frequently ruffling feathers.

Looking back over 20 years it seems to us that *Cite*'s basic ingredient has been its self-regeneration through the breadth and openness of its editorial pattern, a pattern reflected not only in the broad range of subjects covered but also by the variety of people who have served as guest editors. *Cite*'s style and contributor list have been as amorphous as the city it examined. Most writers and guest editors have been architects, and most of those are teachers at the University of Houston or Rice University. But there have also been professional writers and scholars of note, among them John Graves, J. B. Jackson, Karal Ann Marling, David Dillon, Richard Howard, Phillip Lopate, Larry McMurtry, and Rosellen Brown.

Trying to abridge something as diverse as the *Cite* oeuvre has been a daunting task. Believing that order should not precede essence, we began assembling this anthology without preconceptions, except for the notion that this would not be simply a "best of" book, but a book about Houston, one that would give readers a sense of the city. We began by reading the feature articles in all 55 issues, many of them several times. From these readings emerged the plan to organize the book into three thematic sections: "idea of the city," "places of the city," and "buildings of the city." After selecting the articles, we tracked down the authors and invited each of them to write a short update or reflection on their previously published pieces in lieu of our own updates. At the end of each essay we also have provided a bibliography of related *Cite* articles.

Paul Hester's photographs have been essential to *Cite*, and it would be difficult to imagine this book without them. We are grateful that the University of Texas Press also saw it that way and agreed to a generous allotment of illustrations. Hester's photographs are not glamorizing; they capture scenes and situations rather than objects, and ideas more than things. They have amplified, clarified, and vivified *Cite* from its beginning.

Cite has been a group effort, and in the spirit of all amateur efforts, it has been a labor of love. But it could not have persisted without a professional staff, particularly its managing editors: Joel Barna (1982–1983), Linda Sylvan (1983–1995), Ann Walton Sieber (1995–1996), Barrie Scardino (1996–1998), Mitchell Shields (1998–2001), and Lisa Gray (2001–present). Design Directors Herman Dyal (1982–1984), Lorraine Wild (1983–1984), Lisa Bales (1985–1992), and Craig Minor and Cheryl Beckett of Minor Design (1993–present) have ably fulfilled the unenviable task of trying to satisfy a group of architects within the constraints of a limited budget and tabloid format. The formula forced the designers to work outside the mold of glossy architecture magazines. Except for the stunningly beautiful issue (summer 2000) devoted to color photographs by Alex S. MacLean, *Cite* has been decidedly unglossy and mostly black and white, spanning a period of transition from hand-cut and hot-wax practices, where pages were true pasted-together collages, to the computer age, when page layouts can be changed and changed again with lightning speed. Relying on the talent and ingenuity of its designers, the quality of its photography, and a freewheeling approach whereby the publication is graphically reinvented from issue to issue, *Cite* has presented itself in a bold graphic style that has earned several design awards.

Cite has been mostly sustained by the Rice Design Alliance, but generous grants from a number of sources have allowed the publication to raise its sights. Among these benefactors are the Brown Foundation, the Susan Vaughan Foundation, the Anchorage Foundation of Texas, Houston Endowment Inc., Sara H. and John H. Lindsay, the Turner Charitable Trust, the Texas Commission on the Arts, and the City of Houston through the Cultural Arts Council of Houston/Harris County. Six grants from the National Endowment for the Arts have supported enhanced stipends for writers in special theme issues.

Many people have been instrumental in bringing this long-anticipated book to fruition. The Rice Design Alliance board and three of its presidents, Marjory Alexander, Larry Whaley, and Jim Burnett were immediate and continually enthusiastic allies. Their support reinforced our confidence in the success of the project. Writers and photographers whose work is represented here have been gracious in granting permissions for republishing and providing updates.

In addition, we would like to thank those who generously supported this publication: Houston Endowment Inc., Alfred Glassell III and Marli Andrade, Lynn and Bill Herbert, Louisa Stude Sarofim, and Mr. and Mrs. Wallace S. Wilson. We would also like to recognize those who participated in making *Ephemeral City* a reality: Catherine H. Chase, Kevin Roche John Dinkeloo and Associates; Lisa Cuccia, Friends of Hermann Park; Margaret Culbertson, University of Houston Architecture Library; Farez el-Dahdah; Lisa Gray; Julie Grob, University of Houston Special Collections; Robert Heineman, The Woodlands Corporation; Andrew Hempe, Archives, Houston Public Library; Will Howard, Texas Room, Houston Public Library; William Howze; Mrs. Burdette Keeland; Chris Knapp; Richard Longstreth; Vance Muse, The Menil Collection; William O. Neuhaus; Eddy Roberts, Minor Design; Carrie Rushing; Mary Swift; Carolyn Sylvan; Martie Terry, Randall Davis Company; Doug Weiskopf, Texas Room, Houston Public Library; Kevin Williams, Southeastern Architectural Archive, Tulane University; and Lee Willson.

Foremost, we are indebted to Linda Sylvan, executive director of the Rice Design Alliance, for her able management and assistance with all phases of the project. Linda moved into her present position from the managing editorship of *Cite*. She is so much a part of the publication that we are apt to forget sometimes that she is our publisher and therefore, though she would probably deny it, our designated adult.

In the inaugural issue, *Cite*'s editors wrote in the nervous, future conditional tense, "It is our hope that *Cite* can become a forum for the presentation and criticism of issues unique to the developing city." Five years later, after 18 issues, the editors reflected with some satisfaction that *Cite* still possessed its optimistic desire to reach those who cared about Houston and could make a difference. Somewhat wistfully they added a hope "that *Cite* will always be a place of youthful idealism and that its vitality will never stagnate." And in 1993 Joel Barna, *Cite*'s first managing editor, who went on to edit *Texas Architect*, acknowledged *Cite*'s 10th anniversary thus: "In some ways Houston has started to catch up with *Cite* . . . By clinging to its roots — to the ideas that Houston is not a thing but our ongoing fabrication, and that the city's true story lies in structures hidden by surface events — *Cite* is still creating a necessity for itself."

Probably no one back in 1982 thought *Cite* would still be going after 20 years, since such enterprises usually have remarkably short lives. The fact that it thrives attests to a continuing fascination with Houston and with the challenges of constructing a sense of place in a 21st-century city.

Barrie Scardino, William F. Stern, and Bruce C. Webb
November 2002

IDEA OF THE CITY

Introduction

BRUCE C. WEBB

Cities evolve as collections of circumstances, of real events occurring in real time, as records of how each city dealt with its particular potentials and problems. Each generation of Houstonians has seen the city in a different way. Houston is perhaps the least settled down of cities, always growing, always evolving. Where most cities converge on their past, Houston seems to be running away from its history, all too willing to sacrifice its heritage for future prospects, for the lure of the deal. It's not an easy city to describe, as freelance writer Doug Milburn illustrates in an article on Houston: "From my earliest days of thinking and writing about Houston, I have played a little game. I ask people to describe the city in one word, with one restriction: the word cannot be hot, humid, or flat." His collected responses include "reticulated," " fetid," "boring," "festive," "demanding." "Elusive" is his own favorite: "Take the urban complexities and contradictions, racial and economic, so visible in every other American city, add certain peculiar elements of geography, climate, and history, and you have city as conundrum, chameleon. Hard to pin down. Hard even to perceive."

From the beginning, *Cite* has tried to present Houston more in terms of critical observations than as an object of theoretical speculation. In the first essay of this volume, "Pursuing the Unicorn: Public Space in Houston," novelist Phillip Lopate, a New Yorker who taught in the creative writing program at the University of Houston for several years, reflected on his own stream of experiences as he searched for signs of a public environment. Lopate's observations add up to a revealing critique of a city built largely by private interests and one that has invested very little in creating quality public spaces where people can enjoy and appreciate the collective nature of the city enterprise. Part of the elusiveness in Milburn's characterization of the city is attributable to this formless quality of Houston's in-between spaces and the ways the city reflects a calculus of private speculation rather than of deeply held civic intentions.

"The pell-mell of names that accrues to a city in the course of time is a forceful reminder of metropolitan complexity," wrote cultural geographer Yi-Fu Tuan. "In any large urban center, multifarious interests exist, and each will push for a label that suits its purpose. Over time these nicknames become a part of the *genius loci*." In homage to the most prominent natural features of the city, Houston was for a long time known as "the Bayou City." The name linked Houston to Southern and Gulf Coast cultures similar to some in Louisiana, Texas's neighbor to the east. Houston's natural site and its historical formation recall surrealist Marcel Duchamp's definition of *collage*: "the chance meeting on a non-suitable plane of two mutually distant realities." The non-suitable plane in this case was a jungle of swampy woods in a steamy-hot region of clay-bottom land that shares the 30th parallel with the Sahara Desert.

Water — flowing, drenching, rising, as well as invisibly suspended in the sultry air most of the year — has always been a big part of the city's sensorial *genius loci*. Water has presented both problem and opportunity,

Barrie Scardino writes in her essay "H$_2$Ouston." Indeed, the intricate weave of sleepy bayous that crisscross the city has usually been more of an obstacle than an amenity, necessitating hundreds of perfunctory little bridges to accommodate the expanding network of streets and highways. Lined in concrete following the flood-controlling specifications of the U.S. Army Corps of Engineers, the bayous have lost nearly all of their romantic associations. Instead, they are symbols of the city's abhorrence of natural surface water, a breeding ground for mosquitoes, and a reminder of just how flood-prone and low-lying the city is, particularly during a serious rainstorm.

The two distant realities shaping the destiny of the city were both liquid: first, the Ship Channel, an ambitious waterway dredged almost 50 miles to a depth of 25 feet linking Galveston Bay to an inland port in Houston; and second, the liquid gold discovered at nearby Spindletop. They come together as a callous landscape of refineries and an industrial port in a sullied liquid atmosphere. The thick, soupy ether congealing out of the superheated air causes shapes to lose their starch.

Houston's natural site was never sufficiently endearing to discourage people from remaking it into something more temperate, more accommodating. Houston embraced technology with a can-do ethos that said no problem was so large that it couldn't be altered or fixed. With few prominent natural features such as broad rivers, lakes, or hills, the cityscape is dominated by an artificial topography of freeways, the Ship Channel, and buildings. It emerged in the 20th century as the most air-conditioned city in the world, a city flavored by Texas but not exactly contiguous with it.

The precise metaphor for this big-scale modern engineering appeared in 1964, when the NASA Manned Space Center arrived at nearby Clear Lake, and Houston traded its old-fashioned "Bayou City" name for a new title: "Space City." It also showed off an audacious work of earthbound engineering—the Astrodome, the world's first full-size, fully air-conditioned indoor baseball stadium. To complete the theme, the baseball team's name was changed from the Colt .45s to the Astros, trading an old frontier hero for a new one.

It is hard to talk about Houston without talking about its developer-friendly way of doing business. British architectural critic and historian Reyner Banham, after visiting Houston in the 1970s, described the city as a real-life version of a Monopoly game. To Banham, the decorated condo was the prime game piece for developing a real estate fortune in a place where you only had to answer to the banker. And Houston did, indeed, begin as a real estate invention of the Allen brothers, New York sharpies who successfully promoted the swampy site as the great interior commercial emporium of Texas. As game or city, Houston is both wide open and impenetrable at the same time. "Property wheels and deals there with less restriction than anywhere else in the Anglo Saxon world," Banham wrote. "Los Angeles in the *Chinatown* epoch seemed like a socialist economy by comparison."

Some of Houston's reputation for being something of a renegade city can be attributed to the paucity of developmental restrictions Banham refers to, most notably the city's lack of zoning and its light-handed approach to planning. Houston voters have consistently rejected zoning. But as Stephen Fox points out in his essay "Planning in Houston: A Historic Overview," the generally held view about the city's antipathy toward planning may be oversimplified. Still, planning efforts have tended to be short on vision and long on trying to keep up with the city's burgeoning growth. In *Cite*'s very first issue, in August 1982, an article titled "Trading Toilets" recounted a classic case of how even an unzoned and unplanned city must finally account for the implications of its own growth. A lack of sufficient sewage capacity ("sewer hook-ups," in developer parlance) engendered a building moratorium within the inner city while encouraging development in other areas, mainly outside Loop 610. Thus a default form of planning and zoning that favored sprawl was inspired by the most primitive requirement of city building.

More than anything else, Houston's development as a 20th-century city has been shaped by the automobile. *New York Times* architecture critic Ada Louise Huxtable, when she visited Houston in the 1970s, was impressed by the degree to which the automobile had invaded the Houston experience. She wrote something of a paean to the city's kinetics in which she nicknamed Houston "Freeway City," "Strip City," and "Mobility City." Mobility captures an important part of the Houston spirit and helps explain its congenitally spread-out dimensions. But mobility doesn't entirely explain the devotion to the private automobile, a passion that is an expression of the city's culture of freedom and identity.

From the 1950s on, freeways became the most powerful marks on the Houston landscape, providing the city with determined economic and social partitioning and spawning aggressive commercial development along its flanks. Houston freeways have become, like those in Los Angeles described by Reyner Banham, "a single, comprehensible place, a coherent state of mind, a complete way of life, a fourth ecology." But the freeway is always a victim of its own success, as Joel Barna shows in his essay "The Mother of All Freeways," which looks at Houston's legendary West Loop. One of the busiest stretches of freeway in America, it flows through some of the city's most affluent playgrounds. Having created the conditions of prosperity, the issue became how the already oversized highway could become supersized while at the same time fending off vigorous protests from the freeway's upscale adjacencies.

As it spread spiderweb linkages of concentric and radial lines outward from the *axis mundi* at the city center, the freeway system allowed the city to metastasize in a more or less evenly densified sprawl. Suburban living has been an important part of Houston's growth, and architectural historian Richard Ingersoll describes how freeways became the armatures of suburban development. In his article "Utopia Unlimited," Ingersoll looks at three of Houston's planned suburban communities: The Woodlands, Kingwood, and First Colony. These more coalesced, planned developments have been touted as alternatives to less organized and more ubiquitous sprawl. Far from being the salvation of the city, as the garden city reformers of the 19th and early 20th century thought them to be, Ingersoll finds them to be only marginally better. Like the rest of the city's vast hinterlands, they are wasteful consumers of land and natural resources and reinforce social and ethnic segregation, besides having so little noteworthy architecture in them.

David Kaplan in "Suburbia Deserta" shows how the newer suburbs, too, are vulnerable to economic events and ever-changing lifestyle preferences. Houston's suburban neighborhoods have often been pass-through settlements where older and smaller houses serve as stops on the way to bigger houses in newer subdivisions. But as the city's economy began to unravel in the 1980s, many new suburban developments witnessed foreclosures and empty mini-mansions on streets only a decade old or less. Kaplan shows that thoughtful planning and creating a sense of community can make a difference when a neighborhood finds itself in economic distress.

Development in Houston feels the competing tugs of centrifugal as well as centripetal forces that alternately draw the city's growth pattern out to the perimeter and sometimes back into town again. For most of its modern life, Houston invested in the expanding suburbs, dismantling old forms of urbanization in the city core and reconstructing them in entirely new forms on the perimeter. By the late 1970s, the inner city had shriveled into a socially inert collection of office buildings incongruously matched with the city's legitimate theaters that were gathered tightly together, an island of prosperity surrounded by neighborhoods and older businesses in serious decline. During the 1990s an almost unimaginable shift occurred that refocused attention on the downtown—a mini-boom of loft conversions and townhouses that has transformed a derelict central city area into one of Texas's fastest-growing residential neighborhoods. Joel Barna calls this "Filling the Doughnut" in his essay. High-profile projects helped boost the image of downtown, among them the remodeling of the venerable Rice Hotel, which had stood empty on a prominent corner downtown for some 30 years, and the conversion of the architecturally banal 1960s vintage Albert Thomas Convention Center into a restaurant and entertainment center. A new inner-city baseball stadium, replacing the peripherally located Astrodome, together with an impressive array of performing arts spaces and a new convention center, affirmed a new social prominence for the downtown as a companion to its uptown rival in the Galleria/Post Oak district along the West Loop.

Houston left the 20th century with an astounding 620 square miles in surface area and a voracious appetite for annexing whatever settlements appeared on the horizon, even if the intervening distances seemed decidedly un-urban. As Houston grew it became more and more an urban anomaly, a puzzle struggling to find the difference between building a great city and merely housing a huge population — a choice and a warning recognized as early as 1929 in a report from the City Planning Commission. Entering the 21st century, Houston is still elusive. But as in all modern cities, many of its unique qualities are being dismantled, razed, and marginalized, only to be replaced by generic forms belonging to the heterotopia. It is a case, as Italo Calvino wrote, of how "cities begin to resemble one another in a labyrinth of reflections."

In the modern city, there may no longer be anything like a sense of place as it has been understood in the past but only place metaphors that drift across the city, giving it nicknames. As Japanese architect Atsushi Kitagawara reflected, "The city is not streets, buildings, crowds, and freeways. It's just that metaphorical condition we call the city." In Houston, the idea of the city as an organic, historic *genius loci* is hidden away in the cracks and grooves and margins and in things discovered by looking at a smaller and larger scale than the ordinary. Behind the corporate city reaching for seamless resemblance there are still lazy bayous harboring mysteries as they move in a different time frame from the mechanical pulse of the city of our creation. There is a transformative liquidity of the city as it seems to melt, flow, and congeal in new configurations. There are still distinct chunks of the city's old patchwork quilt that reflect places without names or maps. There is a city of profit-making beyond civic control. There is a city of mobility — always restless, always on the move, slipstreaming through space in pursuit of a million individual dreams and destinations. There is a city harboring space, half-empty, part garden, where a persistent background technology makes temperate machines in the garden. There is a city built around characteristic features of modern life: rapid change, built-in obsolescence, indeterminacy, media orientation, a culture of style and gratification. It is a city literally attacked by time and motion. Its existence is formed in a series of conjunctive episodes that hold onto their relationships for relatively brief periods. In the ephemeral city, time conspires to fashion a sense of place.

Cite 8,
WINTER
1984

Pursuing the Unicorn

PUBLIC SPACE IN HOUSTON

Phillip Lopate

Before diving into this critique, let us quickly rehearse some of the charms of Houston: its spaciousness; its trees; its mysterious no-man's-lands of vacant lots, warehouses, and railroad ties with their darkness-at-the-edge-of-town uncanniness. Indeed, this is a city three-fourths of which sometimes gives the impression of being at the edge of town. "Perhaps only through a kind of inattention, the most benevolent form of betrayal, is one faithful to a place," writes Aldo Rossi.[1] If so, Houston invites fidelity, because it is a strangely non-imposing environment. Part of what makes Houston so lovable is that here you can think without distraction, only marginally attending the not-too-stimulating streets.

Nevertheless, Houston for a city its size has an almost sensational lack of convivial public space. I mean places where people congregate on their own for the sheer pleasure of being part of a mass, such as watching the parade of humanity, celebrating festivals, cruising for love, showing off new clothing, meeting appointments "under the old clock," bumping into acquaintances, discussing the latest political scandals, and experiencing pride as city dwellers.

I am not speaking of Houston's public buildings — its courthouses, schools, welfare centers, prisons, and so on — which I am sure are quite delightful in their own way, but rather of those in-between spaces for the public's enjoyment, such as squares, fountains, monuments, parks, and promenades. These amenities tend to be viewed by residents of older cities as their natural birthright, like geographical features cut by glaciers. On the other hand, those who have only known the new car-culture cities understandably must be impatient with these tiresome nostalgic rumors of fabulous public space as they are of tales of a unicorn. The successes of traditional public space increasingly are acquiring a mythological quality, like fairy tales about powerful grand dukes, titans of industry, or Olmstedian wizards who bear no resemblance to present humanity. But we must remember that these treasured places were neither the result of magic wands nor of glaciers, but of strenuous civic activity by people in the past not unlike ourselves.

We have all sorts of wonderful excuses for any deficiencies of urban design in Houston, which we trot out enthusiastically: the weather; the lack of zoning; the too-rapid boom in population; the scarcity of beautiful natural features; the low-density spread; the prohibitive cost of public space in the present economy; the free-enterprise, anti-tax ethos; the business community's stranglehold on municipal government. While these explanations contain part of the truth, taken

McKinney Avenue, looking west.

singly each appears to be a rationalization. For instance, consider the following. Many South American cities abound in attractive outdoor plazas, though their climates are at least as hot as Houston's. Chicago grew from 300,000 to nearly 2 million between 1871 and 1900 and still managed to provide increased public space. Low density in itself need not preclude the establishment of neighborhood *foci*—witness some Scandinavian cities. (Moreover, downtown Houston is hardly low-density.) A zoning law here would by no means ensure improved public space. Good urban design for the public can still be done economically, as demonstrated by the new Battery Park City promenade in Manhattan. Houston has got plenty of untapped natural beauty. Oligarchical control of city governments is the rule, not the exception.

We cannot blame greedy capitalism per se for the underdevelopment of public space. On the one hand, socialist governments have not produced a noticeably better record in this area. On the other, profit-motivated developers elsewhere have been quick to seize on the strategy of creating attractive public squares as a drawing card for their speculative property. Both London and New York have wonderful such squares that continue to benefit generations of city dwellers though long ago lining speculators' pockets. Nowhere does it say that the making of good public space must be motivated only be idealism. Indeed, Rockefeller Center, one of the most profitable real estate gambles in history, sold itself from the beginning as a contribution to the public weal and included enough public space to back up the claim. Closer to home, the Water Gardens of Fort Worth—surely one of the happiest public magnets built recently, drawing a mix of social classes and putting them in a good mood (the one recent work by Philip Johnson that does not invite endless reservations)—also happen to be the hub of a newly developing area ringed by luxury condos, convention center, and a Hilton Hotel.

THE NEED FOR PUBLIC SPACE

When it comes to good public space, Houston approaches the Miesian ideal of "almost nothing." Why should Fort Worth or San Antonio have more to show in this respect? "If the city fathers, the big shots of Houston, had been as civic-minded and as proud of their city as San Antonio's were," offers a local planner, "Houston would be as pretty as downtown San Antonio. Simple as that." Being a relative newcomer, I don't know if this is an oversimplification or the crux of the matter. Nor do I understand why the fortunes that were made in this particular boomtown should have engendered so half-hearted a tradition of civic improvement among its elite. We are not lacking in millionaire-donated hospital pavilions and art museums, but in those gestures that would help to bring the city itself together as a work of art.

Perhaps that much of Houston's population is not only new but transient has a bearing here. Many people use Houston as a stepping-stone to make money quickly and get out of this ugly town. In such an exploitative atmosphere, little thought is given to putting anything back in. I have spoken to native Houstonians who take as a deep insult this rip-off, this sneering violation of their hometown, yet they continue to wear a friendly demeanor. Considering the provocations, Houstonians are a remarkably warm and hospitable people. However, the city itself as a built environment is rather inhospitable, impenetrable, and unfriendly to strangers, because there is so little public space to mediate between private homes and the impersonal corporate world. For all the local media's promotion of Houston as a brash, extroverted cook-off, the outsider is apt to find it a very hidden city, where you need special access, good letters of recommendation, as it were, to begin to uncover its secrets. Every metropolis is finally like that, but there are some that allow the stranger to have the sensation of at least holding the city's throbbing pulse and sharing the best of its personality, merely by inhabiting its public space. Not so Houston.

Public space also has political implications. To the degree that it promotes popular assembly, it raises the potential for, on the one hand, a more direct, participatory democracy, and on the other, anarchic riots. We know that the original seat of Greek democracy was a public square, the agora; medieval and Renaissance cities organized themselves around a marketplace with a communal meeting hall; the American town-hall tradition grew out of this same principle. The toleration of radical orators in Hyde Park and Union Square seems a functional outgrowth of public space.

The public-space tradition is opposed by a strong current of anti-urban thought in America that views crowds as "the mob" or "the herd"; in any case, the enemy of the rugged individualist. Anti-urban values color our Chamber of Commerce religion — Texana. Houston, as the biggest city in a state that is now predominately urban, though it refuses to recognize itself as such, has suffered from this schizoid denial. Its resistance to city planning is partly a way of putting off acceptance of its urban nature and partly a dread of the messy negotiations between conflicting political interests an open planning process necessitates. Houston does not seem to have had much of a town-hall tradition; nor do its democratic institutions at the local community level seem particularly developed. Indeed, the weakness of the neighborhoods politically goes a long way toward explaining the city's shortage of good public space. The creation of public space is the most self-conscious urban act a city can engage in; it signifies a city's maturation through the recognition of its responsibilities to the public right to collectivity.

STREETS

The most basic unit of public space is the street. Has the populace been made to feel it has a right to stroll the streets and that the streets belong to it? Try walking in most neighborhoods of Houston (excluding downtown, which we will get to later). If you are lucky, you will find a semblance of a sidewalk — one narrow square of concrete edged on both sides by grass. After a rain the grass looks like rice paddies, and the concrete is probably cracked, buckled, and in grisly condition. Moreover, it is often only wide enough to walk single file, telling us something about the city's attitude toward walking as a social activity. Even single file, you cannot advance very far without being stopped by a giant puddle, ditch, wall of weeds and vines, the concrete's sudden disappearance, or a fence pushing you onto the road. If you swerve the other way, you will find yourself marching across someone's lawn, where the line between pedestrianism and trespassing becomes paper-thin. This is not only the back streets, mind you, but important thoroughfares such as Bissonnet.

How long can this "City of the Future" get away without putting in decent sidewalks? Outside of downtown Houston, one is not even required to reconstruct a public sidewalk after tearing it up for new construction. Houston's streets give off the blunt message: Don't bother walking. It's not worth it. Take the car. Such a suggestion must be particularly rejecting to citizens who don't have cars. Make no mistake, the shabby condition of our sidewalks is a matter not of neglect but of policy: the sidewalk system will neither be completed nor its present stock repaired as long as the rights of pedestrians are held in such contempt.

What of the rights of streets themselves? I ask not in a fanciful Louis Kahn manner, but in the sense in which "an emphasis on the spatial continuity of the street is an absolute prerequisite for the achievement of urbanity."[2] In Houston, time and again streets are rerouted to dogleg around private homes or office buildings that stand in their way.[3] The result is that oddity of Houston road pattern so confusing to visitors and residents alike: the street that dies in a dead end, only to be reborn with the same name several blocks later, then to disappear, reappear again, etc. In a way, there is something charming about this little hide-and-seek game with its slow, Southern rhythms. The maddening infrequency of street signs and street lamps to read them, or the house numbers, all seem part of the hidden, esoteric, elusive face of Houston. (Or is it a subtle expression of hostility to newcomers?)

I would also invoke the principle of preserving the integrity of the street-wall, if I were not afraid of being laughed at in the Houston context. Here, each owner defends his right to set his building as far off-line as he wants to. The recent setback regulations, which com-pel new buildings to be placed a minimum of 10 feet from the curb, are admirable as far as they go, but what is the point of setback laws when there are no functioning sidewalks to begin with? The next Woodway Canyon may be a little less cheek-to-jowl with its highway, but without the commitment to create more of a walking environment, it will still be a sterile office park, albeit set back to a more orderly starting line.

Whichever way you turn the question, walking and public spaces are deeply intertwined. Great plazas and squares do not bloom in a void; they are fed by the rich pedestrian life of the neighborhood streets around them. What makes Siena's Piazza del Campo work so magnificently, I discovered recently in Italy, was not just the often-reproduced monumental ensemble or the sloping funnel shape, but the circulation pattern of 11 streets leading into it, drawing walkers from the nearby, encircling commercial streets almost inexorably into its magnetic field.

In Houston, the lack of public space inhibits festivity. There is an impoverishment of ceremony, processions, and holiday rituals, because we have not even a modest Piazza San Marco for people to gather. The Galleria is our Fifth Avenue, but you cannot have an Easter parade in a shopping mall. We do have, however, the opening of the Livestock Show and Rodeo in which the city elders ride horseback down Main Street. Here horses and ponies are less out of place than pedestrians.

MONUMENTS AND STADIUMS

Houston is a city without a symbol. You cannot conjure up its image with simply an arch, an Empire State Building, a landmark like the Alamo, an Eiffel Tower. Not that this is necessarily bad. It permits the imagination to roam; and better the honesty of no symbol than a trumped-up logo rushed in to fill the void. Still, there is much talk now of monuments anchoring various neighborhoods. While I doubt strongly that the weightlessness of Houston—its eerie, flat, floating quality—

Jefferson Avenue, looking west.

can be counteracted by a series of anchoring monuments strategically placed (a literal picture of Oldenburg's anchor comes to mind), I applaud the effort and look forward to results. The tricky thing about contemporary monuments is that it seems a little too late in the game for the solemn, patriotic bronze celebrations of civic pride, while the anti-heroic, post-modernist approach still smacks of coyness and calculation.

Monuments are meant to outlive us, to be passed from one generation to the next. In *The Human Condition*, Hannah Arendt's crucial discussion of the public and private realms, she makes the point that love of glory drove powerful men in ancient times to leave behind triumphal arches and other beautifying monuments. This perfectly valid motivation—glory—has been undercut, first by Christian anti-*vanitas* morality, and more recently and seriously, by anxiety about the earth's very capacity to endure, and with it, a shifting of the image of the future to outer space. "Only the existence of a public realm," wrote Arendt, "and the world's subsequent transformation into a community of things which gathers men together and relates them to each other depends entirely on permanence. If the world is to contain a public space, it cannot be erected for one generation and planned for the living only: it must transcend the life-span of mortal men."[4]

The architect Bruno Taut believed that every municipality should have a *stadtkröne* or city crown, a sort of shrine to inspire the rebuilding of society. Our *stadtkröne*, if you will, is the Astrodome. It could indeed become a cult building if the Oilers ever put together a championship season. The Astrodome is a moon rock on a lunar landscape. Built during Houston's love affair with the space program, its forbidden planet iconography has more to do with NASA than baseball. On a hot day, you are well advised upon leaving the stadium to make a beeline for your car. In any case, there is nothing to detain you. The Dome, which could have been the hub of cafés and bars where people gather to discuss the game afterward, is like a giant vacuum cleaner sucking in tens of thousands and a few hours later spitting them out onto the heat-blasted parking lot.

Imagine a city park landscaped over that parking lot, where fathers could take their sons and daughters afterward, where friends could play catch and people lie under the shade trees. At our sports stadiums, though subsidized by tax money, the public is made to feel redundant and unwelcome the moment an event is over. Greenway Plaza is dead late at night. No matter how keyed-up you may be after a basketball game or rock concert at the Summit, you have no alternative but to sit in your car for half an hour, inhaling exhaust fumes and waiting for the opportunity to squeeze into a moving lane of exiting cars. Compare this situation to Madison Square Garden, Wrigley Field, or the Boston Garden, where fans spill directly into the streets and walk off their exuberance or disappointment.

There are so few opportunities in Houston to linger en masse after an event and savor oneself as part of the emotional crowd. Better public transportation would help. Then you would have an alternative to driving; you could walk friends to the next bus/train stop. Mass transit also holds a crowd together. Anyone who has ever taken the train to or from Yankee Stadium on the night of an important game and seen the subway cars fill up with fans can attest to the carnival atmosphere — liberating and sometimes a little frightening. The Astrodome and Summit exit plans prevent any possibility of rampaging teenagers taking over the streets; crowds are dispersed immediately into atomized, separate automobiles. But a city that takes the bigger chance with a crowd's freedom is also the livelier city.

It has been suggested that the true monuments of our age are the freeways. Certainly this is the one public space on which the most money and constructional attention has been lavished. The freeways do give us the vantage point for an urban experiencing of Houston, which is no longer obtainable on foot; and, if ever-increasing density and utilization are marks of successful public space, then our highways are a hit. However, they do not promote interactional conviviality — conversation between citizens may be undertaken only at risk and generally is limited to a few words just preceding and following catastrophe.

DOWNTOWN: TUNNELS, PLAZAS, FOUNTAINS, ARCADES

In a city with few distinguishing landmarks, few real places, the downtown will inevitably be regarded as a quasi-public space. The tragedy of Houston as an urban place (and it only occurred in the last 25 years) is the gutting of its downtown as a multi-use, retail, walking area and its conversion to a single-use, corporate office function. This became inevitable when the old movie

Greenway Plaza, The Underground.

theaters were torn down, many of the small stores scrapped, and freestanding slab towers erected whose street levels were given over to garage entrances or bank lobbies. Now corporate headquarters alternate, for the most part, with surface parking lots, and it is no longer inviting to window shop or even dally downtown. Park, do your business, and get out.

It is regrettable that at the same historical moment Houston moved from being a racially segregated to an officially integrated city, it also converted its old downtown into a more monolithically white-collar (if not white) universe and redistributed its shopping and entertainment functions to outlying malls, where pre-existing residential patterns would reinforce de facto segregation. I do not mean to take away anything from the nobility of that struggle for Houston's integration in the

1960s or to question the genuine gains made since by some minority members in the corporate workplace, but simply to note that the social mix role, which the older sort of downtown might have played, was considerably diluted by these changes. At the same time, the city moved to place one particular type of entertainment downtown whose ticket prices and aesthetics would likely attract only the middle and upper classes — high culture.

There are still pockets of downtown, mostly along Main Street, where the down-and-out hang out, clinging to (and tacitly permitted to retain) certain storefronts and street corners by reasons of historic territoriality. However, the poor almost never venture into the underground tunnel system, which is strictly for the socially homogenized office-staff population. The decision

Paul Hester, 1984.

to put so many of downtown's retail functions below ground — in tunnels built by office buildings — is a key example of the movement away from the public space toward privatization. The tunnels have leeched an entire economy from ground level and taken much of the street life and energy of downtown with them. That would be a fair enough exchange if they were more open to the general public. But whereas any damn fool can happen upon interesting shops while walking daily through a city's streets, you need a guide to take you into the tunnels.[5] Their random growth, in the absence of an overall coordinated construction, has made it very easy to get lost down there. In fact, the only real way you can master the maze and become one of the tunnel cognoscenti is to work downtown.

In some ways, the tunnels are rather congenial. They offer a more urban stream of foot traffic than is found in most parts of Houston; people bump into each other, stop, and chat. The occasional glimpse of a boiler room is like coming upon a construction site. In these minimalist corridors, slight differentiations of material or lighting become giddy refinements, while the sudden entry into plaza-like openings seems a thrilling event. Ultimately, though, it is a mole's life, with vista constrictions that induce a monotonized torpor. Monotonous, too, is the duplication of store offer-

Hester + Hardaway, 2002.

Hermann Square, Reflecting Pool at Houston City Hall.

ings — soup and salad bars, travel agencies, card novelty shops — lopsidedly designed for lunch-hour trade. This lack of merchandising variety ensues from the folly of each office tower trying to be its own self-sufficient city in miniature. No surface downtown retail area could ever get away with so little mercantile specialization or so clone-like and mediocre a level of food quality. But without access to the general public, there is no real spur to excel.

Above ground, most of the so-called plazas, which our office towers extrude like pseudopodia, are sad drawing-board abstractions, hard on the bottom and brutally unshaded — fine places for sculpture, not people. One is grateful for the good sculpture, like the Barbara Hepworth ensemble in front of the First City Tower. But this corner seems donated to the public by the angle of the building's setback and would be much more satisfactory if there were also plenty of tables and chairs with umbrellas or shade trees. As is, it seems ambiguous whether the space is meant to be private (still part of the building) or for the public's enjoyment. The message I get is: pause a moment to admire the art, then keep moving.

In general, corporations do poorly at providing public space. Either their plazas are deserted, or, if they become popular like the one at New York's Seagram Building, security guards are hired to keep off the "undesirables." Corporate plazas cannot be considered true public space, as the urban designer Stanton Eckstut has argued: the only way you are going to get true public space is if the city provides it and maintains it.[6]

A much more useful corporate architectural contribution to the public good in Houston would be the addition of porticos. We have an excellent prototype in the gracious arcade attached to the downtown Texaco Building, with its Guastavino tile vaulting designed by Warren & Wetmore. There is also a rather nice arcaded sidewalk on the Rice Hotel. Think of a downtown Houston arcaded like Bologna (another city with problematic weather), where you could walk along for blocks sheltered from rain or excessive heat, under air-cooled stoas, looking into windows of shops, chancing the elements only at street corners, where a pedestrian tunnel might come in handy. A total fantasy? I can't help thinking that these covered promenades would have been no more costly to build than the underground tunnel system. Of course, the tunnels had the economic incentive of providing another layer of rental real estate. But in the long run, that decision may prove to be uneconomic, since it detracts from downtown's potential viability as an 18-hour-a-day center of commercial activity.

One of the most popular downtown public spaces is around the Hermann Square reflecting pool in front of City Hall. Anything with water has a primitive attraction, as everyone knows. So where are all the fountains in Houston? Of the few I have seen, most double as directional barriers, placed in the middle of traffic circles, undercutting any calming and/or romantic effect they might exert. The nice thing about fountains is that they suggest nature without, like parks, obliging one to abandon one's *flaneur* love of the street, one's whole urban mentality, for metaphors of country and wilderness.

That may be one reason why lunchtime workers are so fond of the reflecting pool — they can enjoy the shade, the water, and the jabbering city scene, making an easier transition to and from their jobs. By contrast, people tend to shy away from nearby Tranquility Park and Market Square. The open greensward of Tranquility Park seems designed more as a visual eye rest for people in offices looking down than for actual enjoyment. Indeed, the underutilization of both Tranquility Park and Market Square has become such an embarrassment that the City Council recently discussed allowing street vendors (perish the thought!) in these two places, if nowhere else. Perhaps the municipal government is beginning to learn what Jane Jacobs taught

Hester + Hardaway, 2002.

Galleria I, interior.

streets and below ground, shuttling from tunnels to their cars? The whole habit of public space has dwindled here.

I still like to believe that the mistakes of downtown Houston are not irreversible. With 40 percent of the workforce situated in this one area, it remains too important a focus of capital and civic identity to be left so uninviting. Perhaps when there is more of a residential mix, and when mass transit is added to the equation, the CBD (central business district) will become a livelier place, night and day.

THE GALLERIA, AND A DIGRESSION ON WEATHER

One area I consistently try to avoid is the Galleria. As soon as I come within sight of its concrete panels, I feel a migraine approaching. Managing to combine the twin nightmares of claustrophobic congestion and anemic vacuity, the Galleria is my idea of hell. The whole Post Oak area around the Galleria is noteworthy for having the most concentration of buildings possible to assemble without achieving anything like an urban texture. Architects are trained to build freestanding objects, but quite apart from whether the object is good or bad, if you keep placing one freestanding object next to another you get a proliferation of objects. What are needed now are not objects so much as places.[7] Houston suffers from this malaise of placelessness, and nowhere more so than in the Galleria area.

Memories of a recent trip to Italy will not leave me

long ago: that a city park that becomes too solitudinously tranquil gets a bad reputation as a dangerous no-man's-land. Besides, Houston is not such a jangling, frantically tense place that it needs zones of quiet everywhere. Quite the contrary, downtown Houston could do with some brash corners that intensify excitement. It is a scandal, in a downtown with such minimal public space, that two of its parks are so underused. But what do you expect when the entire strategy of the new downtown has been to keep people off the alone. I cannot help comparing Houston's Galleria to the famous one in Milan. You enter the Galleria Vittorio Emanuele on foot, crossing over to it as a continuation of a busy square. It has a spatial clarity, which one perceives, even from the outside, as a perpendicular intersection of two elegant avenues placed under a ferrovitreous dome. The curious fact that the indoor buildings facing each other under the dome have exterior façades adds to the sensation that you are still walking in a street — albeit an enclosed one — with sidewalk cafés and people in the apartments above looking down at you.

The Houston Galleria is a suburban mall so turned away from the street that one is advised to enter it from the rear or the basement garage. The sidewalk in front of the Galleria is nothing — a taxi-dumping stop, a ramp at best, cautioning that any other mode of entry but the preferred vehicular one would be perverse. You take your life in your hands if you hoof it across from the Sakowitz side of Westheimer. A raised pedestrian bridge might help, of course.

Once inside, the whole complex presents a disorienting multiplicity of undifferentiated corridors, especially since the addition of Galleria II, so that it is necessary to consult a map to get one's bearings. Again, as with the tunnels, we see a disturbing Houston pattern: the interiorization of city life has led to a confusing, insufficiently inflected space, bland as an airport terminal and negotiable with ease only by those in the know. A disadvantage of indoor corridors compared to outdoor streets is that one cannot see the reassuring building tops of distant avenues; one goes forward wearing blinders in this miniature city that is insulated all too successfully from the real city. Contact with the weather outside is minimized both by climate control and introspective design.

By contrast, if you are sitting or strolling in the Milan Galleria, it is an event to see the heavens open up and a rainstorm gusting just beyond the vaulted entrance. Weather has always stood for nature in cities — the saving reality of that which is out of our control and provokes our amused resignation. It makes for solidarity among the urban mass, a good conversation starter for strangers thrown under an awning. In Houston, however, efforts to immunize the place against its own atmospheric conditions threaten to reach a phobic level.

Everyone knows about the interrelationships between air-conditioning technologies and Houston's building boom. We ought to ask ourselves, though, whether we have overdone this moving of life indoors for comfort, especially since Houston's weather is not so terrible. Actually, it has one of the most pleasant climates of any North American city for seven and a half months, and if the remaining four and a half come close to insufferable, that average is no worse than New York, San Francisco, New Orleans, or London — all excellent walking cities. It seems paranoid to plan only for the few difficult months. Besides, even in August, the evenings usually cool down enough to be walkable. The reason people don't walk in Houston is not because of the weather, but because the streets are too boring and spread out. I do not want to overstate the case. I bow to no one in my hatred of a 95°F, muggy Houston afternoon, with air pollution at the danger level torturing the sinuses. There are times when crossing a large street like Kirby at noon is like *Duel in the Sun*. For this reason, the *sine qua non* of a good public space in Houston will always be shade.

One of the shadiest and most agreeable sections to walk in the city is in Broadacres (laid out in 1922) on parallel blocks of North and South Boulevards with their double lanes of live oaks touching over a pretty brick walkway to filter the sunlight into sunspots. Even on the hottest days, one feels invited to stroll down the esplanade and peek at the mansions on either side (certainly more inviting than in other wealthy divisions, like secretive Shadyside, or Courtlandt Place, which

Broadacres, live oak promenade along South Boulevard.

has recently put up an excluding fence). North and South Boulevards spoil us for the rest of Houston because they make us realize how beautiful a city this could be. Houston's climate is ideal for any number of oak-lined avenues. If only a 10th of the streets looked this way, what ravishment! The glory of Houston is its trees. Yet every time a new activity center is built, this seems to be forgotten. The new is all covered with concrete, which is why those who have never been here picture us a city of concrete. The Astrodome, downtown, the Galleria, and the whole South Post Oak area would be so much more appealing and cosmopolitan if they were somehow pulled together by majestic rows of live oaks.[8]

Parkway along Buffalo Bayou, looking toward downtown Houston.

PARKS, BIG AND SMALL

The most important public space at present in Houston is probably Hermann Park. It is certainly the people's choice. The zoo is one of the few places in town where families of all social strata show off their children on a weekend, and the energy of urban life is both concentrated and mellowed by its surroundings. The Juneteenth concerts at Miller Outdoor Theater provide some of our city's finest hours in the making of community. Still, there is no disputing that "Hermann Park remains a conspicuously underdeveloped scenic and recreational resource,"[9] especially compared to what was meant to be our own Golden Gate or Central Park. The city ought to concentrate on upgrading Hermann Park instead of acquiring more parkland.[10]

One does have the impression that there are not many parks in Houston. This is largely the result of geographical maldistribution: most parkland acreage is located in outlying, low-density areas. Memorial Park is larger than Hermann Park but not as centrally located; nor, for all its size, does it contain the number of insti-

tutional and recreational amenities Hermann Park has. When you subtract Memorial Park's golf course, arboretum, and semi-impassable thickets and swamps, you are left with barely more than a strip on the outer perimeter for convenient recreational use. Memorial Park remains basically a hunk of donated land: it is not yet truly a park in the cultivated, municipal sense of the word, but it does have splendid untapped potential.

Even more promising are the long, hilly (for Houston) grasslands along Allen Parkway that slope down to Buffalo Bayou. They could make a terrific Grande Jette picnic grounds and swimming hole, if the bayou water were ever cleaned up and if the park were not so isolated by the road. How much more pleasant and usable it would be if the neighboring streets were designed to meet the bayou instead of being cut off by a six-lane highway. As it is, more and more people seem to discover this green space each year, especially around the time of the Houston Festival's commendable Bayou Show, an exhibition of site-specific sculpture.

The whole bayou system represents a new juicy

opportunity for Houston. A series of walks along the bayous could dramatically increase public space while creating a boon for tourist trade and commercial development. I realize a developed bayou would pose serious engineering challenges, given the area's flood-control problems, but surely we can figure out something better to do with this network of streams passing through the city than to line them with concrete and make them scenery for passing cars.

Houston has a paucity of small neighborhood parks. In a city of private lawns perhaps there is diminished incentive to build them, thinking there is enough green already. There is also no shortage of vacant lots in the inner city, often the sites of old fires, now held in limbo for speculation, growing waist-high weeds, wildflowers, and beer bottles. If only the city would cajole a few owners to donate their land or could buy it and convert some of these lots into neighborhood parks. As it is, some are probably used now as impromptu, if unsafe, playgrounds.

Bell Park is one of Houston's rare exceptions: an exquisitely landscaped, snug, well-kept garden which has all the civility of a London block park tucked into the urban grid. Its small space seems enlarged by the division into florally distinguished areas with a suggestion of topography, augmented by the Japanese wooden footbridge, which passes over the semblance of a brook. And yet, one never really loses site of the park's modest scale. Albeit a little precious, it is like being in a bonsai garden. We could do with a dozen Bell Parks.

Of course, Bell Park has the luck to be situated in a gentrified section of Montrose, surrounded by museums and townhouses. By comparison, the little neighborhood parks over in the black and Chicano sections of the East Side look untouched by a gardener's hand. Of playgrounds like Emancipation Park in the Fifth Ward, all one can say is that they are absolutely necessary—and essentially unfinished.

In the barrios and the black wards there is more street life, perhaps reflecting cultural tendencies to utilize whatever is at hand as improvised public space. Men and women hang on porches and at corners, bantering, arguing, singing, listening to the radio, practicing jabs—a spectacle for which the rising minority unemployment rate does wonders. While the poor may indeed be better at appropriating their streets as communal recreation space, that is no excuse for assuming their vitality should somehow be made to compensate for the lack of proper parks and facilities. On the other hand, what they do not need is a strategy that would embrace their whole neighborhood in a greenbelt, such as the one the University of Houston seems to be proposing for the area around its central campus, now ominously renamed University Park.

Houston has very little good public space. Yet fragments and models exist, scattered across the cityscape that could reasonably be multiplied: the reflecting pool at City Hall, Bell Park, the Texaco Building arcade, Broadacres, the Bayou Show, Hermann Park's zoo, and Miller Outdoor Theater. We could benefit from more lively gathering places that promote a sense of play, collectivity, ritual, and urbanity. Everywhere two major streets come together could be celebrated with an urban design that concentrated vitality. Instead, these crossroads are usually occupied with gas stations.

Maybe I feel this lack of public space because I come from New York and consequently could be applying an inappropriate standard. Certainly, most native Houstonians do not experience their city as suffering from placelessness. A longtime Houstonian suggested to me the following intriguing thesis: that older cities had more of a need for articulated public space because homes were less comfortable. Houston does offer a much higher standard of domestic comfort for the individual, but far less public space.

Finally, I would be remiss if I did not address an unspoken fear: that providing public space is asking for trouble, because such places can become havens for junkies, rapists, muggers, vagrants, and so on. It is beyond the scope of this essay to disentangle undercurrents of racism and classism from legitimate safety concerns, or to examine the legal and civil rights of junkies, vagrants, etc. to free assembly; or, more problematically, to understand the tricky dynamics by which one public space maintains a healthy diversity and territorial balance among competing users, while another is abandoned by the middle class to what is pejoratively called the underclass. All I can do is reiterate that, in my view, the inhabitants of a city have a right to public space and that the rewards of good public space are so lavish, in terms of fostering a democratic sense of community and a reality of well-being, it seems more than worth the struggle to solve whatever problems might arise from such an effort.

If, as both Hannah Arendt and Richard Sennett (in *The Fall of Public Man*) have argued, mankind has undergone a radical shift toward privatization,[11] and resistance to public life is now embedded at the level of the human condition, then why bother? We have seen the last of good public space in our time. If, on the other hand, the problem is not so profound, then with some goodwill, higher urban-design expectations, and a lot of money, Houston can catch up with other cities in this respect. Money: there's the catch. How will we do it in the present economy? I don't know, but I doubt that Houston is in a worse economic hole than all the cities of the past and present that somehow have found a way. Moreover, Houston is dreaming if it thinks it can reach the status of a world city by cash transactions, without lifting a finger to create inspiring public space.

Notes

1. Aldo Rossi, *A Scientific Autobiography* (Cambridge: MIT Press, 1981), 72.
2. Kenneth Frampton, *Modern Architecture 1920–1945* (New York: Rizzoli, 1983), 213.
3. "This is a condition of post–World War II subdivisions and results from two conflicting principles of then-current city-planning wisdom: subdivisions should have non-continuous streets

to discourage through traffic; street names should be continuous to avoid confusion." Stephen Fox, letter to the author, 1983.
4. Hannah Arendt, *The Human Condition* (Chicago: University of Chicago Press, 1958), 55.
5. I thank Ceil Price for being that able guide.
6. Stanton Eckstut, conversation with author, November 1983.
7. This interpretation was suggested to me by Kenneth Frampton, in conversation, December 1983.
8. I specify live oaks because they flourish in this climate. Palm trees, which provide little shade, have unfortunately become the preferred status symbol in Houston.
9. "Reclaiming Hermann Park," *Cite* 3 (spring 1983).
10. Stephen Fox, "Big Park, Little Plans: A History of Hermann Park," *Cite* 3 (spring 1983).
11. Much as I am drawn to Arendt and Sennett's rise-of-privatization thesis, I wonder how much hard historical evidence there is for this line of thinking, or if public man is, in his own way, just another lost Golden Age myth, a Noble Savage in reverse, with which we torment ourselves. After all, the agora tradition was never so robust that we can blame a whole decline scenario on it.

2002 UPDATE

Although Lopate's discussion of public space, or the lack of it, in Houston appeared in *Cite* 18 years ago, many of his observations still apply. Newcomers to the city continue to register dismay at the paucity of pedestrian accommodations. The most dramatic change has been in the redevelopment of downtown and Midtown. The new baseball stadium has brought new crowds that mix with the theater-district patrons to create some of the camaraderie in Houston's central city that Lopate found missing in Greenway Plaza and the Astrodome. *Editors*

See other articles in this collection: "Filling the Doughnut," "Big Park, Little Plans," "Fair or Foul," "Evolving Boulevard," and "Deconstructing the Rice."

Peter C. Papademetriou in "Houston in the '80s: In Search of Public Places," *Cite* 18 (fall 1987), furthers Lopate's discussion.

Cite 46,
FALL 1999
WINTER 2000

H₂Ouston

Barrie Scardino

Allen's Landing, foot of Main Street, 1910.

In Houston, water has been as much obstacle as opportunity. As both, it has changed the face of the city.
Paris has the Seine; Boston, the Charles; Memphis,
the Mississippi; London, the Thames. Houston has
Buffalo Bayou. Even the little San Antonio River makes
us look bad. Chicago has Lake Michigan, and Houston
has the Lake on Post Oak.

Most great cities are easily identified with some
body of water. The reasons aren't hard to understand.

Until 19th-century industrialization brought railroads
and 20th-century ingenuity perfected the automobile,
watercourses were the fastest and safest means of
transportation for people and cargo. Even more important than commercial reasons for planting a settlement
on a waterway has been the practical human need for
drinking and bathing water. But the most subtle and
perhaps most powerful draw for situating oneself near
some form of water is an emotional one. Poets and

theologians have for all time pondered water as the central life-giving force.

So it was with good reason that Houston's founders greatly exaggerated its water features. In the famous *Telegraph and Texas Register* advertisement of August 30, 1836 (six months before there actually was a town), promoters audaciously claimed that Houston was situated at the "head of navigation" on Buffalo Bayou and went on to say that "tidewater runs to this place and the lowest depth of water is about six feet. It is but a few hours sail down to the bay, where one may take an excursion of pleasure and enjoy the luxuries of fish, fowl, oysters, and sea bathing."

In fact, Harrisburg, at the confluence of Brays and Buffalo bayous just east of Houston, was the closest thing to the head of navigation, if indeed Buffalo Bayou could have been considered a serious navigable waterway. Today, the turning basin of the Ship Channel is near Harrisburg, not downtown Houston. The Allen brothers initially tried to buy the site of Harrisburg, founded in 1822, but were unable to complete a land purchase there. Good promoters that they were, the founders never let on that the site at Buffalo and White Oak bayous was not their first choice.

Although tidewater does technically reach Houston, the water is brackish and in no way aids navigation. Nor was it a pleasant sail from Houston to the bay, given the tangled vegetation and dangerous stumps as well as obstructive overhanging trees draped with bug-infested Spanish moss and snakes. Furthermore, alligators ruled the swampy shores and freely swam wherever they pleased. Galveston Bay did and still does provide the luxuries of seafood and pleasant recreation, but it was not an easy destination from Houston in the early decades.

At the time of its Anglo settlement, Harris County had a substantial watershed from the San Jacinto River and 22 natural streams that included 44 miles of bayous, in addition to uncountable gullies. Once part of the ocean floor, this part of Texas is not sufficiently elevated above sea level to promote effective runoff, and dense clay soils exacerbate poor drainage. The elevation in Harris County rises from zero feet above sea level to barely 100 feet at the northern tip of the county. Rainfall in the Houston area, while not excessive (on average, there are 100 days per year with some rain, for a total of 48 inches) is problematic given the makeup of the vast watershed.[1] So Houston began its history paradoxically touting water features that were, in fact, its main detraction. As this truth dawned on residents who experienced mud and flood almost annually, Houston developed a reputation as a place shaped by water. However, that water has shaped Houston in any profound way is far less intriguing than the way in which Houston has shaped its water.

IN THE BEGINNING

That Houston was founded on myth and greed is no secret. The great mystery is that it succeeded so wildly. One writer has bluntly stated, "Houston has never been so much a maker as a beneficiary of history, and disaster has often served it well."[2] The first of those disasters was the Battle of San Jacinto in 1836, from which the Republic of Texas emerged with the war hero Sam Houston as its president. Harrisburg, the more established and better-located spot for a capital, was destroyed in the fighting. So the Allen brothers, through political manipulation (the usual promises and personal favors), managed to make Houston the Texas capital. The lawmakers and their entourages swelled the infant town for only two years, leaving in 1839 for two reasons: politics and climate.[3] Houston was an impossibly unpleasant and unhealthy swamp.

When Sam Houston was reelected president of the Republic of Texas in 1841, Houston made a bid to move the capital from Austin back to Houston. At issue were the archives of the Republic, which Houstonians believed were unsafe in Austin because of the threat of Indian attack. What became known as the Archives War ensued when the people of Austin bitterly opposed the removal of the archives, seen as symbolic of the whole government, to Houston. On December 30, 1842, a contingent of Houston "soldiers" mounted a secret foray into Austin in which they filled wagons with the archives and escaped under cover of darkness, only to be apprehended by Austinites on the way to Houston. Under armed guard the papers went back to Austin. It was lucky that happened, for in 1843 Houston endured it first major flood, which would have utterly destroyed the archives, as the entire town was submerged.[4]

Despite such problems, Houston devotees, with totally unreasonable optimism, had begun almost from the start planning to deepen and widen the channel of Buffalo Bayou, determined to make their city into a commercial emporium. Since Houston was poorly suited for agriculture (with the exception of rice plantations in northwest Harris County), the settlement attracted merchants and artisans instead of farmers and ranchers. In 1840, Houston received authorization from the Texas Congress to build and maintain wharves, and in 1841 the Port of Houston was established at the confluence of White Oak and Buffalo bayous. For a brief time the port charged wharfage fees and taxed boats using the channel, but it discontinued the practice when it became evident that captains would rather put off goods and passengers at Harrisburg (which had been rebuilt after its destruction during the Battle of San Jacinto) than pay for the privilege of docking in Houston. Sporadic dredging occurred, but only shallow-draft vessels could navigate Buffalo Bayou until after the Civil War.

An 1851 newspaper article summarized the town as a place with a "warm, wet climate, poor drainage and sluggish bayous."[5] After the flood of 1843, drainage ditches were dug throughout the town, which helped somewhat, though ladies still tiptoed across streets and wore dresses permanently mud-stained at the hems. Raw sewage was dumped into the bayous from which Houstonians obtained most of their water. Cisterns and barrels in every yard collected rainwater for household use, but these were not always full. Though Houston held its own, managing to grow and thrive despite yellow fever and cholera epidemics, which were directly linked to wet climate and poor drainage, there was little evidence that the city could realize its vision for a grand future.

But then another disaster, the Civil War, worked to Houston's benefit. Just as the Battle of San Jacinto had destroyed the challenge of Harrisburg, the War between the States gave Houston an advantage over its rival Galveston. Unlike Galveston, Houston was not occupied by federal troops, and Buffalo Bayou provided a fine waterway for blockade running. Houstonians, including William Marsh Rice, made fortunes supplying inland troops. Following the war, Houston, having been spared the devastation that occurred in much of the South, emerged with considerable capital brought to town by war profiteers. Such civic projects as dredging Buffalo Bayou could be comfortably financed. By 1870, it was clear that Houston's relationship with water was based not on recreation or quality of life issues, but on money.

In 1866 Houston municipal officials had established the Houston Direct Navigation Company with the hope of dredging Buffalo Bayou to a depth sufficient for oceangoing vessels. In 1870 the Buffalo Bayou Ship Channel Company began dredging, and the federal government declared Houston a port of entry, establishing a customs house. In 1872 Houston received its first federal grant of $10,000 to aid in completing the dredging project, one designed to create a 100-foot-wide channel nine feet deep. Work was slowed by a hurricane that hit Houston in September 1875 and caused $50,000 worth of damage. During this storm all but one bridge across Buffalo Bayou were swept away. Nevertheless, in April 1876 the first ship sailed through the new channel. The ironclad Clinton, a schooner-rigged side-wheeler, came into Houston with 750 tons of freight and left with 250 cattle. Although it took a full 10 years to realize the first "ship channel," the effort was but a baby step toward the dream of establishing a great port in Houston.

During Reconstruction after the Civil War, Houston fared well despite continued high water and poor drainage. In a second effort (after construction of drainage ditches) to improve these conditions, the city began to build large open channels to direct and control the flow of excess water. The two largest, along Caroline and Congress avenues, emptied directly into Buffalo Bayou. At the same time paved roads were built across the swampy plain into which Houston continued to expand. By the 1880s, ditches, channels, and both plank and gravel roads crisscrossed the town, creating a more or less effective drainage system. In 1878, James M. Loweree of New York was awarded a contract by the city to build the first waterworks to supply Houston with water from Buffalo Bayou. Loweree installed a dam above the Preston Avenue Bridge and laid pipes throughout the city. This water was not purified, and the water pressure proved too low for a consistent supply or for fighting fires.[6] It was not until 1891 that a successful water works company supplied city water from 14 wells.[7]

During the last quarter of the 19th century Houston developed and prospered as a commercial rather than manufacturing community, in large measure due to the fledgling water channel and the establishment of important railroad connections. By 1890, the Deep Water Committee was busy planning further improvements to the Ship Channel. Houstonians had enjoyed the Gay Nineties with the rest of the country, and on New Year's Eve 1899 there was much to celebrate, including the fact that the U.S. Congress had approved the construction of a yet deeper channel.

Then came the Great Storm of 1900. This tragedy nearly caused Galveston's physical and economic demise, but it left Houston, Galveston's chief commercial competitor, in an advantageous position to take over Gulf Coast shipping. Plans were underway to widen and deepen Houston's Ship Channel yet again, and Houston already had a railroad network that enhanced its port position in a way that could not be duplicated on the island. Galveston's spirit had been crushed, while Houston's continued, perhaps naively but indomitably. No historian analyzing the city of Houston should underestimate its brash can-do attitude, which for more than 150 years has shaped and reshaped its natural resources to great advantage.

WATER AND OIL

With increasing sophistication and leisure time, well-to-do Houstonians concentrated on the pleasures of dining, dancing, and water sports. Boating and fishing, once necessities and chores, became diversions, and several male-only clubs were established: the Redfish Boating, Fishing, and Hunting Club (1865), the Andrax Rowing Club (1874), the O. O. Boat Club (1882), the Houston Yacht Club (1898), and the Aquatics Club (1900). The Houston Yachting Club (1903) met on a houseboat on Buffalo Bayou at the foot of Travis Street, and the Houston Yacht and Power Boat Club (1905) was organized to encourage scientific navigation.[8]

Those who did not belong to clubs or own fancy boats also had a recreational relationship with the bayous. For health and safety reasons, city ordinances had since the 1840s forbidden bathing and swimming in local streams. And even though daring youngsters had always defied the rules, swimming in the bayous, for obvious reasons, never became popular. And, curiously, neither did sport fishing. Until late-20th-century pollution decimated their ranks, fish abounded in the inland waters around Houston. But local fishermen preferred the smaller creeks and bayous, usually catching only enough to provide supper for their families. Until the 1930s even crawfish were plentiful and easy to catch in swampy areas away from downtown. As for Buffalo Bayou, it was too full of commercial boat traffic to make a good fishing ground.

But the local bayous, including Buffalo, were not too overwhelmed with boats or fish to deter another group from using them. Christian sects that required baptism by immersion understood the sacredness of the local waters. For these baptisms an entire congregation would gather on the bayou banks to welcome new members, and often after the religious service most people remained for a picnic.[9] Even so, Houstonians' recreational and religious relationship with local waters has been and still is limited. It was commercial promise that captured official recognition. With a pervasive "we can overcome anything" spirit, local citizens were determined to conquer the swamp and build a mighty river. That the inland city had withstood strong wind and high water in 1843, 1875, and 1900 while nearby cities were destroyed was a selling point that profoundly affected Houston's future.

Only in Houston has it been proven that oil and water mix. After the founding of the Texas Company in Beaumont in 1902, its director, J. S. Cullinan, began looking along the Texas coast for the best site for his headquarters and refineries. What he wanted was large acreage, fresh water, deep-water shipping, and protection from storms and floods.[10] He chose Houston, convinced that a sufficiently deep channel was under construction in Buffalo Bayou and that the threat from flood and hurricane was a thing of the past. This 1905 move to Houston of the oil giant that became Texaco is considered critical in the establishment of Houston as the oil and gas capital of the nation.[11] In 1908 redredging of the Ship Channel was completed to a depth of 18 feet, with a turning basin just above Harrisburg.

Many writers have credited the oil industry with the development of the Ship Channel, but it well may be the other way round. Influential residents had decided long before Spindletop that a channel with a depth adequate for large oceangoing vessels was a must for Houston. As oil companies stacked themselves along the bayous, advances in marine technology produced vessels that required deeper drafts, making Houstonians once again question the sufficiency of their Ship Channel. They created a navigation district to control the watercourse and issued bonds to finance an even deeper channel. With the approval of Congress, the federal government matched local investment, and construction began in June 1912. On November 10, 1914, President Woodrow Wilson pushed a button in Washington that fired a cannon at the new turning basin, opening the 25-foot-deep channel with great fanfare.[12] This event ush-

Courtesy of George Fuermann "Texas and Houston Collection," University of Houston Libraries.

Baptism in Buffalo Bayou, ca. 1904.

Houston Ship Channel, 1999.

ered Houston into position to become a lucrative port and an economically stable city.

Before oil products became Houston's chief export, though, the wharves at the foot of Main Street and then from the port near Harrisburg were stacked high with bales of cotton. A local cotton carnival, the social event of the year, began in 1899. "According to an elaborately devised mythology, No-Tsu-Oh (Houston spelled backward) was the capital city of the Kingdom of Tekram (market) in the realm of Saxet (Texas). King Nottoc (cotton) emerged annually from the depths of the sea, or rather Buffalo Bayou, at the foot of Main Street to rule over his Court of Mirth."[13] His arrival began a weeklong commercial exposition and nonstop carnival activities. In 1914 the name of the carnival was changed to the Deep Water Jubilee to celebrate the opening of the Ship Channel; however, the festival was discontinued the following year.

FACE IT: HOUSTON FLOODS

In August 1915 a hurricane with 80-mile-an-hour winds struck Houston, killing three people. But the idea that Houston was not safe from high wind and water still did not sink, as it were, in. After Brays Bayou was hard hit by major flooding in 1919, the first serious flood-control measures were begun in Harris County. In 1923 a project to drain the 80,000-acre watershed of Brays Bayou started with the presumption that this

Preston Avenue Bridge during 1929 flood.

would control flooding in Houston. It didn't. In 1929, after a 14-hour rainstorm, all of the bayous around Houston, including Brays, overflowed, and the San Jacinto River rose 30 feet above its normal channel. Although losses in Houston were close to $1.5 million, this sum did not touch the losses six years later from the most devastating storm in Houston's history.

In 1935 the buildings and streets of 25 blocks downtown flooded along with 100 residential blocks. Seven people were killed, and the Port of Houston was crippled for six months due to submerged docks and a Ship Channel clogged with tons of mud and wreckage. Uprooted tracks disrupted vital railroad connections. And nature finally got Houston's attention.

Politically, the timing of the hurricane was perfect. Federal works projects, particularly huge water infrastructure programs, were being created all over the country during the 1930s. In 1936 the U.S. Army Corps of Engineers stepped in to begin planning a limited flood-control program that would move high water away from Buffalo Bayou. To facilitate interaction with the Corps and process requests for federal grants, the Texas Legislature on April 23, 1937, created the Harris County Flood Control District. Two years later, taxpayers in Harris County approved the first bond issue ($500,000) for an expanded drainage program. Meanwhile, federal and county programs were approved, adding over $35 million for the project. In February 1940 a comprehensive flood-control plan was announced that called for the retention and diversion of floodwaters (Addicks and Barker Dams) and two canals, one to extend from White Oak Bayou to the San Jacinto River, the other to run from a retention dam on Buffalo Bayou to Galveston Bay. These canals were "designed to protect the city and harbor from superfloods."[14]

The story of this massive plan was basically an attempt to move Harris County's excess water out into Galveston Bay with little regard for the natural environment. The arrogance of Houston planners once again raised its head with the notion that technology could fix anything. Not only did the storms and high water refuse to desist in the face of concrete channels and the like, they seemed to continue at a heightened pace. For example: heavy rains drowned 10,000 head of cattle and displaced 400 families (1940); Hurricane Audrey and another heavy thunderstorm caused flooding in Houston (1957); Hurricane Carla caused heavy flooding in southeast Harris County (1961); Texas Medical Center flooded and eight drownings occurred in three major thunderstorms (1976); a new U.S. 24-hour rainfall record of 45 inches was set in Alvin (1979); Hurricane Alicia and three other hurricanes caused severe flooding throughout the county (1983); and a major storm sent many bayous over their banks, flooding 1,500 houses and putting I-10 under water (1992).[15] It has been five years since significant flooding has occurred in Harris County, but officials warn that it is only a matter of time until the next big one comes.

What's going on? Claiming that all this recent flooding is new, environmentalists blame developers for paving over so much land in the county's watershed areas. Houston's rapid and often nearsighted development does retard natural runoff, but the gumbo soil that has been paved over was little help in absorption anyway. The hard, cold fact is that Houston has dangerous and destructive rainstorms, just as the Midwest has tornadoes and California has earthquakes. No one, not even rich Houston boosters, nor well-meaning engineers, nor tree-hugging naturalists can stop the water. Gary Green, operations manager of the Flood Control District, says that we have only three choices to deal with excessive water: move it, park it, or get out of its way. The move-it school had its day with channelization. And the park-it school continues to build dams and huge retention areas (such as the Barker and Addicks reservoirs). The get-out-of-the-way philosophy has established a federal buy-out program

Championship Park, White Oak Bayou near downtown.

in Harris County that encourages those who live in the most flood-prone areas to sell out and move on. Rather than a program of flood control, which is impossible, Harris County now has a much more realistic program of flood management.

Even if the environmentalists are wrong in their assessment of the reasons for flooding, they appear to have won the day. Since Arthur L. Storey Jr. took over management of the Harris County Flood Control District in 1989, the way in which Houston deals with water has changed. Much of the work has become privatized, allowing resources and time to be spent on careful planning.[16] Young planners and engineers responsible for current flood management programs seem much more sensitive to nature than their predecessors from the Corps of Engineers. For example, instead of channeling water in concrete culverts from natural wetlands, flood managers are planting marsh grasses that will filter standing water (which could be unhealthy) and stop erosion (which could lead to flooding). New detention basins are now designed to retain as much established vegetation as possible. Concrete channels are being removed in some areas, and new approaches tried. The idea of straightening out bayous and creeks to enhance drainage speed is no longer considered a good one.

Houston's developing ability to deal effectively with its own peculiar characteristics, including humidity, mud, and flooding, is a sign of its growing maturity as a city. Houston was founded on the myth that its lo-

cation and natural resources were good things. It was also founded as a real estate venture, ironically one from which the Allen brothers never profited. Despite the fact that neither a beautiful lake nor a wide, high-banked river sits by its side, Houston has emerged at the end of this millennium as a great city because of the unrelenting arrogance of successive generations of leaders who have understood how to capitalize on external disaster and how to control the natural environment. They have effectively managed heat and humidity with air-conditioning and managed commerce through manipulation of the waterways. The masters are still in the process of gaining control of rains that cannot penetrate the nonporous soil or easily run off the flat land.

Notes

1. Gary M. Green, P.E., director of operations, Harris County Flood Control District, interview with author, November 15, 1999.

2. Jerry Herring, *Guide to Understanding and Enjoying Houston* (Houston: Herring Press, 1992), 14.

3. Margaret Swett Henson, "A Brief History of Harris County," in Dorothy Knox Houghton, Barrie Scardino, Sadie Gwin Blackburn, and Katherine S. Howe, *Houston's Forgotten Heritage* (Houston: Rice University Press, 1991), 6.

4. *Houston, A History and Guide,* compiled by workers of the Writers Program of the Work Projects Administration in Texas, (Houston: Anson Jones Press, 1942), 56–60.

5. David McComb, *Houston: A History* (Austin: University of Texas Press, 1981), 60.

6. Ibid., 87–88.

7. *Houston, A History and Guide,* 92.

8. Ibid., 341.

9. Dorothy Knox Houghton, "Domestic Life" in Houghton, et al., *Houston's Forgotten Heritage,* 259.

10. McComb, Houston, 80.

11. Marta Galicki, "The Architecture of Oil," *Cite* 39, (fall 1997): 47.

12. Henson, "Brief History," 10.

13. Houghton, "Domestic Life," 312.

14. *Houston, A History and Guide,* 124.

15. "Riding the Waves of Change: 60 Years of Service" (Houston: Harris County Flood Control District, 1998), 7–15.

16. Green interview.

2002 UPDATE

From June 5 to June 9, 2001, Tropical Storm Allison pounded Houston with extremely heavy rain, producing the worst flooding Houston had seen in years. Sections of all highways and numerous secondary roads were closed; thousands of automobiles were abandoned; and at least 22 deaths were attributed to the storm. Some areas of greater Houston received more than 30 inches of rain, causing damages totaling several million dollars. The Medical Center was one of the hardest-hit areas: flooding of basement labs destroyed years of research data, and hospitals were closed for more than a week. Much of the city was without electricity.

This catastrophic occurrence should not have been a surprise. But, like storms of the past, it was met with awe and confusion. Houston, as always, recovered. But the scramble and the controversy continue as to how to improve drainage and prepare for the next flood. *Barrie Scardino*

Two articles published earlier in *Cite* also addressed the ongoing problem of Houston's water: Mary Ellen Whitworth, "Bayou Degradable: Up Against the Corps Again," *Cite* 28 (spring 1992); and Barry Moore, "The Nature of Control: the Greening of the Flood Control District," *Cite* 33 (fall 1995 / winter 1996).

Courtesy of *Houston Chronicle*.

Flooding caused by Tropical Storm Allison, June 2001.

Cite II
FALL
1985

Planning in Houston

A HISTORIC OVERVIEW

Stephen Fox

Houston's reputation as an unplanned city is the result of selective and uncritical historical reflection. It is more accurate to say that Houston is a partially planned city in which successive episodes of rapid expansion have outstripped whatever planning progress might theretofore have been achieved. The notion of planning Houston's urban growth and development is not new. But support for constructing a public policy of planned development has been sporadic and inconsistent, dependent upon the personal commitment of individual citizens or public officials rather than institutionalized city policy.

City planning in Houston began as a result of local interest in developing a park and boulevard system tied to the regional network of bayous. Between 1910 and 1917 a city plan document, *Houston: Tentative Plans for Its Development*, was prepared and published by the Cambridge, Massachusetts, landscape architect Arthur Coleman Comey.[1] The first increments of a citywide park and parkway system were carried out under the direction of the St. Louis landscape architect and planner George E. Kessler; its centerpiece was the development of Hermann Park and Main Boulevard.[2]

Comey's recommendations, although received with interest, must have seemed politically and administratively too ambitious, for they were not implemented. Comey addressed not only the development of a citywide park system, but also the compilation and use of data, traffic and transportation planning, control and regulation of housing and building construction, and legal measures that might be taken to establish a "Metropolitan Improvement Commission" to plan, regulate, and coordinate the city's and county's public works projects.

The enthusiasm that sustained Houston's forays into public and private planned development in the 1910s ran its course by the end of World War I. The subsequent revitalization of the cause of planning during the 1920s at first may appear as a logical — and even more successful — sequel to the achievements of the previous decade. Yet this revitalization masked radical weaknesses that eventually retarded efforts to establish public planning as a normative procedure in Houston: an exclusive dependence on individual citizens committed to planning; the apathy, if not hostility, of the general public to the purpose and mechanisms of public planning; and the ambivalence of public officials who supported the "progressive" appearance of planning, while only reluctantly according statutory authority and financial support to public planning agencies.

Mayor Oscar F. Holcombe (left), City Planning Director Ralph S. Ellifrit (center), and Planning Commission Vice Chairman M. E. Walter reviewing Houston zoning map.

ACHIEVEMENT AND FAILURE

From the 1920s, three individuals stand out prominently in the history of Houston planning: Will C. Hogg, the rich, mercurial, impulsive lawyer who made public planning his personal cause; Oscar F. Holcombe, who, between 1921 and 1957, would serve 11 nonconsecutive terms as mayor; and S. Herbert Hare, who, from the time of Kessler's death in 1923 until his own death in 1960, was the city's professional planning consultant.

In terms of achievements, the record of the 1920s was impressive: creation of a City Planning Commission; acquisition of Memorial Park and smaller parks; creation of the Buffalo Bayou and Brays Bayou Parkways; planning of a downtown Civic Center; preparation of a major street and thoroughfare plan; and publication of a second city planning document, *The Report of the City Planning Commission* (1929), issued as a

record of the commission's recommendations and achievements.[3] Moreover, the effects of public planning were adumbrated by those of private planning, especially in the development of planned garden subdivisions. The largest and most comprehensively developed of these was Will Hogg's River Oaks, begun in 1923 and carried out by Hogg, his brother and sister, Mike and Ima Hogg, and his associate Hugh Potter as a model of the benefits of planned community development.

However, when these achievements are balanced against the shaky course of planning as public policy, the complete dissolution in 1930 of public planning in Houston, during the first attempt to adopt a zoning plan, becomes comprehensible. Mayor Holcombe appointed the first City Planning Commission in 1922, but the City Council neither established it by ordinance

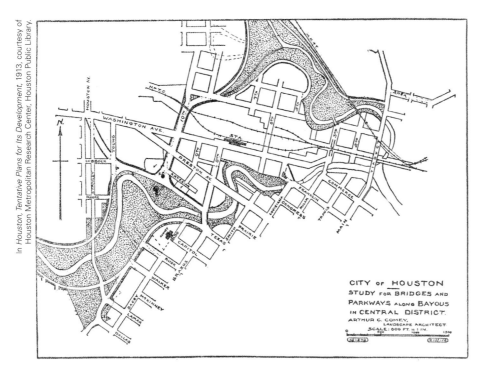

Proposed Parkway System: Buffalo and White Oak bayous (Arthur C. Comey, 1913).

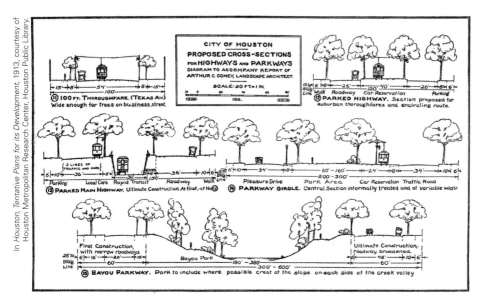

Street Standards (Arthur C. Comey, 1913).

nor authorized any funds to support its work. The members ceased meeting, and in 1924 Holcombe had to appoint a second commission, this time established by local ordinance and provided with a budget and a charge by the City Council. Hare & Hare, the landscape firm from Kansas City, was retained by the new commission to prepare a zoning plan, a Civic Center plan, a park plan, a major street and thoroughfare plan, and plans for beautifying the city's bayous. By 1926 Hare & Hare had produced a series of proposals for physical improvements, particularly for the Buffalo Bayou Parkway and for the Civic Center. However, when the commission's appropriation was depleted, its work ended and the commission members again ceased meeting.

It was Will Hogg's intervention and his willingness to spend his own money for a cause that he supported that enabled property to be acquired for the parkway between downtown and River Oaks and for the Civic Center.

In acknowledgment of Hogg's work (which included securing passage of legislation by the Texas State Legislature in 1927 enabling cities to adopt zoning laws and to control the platting of subdivisions), Holcombe appointed him to chair a third City Planning Commission in 1927. But Hogg resigned in 1929, the year before his death, in part because he felt that local political support was so inadequate. In 1928 he helped defeat Holcombe's re-election after he discovered that

Proposed Civic Center (Hare & Hare, 1925).

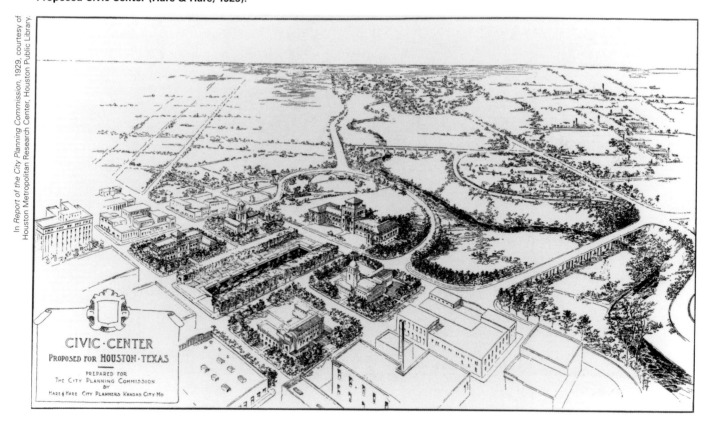

In *Report of the City Planning Commission*, 1929, courtesy of Houston Metropolitan Research Center, Houston Public Library.

the mayor had profited from the sale of property that the city was to acquire for the Civic Center. Following Hogg's resignation, the City Council and Holcombe's successor as mayor, Walter E. Monteith, began hearings on the zoning ordinance and plan drawn up by Hare & Hare. Taken aback by a display of concerted opposition, the council tabled the proposal and once again allowed the City Planning Commission to lapse.

In reaction to the laissez-faire attitudes of the 1920s, public planning nationally gained prestige during the 1930s. In Houston, however, it remained dormant until, as Barry J. Kaplan has pointed out in his study of the zoning issue in Houston, a single crisis renewed public interest in planning: the expiration of deed restrictions in Montrose Place in 1937.[4] Oscar Holcombe, re-elected mayor in 1932, 1934, 1936, and again in 1939, established a fourth City Planning Commission in 1937, with Hugh Potter as chairman, to prepare a zoning plan. Again, concerted opposition developed, and Holcombe's successor, R. H. Fonville, responded by tabling the issue and permitting the commission to go out of existence in 1939. But immediately upon being re-elected to succeed Fonville, Oscar Holcombe re-established the Planning Commission in 1940 as well as constituting a new Department of City Planning. To head the department, Holcombe chose a young landscape architect, Ralph S. Ellifrit, who came to Houston in 1939 as Hare & Hare's local representative.

Ellifrit retained the position of director of the Department of City Planning for 23 years, and he brought to this position a sense of professional responsibility and continuity that compensated for the lack of an effective planning constituency in Houston. During the war years Ellifrit and Herbert Hare revised the 1929 plans for parks and major streets and thoroughfares. At the same time, Ellifrit began planning a freeway network that became the basis for the Texas Highway Department's eventual Houston system. Ellifrit was responsible for the westward extension of the Brays Bayou Parkway, the creation of a White Oak Bayou Parkway, and the addition of many neighborhood parks. He set standards for subdivision planning and produced a new Civic Center plan in 1957 that led to the renewal of the Civic Center district.[5]

POSTWAR ATTEMPTS AT ZONING

After World War II Houston entered a period of unprecedented territorial expansion. It was during this period, as Peter C. Papademetriou demonstrated in *Transportation and Urban Development in Houston, 1830–1980*, that streets and freeways replaced parks as the basic element of public planning in Houston.[6] As a result, the Major Street and Thoroughfare Plan of 1943, enforced and periodically updated by the City Planning Commission, became the city's de facto comprehensive plan. At the same time, a fragmentation in planning authority began to become evident as planning agencies not directly subject to the City of Houston, such as the State Highway Department and the Harris County Flood Control District, emerged. However, the symbol of planned municipal development in the United States — the zoning ordinance — continued to occasion tremendous controversy in Houston, despite the considerable support it received from established local interests. Mayor Otis Massey, in 1946, and Mayor Lewis W. Cutrer, in 1959, initiated public planning and hearing procedures to draft a zoning plan. In each instance, after several years' work, a plan was submitted to the voters, first in 1948 and again in 1962, and both times zoning was soundly rejected.

The year following the 1962 referendum, Louis Welch was elected to the first of five consecutive terms as mayor of Houston. During these years, 1964 to 1973, Houston continued to expand rapidly, eclipsing even the dramatic growth periods of the 1920s and 1950s. Welch replaced Ralph Ellifrit as director of the Department of City Planning with Roscoe H. Jones, who retained the post from 1964 until 1983. Jones did not adopt Ellifrit's role as a public planning advocate.

Instead, the Department of City Planning concentrated upon documentation, trying to maintain accurate records in the face of Houston's expansion. The function of the City Planning Commission also was limited strictly during these 20 years to the approval of subdivision plats. Welch's successor as mayor, Fred Hofheinz, even created divisions of Economic Development and Community Development within the mayor's office to carry out many of the functions that in most American cities were the responsibility of a planning department.

After the zoning referendum of 1962, planning subsided as a public issue in Houston. Yet, in the middle 1960s, it began to re-emerge as a factor in commercial real estate development. Master plans of development, restrictive covenants, and legal associations charged with maintaining these covenants had been commonplace in Houston residential development since the 1920s. With the advent of suburban office and industrial parks, regional shopping centers, and massive garden-apartment and townhouse communities, these mechanisms began to be employed by developers of commercial real estate to establish and maintain standards—and property values. The co-existence of private planning and public laissez-faire was sustained by the belief that unceasing economic growth would result in the correction of dysfunctional conditions, once they had become apparent, on an ad hoc basis. Indeed, the real estate lawyer Bernard H. Siegan used Houston as the model of an economically self-regulating city in his book *Land Use without Zoning* (1972).[7]

The imposition of a moratorium on new construction in many parts of Houston in 1974 due to the city's insufficient sewage-treatment capacity indicated, however, that even without a zoning ordinance the municipal government had to play more than a passive role in urban planning. The dizzying intensity of growth and development that lasted until 1982 demonstrated that even the most farsighted and comprehensive private planning could not address the sort of issues that were becoming more and more problematic: traffic congestion, flood control, air and water pollution, and uncertain public services. Symbolic of a cautious shift in official attitudes toward public planning were a series of actions by the Houston City Council and by a new mayor, Kathryn J. Whitmire, who was elected in 1981. Passage of the Development Ordinance in 1982, authored by council member Eleanor Tinsley, marked a tentative first step toward defining a public planning policy. This was followed by Mayor Whitmire's revitalization of the City Planning Commission, chaired by Burdette Keeland, and the appointment of Efraim S. Garcia as director of City Planning in 1983 to succeed Roscoe Jones.

Yet for Houston the critical issue remains one of public understanding of, and support for, a public planning policy. This was true in 1913, and it remains no less true in 1985.

Notes

1. Arthur Coleman Comey, *Houston: Tentative Plans for Its Development* (Boston, 1913).
2. Stephen Fox, "Big Park, Little Plans: A History of Hermann Park," *Cite* 3 (spring 1983).
3. *The Report of the City Planning Commission* (Houston, 1929).
4. Barry J. Kaplan, "Urban Development, Economic Growth, and Personal Liberty: The Rhetoric of the Houston Anti-Zoning Movements, 1947–1962," *Southwestern Historical Quarterly* 84 (October 1980), 137–168.
5. "Planning the City: An Interview with Ralph Ellifrit," *Houston Review* 3 (winter 1981), 203–219.
6. Peter C. Papademetriou, *Transportation and Urban Development in Houston, 1830–1980* (Houston, 1982).
7. Bernard H. Siegan, *Land Use without Zoning* (Lexington Books, 1972).

2002 UPDATE

While suburban communities continue to proliferate in a fashion "planned" by developers, the city of Houston itself still holds to its maverick no-zoning ideals. Many special interest groups (the preservationists, the flood

controllers, the environmentalists, and others) have taken on grassroots advocacy roles. But Houston still eschews most comprehensive efforts at planning.
Editors

Planning (or the lack of it) has been well documented in *Cite*, including: Joel Warren Barna, "The Development Ordinance and Its Discontents," *Cite* 5 (winter 1984); William F. Stern, "The Quilted City: Planning for Houston," *Cite* 24 (spring 1990); "A Stranger Here Myself: *Cite* Talks with Planning Director Donna Kristaponis," *Cite* 27 (fall 1991); William F. Stern, "Tools of the Development Trade: Interpreting Building Codes and Planning Ordinances," *Cite* 42 (summer / fall 1998); George Grenias, "Shadow Planning," *Cite* 42 (summer/ fall 1998); Mitchell J. Shields, "Revising Chapter 42: Houston Readies a New Development Ordinance," *Cite* 43 (winter 1999); Rives Taylor, "Starting at 42: Houston's New Development Ordinance," *Cite* 44 (spring 1999); and Mitchell J. Shields, "Reviewing Chapter 42," *Cite* 48 (summer 2000).

Zoning in Houston, an important aspect of local planning initiatives, also has commanded a good deal of attention in *Cite*: "Trading Toilets," by William Anderson and William O. Neuhaus, *Cite* 1 (August 1982); John Mixon, "Honor Thy Neighbor: A Zoning Starter Kit for Houston," *Cite* 24 (spring 1990); "Through the Zoning Glass," *Cite* 27 (fall 1991); Tom Curtis, "5,000 Voters Can't Be Wrong: How Zoning Came to Houston," *Cite* 27 (fall 1991); "Beyond the O-Zone: Shaping Up Houston," *Cite* 27 (fall 1991); John Mixon, "Zone First, Ask Questions Later," *Cite* 27 (fall 1991); "Zoning Houston: A Guide," *Cite* 29 (fall 1992 /winter 1993); Donna H. Kristaponis, "Zoning Houston — Not," *Cite* 31 (winter / spring 1994); Bruce C. Webb and William F. Stern, "Houston-Style Planning: No Zoning but Many Zones," *Cite* 32 (fall 1994 / winter 1995).

Cite 28
SPRING
1992

The Mother of All Freeways

MAINTAINING THE STATUS FLOW ON HOUSTON'S WEST LOOP

Joel Warren Barna

West Loop 610, looking north from US-59.

The Uptown section of the West Loop has always enjoyed a certain apartness among Houston's major traffic arteries. Until recently, this 4.1-mile-long stretch of Loop 610 between I-10 and US-59 in the heart of post-downtown, smog-bound Houston was destined to become the widest freeway in the world. Other freeways may be ordinary, land-despoiling paths of commerce taking farmers to market, connecting the port to its hinterlands, collecting workers for their trudge to the still-shimmering office towers downtown or the incendiary chemistry mills along the Ship Channel, and speeding harried salary men to and from the airports. Houston's other freeways have always been levelers of humankind, the domain of off-price malls, budget motels, and used-car lots, where billboards broadcast the forbidden impulses of the city's autonomic nervous system, flashing images of whiskey and cigarettes, psychiatric hospitals for women and children, and vasectomies for men.

Not so the West Loop, the flagship of Houston's head-over-wheels embrace of the automobile age. By a happy coincidence of its birth—an engineering decision that reportedly ratified a deal cut in Houston City Council in the 1950s to benefit R. E. "Bob" Smith, then a major financial backer of Mayor Roy Hofheinz—the West Loop passes through the western end of Memorial Park, ensuring its safe transit south through Smith's holdings, close to and paralleling Post Oak Boulevard.[1] The West Loop is relatively free of billboards and therefore is more purely itself—a connector, like the other Houston freeways, but insulated by them into a field of activity without poles.

THE LOCAL (NOT THE EXPRESS)

Metaphorically, the West Loop is not electrical path but Brownian motion. This shows in the difference between its traffic patterns and those of other freeways. Other freeways are congested at peak hours or when there are wrecks or floods or roadwork to contend

with. The West Loop, by comparison, evolved past that point in the mid-1980s, when, for a while, it was the busiest stretch of freeway in the nation, with an average daily traffic count of 231,000 vehicles. The latest published daily average, for 1990, is a mere 224,000, making the West Loop still the busiest freeway in the city but only the second busiest in the state, after a stretch of the LBJ Freeway in north Dallas (227,000 vehicles per day for 1990). The Nilotic inundations of the West Loop's traffic stream have been almost unbelievably stimulating, turning the freeway's frontage roads and the commercial zones visible from its overpasses into a valley of giants ruled by Philip Johnson and John Burgee's beacon-topped Transco Tower, in company with lesser marvels by Johnson, Cesar Pelli, and Skidmore, Owings & Merrill and the enfilade of the Woodway Canyon. Uptown Houston, as this aggregation is now called as a public relations convention in preference to the earlier designation Magic Circle, is the eighth-largest business district in the United States and is expected to double in worker population over the next 20 years.

Best of all, the West Loop joins what is perhaps the most exquisitely symbolic pairing in the American landscape. On the west side in the Houstonian, shielded by scraggly pines within a gated sports-health center for stressed-out executives, is the hotel room that serves as the primary private residence of the President of the United States, at least for tax and voting purposes. On the east stands the Houston headquarters of the Resolution Trust Corporation, a $500 billion-revenue-producing workout center for the real estate lending industry, created to ensure that profits stay private and losses are duly socialized.

All development in the corridor was predictable, but little of it was understood in the 1950s, when Loop 610 was planned. Back then the Loop was intended simply as a bypass route to relieve congestion downtown and on the city's thoroughfares through the end of the century. But, as Peter C. Papademetriou explains in his authoritative *Transportation and Urban Development in Houston, 1830–1980*, the Texas Highway Department's decision to develop the Loop and the new freeways of the 1950s and 1960s with parallel frontage roads embodied "a philosophy that it was less costly to build more roadway than [to] buy out access rights."[2] This all but guaranteed that the Loop would also function "as a local street, or a collector street, conceptually at the opposite end of the traffic spectrum [from a freeway loop]." This potential was nowhere more heroically realized than on the West Loop, in part because of the spectacular high-rise building spree that acquired a self-fulfilling momentum with the development by Gerald D. Hines Interests of the Galleria complex, thereby exploiting the market demographics inherent in the charmed geographic area that the West Loop passes by.

HIGHWAY TO HEAVEN

To the east of (inside) the West Loop, Memorial Park shields the exclusive subdivision of River Oaks from the freeway, while to the west (outside the Loop) Tanglewood and the incorporated Memorial villages spread out seemingly forever. These neighborhoods west of the freeway have a peculiar unity: in them, low-scaled fifties and sixties ranch houses are set behind open drainage ditches. A remnant of the not-so-distant agricultural past, these ditches link the region visually as much with Bordersville and West Columbia as with River Oaks. Even so, these neighborhoods are in the top tier of Houston's elite residential areas, and all predate the West Loop. It was the proximity of these top-dollar demographic swatches, in fact, that made the Galleria, precociously conceived as specialty retail on a quasi-European theme, Houston's special contribution to high-speed consumer-urbanism.

Stands of old trees and the topographical variations afforded by Buffalo Bayou (its waters laced at the Loop only with effluent from the nascent communities of the pine forests and prairies to the west) were among the chief attractions abetting the creation of these enclaves, insulated, like a piney dream of southeastern Connecticut, from the unpleasantness found in working-class neighborhoods. This preservation of primeval identity was embraced by area residents as a matter of both principle and interest; they strove to keep the bayou free from such unwelcome intrusions as continuous north-south roads. As a result, until 1989 not a single north-south street crossed the Buffalo Bayou to link I-10 and US-59 between Shepherd Drive and Voss/Hillcroft. An impregnable green curtain meandering along the bayou across the western half of the city secured the social position of a relative handful of houses. Consequently, all the area's local north-south traffic, not just that coming from outside the West Loop corridor or generated by Uptown growth, was pushed onto the West Loop, creating constant congestion where the green curtain parted.

Interestingly, the routing of the freeway through the edge of Memorial Park actually helped preserve the development options for privately held land to the west. Plans for a second breach, the 1989 extension of Chimney Rock across the bayou to join Memorial Drive with I-10, resulted in an acrimonious process that, as former Houston Planning Commission Chairman Burdette Keeland notes, took from the 1940s to the 1980s to effect (*Cite* 25, fall 1990, p. 24). The maintenance of the bayou barrier was a strategically brilliant social and political achievement, in view of Houston's zoning-free, no-lands-barred pattern of development. For as anyone who has bought a house in a subdivision or even merely studied ads for residential real estate knows, all new suburban houses, from the Houston Heights in the 1890s and Montrose in the 1910s to Kingwood and First Colony today, were sold with an implicit promise: "Move out here, live in tamed but otherwise unspoiled nature, and you will be a happier, more fulfilled person.

In addition, you will be spared, forever, from the churning real estate market that afflicts the rest of the city. Your neighborhood won't turn into a slum, and it won't skyrocket up in value so much that speculators will drive you out to build a mall or an office park."

And as anyone who has lived in Houston more than half a boom-bust cycle knows, in a city that thrives on the unabated churning of the real estate market, the sellers of most subdivisions have no intention of honoring any such promise, which evaporates like a sulphurous Clinton Drive fog as soon as the developer's investment is recovered, and control of his municipal utility district is sold out to the home buyers. From that point on, the dynamism of the market takes over, and the subdivision's value begins to fall or rise, almost never standing still. As Houston's long-deferred experiment with zoning begins to counteract relentless neighborhood displacements occasioned by unbridled speculation, neighborhoods to either side of the West Loop hold certain lessons.

Of all the participants in the great real estate casino that Houston has been since the Allen brothers began selling lots in 1836, only the residents of the Buffalo Bayou barrier have managed to achieve stasis for more than a year or two. Unfortunately, the lesson of the bayou-side communities is that the only thing that actually worked was sufficient spare cash to create economic and political buffer zones. Now it appears that, zoning or no zoning, the buffer zone that held for the past 40 years will not be enough. Because the West Loop has in effect redefined the city's physical center and become its central artery, the bayou-side communities have become, in essence, part of a new inner city. If Billy Joe Doe needs to get from FM-1960 to Pearland, he doesn't much care that the residents of Tanglewood wish to maintain what remains of its traditional connection with Memorial Park. All he knows is that the West Loop is bumper to bumper.

BIG, SCREAMING DEAL

The political power of Tanglewood and its neighbor communities remains enormous, but it has been perceptibly eroded over the 1980s, with changes in the Houston City Council that emphasized (and may soon eliminate altogether) at-large representations in an effort to increase minority-group membership. Most of all, the residents of the barrier have to contend with the patchwork emergence of the Uptown business district, which has established itself as a formidable economic generator and political force, and which is beginning to tire of the rustic-domestic pretensions of its neighbors. It is in this context that the plan to expand the West Loop became a big — often literally screaming — deal. The Texas Department of Transportation (a 1991 renaming of what, since the 1970s, had been called the Texas Department of Highways and Public Transportation) sees itself as responsible to the through-traffic commuter and has been planning to expand the West Loop for over a decade to alleviate congestion and to deal with actual and projected growth in traffic. From the start, the department has sought to achieve this expansion by double-decking the West Loop, like the portion of I-35 that runs to the east and north of downtown Austin. The state's intentions have been reflected as a matter of course in its long-range planning and also in studies released by Metro, the Houston-Galveston Area Council, and other local planning bodies over the years.

The first public controversy over the plan arose in 1989, when highway officials released a double-decking scheme for public comment. This much must be said for the scheme: it had a certain physical grandeur. Two elevated lanes in each direction would have started on the Southwest Freeway near South Rice, risen above the 610/US-59 interchange to a height of about 100 feet, run some 50 feet above the outer lanes of the West Loop, crossed over the top of the 610/I-10 interchange, and extended along I-10 eastward to T. C.

Jester Boulevard and westward to Antoine. At the same time, the current width of the West Loop would have been expanded by two lanes in each direction, increasing the total number of lanes (not counting frontage roads) from eight to 12. And the area's access ramps would have been reconfigured to make entering and leaving the freeway less difficult and hazardous.

Engineers at the highway department estimated that the designed capacity of the West Loop would increase from the then-current 200,0000 average daily trips to 275,000; this capacity, they said, would be reached in 2010. The specific purpose of the double-decked lanes would be to reroute long-distance traffic, taking it out of what one engineer called "the turbulence in the corridor that is caused by all the entering and exiting vehicles." Hedging their bets, officials said that the proposal for elevated lanes was only one of three options under consideration. They were also studying widening the West Loop at its current grade level and sinking the roadway below grade. But both alternatives to double-decking had big problems, they said. Widening the freeway at grade would have demanded that state officials acquire an additional 40 feet of right-of-way on each side of the freeway, and this was complicated by the fact that several large structures would stand just over 20 feet from the freeway frontage roads. The cost of acquiring the buildings and land would have added perhaps $100 million to the $80 million needed for the freeway improvements. Sinking the roadway would have taken even more land, to account for the thickness of retaining walls. And it would have been complicated by the proximity of Buffalo Bayou, which has a tendency to overflow into low-lying areas during heavy rains.

Local residents argued against the highway department's plan. Mike Globe, president of the Afton Oaks Neighborhood Association, said: "Elevated lanes would introduce additional noise into what is already a very noisy area, and it would be visually degrading to

what is now an attractive portion of Houston. The scope of the type of structure they are talking about is such that it removes any human scale from the area." By proposing a least-cost engineering solution for West Loop traffic, Globe maintained, officials risked exacting a greater cost from the neighborhoods and work centers that would be damaged. "A neighborhood without zoning like ours is extremely fragile; it only takes a little to tip the scales toward urban decay, and we already have the roar of two freeways." Don Olson, director of the city's parks and recreation department, also condemned the double-decking proposal, saying the noise it would generate would threaten Memorial Park. "From the standpoint of the city, we own some highly scenic parkland that has already been cut into by the West Loop and by Memorial Drive and that already has significant noise problems," Olson noted in a 1990 interview. "We don't want to lose any more land to highway projects. And we want to see the mobility problems of the area solved in a comprehensive way that has the least impact on the park, instead of having them dealt with piecemeal." Olson said he was concerned about any solution "that will just push more traffic through the corridor, making the relief valves more congested"—and leading inexorably to calls to widen Memorial Drive. But it was opposition from Uptown Houston and individual commercial-property owners in the area that killed the double-decking plan. John Breeding, the director of the Uptown Houston Association, said in an interview in early 1990, just before highway officials abandoned double-decking, that "an elevated expressway is inconsistent with an urban situation like this" and urged highway department planners to design a sunken roadway.

The matter moved out of public discussion in early 1990, and a West Loop Task Force was constituted, with two representatives of the highway department (including then-highway commissioner Wayne Duddlesten of Houston), five representatives of Post Oak

Proposed 24-lane widening of the West Loop, computer simulation.

business interests, and representatives from Metro, the City of Houston Parks Board (including Don Olson) and Planning Department, the Greater Houston Partnership, and the Citizens Environmental Coalition. Late in 1990, both Duddlesten and Olson were quoted in press accounts as saying that widening the freeway at grade level looked like the best compromise, even though it meant some loss of parkland, which Olson put at 1.5 acres.

TWENTY-FOUR-LANE WORLD WONDER

Again, there was little reaction to this testing of the waters. Then came the public presentation in late No-

vember at the Doubletree Hotel at which department officials hoped to release details and answer questions about their quietly negotiated compromise: a $280 million, 24-lane wonder that would require three acres of Memorial Park and provide five lanes in either direction for express traffic, four in either direction for local freeway traffic, and three on either side for frontage, so as to accommodate not 275,000 vehicles daily but 350,000. The department officials did not want to emphasize what they saw as the true but misleading fact that this would produce the world's widest single freeway; after all, it was only an addition to what was already a 14-lane project. They came armed with computer-generated views of the new freeway, showing how it could incorporate landscaping in its medians, and they were ready to talk about some new sound-absorbing structures to cut noise. Instead, they found themselves confronted by an angry crowd of 500 to 600 people, including City Council members Jim Greenwood and Sheila Jackson Lee and a well-coordinated series of parks advocates, neighborhood representatives, and emissaries from citywide environmental groups. All expressed outrage at the scale of the project, its violation of the park, and its obvious intent to stimulate automobile traffic through the corridor. The project would turn Houston "into one big shoulder to Loop 610," said Greenwood, who suggested that the department turn instead to comprehensive planning to expand other traffic routes and alternative mobility measures. Lee was quoted as saying, "This expansion goes right in the face of the city's efforts to comply with the Clean Air Act."

In December the Houston City Council voted 13–0 to oppose the 24-lane expansion plan. Outgoing Mayor Kathy Whitmire spoke against the plan, even though officials of her administration had been involved in negotiations and proceeded with her apparent blessing. Incoming Mayor Bob Lanier waffled on the matter, saying that the highway department's plan should proceed if it was the right thing to do. Of those involved, only the Uptown Houston representatives held firm. In an interview in early 1992, John Breeding said that his group had given up the sunken-freeway option, convinced by highway department officials that it would be too costly and technically too difficult: "The widening option would bring the freeway within a few feet of some buildings, but at ground level. We feel that is a lot more acceptable than at the third or fourth floor." Breeding also vowed that, if the compromise plan unraveled, his group would oppose any attempt to reintroduce the elevated-express-lane option. "There are groups that have fought freeway proposals for 30 years and eventually won, and we are prepared to go to similar lengths if necessary," Breeding said.

WHAT NEXT?

With the compromise apparently undone, highway department officials again dropped back. The 24-lane proposal was only one of 12 options they were studying — everything from "no-build" ($50 million) to closing the West Loop's entrance lanes to local traffic ($450 million) to variations of a sunken freeway ($500 to $800 million, not counting air-handling equipment, water pumps, and generators). While highway officials ran their numbers, the focus shifted again. In a manner typical throughout modern Texas, private interests began to develop the comprehensive vision that public entities had failed to achieve.

Uptown Houston, which as a group knows that expansion of mobility represents the difference between its own growth projections and stagnation, has had consultants working on plans to incorporate some form of public transit into a reworked street network for the business center. What form that transit will take keeps changing. Until last fall, it looked like it would be monorail. With the election of Bob Lanier, that changed to light rail on existing railroad lines, and in February it shifted to a regional bus plan. By then John Breeding said he believed that rail transit in Houston was dead and that an all-bus system would be the choice of the future. With that realization, he hoped to ensure that the future expansion of the West Loop would at least be coordinated with the plans emerging for increasing mobility in Uptown. "There's no way you can justify having 24 lanes of concrete out there," he said. What he anticipated at that point was forgoing one lane in either direction of both the express and local highway lanes in favor of a single lane for high-occupancy or "fixed-guideway" vehicles — buses, or even trains.

Neighborhood activists were still hoping to kill every expansion option but the sunken freeway. Dr.

Robert Silverman, representing one resident coalition, felt that the 1990 amendments to the federal Clean Air Act, which require city and regional planners to find ways to cut automobile emissions, would help block the expansion. He also was of the opinion that the 1991 Intermodal Surface Transportation Efficiency Act (signed into law by President Bush in Arlington the day that General Motors announced it was planning to cut 70,000 jobs from its workforce), which requires that future highway-construction projects not contribute unnecessarily to expanding the demand for automobile use, might make it possible to kill the project altogether. Moreover, according to Silverman, with the Houston City Council on record opposing the project, state officials would be compelled to bring forth a locally acceptable solution.

STATE VS. FEDS

Not so, according to Don Garrison of the Texas Department of Transportation. "Legally, under the new federal funding bill, it's between the state and the feds," says Garrison. He added that his office had kept both the Environmental Protection Agency and federal highway administration officials abreast of plans from the start. Clean-air requirements would be met by expanding the freeway, he said: "Having cars in stop-and-go traffic produces a lot of pollutants. If you can get them moving faster, you actually reduce the amount of pollutants in the area, which satisfied the EPA. Same things with noise: get the traffic moving faster and it decreases." Silverman and other neighborhood activists vowed to test Garrison's assertions in court and through the political process and to do their best to knock the freeway-expansion plan off the tracks.

Whether elevated, at grade, sunken, or even not at all, the expansion of the West Loop seems to have settled back down into the realm of technicalities. By April its future appeared seriously, if not fatally, imperiled, as Silverman had predicted, by the impending application of the 1991 Intermodal Surface Transportation Efficiency Act, the effect of which even in Houston was to shift substantial appropriations originally intended for highways to mass transportation. Milton Dietert, district engineer for the Houston district of the Texas Department of Transportation, was reported in April as hoping simply "to do small projects such as the Westheimer entrance ramp, and leave the Loop widening headaches for the next century."[3]

But whatever its fate, the 24-lane compromise that had emerged under the guidance of business leaders with the power to forge a working political consensus in the vacuum left by city and state officials signaled a shift in the city's political geography of far greater significance than the size or arrangement of the freeway itself. The West Loop, which in a sense came into being as a guardian of the neighborhoods through which it passed, had at last become an indistinguishable extension of Uptown, the business center it had done so much to make possible. In the process, the West Loop had been socially leveled and was now, like the other freeways of Houston, just another massive culvert of cars. Let Houston zone itself blue in the face, but if economic motives could override the Buffalo Bayou barrier, no force for neighborhood stability could be depended on to count for anything, anywhere, any longer inside the Beltway.

Notes

1. Mel Young, "Loop Freeway Gets Tough Punch," *Houston Chronicle,* December 23, 1954.
2. Peter C. Papademetriou, *Transportation and Urban Development in Houston, 1830–1980* (Houston: Metropolitan Transit Authority of Harris County, 1982), 85.
3. Karen Weintraub, "Mass Transit Gets a Leg Up at Expense of Area Highways," *Houston Post,* April 13, 1984.

2002 UPDATE

TxDOT's current plans for the West Loop call for re-working its complex intersections with US-59 to the south and I-10 to the north. State officials argue that these interventions will go a long way to alleviate traffic congestion and air pollution—at a price of $1.2 billion and not until completion in 2009.

Uptown Houston maintains its steely opposition to expansion through elevated or sunken lanes. Any hope that park advocates and neighborhood groups had of convincing state officials to proceed with a sunken freeway drowned in June 2001's cataclysmic flooding. If there's any good news for mobility in the West Loop–Uptown area, it's that the intersection plans don't seem to preclude connection to a likely rail corridor along the Southwest Freeway linking Sugar Land to downtown and the Medical Center.

But obscenely wide freeway plans never die; they just get moved around. Now TxDOT is planning to expand I-10 from the 610 Loop westward to Katy to 18 lanes. Until recently, some of those lanes were to be devoted to Metro high-occupany vehicle (HOV) lanes and, potentially, to light rail.

A new plan has emerged from the smoky back-rooms of power, announced at a recent press conference by Harris County Judge Bob Eckels and Congressman Tom DeLay (always willing to set aside his other good works for a chance to stick his finger in Central Houston Inc.'s eye). Metro's lanes have disappeared, replaced by a county-owned tollway down the middle. So Houston may still have a 24-lane wonder to look forward to. *Joel Warren Barna*

Transportation, like zoning and planning, has been a forefront topic in *Cite*. Joel Barna in *Cite*'s second issue (a special on transportation, November 1982) wrote "Just As Soon As I Understand What They're Talking About" and in the third issue (spring 1983) "Congestive Failure." Other articles on Houston's transit woes have included: Jerry Wood, "From Loop to Loop to Loop," *Cite* 10 (summer 1985); Jeffrey Karl Ochsner, "Metro Regional Plan 1985," *Cite* 11 (fall 1985); Alan M. Field, "Light Rail and the Future of Houston," *Cite* 18 (fall 1987); Bruce C. Webb, "Busing Up to Rail: Metro's Park-and-Rides," *Cite* 25 (fall 1990); "Funnel Vision," *Cite* 27 (fall 1991); "Down with the Southwest Freeway," *Cite* 31 (winter/spring 1994); Dan Searight, "The Train Stops Here," *Cite* 47 (spring 2000); and Christof Spieler, "On Track: Metro Unveils Artist-Architect Collaborations," *Cite* 52 (fall 2001).

Cite 31
WINTER /
SPRING .
1994

Utopia Limited

HOUSTON'S RING AROUND THE BELTWAY

Richard Ingersoll

Hester + Hardaway, 1994.

First Colony, new grove of trees.

Houston has few topographical impediments to its continuous centrifugal expansion. The network of concentric, radially connected freeway loops has provided an armature for suburban tracts that saturate the land like huge oil bolts, oozing across an incorporated territory of about 580 square miles. Four of the largest and most successful master-planned developments in the United States are tethered at the outer edges of this unrepentant sprawl. The Woodlands, First Colony, Kingwood, and Clear Lake City are the most prominent of a series of self-zoned subdivisions smugly surrounding a city that would not allow itself to be planned.

NEW TOWNS

Distinct from mere subdivisions and planned unit development schemes, these new towns have a considerable mix of land uses, including retail, commercial, social services, and parks. Each has a population ranging from 30,000 to 40,000 and an area varying from 10,000 to 25,000 acres (the grid of downtown Houston covers approximately 2,000 acres). During the 1980s the majority of new-home starts in the Houston metropolitan area gravitated to the master-planned developments, indicating a victory in real estate terms for the fully planned suburb over the rest of the city.

A master-planned development is different from a city in that the development corporation guarantees infrastructure and services that otherwise would be the result of a democratically mandated municipal authority: it privatizes what has traditionally been the prerogative of the community. Associations for maintenance of services (something like 60 cents per $100 assessed value) are attractive because these havens of zoned orderliness appear free of the problems of the city, such as poor public schools, lack of recreation space, and high crime rates. These developments are, moreover, the ultimate eugenic experiment for PLU (People Like Us), since they are generally reservations of that rapidly declining species — the aspiring white middle class. A great deal of breeding goes on out in what might be called Houston's fertility crescent, where the safety of children, access to good public schools, and well-organized sports programs are the highest priorities.

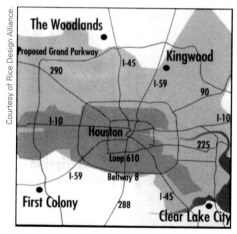

Metropolitan map showing The Woodlands, Kingwood, First Colony, and Clear Lake City.

Like the original Humanist paragon of planning, Thomas More's *Utopia*—the name of which is a play on words meaning "no place"—these settlements on Houston's edges cultivate a certain placelessness. Although each of the four developments described below reflects distinct topographical characteristics and a great deal of design effort has been applied to their landscaping to create a market identity and special physical attributes, all give the strong impression of being nowhere in particular and are in some ways interchangeable. The resounding lack of orientation created by looping roads and the anonymity and remoteness caused by the setback fabric of these environments suggest a kind of existential camouflage.

All the cities on the island of Utopia were identical and were located approximately 24 miles, or a six-hour walk, apart. The Woodlands is 27 miles and First Colony, Kingwood, and Clear Lake City each 22 miles from downtown, all on the circuit of the proposed Grand Parkway, Houston's beltway beyond the Beltway. All the houses in Utopia were of the same model and were arranged 30 to a street with a community house in the center; this bears some correspondence to the conformity of suburban houses, now marketed by national mass builders like packages of potato chips, built on cul-de-sacs with a tot lot or neighborhood park in the center. Utopians were obligated to change houses every 10 years so they would not feel proprietary about their dwellings. Americans change their homes on the average of once every five years, usually for the purpose of trading up, and thus the house is always conceived in terms of the value it will have for some normative other who will be the next to acquire it. Utopia, now with the goal of private rather than communitarian well-being, is closer than was previously thought.

Suburban, low-density developments have, in the half-century since World War II, become the site of the new majority of population distribution, accounting for more than 40 percent of the U.S. population in 1990. The suburbs are in general architecturally undistinguished and difficult to represent in plan or through perspective means, and they seem beyond the pale of human drama, only suitable for the bathos of television serials. Nothing can happen in the master-planned landscape except sheltered breeding to ensure the survival of *Homo suburbanis*. Because of the suburbs' exceptional banality but overwhelming economic and social importance, there is something unexpectedly meaningful about their ascendancy. Life on the edges of Houston is yet another instance of space apparently overcoming time.

The ambivalence of the suburbs as placeless places and history-free shapers of civilization is symptomatic of the semantic crisis of the late 20th century, when meanings no longer seem to adhere to words, when signs and referents are constantly betraying rather than portraying. Take, for instance, the fact that new suburbs such as The Woodlands or First Colony are generically called "new towns," their advertisers promote them as "communities," and they are usually broken down into 1,000- to 2,000-acre packages referred to as "villages." Not formally, structurally, socially, or in any other way do these developments resemble the entities referred to by the words attached to them. Was there ever a town without a commercial nucleus, a village without a main street, or a community without historical continuity? The language is so delusional that recent arrivals to this real estate package deal, such as the offices of Duany & Plater-Zyberk or Peter Calthorpe, have felt it their rhetorical mission to supply a form that better corresponds to the name, in hopes of restoring the "traditional" values of the phenomenon the original words describe. But the rupture in meaning has already occurred, and there is no turning back.

The master-planned development's street patterns derive from the picturesque, curving streets deployed by Frederick Law Olmsted in such plans as that of Riverside, Illinois (1869), and from the patterns used to separate traffic that were devised by Raymond Unwin for the early garden cities in England during the first decade of the 20th-century street configurations that avoided frequent intersections and provided secluded streets. Arterial fast streets with internal loops and cul-de-sacs were the ingenious solutions.

Houston's master-planned developments aspire to a combination of the elite 1920s Olmstedian subdivision of River Oaks, which was given easy automobile access to downtown by Allen Parkway, and the quick-profit middle-class development of Sharpstown, Houston's version of Levittown. Sharpstown, begun in the mid-1950s, supplied more-affordable houses on smaller lots with such amenities as schools, a golf course, and a shopping mall. The decline in the status and security of Sharpstown, which now embraces a significant minority population, is not likely to be repeated in the current new towns. The new towns are not named after their developers but have neighborhoods named after natural features, such as Bay Oaks in Clear Lake City, Sweetwater in First Colony, Panther Creek in The Woodlands, and Elm Grove in Kingwood. Although The Woodlands has some commitment to the concept of human diversity, the process of real estate competition has confined it to marketing strategies that inevitably focus on a middle-class clientele.

Squiggly street patterns as an alternative to the conventional grid made particular sense to developers during the car-crazed 1950s and were encouraged by the FHA guidelines for subdivisions, because they provided a method for keeping houses from facing directly onto loud and dangerous thoroughfares. But while such systems facilitated movement on a larger scale, they tended to fragment the urban fabric and limit interaction at the local scale. The irresistible logic of these street patterns is determined by the automobile. To drive in Houston is a political act. It means support of the industry that linked the city's economy to the destiny of the nation. The settlements at Houston's outermost limits are so intimately linked with the oil economy that the relationship cannot be seen as casual: Friendswood Development Company, an Exxon subsidiary, developed Clear Lake City (1963) and Kingwood (1972); Mitchell Energy developed The Woodlands (1974); and the Royal Dutch Shell Pension Fund has replaced the Ford Foundation as the primary financial partner of the Gerald D. Hines–initiated First Colony (1976). (Mobil Oil is currently developing 11 master-planned suburbs throughout the Sun Belt.) It is, of course, in the interests of the oil and automobile industries to encourage development on the edge, thereby making the demand for their products integral to a way of life—a round trip to one of these new towns is equivalent to half a tank of gas in my car. That Gerald Hines and George Mitchell supported both light rail and zoning does not necessarily contradict this scenario, since these measures would benefit the center and the edge, where both developers have a lot at stake.

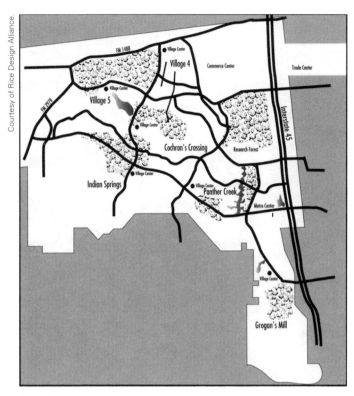

Courtesy of Rice Design Alliance.

The Woodlands, map.

THE WOODLANDS

The largest of Houston's master-planned developments, at 25,000 acres for a projected population of 150,000, is The Woodlands, and it is by far the most utopian. The developer, George Mitchell, has persevered with undying idealism in planning a real estate domain that will foster social diversity and respect for environmental concerns while attracting employment and culture. Mitchell is one of the great, self-made *eondottieri* of the energy business, one of the last of the Texan "can-do" entrepreneurs, and it is hard not to admire his progressive approach to environmental and social issues. The Woodlands indeed aspires to provide an alternative to existing urban and suburban conditions. But despite the expenditure of so much talent, imagination, and investment, the question lingers as to whether The Woodlands is appreciably different from the suburbs or its rival new towns.

The most frequently quoted reason George Mitchell gives for having created The Woodlands is that the new town represents a sort of fiscal *realpolitik* which arrests the drain of tax dollars to autonomously controlled suburbs such as West University Place and Bellaire. Mitchell advocated a well-planned suburb that would remain within the city's ultimate jurisdiction. The Woodlands is unincorporated, and although currently it is more dependent on the services of Montgomery County and the more proximate city center of Conroe, it nevertheless lies within Houston's statutory extraterritorial jurisdiction. But even if the tax base of The Woodlands is ultimately retrievable, the drain of employment,

The Woodlands.

cultural, and housing possibilities it encourages is less than salubrious for the vitality of the urban core.

Mitchell started planning The Woodlands with an eye to obtaining federal subsidies and loan guarantees as part of the U.S. Department of Housing and Urban Development's Title VII New Community Act. Approximately $30 million of an overall $2.8 billion investment came through federal grants. The public funding is one of the reasons The Woodlands is so much better documented and more accountable in social terms than its confreres. It is also more conscientious about fostering public resources such as HARC, the Houston Advanced Research Center, to which Mitchell recently pledged $65 million in matching funds, and the Houston Symphony summer program. The terms of the New Community Act of 1970 stipulated that loans for development were guaranteed in exchange for provision of 15 percent low-income or assisted housing. Somewhat akin to the New Deal strategy of creating well-planned suburbs, such as the one built at Greenbelt, Maryland, for absorbing lower-income people from the inner cities, The Woodlands has continued to maintain, even after the terms of the initial contract lapsed, a small number of publicly assisted apartments. These constitute a far larger percentage of the available local housing than do the similar rental units available in Houston. Until recently, The Woodlands mixed the price ranges of houses in each subdivision, a strategy contrary to the prevailing practice in other master-planned developments. Currently about a third of the population of The Woodlands is employed there, predominantly by corporate and research facilities. Light industry, projected for the future, would help diversify the class and racial mix.

From the outset, The Woodlands was intended to be a new type of development, closer to nature. The expertly prepared marketing literature emphasizes environmental preservation "so that people may live in harmony with nature." In the first areas developed in The Woodlands, in the village of Grogan's Mill, the buildings are concealed with remarkable consistency by obligatory trees and shrubs. The result, however, is anti-architecture. The houses of this era, mostly modest and wood-sided, are completely hidden in the trees. The five-story office buildings, just barely taller than the treetops, are sheathed in mirrored glass that makes them disappear in the reflection of the sky and other natural features. Every act of building in these early stages followed a strategy that pardons uninspired design through the mitigation of the forest.

Mitchell, who in the 1950s commissioned Karl Kamrath to design one of the more interesting houses in Houston, was conversant with the principles of Wright's organic architecture. His own house was a variant on Wright's Hanna House (Palo Alto, 1936), which used hexagonal planning and broad sloped roofs to blend in with natural features. Among those working on the planning stages of The Woodlands, including Kamrath and William Pereira, was Ian McHarg, the Scottish-born doyen of environmental landscape planning. McHarg made studies, including an aerial survey, of the site's ecosystems and recommended ways of placing drainage to reinforce the effluent patterns of the land. The result has been a noticeable environmental difference in The Woodlands. The ethic is to live

in the forest, and thus everything in The Woodlands is set back and hidden by trees. The architectural guidelines encourage saving as many trees on a lot as possible and then planting indigenous trees and undergrowth wherever needed. There were no front lawns in the earliest subdivisions, which for the suburbs was revolutionary.

Recently the guided "natural landscaping" has given way to more conventional front lawns and fences in order to remain competitive with the norms of upscale real estate. The development company itself is an agent of this stylistic transition, sponsoring such projects as the newly finished Bear Branch Recreation Center (designed by Royce R. Leachman), which uses classical compositional strategies, arches, and monumental massing in diametric opposition to the earlier passive approach to the same program. The design of houses in The Woodlands has also evolved, from humble, faceless wooden structures to large houses with imposing façades cluttered with pseudo-historical decoration and a foreground of high-maintenance yards.

About 25 percent of the land in The Woodlands has been set aside as public space for parks and recreation. This is considerably more than any of its competitors can boast, and the green spaces, which include 40 neighborhood parks and four golf courses, are easily accessible and often quite impressively unspoiled. The minor streets retain the look of country roads because they have soft shoulders without curbs or sidewalks. Instead of sidewalks, 64 miles of paved hike-and-bike trails depart from the 150-mile road network to form an independent system through the less-disturbed natural habitats. Unlike trails in other master-planned new towns, those in The Woodlands break away from visual contact with the subdivisions — a virtue that someday may become a liability. Although the crime rate in The Woodlands is relatively low, there have been isolated incidents in the past few years of

Grogan's Mill Village, plan, The Woodlands.

minor crimes or intimidating confrontations on these paths, which, because they are not visible from the road, are perceived as less safe.

Although the efforts to coordinate the hydrological impact of settlement and to disturb the forest as little as possible proved less damaging than conventional clear-cutting, The Woodlands does not discourage the use of automobiles, which remain the most deleterious threat to the environment. Shopping, schools, recreation, and employment are not situated in a way to make walking a realistic alternative. Express charter buses take commuters to downtown Houston, the

Texas Medical Center, and the Uptown Galleria area, and there is the future possibility of a light-rail connection with downtown. But these services cannot remedy the spread of local automobile-dependent patterns of movement. The needs of commuters in The Woodlands played a big role in construction of the Hardy Toll Road, which provides a faster highway to downtown. This commitment to automobile traffic has been implicitly acknowledged in The Woodlands by the placement of public sculptures at major intersections of the arterial parkways, where there is no pedestrian activity.

Also problematic is the promise of community in The Woodlands. Unlike conventional suburbs, The Woodlands promotes the idea that it will gather a diverse population and become a real hometown. Ancient Sparta or Mayan settlements in the Yucatan may have maintained a strong culture with a diffusely settled population, but overriding military and religious commitments provided the social glue in a way that is hard to imagine in an American suburb. During its early years, with only a few thousand residents, there was a stronger sense of togetherness in The Woodlands. Everyone picked up mail at the post office in the Grogan's Mill village center. Children went ice skating at the Wharf or swimming at the YMCA. The residents, who mostly came from out of state (currently 46 percent come from outside the region), were eager to participate on the conscientious terms of the developer. Now that the population has grown to about 35,000 (the ultimate projected population is 153,000) and starting a new town is less of a novelty, the initial sense of intimacy has declined. The post office was moved to an anonymous site, and mail is now delivered to each cul-de-sac. The skating rink has been closed because it was too expensive to maintain, although the Y is still a popular place.

The most frustrating impediment to a sense of community in The Woodlands is that there is no center;

there is no place where the community can come to-gether. The first village center at Grogan's Mill failed as a retail center—perhaps because the architecture was overly passive. On one side of the narrow pond of Lake Harrison is The Woodlands Country Club and Confer-ence Center, designed by Edward Durell Stone's office in the mid-1970s with a vague suggestion of Wrightian, wing-spread eaves. This building is connected to retail facilities on the other side of the narrow lake by a glass-enclosed wooden bridge. The structures were somewhat cheaply built and, like all the first buildings

of The Woodlands, recede timidly into the trees, mak-ing impossible the creation of visual connections that make urban space interesting. It is difficult to see the parts of this so-called center, let alone the whole. Lack of visibility from the road is particularly disadvanta-geous to retail.

The Woodlands Information Center (Bennie M. Gonzalez, 1975), an expressionistic collection of irregu-larly shaped wood-sided wedges in the midst of tall pines, is perhaps the consummate example of the camouflage style, building too carefully according to

Hester + Hardaway, 1994.

Cynthia Woods Mitchell Pavilion (Horst Berger & Sustaita Associates, 1990).

the dictates of the trees. Even a building of modest civic intent such as Taft Architects' Water Resources Building is lost behind a thick buffer of trees that thwarts an axial view of the building's portico. The recently expanded HARC campus has indulged in more monumental tactics, with a framed gateway, emulating Rice University, and a stout brick-clad, limestone-corniced administration center. All signs in The Woodlands are restricted to two-foot-high, sand-blasted wooden panels, a non-aggressive touch that only increases the difficulty of finding things for the driver.

The major public building of The Woodlands, the Cynthia Woods Mitchell Pavilion (Horst Berger & Sustaita Associates, 1990), which because it is the site of numerous rock concerts and the summer residence of the Houston Symphony should be the place easiest to find, is hopelessly sequestered in the middle of the forest. The thrusting peaks of its white Teflon tents, held up with soaring web trusses, make it the most interesting building of the development, yet it is not visible from any major roads.

The combination of too great a respect for natural features (many of which, like the concrete-lined Lake Woodlands, are artificially induced anyway) and a self-effacing desire for humble structures (which became instead an excuse for cheap ones) failed to create places of assembly where a sense of social involvement might continually be generated. The supermarket at Grogan's Mill went through several tenants without success and is currently used as a public library. Most people went back to the strip malls, just outside The Woodlands on I-45, to fulfill their shopping and entertainment requirements.

The new village center at Panther Creek shows that some lessons have been learned. Randall's has opened a quite successful hypermarket that encourages more social contact than previous retail developments in the new town. The trees have been thinned a bit so that the complex of stores surrounding the market is visible from both Woodlands Parkway and the secondary artery. This ensures a better psychological connection. But it still does not foster the idea of public assembly the way a small-town Main Street does.

Standards of house design have also changed in response to the competition from Kingwood and First Colony. Many builders are producing grandiose mansions in the West University–South Fork Ranch idiom, with phony brick details, mammoth arched entries, and blind corners. Natural landscaping is not appropriate to these statements of bourgeois self-importance, and high-maintenance yards have become the rule.

The new regional mall at The Woodlands, currently under construction and planned to open in 1994, may change its entire social complexion. Optimistically called the Town Center (the same term is employed for the mall planned at First Colony), it does not promise to add a greater sense of architectural or urban identity to The Woodlands. Co-developed by Homart, a Sears subsidiary, the mall, designed by E.I.S. of Berkeley, has a classic enclosed, double-loaded spine with anchor stores at each end. Rather than occupy a position in the physical center of the new town, the mall is located on the easternmost edge of The Woodlands, adjacent to I-45, to catch freeway shoppers. It is completely surrounded by a broad apron of surface parking except on its southern side, where a link with Main Street is planned. The trees envisioned for the lot are insufficient to relieve its openness. An artificial lagoon has been dug to offset the center from the freeway and to connect the mall to a mile-and-a-half-long canal leading past the concert pavilion to Lake Woodlands. A transportation link is being planned at the canal level. Judging from published plans, none of the buildings will come close enough to the edge of the water to integrate the water feature with commercial and social functions.

The single factor that might engender true solidarity among the residents, something equivalent to the threat of war, is the teenage problem. Teenagers in The Woodlands, like suburban teenagers everywhere, are the unanticipated factor that upsets domestic tranquility. The energy of sexual awakening is simply incompatible with the confinement of the single-family house, and there comes a point in a suburban child's life when sports no longer fulfill all of one's desires for contact with the world. Stuck out in the middle of nowhere, in an empty house (since both parents usually work), informed and stimulated through telematic

excess, teenagers often become resentful of the ennui of planned environments and devote all their energies to transgressing the local limits. This had its most tragic expression a few years ago when a group of Woodlands teenagers went on a gay-bashing spree and murdered a man in the Montrose district. Last year, in an attempt to confront the problem, The Woodlands opened a teen center, a large clubhouse designed by Ray Bailey Architects, with a basketball court in the middle and video games in the side rooms. It is

The Woodlands Lake.

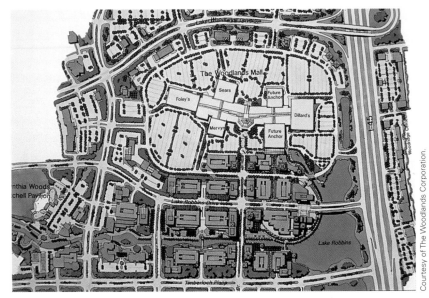

The Woodlands Town Center, plan (Elbasani & Logan, 1994).

The Woodlands Town Center, model (Elbasani & Logan, 1994).

doubtful, however, that a mere container will be able to sublimate teenage aggression. Surveillance does not usually coincide with the concept of liberation or transgression. The weakness of the scheme for the town center is that it was not designed to answer these problems. It fails to provide enough interstitial room for slackers and, because it is hermetic, is unable to foster the streetlike connections that might permit casual socialization.

FIRST COLONY

The problems described in The Woodlands are present in all the other suburban new towns, where perhaps because there is so little idealism, the contradictions seem less apparent. If The Woodlands is the best intended of Houston's new towns in terms of social conscience, First Colony is the most socially unconscious. It offers no promises regarding nature, diversity, or any culture beyond that of sitcoms; its only reality is that this is status real estate. Adjacent to Sugar Land, which was the center of agricultural processing in this area, First Colony was preceded in the 1960s by Venetian Estates, a smaller subdivision of mostly one-story, ranch-style houses situated on a series of artificially generated lagoons. Quail Valley, southeast of First Colony, and Sugar Creek to its northeast are smaller subdivisions begun shortly before First Colony opened in 1976. Since then, this area of Fort Bend County has seen a proliferation of

The Woodlands Town Center, interior.

Courtesy of The Woodlands Corporation.

Hester + Hardaway, 1994.

First Colony billboard.

master-planned subdivisions, including Greatwood, New Territory, Lake Olympia, Kelliwoods Green Trails, and Cinco Ranch, none of which has the size to sustain as many amenities as First Colony. Many of them in fact rely upon the higher degree of amenities and services, in particular the retail oppor-tunities, of First Colony. (As investments, the smaller 1,000- to 2,000-acre developments reap the greatest profits, because they can be realized in the shortest time and have fewer infrastructure costs.) Fort Bend County has the fastest-growing economy in the region, with the lowest percentage of low-income and highest percentage of high-income residents in the Houston area. The county offers aggressive tax-abatement programs, and more than half of the businesses relocating there receive reductions according to the benefits they will confer on the county.

The success of these zoned packages was due at first to the decision of major oil companies such as Conoco, Shell, British Petroleum, and Amoco to locate their corporate campuses outside Loop 610 along Highway 6, in what has come to be known as the Energy Corridor. These postindustrial forms of high-income corporate employment are the perfect patron group for master-planned communities, and the relationship has become symbiotic, so that it is difficult to distinguish

which has had a greater impact on the other's choice. Schlumberger Well Services recently decided to consolidate its administrative offices in the area, partly because of the access to this type of housing.

In many ways First Colony reverses the strategies of The Woodlands. The landscape, mostly old rice and sugarcane fields, had few trees. The look of the development was created by introducing a new, formal landscape. The SWA Group, which specializes in the landscaping of corporate campuses, has given an orderly look to the streetscape. The regular rows of teardrop-shaped, nonbearing Aristocrat pear trees that frame the last of First Colony's three freeway exits at Sweetwater Boulevard are a stunning reminder of the displacement of the regular agricultural striation of the land by the cash crop of single-family homes. During the past 15 years, 10,000 street trees have been planted and paved sidewalks laid along every street to give the edges of the streets more definition. Some streets have the charm of Houston's older oak-lined boulevards, although the plantings have not been uniformly successful: Palm Royale Boulevard was lined with tall palms that were unable to survive winter in this climate. In the more expensive neighborhoods, decorative landscape features such as pergolas and fountains give a lush quality to the outdoor spaces. Because the landscaping is so ambitious, all of the houses and retail buildings are much more visible than in The Woodlands. This should not imply that they are more pleasant to look at, only that it is easier to orient oneself.

First Colony spreads out over 9,700 acres with a population of over 30,000 (projected build-out population is 50,000). The name implies the good WASPy stock of Pilgrim fathers but actually refers to the fact that Stephen F. Austin established the first (Anglo) colony in Texas nearby. What is so astounding about First Colony is the sense of crowding where there is so much space. It is difficult, of course, to squeeze four-car garages onto standard suburban lots. If there is a

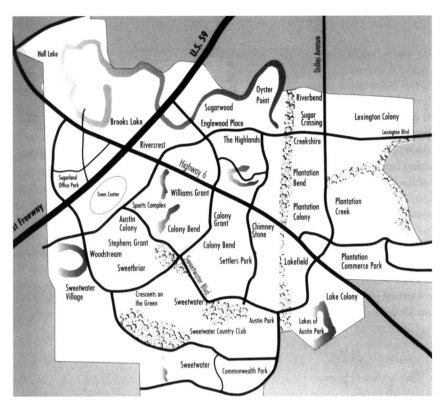

First Colony, Fort Bend County (Llewelyn-Davies Associates, 1976).

style that is emerging in the expensive houses, it is not by accident. Sugar Land Development Company hired the firm of Ray Bailey Architects to develop design criteria. The builders were then educated through presentations and booklets about "enduring design characteristics" culled from the most admired parts of River Oaks and Shadyside. "Contemporary" houses (i.e., modern style, with flat roofs or strip windows) were thought to be inappropriate, as were styles not of Anglo derivation. A design for a house with onion domes and pointed arches was successfully discouraged. Many houses in First Colony, especially the high-priced ($300,000 to over $1 million) ones in Sweetwater Village, aspire to the girth of River Oaks houses with only a quarter of the land. They are abnormally high, capped with a big-hipped roof, studded with fake dormers, and smeared with Georgian or Colonial regalia. In contradiction to wood-frame construction, the typical First Colony house is liberally encrusted with gables, brackets, quoins, rusticated brick patterns, and pilasters. The rear elevations of these houses are almost invariably surfaced with cheaper siding materials. Such regular features as cathedral ceilings for the living rooms and private baths for each bedroom boost the square footage well beyond the needs of a modest family.

The developer, Gerald D. Hines Interests, owes some of its fame to its practice of hiring celebrity architects to make distinctive packaging for large commercial projects. In the privatization mentality of the 1980s, this meant that the developer took over as provider of the public realm, a transfer brilliantly portrayed in the fountain park at the base of the Transco Tower. At First Colony the firm of Johnson / Burgee was hired in 1982 to design an office park at First Colony's first freeway intersection. The only one of the buildings

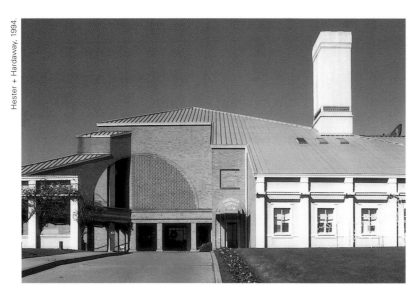

Sweetwater Country Club (MLTW/Turnbull Associates with Richard Fitzgerald & Partners, 1983).

to be constructed is brick-clad, with a neoclassical tympanum placed at the top of the central wing and two wings spreading out at a 45-degree angle. It looks stranded, especially when glimpsed with the shimmering Fluor headquarters, the star resident of the office park, looming in the distance. Charles Moore and William Turnbull designed Sweetwater Country Club in 1983 for the high-income neighborhood. Despite some interesting interior plays with light in this structure, its construction is generally cheap, and the overall impression is that it has the biggest hips of the high-hipped roofs in the development.

Sugar Land Development Company has helped establish the First Colonial style with the design of several commercial buildings such as the Williams Trace Shopping Center, where brick elevations are given some articulation with striated bands of different-color brick, string-course moldings, and limestone corners. One of the neighborhood recreation centers uses a prominent Palladian archway for its bathhouse. By far the finest buildings are not those of the famous architects, but the excellent design for elementary schools by Spencer Herolz Architects. At the Austin Parkway School, an arresting freestanding wall shoots out on a

45-degree tangent to serve as a canopied walkway from the automobile drop-off point. The design was so successful that it was repeated on another site for the Colony Meadow School with only a slight variation in brick color.

There are bike paths and greenswards at First Colony, but they are not conceived with the conviction of The Woodlands and are apparently little used except by joggers. First Colony is designed for those who like to drive. The ample retail areas have huge parking lots. Also surrounded by parking, a new mega-mall will be similar to the one planned for The Woodlands, except that its main axis will run parallel to the freeway. Among the largest green spaces on the First Colony map is the right-of-way for high-voltage power lines. Another idea currently being discussed is to import white sand from Florida to create an artificial beach at the recreation center lake, which was done first at Cinco Ranch. There is diversity at First Colony—the only pedestrians are domestics and gardeners, people of color working hard to maintain the look of the American Dream while the occupants are off working hard to pay for it.

Hester + Hardaway, 1994.

Clear Lake City.

CLEAR LAKE AND KINGWOOD

Both Clear Lake City and Kingwood are products of Exxon's Friendswood Development Corporation. They use nearly identical promotional literature and follow very similar layouts. Clear Lake City, the first master-planned new town in Texas, was begun in 1963 by Humble Oil and Del Webb. It is located at the southeastern edge of Houston off I-45 and near NASA, which opened in 1964. Kingwood is at the northeastern frontier, just north of the Humble, Texas, from which the Humble Oil and Refining Company (now Exxon) took its name. In the northwest quadrant of Houston, Friendswood has also developed Copperfield and Fairfield, which are considerably smaller but similar in concept.

The logic of Clear Lake City, which has a population of 40,000 on 15,300 acres, is to provide a suburban setting for a major new employment center; about 80 percent of the residents work in the immediate area. Following the success of Sharpstown, Clear Lake City offers fewer amenities than new towns founded a decade later. It occupies dubious land that once was used for oil exploration but no longer yields oil. From the off-ramp of I-45, large oil pipes undulating in and out of the ground greet the Clear Lake City visitor.

Breezes from the Ship Channel are seasoned with the trace of petrochemicals. Clear Lake City, which is not a city, was incorporated into Houston in 1977 after one of the most hotly contested annexation disputes. One of the big attractions of this development is Clear Lake, which is not clear. The brackish inlet, located nearby but not adjacent to the development, contains the third-largest marina in the country and is the site of great sailing activity. There is some genuine Gulf Coast feeling around the lake, probably because the master planners were not able to include its periphery in their package.

Like Sharpstown, the first plots of Clear Lake City were tightly packed on long, wavy blocks. The later subdivisions seem to have learned from The Woodlands and First Colony and use cul-de-sacs and loops more astutely for greater privacy. One of the chief characteristics of Clear Lake City is that the major thoroughfares are lined with 10-foot concrete walls to shelter adjacent backyards. This gives the subdivision a particularly impermeable and forbidding feeling. There are schools, big churches, and strip retail centers for the spiritual and physical needs of residents, but the landscape exudes about as much sense of community as a Motel 6. The Wetcher House by Peter Waldman, with its fanciful metal extrusions visible from across the Bay Oaks golf course, is one of the few instances of architectural achievement amid some very cheap-looking, expensive property.

Clear Lake City and Kingwood have none of the landscaping coordination of First Colony, nor do they pay much attention to the natural features that are implied in their names and ads. Their approaches to siting and subdivision are more perfunctory. Kingwood was developed on 13,000 acres belonging to the King Ranch on the edge of Lake Houston. The current population is 37,000. Built in a forested area much like the site of The Woodlands, it bills itself as the "livable forest." But in spite of some good intentions such as Charles Tapley's design for a nature trail (which won a *Progressive Architecture* award in 1971) in Trailwood Village, the first subdivision, there is no apparent crusade here to preserve the forest. The publicity brochure shows a lush carpet of forest, but the trees of Kingwood have been unceremoniously cleared for construction. House sites are quite visibly scraped, and front lawns are uniformly installed. Wetlands around the lake are preserved by law, so very few houses are close enough to see the water, and the golf courses exploit unbuildable land. As in Clear Lake City, retail is clustered in ubiquitous strip-centers. Each of the subdivisions within Clear Lake City is segregated by price range. The schools and churches are there, and publicity boasts that 95 percent of high school graduates go to college—but with incomes averaging $83,000 here, should that be any surprise?

Kingwood has bike paths (Clear Lake City is apparently the only new town without them), but they are fairly pathetic grassy alleyways rather than wooded paths. Houses look too large for the single families that live in them but because of the trees do not seem as cramped on their sites as similar houses in First Colony and Clear Lake City. Like all the other new towns, Kingwood is spread out in such a way that people can avoid each other.

The lack of life and spontaneity in the new towns is unsettling. While The Woodlands offers unique access to natural features and First Colony provides a cheery revival of grand landscaping, there is something mortifying about the way the new towns evade human problems while invading the forests and fields, displacing natural landscapes and transmuting them into a name, as the ultimate act of semiotic instability.

2002 UPDATE

Houston is no less a city of ever-expanding sprawl than it was in 1994 when Richard Ingersoll wrote about Houston's most successful master-planned communities. A lack of geographic impediments to growth has encouraged the city to expand its metropolitan boundaries, spreading new development that follows characteristic patterns of Sun Belt suburbs. But new subdivisions don't often aspire to the standards of community planning set by the Woodlands, nor do they see themselves as becoming towns. The Woodlands itself continues to mature. The Woodlands Mall, built in 1992, the suburban equivalent of Main Street, has been commercially successful and provides a social focus for the town. An outdoor extension to be built around a waterway is presently being planned. *Editors*

Mark A. Hewitt writes about suburban housing typologies in "The Stuff of Dreams: New Housing Outside the Loop," *Cite* 10 (summer 1985).

Cite 16
WINTER
1986

Suburbia Deserta

David Kaplan

In only 12 years' time, a multitude appeared: neighborhoods whose names evoke the country, aristocracy, and the past, places that sound like dreams come true — Kings Forest, Whispering Pines, Mandolin, Windsong, Vienna Woods, Woods of Wimbledon, Pecan Grove Plantation, Sha-De-Ree. For many, these places represent lifelong dreams, even though the dream is way the hell out. The suburb for many is the preferred setting for raising a family and making a life.

Bruce C. Webb, 1994.

Swallows Meadow subdivision.

IDYLL TO WAR ZONE

But with the sudden economic downfall, some suburban neighborhoods have turned into what city planners call "war zones," a description formerly reserved for inner-city ghettos. Houston is often called the city of change, the city in process, but drive to certain middle- and upper-class neighborhoods and you'll see where things just stopped. One section of the city has seen so much suburban breakdown, so much abandonment it has been nicknamed the "foreclosure rainbow." It is an 18-mile arc of newer subdivisions in West Houston, stretching from US-59 South to US-59 North. Many of these subdivisions were built to be near the Energy Corridor, a series of energy-related office buildings along the Katy Freeway (I-10).

A TOUR WITH JIM

A real estate salesman, who will be called Jim, takes me into the foreclosure rainbow. We drive along the I-10 feeder road, near Mason Road. "This area was supposed to be the center of Houston," Jim says, driving

Houses in the "foreclosure rainbow."

past great expanses of unmowed fields. The area was once rich rice land. Driving through a healthy-looking suburb, he explains why many of the two-story brick houses look alike: "One builder tried it and it worked." He gives away a few quirks of the trade: "If there's no sidewalk, it's called an estate."

Jim drives to a different subdivision, where there are few signs of life. The houses are in the $100,000 to $200,000 price range and only a few years old. Toward one horizon is a desert of empty lots. Jim parks his car at a half-completed block, where a few houses look lived in and the rest appear vacant. We enter one of the vacant houses, where carpeting has been ripped up and sinks are missing. "Reclaimed by their builder," Jim speculates. But teenage vandals have been responsible for most of the destruction. "There's nothing else for these kids to do out here," he says. A message has been painted in every room: "Rock 'N Roll" over the kitchen cabinets.

OVERLY OPTIMISTIC OVERBUILDING

Scenes like this are common in Houston for a number of reasons. First, there is the economy. Houston developers gambled that economic lightning would strike Houston a second time, but it did not, according to Barton Smith, director of the University of Houston Center for Public Policy. Our first boom, which began in 1975, was counter-cyclical in that the rest of the nation suffered during that period, prompting many Americans to migrate here. In 1981, foreseeing another great counter-cyclical boom, builders went wild, especially in the outlying regions of town. But there was no second boom. In 1982 the oil market began to slip. In a 15-month period between 1982 and 1983, 160,000 people lost their jobs here.

With a tremendously overbuilt real estate market, property values dropped. This sent shock waves through a town that had come to believe that the value of anything in Houston was bound to go up. At the same time, interest rates were rising. To make home-buying more appealing, mortgage banks introduced the graduated mortgage, which allowed a buyer to initially assume low monthly payments, then pay more with time, creating a situation where the buyer eventually made steep monthly payments as he or she watched the home's value decrease. This, along with

job losses, encouraged foreclosure. If Houston had been a state during the summer of 1985, it would have led the nation in foreclosures.

But the economy does not tell the story. It doesn't explain why one subdivision makes it, while another in the same area does not. Other factors come into play, most importantly quality of life. According to University of Houston sociologist John Gilderbboom, too many projects were built by inexperienced developers who were "unable to see the big picture," who were looking for a quick buck. Rather than rely on the wisdom of professional planners or borrow from the examples of successful neighborhoods, these developers, says Gilderbboom, "acted too much on a whim." Gilderbboom believes that the neighborhoods that worked are those that were founded by developers who not only believed in planning, but who also committed to stay with their projects.

Suburban houses for sale during the 1980s bust.

Paul Hester, 1986.

THE GOOD, THE BAD, AND THE UGLY: NOTTINGHAM VILLAGE

A viable neighborhood also requires a sense of community, a sense of "we-ness," Gilderbboom said. Often, he laments, buyers choose their homes solely for the deal they can get, overlooking who their neighbors might be and whether they will be the kind who will look after one another. If a neighborhood possesses those attributes it can flourish, even in these rough times, even way out in the foreclosure rainbow. Cathy Lecky enjoys living there, in the suburb of Nottingham Village. She and her husband have been there since 1980. From her screened-in porch, we look out on her flower garden, the centerpiece of her spacious backyard. Her fence blocks the view of I-10, although we still hear the traffic. Lecky brags about her 2,875-square-foot home. "We got a super deal," she says. "It's sturdy, energy-efficient, and it doesn't leak." She adds that in the house's early stages, their builder, Ray Braswell, was cooperative. "A lot who built out here have left town or have gone out of business," she says, "but he still builds out here."

Nottingham Village, built by Kickerillo Company, is nicely landscaped and offers recreational facilities and good schools. But despite its well-laid foundation and active civic group, Nottingham now has its troubles. When Kickerillo sold out, the new developer built a big apartment complex near the country club, which angered homeowners. Crime also has increased. Teenage crime is a minor nuisance: recently kids knocked over mailboxes and stole the yard-of-the-month sign. There are more serious crimes as well. A security man told Lecky that because of the economy, more and more people are stealing jewelry, guns — anything they can sell quickly.

But things are good in Nottingham compared to other nearby subdivisions, where, says Lecky, "a world of people" have been foreclosed upon. Some have lost their jobs, others are unhappy with their subdivisions. Many houses leak badly. A developer in one subdivision built $300,000 to $400,000 houses and never got around to planting trees. Homeowners in another expensive suburb were startled when they discovered that the road connecting I-10 to their houses would be lined with strip centers. Lecky knows a couple who is considering walking away from a poorly constructed $200,000 home. Their monthly payments have shot up to $3,000; they've paid $180,000 on the house — almost its original value — yet they still owe $215,000.

Some Houston streets have as many as a half-dozen or more foreclosed houses in a row. When faced with such extreme abandonment and eventual deterioration, the best response for remaining residents is to draw on the strength of their homeowners association (HOA). The north Houston subdivision of Forestwood offers a case in point. Built in the late 1970s, its inexperienced developer sold out to another one who went bankrupt in 1985. The developer had been acting as Forestwood's homeowners association, so that when it went under, there was no longer a HOA, and no deed restrictions could be enforced. Residents who couldn't pay the private garbage collector let months of garbage pile up in the backyard. One man raised goats. There was no street lighting; the club pool was covered with slime.

PILOT PROJECT: FORESTWOOD

One resident, a schoolteacher named LaSandra Sanders, decided to save the neighborhood. She knocked on doors and tried to clean up things. "My husband and sons would mow nearby vacant lots, and it kind of caught on," Sanders says. They enlisted more neighbors by holding outdoor socials and literally stopping passing cars. Sanders and her neighborhood posse then tried to get the owners of the abandoned homesites to maintain their own properties. It often took them a while to figure out whether a house was actually vacant, suburban life being what it is. Once they were sure a house was abandoned, it could take several more months to track down the owner.

Making Forestwood their pilot project, the Center for Public Policy and Houston Proud stepped in to assist the Forestwood residents. In October 1986 Forestwood achieved a milestone. By getting approval from the necessary 50 percent of property owners, Forestwood could recharter its HOA, giving it legal power to maintain restrictions and collect fees to pay bills. Forestwood's destiny was in the hands of its homeowners.

In Forestwood, or anywhere else, when people walk away from their homes they go in many directions. They leave town, they rent apartments or buy trailer homes. Some obtain bigger houses at lower prices. It is not uncommon these days for a person making huge payments on a house to let the lender foreclose and, in the same neighborhood, find an identical house which has been repossessed by the Department of Housing and Urban Development and is being offered for $20,000 less than the value of the original home. To pull this trick, one must sign on to the new home before leaving the old one. Many desperate people find "creative" negotiating. David Montgomery, a Forestwood resident, says, "All kinds of deals are taking place. You see a lot of 'save my credit' listings in the classifieds. It's unbelievably chaotic. It's a flood. Lenders are swamped with property now; they don't really want to be in the property management business; it's a great buyer's market right now. You can get good prices and good financing, if you've got a job."

STRATEGIES FOR COMMUNITY ACTION AND PERSONAL PROFIT

Charles A. Fuller has made a business out of the chaos. He goes door to door buying houses about to foreclose, cleans them up, and resells them. Three years ago, he was himself in dire financial shape. Now he nets a six-digit income and trains teams of foreclosure buyers in seminars across the United States. Fuller sees himself as an entrepreneur who generates a previously stagnant market.

On September 13, 1986, the University of Houston Center for Public Policy and Houston Proud hold a half-day conference called "Neighborhoods at Risk: Strategies for Community Action." It takes place in a ballroom of the Marriott Brookhollow. Water is served. Tables surround the room staffed by various private and government groups. At one table sits Darryl Keller, owner of Lifestyle Management. For the right price, his company will manage a neighborhood, overseeing security, trash, landscaping, and mosquito control. Keller brags: "We take the place of the local government." The purpose of the conference is to stress the importance of a homeowners association in improving a community's quality of life by voicing their concerns to developers, local government, banks, and residents. Conference organizers also hope to cultivate future neighborhood leaders. Barton Smith speaks frankly to the audience of concerned homeowners, saying Houston is experiencing the greatest home market decline since the Great Depression.

During a break, a member of the conference steering committee tells me that Houston could tumble because of its distressed neighborhoods. He hears that New York banks are getting nervous about insuring loans here. He also tells of neighborhood civic groups going to mortgage banks, trying to renegotiate by making trade-offs. "We'll mow lawns of foreclosed properties if you'll lower mortgage rates."

Difficult years lie ahead for suburban dreams. Some literally may be plowed under, according to Smith. Others may revert to what he calls "mixed land use." But when all is said and done, Houston may grow wiser. Perhaps we'll build suburbs with more care and add meaning to our existing neighborhoods. Says David Montgomery of Forestwood, "These are tough times, but the world's not coming to an end. At least in Forestwood, we're now talking to one another."

2002 UPDATE

After the oil bust, homes in the "foreclosure rainbow" and other subdivisions in outer Houston found new life. When the local economy revived, builders went back and filled in, partly because they could get cheap lots from bankruptcy court, according to Barton Smith, currently the director of the Institute for Regional Forecasting. The healing was complete by the mid-1990s.

Houston's urge to move continually outward shows no signs of letting up. Residential development is taking place way beyond the FM 1960–Highway 6 arc, and within five to 10 years, the primary ring of development will be around the Grand Parkway, Smith said. Within the past decade there has been a trend of housing development within the inner city, an area that had been losing people since the 1960s. But suburban expansion is still the main trend.

In Forestwood on a recent spring day, the sprinklers were turned on at the entranceway, the relatively modest homes seem to be in good shape, and the trees have filled out nicely. Some of Forestwood's streets lead to dead ends with vast fields and frontier beyond. A group of teenage boys cut through the neighborhood on the way to a basketball court, but few other residents were out on this beautiful weekend day. In a newer section of Forestwood, a young couple was in the front yard with their small children. Heavy winds had been forecast. The woman knelt to place rocks on a tarp to protect a seedling. *David Kaplan*

Cite 42
SUMMER /
FALL 1998

Filling the Doughnut

Joel Warren Barna

It wasn't all that long ago that someone driving through the neighborhoods inside the Loop would have noticed an air of, if not decay, at least stagnation. Houston's energy was to be found elsewhere, out along the rim, where planned communities bloomed and new commercial complexes carved out space next to the freeways. But now that's changed. Anyone cruising the real estate circumscribed by Loop 610 today can't help but be struck by the suggestion of a city being reborn, for good or ill. The area within two miles of the center of downtown Houston has been experiencing growth rates of nearly 33 percent per year in the number of dwelling units being built, a boom that is fast transforming what was only recently a struggling business district into one of Texas's fastest-growing residential neighborhoods. One statistic makes the point: in early 1995, there were some 900 apartment and condominium units available in Houston's central business district. By the end of next year, that number will grow to almost 2,000.

The change is dramatic throughout the city. Between January and June of this year, Houston's Planning and Development Department recorded applications for 3,819 new multi-family dwellings inside the Loop and 2,921 more outside. In addition, 695 applications for single-family structures were logged inside the

Hester + Hardaway, 1998.

Clearing for new townhouse and apartment construction southwest of downtown.

Loop and 1,432 outside. This influx is touted by some as bringing new life to a number of historic properties and, more important, bringing renewed vitality to several threatened neighborhoods. Others, less sanguine, have complained that too many of the changes are destroying history rather than saving it and that the new Houston being born is not a particularly pretty one.

In terms of size, the sections of downtown and Midtown undergoing the most rapid growth are only a small part of an awesomely sprawling whole — little more than 12 square miles out of a total geographic area of 617 square miles. In urbanistic impact, however, the current change in downtown and Midtown is the most important shift of pattern since the creation of Loop 610 in the late 1950s.

Factors as diverse in scale as a rebounding national economy, an activist mayoral administration, and the end of the sewer moratorium inside 610 have combined to stimulate an interest in the central city among both builders and buyers, creating the first major centripetal force for development in Houston in more than 30 years.

DOWNTOWN DECLINE: 1960–1994

The creation of Loop 610, which linked the spokes of Houston's radial north-south and east-west freeways, made vast tracts of land accessible from high-speed motorways, opening huge areas for new suburban subdivisions by providing fast connections to the rest of the city.

Loop 610 turned Houston from a fragmenting but still centrally focused spatial entity into something more like a doughnut, with the field of development and growth focused at its edges, and it took only a few years from the Loop's construction for the center of the doughnut — downtown — to start turning into a hole.

Interchange connections between Loop 610 and Interstates 45 and 10 and U.S. Highways 59 and 290 afforded a huge jump in accessibility for each of those junctions, giving them the same status as centers for retail and office development that downtown had previously enjoyed. Downtown became just another node in a multi-node grid and a has-been at that, with already established high densities and high land prices. Although signature high-rise buildings continued to be built downtown throughout the 1970s and early 1980s, after 1979 the volume of office space outside the city core outranked that downtown by more than three to one. Downtown began a decline that turned precipitous in the mid-1980s, when the bank and savings-and-loan crisis drove the high-dollar-name tenants of the downtown towers first into retrenchment and then, in many cases, completely out of business. The economic bust hurt the suburban real estate market too, of course: the statistics for suburban office vacancy were almost always higher than for downtown. But those figures masked a deeper abandonment of the central city. By the late 1980s, almost 35 percent of downtown Houston was given over to surface parking.

Similar scary conditions developed just outside the downtown core, where increasing numbers of properties went vacant. Residential and small commercial properties on and around Main Street south of the Pierce Elevated were abandoned; many burned, leaving gaps in the city fabric. The decline, already pronounced in the Scott Street area east of downtown, moved westward from the central business district, clearing away blocks of Fourth Ward and traveling through Midtown along Dallas and West Gray, up through the eastern ends of Westheimer, Alabama, and Richmond, into Montrose and across Waugh Drive to finally lap the edges of River Oaks along Shepherd Drive.

DOWNTOWN REDUX

It is in reversing this trend that the present resurgence of development is so significant. The nodes of Loop 610 have almost filled in, and now that Beltway 8, some five to seven miles farther out, is nearing completion, it seems that a sizable market of home buyers and renters who want to escape the suburbs and the time demands of commuting has developed. It's as if Houston had stretched out so far that its sprawl began doubling back on itself. The hole in the doughnut has turned into a city edge on a par with the edges outside Beltway 8 and is now open for the big shifts in density that used to be the sole province of suburban tracts. Builders and buyers have discovered that the downtown skyline is a unique amenity, something that turns the in-town segment of the multi-node grid into a memorable, affecting place.

This is a historic moment for Houston, albeit one that is not unique (similar interest in downtown living has been developing in Fort Worth, Dallas, and Austin).

Not only are the young and the hip gravitating in increasing numbers to inner-city loft spaces, but they are accompanied by a sizable number of older "empty nesters" uninterested in suburban schools and bored by suburban sameness. Still, these trends have existed, at least in an attenuated form, for a long time. The real surprise is that a major suburban residential developer is doing a booming business within a stone's throw of downtown, selling the equivalent of regular suburban houses to people who are very much like regular suburban buyers.

This is a remarkable change, and it's worth tracing the factors that have combined to stimulate the market for housing in and near downtown Houston. First, at the national scale, the economy recovered from the re-

Hester + Hardaway, 1998.

Midtown housing, 1998.

cession of the early 1990s, and Texas, now much more closely aligned with the national economy than before, completed its recovery from the effects of the real estate and oil busts of the 1980s. Interest rates for commercial and residential loans fell. Then, for reasons that are still being debated across the country, crime rates began to fall. The fear of walking on downtown streets began to decline. Throughout the city there was confidence in the economy, money available to finance construction, and a new perception about Houston's safety.

So all of a sudden, young couples, single people, and empty-nesters could contemplate living in one of those hip loft spaces that were in the news and not feel that they were placing themselves in danger.

THE MAYOR MATTERS

Given the state of the inner city, however, a falling crime rate was not in itself enough to induce a flood of new residents. Simply decreasing one negative aspect wasn't sufficient. There were other issues to deal with, from the presence of the homeless to the area's many empty blocks and buildings. What was needed to attract people downtown was something new and positive.

Over the years, many attempts had been made to come up with any number of positive changes downtown. The American Institute of Architects, the Rice Design Alliance, and the architecture schools at Rice and the University of Houston were among a number of groups that sponsored a steady stream of design workshops, shows, and think-a-thons aimed at helping developers and the city government see the potential for redevelopment in particular properties and various neighborhoods.

What may have turned the tide were the transformations of two hulking derelicts: the Rice Hotel and the Albert Thomas Convention Center. Both had long been the subject of protracted brainstorming and negotiations that went nowhere. The turning point for

these two projects, and for the attractiveness of downtown residential property in general, came with the election of Bob Lanier as mayor. A suburban apartment developer whose antipathy toward a mass transit rail system was an important part of his campaign, Lanier wasn't expected to be particularly interested in the fate of the inner city. That expectation turned out to be wrong.

"Bob Lanier was very focused from the first of his administration to the last on inner-city redevelopment. For the first time ever, he directed city resources to rebuilding central-city neighborhoods," claims Guy Hagstette, who as director of capital projects and planning for the Houston Downtown Management District has a particular interest in seeing downtown grow. "He deserves a huge amount of credit for the good things that are happening downtown now."

Lanier's point man in pushing the rebirth of downtown was Michael Stevens, who was tapped to head the Houston Housing Finance Corporation (HHFC), a city agency that had been created to use federal funds to build affordable housing. Stevens, a real estate developer who left city government following the election of Lee Brown and who is now pushing the creation of new arenas for basketball and football, says that he began at HHFC by "scouring the HHFC's outstanding bonds." The agency, he says, had borrowed lots of money for projects in the late 1970s and early 1980s and was still paying for the bonds at high rates of interest. "We refinanced those bonds," says Stevens, "and generated $20 million in liquidity for HHFC."

That bankroll enabled HHFC to buy 2,500 abandoned apartment units around the city, rehabilitate them, and sell them to developers for a profit of $9 million. Though some critics claimed that the city was getting too deep into being a real estate developer and forgetting its commitment to affordable housing — restrictions on the apartment sales were supposed to keep 30 percent of the units affordable, but there was some debate over how seriously those restrictions were enforced—Stevens says, "My concept was to only do the deals that needed doing. If a building is having a positive or a neutral impact on its surroundings, don't get involved in it. But if it's having a negative impact, hurting tax revenues from property values around it, that's the type of project where involvement by the public sector can have the maximum benefit on public funds."

BAYOU PLACE AND THE RICE HOTEL

Stevens brought this concept, funds from the HHFC, and his experience with financing commercial projects to bear on both the Rice and the Albert Thomas Convention Center. The latter was metamorphosed into Bayou Place, which, while not exactly perfect (there's lots of interior space that remains unfinished), is already a remarkable success in urban terms. The Angelika Film Center is bringing in moviegoers from across the city, while the center's restaurants and music clubs provide ancillary attractions. The result at Texas and Smith is, at least in the early going, one of the most successful public spaces that Houston has seen. The connection between Bayou Place's sidewalk cafés and the formerly all-but-dead plaza in front of the Wortham Center crackles with energy by day, and by night, with a full complement of people on the street, it's even better.

When the Rice renovation is finished—something that's projected to happen this fall—it promises to have a similarly stimulating impact on downtown life. The Rice Hotel project will have 312 lofts, but equally important, it will have 25,000 square feet of retail space, meaning, at least potentially, services for residents who will be able to shop for groceries without getting into their cars to drive outside downtown. The hopes for this retail space are big, perhaps unrealistically so. But it's clear that the interest in properties in and around Market Square is having important spin-off

effects. For example, some 25 new restaurants have opened in the area in the past year.

"The number of restaurants that have opened in the north end of downtown is amazing," says Steve Flippo, associate director of the Downtown Historic District. As someone who works to give historic buildings new uses rather than see them cleared by the wrecker's ball, he is delighted that restaurants have opened in the street-level spaces of the Brashear Building (1882), the Hogg Building (1921), the Hermann Estate Building (1916), and the Roco Building (1870).

WHO IS BUILDING WHAT, WHERE?

The perceived success of high-profile projects such as Bayou Place and the Rice Hotel add cachet to downtown living and have helped encourage a broader residential boom, something that has been building since the early 1990s, when the Houston central business district contained just under 900 dwelling units in four high-rise apartment/condominium projects: the Beaconsfield, built in 1908; 2016 Main, built in 1964; Houston House, built in 1965; and Four Seasons Place, which opened in 1982. In 1993, however, Randall Davis, who went on to become the developer of the Rice Hotel, opened his Dakota Lofts project, 53 converted industrial/warehouse spaces on William Street north of downtown. He followed this in 1995 with the Hogg Palace on Louisiana, with 79 loft spaces. The loft concept—high ceilings and tall windows, open plans with floating interior walls, exposed brick walls and ductwork, and industrial flooring—has been a staple of artists' live/work spaces throughout the country since the 1960s. Indeed, that's part of what makes them attractive to a wider market today. With the opening of Davis's properties, the loft apartment concept took on a new marketability in Houston. It formed the basis for the redevelopment of the Rice, and it provided the pattern for scores of smaller projects, either of conversion

The Metropolis, Waugh at West Gray (PageSoutherlandPage, 1997).

or new construction, built or planned north and west of downtown, with high windows turned to the Houston skyline. (Davis himself developed the most visible of these projects, the Metropolis at Waugh and West Gray, a new building in a loft style with silly-looking gargoyles, but with huge expanses of glass facing downtown.)

Other high-dollar loft residences under way for downtown include 220 Main, a 30-unit condominium project developed by Q Ratio Texas; Bayou Lofts at 907 Franklin, developed by Spire Realty, which will have 107 units; Main Street Plaza, a 110-unit project at 705 Main, developed by Randall Davis; and the 90-unit Humble Building at 1212 Main, developed by HRI. All these projects are set to open in 1999.

At the opposite end of the spectrum in terms of price, but no less significant for downtown, are four projects developed by New Hope Housing Inc., and Houston Area Community Development Corporation. These are single-room-occupancy residences at 320 Hamilton and 1414 Congress that are designed to house the formerly homeless.

As significant as this stream of projects is, the numbers are almost certain to change drastically over the next year as the Rice Hotel comes on line. As Michael Stevens notes, "The more people you have walking around downtown, the more people will feel comfortable there, and the more people will feel that living downtown is a viable option."

In addition, other developments will add to the interest in downtown. Hagstette, who lives downtown, says that four of his neighbors moved into the building where he lives when their employer moved its offices to the central city from the suburbs. He expects to see similar effects later this year, when Continental Airlines moves its headquarters downtown.

MIDTOWN MOMENTUM

All the factors that contributed to downtown's decline, and all the factors that are now contributing to its resurgence, have also affected the Midtown area, the section of the city south of downtown and west of I-45 and US-59. Like downtown, Midtown has a street grid turned 45 degrees from the north-south grid of neighborhoods to the west. And like downtown, Midtown has a lot of open land.

Hester + Hardaway, 1998.

Old, tree-lined residential streets with new multi-family apartment units.

There is a special factor at play in Midtown and the neighborhoods to its west — the lifting of the city's sewer-connection moratorium. Previously, builders were limited by the local sewer capacity to the density of previous uses of a given piece of land (or to the number of sewer connections they were able to buy elsewhere for use with the land), but now they're free (for a fee) to develop properties at much higher densities.

Townhouse project, 44 units, Tuam at LaBranch (Perry Homes, 1998).

The effect of this change can already be seen in four projects that occupy no more than a 10th of Midtown's area. Post Properties is developing Post Apartment Homes of Midtown, a project in three phases with some 600 units on the Bland Cadillac property at the corner of West Gray and Bagby. Design for the project is being provided by RTKL Associates of Dallas. Jenard Gross, who built the Rincon, a 1996 apartment project on Dunlavy at Allen Parkway, is building The Oaks, a 190-unit complex three blocks away from the Post Properties project. JPI Texas, a Houston-based firm, is constructing the Jefferson at Oak Place, designed by Kaufman Meeks Associates, on property situated between that belonging to Gross and that belonging to Post Properties. Four blocks away, Camden Realty Trust is planning a project that will take up the equivalent of six city blocks.

As construction on these projects goes forward, improvements to the streets, sewers, and water services are being undertaken with the support of the Midtown Tax Increment Finance Reinvestment Zone, or TIF, another quasi-governmental entity using the improved tax revenues from new development as seed money to get the projects the infrastructure and services they

need. As those improvements are made, the rest of Midtown will be primed for even more development.

Another significant factor in the area south and west of downtown has been the work of Perry Homes. This residential builder, best known for suburban developments, has since 1994 built scores of townhouse projects in the River Oaks Shopping Center area around Fairview Street west of Shepherd Drive.

Barbara Brown Tennant, vice president for planning and design at Perry Homes, says that she moved into the area, a neighborhood of 1920s-era bungalows with numerous rental properties, in 1992. At the time, it had seen only a few small-scale conversions to townhouses. "We saw the opportunity to deliver a new product with efficiency," Tennant says. "There was no new housing in the area at all, and I could see that there was a real market for new townhomes."

The projects built by Perry Homes and others have featured townhouses ranging in size from 2,500 to 3,900 square feet. They are built on vacant lots or on the sites of houses that, according to Tennant, can't be remodeled for new buyers. Typical townhouse buyers, she adds, are older people, many of whom have second homes. "They want a simpler lifestyle than they had in the suburbs," says Tennant, "and a townhome is easier to maintain — [it's] something you can lock up and leave for the weekend to go to the country or the beach."

Perry Homes's newest project is Baldwin Square, a 44-unit townhouse project near the intersection of Tuam and LaBranch, adjacent to Elizabeth Baldwin Park. "This is a pioneering project for us," says Tennant. Indeed, Perry Homes is creating a significant expansion of the housing stock in an area that hasn't seen any new residential construction in perhaps 65 years. Two other projects are also on the drawing boards, Tennant says. All told, Perry Homes plans more than 100 units in the area. The units will sell in the $130,000 to $160,000 price range and will be between 1,600 and 2,000 square feet in size.

The Midtown TIF played an important role in stimulating Perry Homes's interest in the area, notes Tennant. "The TIF is reimbursing us for the streetscape improvements in the right-of-way we are putting in: street trees, landscaping, sidewalks, streetlights, benches, and so on," she says. "This reimbursement helped spur all the development that is going on the area, and it's going to have a real impact on quality of life. We're not just doing sidewalks and grass. It'll be a lot nicer, because of what the TIF is willing to pay for."

A QUESTION OF QUALITY

The financial assistance and urban-design guidance of the Midtown TIF could help the Baldwin Square area avoid the problems that have plagued some other townhouse projects. Indeed, more financing for infrastructure and lots more design guidance will be necessary in the future as Midtown and downtown develop if these areas are to become the vibrant population centers that are hoped for rather than the sea of dull townhomes some fear.

One has only to look at the development around Fairview and Shepherd created in recent years by Perry Homes and others to see what should be avoided. There, the modicum of urbanity attached to the previous fabric of 1920s-era duplexes, with their classical massing and uniform setbacks, and to the bungalows from the same period, with their porches and gardens, has been replaced by inexpensively built stucco and pseudo-masonry townhouses that crowd the street, turning streetscapes of measured expansiveness and layering into areas of high density and blunt juxtaposition.

This doesn't have to be repeated; there are well-known ways to deal with the types of problems that townhouse development can create for the urban texture, and

Hester + Hardaway, 1998.

Midtown apartment complex, 1998.

the presence of TIFs as mediators and facilitators for new development holds out hope for Midtown and neartown Houston. Still, all that is required for the triumph of the really dreadful will be for the TIF oversight mechanisms to relax.

For now, I would argue that the mere fact that residential developers want to create residences in these close-in neighborhoods, many of them otherwise perilously close to abandonment, is a positive factor that should outweigh design-related concerns, at least for the present. Although concerns about the type and quality of development in these areas have been voiced and should be pursued, overall this is an enormously positive change for Houston.

However the development is carried out, one thing is for sure: it will be carried out. Further construction is taking place, linking the central city with the more stable residential areas west of Shepherd Drive. Within the next few years, downtown Houston and many of the close-in neighborhoods will be vastly different places than they have been for the past two decades. Residential and commercial development, fostered by the Lanier administration and carried forward by the tax increment districts and other entities created during the past 10 years, will increase the uses of downtown land and property to the west to form a zone of relative high density that stretches from the central business district to the Galleria/Post Oak area. In effect, Houston's core will be redefined to embrace everything in between those two nodes, giving the city a new, bipolar center. Houston is filling the doughnut.

2002 UPDATE

When I was editor of *Texas Architect* in the late 1980s and early 1990s, I decided to treat every new downtown revitalization project anywhere in the state, particularly if it involved housing, as if it were a big deal. The projects described in "Filling the Doughnut," finally, were the real thing, as was the municipal involvement that brought them about, changing negatives into (aesthetically qualified) positives over a wide area of Midtown. A bigger potential change lies on the horizon when Metro starts transit-related development along its first seven and one-half miles of light rail. That is, if Houston's experience mirrors that in Dallas, where DART's light-rail system has been so successful that in 2000, area voters approved $2.3 billion in long-term financing so the agency could extend its service another 53 miles. The most enthusiastic proponents of the expansion were the leaders of suburban communities, such as Farmer's Branch and Irving, that decades ago did their best to kill DART rail. These towns see the billions of dollars invested in new housing, retail, and office development clustered around DART's in-town Dallas stations and glimpse a way to save their own inner cities. The president of DART in 2000 even dared to predict, "Instead of a family having two or three cars, it might be able to have one car and still be able to do everything." Metro won't have some of DART's advantages for its first route: in Dallas, the first line linked downtown with southern and northern suburbs along choked freeways. But the South Main Corridor, with its enormous stock of vacant and underused properties, awaits. This could be a significant change for Houston. *Joel Warren Barna*

PLACES OF THE CITY

Photograph on preceding page:
**Bayou Bend Gardens
(Fleming & Sheppard).**

Introduction

BARRIE SCARDINO

The concept of place is as fundamental to the identity of community as it is to the identity of the individual. Like all cities, big or small, Houston is a constellation of places — hidden and exposed, public and private, ordinary and special, peaceful and crowded. In looking at various areas of the city over the past 20 years, *Cite* has been fascinated by the ways places grow and change as well as by the diversity found within any given place. Houston places, we have discovered, are neither so easily recognized nor so well behaved as the piazza or promenade, and sometimes the most authentic among them are found outside the city's mainstream.

In his exploration of the Montrose district in "Evolving Boulevard," Bruce Webb begins: "There are places that hold our interest because they seem to compress time and space into a picture of the city in miniature." Such places have been called "epitome districts." Houston has other epitome districts — areas that seem to encompass a range of history and culture and that give "clues that trigger our awareness of the larger scene" — but not many. The essays that follow are about places "inside the Loop," which in Houston means the older, more densely settled areas. *Cite* also has ventured into the vast expanse of Houston's suburban sprawl, where loose, inchoate communities of subdivisions, automobile strips, and shopping malls form cities of the non-place urban realm. In seeking those areas of Houston that are the most revealing and significant, it was not surprising that we found them in areas with longer and more complex histories. Webb's walk down Montrose Boulevard is a journey from the high culture of the Museum of Fine Arts to the low culture of tattoo parlors and condom shops. It is also a journey back in time, for the closer one gets to downtown, the older and seedier the scene becomes. Nevertheless, this particular seam in the fabric of Houston, with more substantial neighborhoods to its west and developing neighborhoods to its east, serves as a place where Houstonians can walk together and feel comfortable.

Houston's Freedman's Town grew up in a very different way from the streetcar suburb of Montrose. A part of the city's Fourth Ward partitioned in 1837, Freedman's Town became a community of freed slaves following the Civil War. The historic legacy of the area with its tight, brick-paved streets and wood-frame shotgun houses was acknowledged when Freedman's Town was designated a National Register Historic District in 1985.

Because of its adjacency to downtown, some of the land within the designated district had valuable developmental potential, particularly the land on which Allen Parkway Village was located. The large, architecturally distinguished housing project from the 1940s, with beautiful mature landscaping and views out to the greensward along Allen Parkway, became the prize in a struggle that was seen as pitting mercenary developers abetted by city officials against a powerless minority community. Among several *Cite* stories on the subject is one by Diane Ghirardo called "Wielding the HACHet" (Housing Authority of the City of Houston). Ghirardo centered her discussion around two critical questions: "How does the community treat its least advantaged members?" and "How are decisions made in Houston?" Ghirardo not only describes the place called the Fourth Ward but also hints at its meaning as a part of Houston's social conscience. Allen Parkway Village was not saved, but neither was it turned into an expensive high-rise neighborhood near downtown. Compromises were reached on all sides, and no one was completely satisfied. Most of the solid, old units have been replaced by suburban-looking apartment houses painted beige and blue with pitched roofs—making no reference whatsoever to the historical associations of the area. If any generalization about the city and its decision-making processes can be gleaned from this neighborhood's struggles, it is that Money Talks—this is the one constant that has made most of the places in Houston what they are today.

Some of those displaced from Allen Parkway Village were Indo-Chinese immigrants. But these nomads seemed content to relocate, since their cultural identity is not in where they live but in places where they shop and meet and worship. Deborah Velders (then Deborah Jensen) documented this in her study of the Asian hold on part of Midtown, not far from the Fourth Ward. She found a bustling community of Vietnamese, Indonesians, Cambodians, Laotians, Thais, Chinese, Malaysians, and Filipinos generally appreciated for their Asian restaurants and discount fabric stores. But she also discovered that such cultural communities are held together by deep ethnic and social ties that leave an imprint on the places where they gather.

Houston, like big cities everywhere, has a myriad of both hidden and visible ethnic neighborhoods. Hermann Park, the city's oldest and most heavily used park, provides an extraordinary opportunity for the city to come together in a relaxed, bucolic setting. The automobile culture may have stripped Houston of a pedestrian-friendly urbanity, but this park goes a long way toward offering the in-town diversion city-dwellers crave.

Hermann Park is, like Webb's right bank–left bank notion about Montrose Boulevard, a place in between. It borders one of Houston's most exclusive subdivisions (Shadyside) on one end and honky-tonk Almeda Road and poor neighborhoods on the other. Residents of both enjoy the park and its facilities, including the golf course (the first racially integrated golf course in the country), the zoo, Miller Outdoor Theater with free summer evening performances, the Museum of Natural Science with an IMAX theater and glass butterfly house, as well as picnic areas, playgrounds, formal gardens, and woodland trails. In "Big Park, Little Plans," Stephen Fox recounts the history of this park and hints at still greater possibilities within its borders.

Most of the city's museums are gathered just across the street from Hermann Park. In "Loose Fit," Peter Papademetriou explores the idea of an identifiable district in this collection of institutions. The impressive list includes the Museum of Natural Science, the Museum of Fine Arts, the Contemporary Arts Museum, the Children's Museum, the Holocaust Museum, the Lawndale Art Center along Main Street, and the collection of Menil-associated museums a short distance away on Montrose. This latter group of private museums, sponsored by the late Dominique and John de Menil, is brought into sharp focus in William F. Stern's "The Twombly Gallery and the Making of Place." If the museums around Hermann Park form the nucleus of the district, the Menil museums float on the edge, adding considerable content to the whole. Papademetriou concludes that Houston's major museums do form a "loose" sort of district, though he points out the difficulty of walking in an orderly fashion from one place to another.

The same could be said of the Theater District downtown. It's cozy to think of the opera, the symphony, a play by Edward Albee, and the road-show of *Cabaret* all happening at the same moment in a clustered menagerie of theater buildings—but you only go to one show at a time. While the heart of downtown may constitute a more cohesive district than the museum area, it is not a place in the sense that Broadway and Times Square are. Drexel Turner in "The Neighborhood of Make Believe" notes that while the Theater District is "conspicuous, [it is] still somewhat disjointed." The nightlife in Houston had not yet developed to make the place as memorable as the show when Turner wrote this piece in 1998.

Houston's universities are memorable places. Larry McMurtry admitted that Rice University, where he once taught, was one of his favorite Texas places (*Cite* 37, fall 1997): "Rice is one of the nicest campuses in the nation. What I like about it is that it's the center of a really dynamic city, and yet it doesn't dominate the city, nor is it dominated by the city . . . [I] like a university that can sort of hold a dignified place in the center of a huge city. I still feel very attracted." High praise for a place that Richard Ingersoll, in "Academic Enclaves," worries might be less involved with the city than it should be. Each of the city's universities has a specific identity that reflects its social community: Philip Johnson's compact, Miesian cloister at the University of St. Thomas; the classical quadrangles at Rice; the painted trees and student murals inspired by the African-American artist John Biggers along the central mall at Texas Southern University; and the huge, proletarian, commuter campus of the University of Houston identified from the freeway by the *tempietto* atop the Gerald D. Hines College of Architecture building.

While some of the seven essays that follow show the rich and evolving cultural spectrum provided by Houston's museum and theater districts, others discuss places less easily discovered—the precincts of specific social or ethnic groups. The writers provide us with a unique way of seeking the city by looking through the veil of refinement, surface spectacle, and boosterism to find a more authentic experience. These essays examine only a select few from among Houston's landscape of places. Other places that bolster a sense of its identity include NASA's Johnson Space Center in nearby Clear Lake, the Texas Medical Center, and the Galleria. Along with the Astrodome complex, still a strong Houston icon, these places are prominent on the visitor's map of the city.

Houston is a restless city, constantly changing, and the concept of place is often at odds with these shiftings. Houstonians like the novelty more than the substance of the new, but they also cling to the stability of the familiar, even — ironically — when it means rejecting protective land use controls. Uniquely and paradoxically, Houston is a city of ever-renewing old places and new places designed to provide comfortable familiarity.

Cite 49
FALL
2000

Evolving Boulevard

A WALK DOWN MONTROSE

Bruce C. Webb

Montrose Boulevard, 1911.

There are places that hold our interest because they seem to compress time and space into a picture of the city in miniature. Grady Clay, a longtime editor of *Landscape Architecture Quarterly* and a keen observer of cities, called them "epitome districts"—places that are crammed with clues that trigger our awareness of the larger scene—things around the corner, processes out of sight, history all but covered up.

Montrose Boulevard in Houston is one of those places. In a city with few notable contenders, it, or at least that portion of it that begins at Mecom Fountain and ends at the intersection with Westheimer Road, is arguably Houston's most urbane street. It serves as a bridge between the refined, right bank culture of the Museum District and the left bank counterculture strung out along Westheimer. Along the way it gathers up an eclectic collection of businesses, cultural institutions, apartments, and restaurants—a few of them squeezing alfresco dining into the narrow sidewalk—and arrays them in a way that has the look and feel of that rarest of Houston happenings: a pedestrian zone. It is also the source of curious discoveries, among them such entities as the Consulate General's Office of the People's Republic of China, a proletarian, concrete-block stronghold with a small signboard holding a brace of fading photographs of Chinese celebrations.

You can actually take a decent stroll along Montrose and feel reasonably well accommodated and diverted. North of Westheimer, the boulevard sheds some of its dignity, unravels into an inner-city version of a strip, and becomes more aware of the view from the automobile than the view from the sidewalk.

HISTORY

Epitome districts change, leaving only traces of a former life surviving from one generation to the next. Present-day Montrose Boulevard is a product of such changes. It is a far cry from its original formulation as the spine of a 260-acre subdivision built on the then-outskirts of Houston in 1911. Montrose, one of several early 20th-century streetcar suburbs, was put together by J. W. Link, a lawyer, lumberman, and former mayor of Orange, Texas. Link assembled land between Richmond, Pacific, Taft, and Graustark Streets from 25 separate owners and set out to create Houston's poshest neighborhood, naming it after the Royal Borough of Montrose in Scotland. In a precursor to what would happen in dozens of later themed subdivisions that sought metaphorical respite from the heat and relentless flatness of Houston's topography, he gave Scottish Highland names to most of the streets as well.

The Houston Land Corporation, which Link formed with several other leading Houston businessmen, provided a modern, comprehensive infrastructure for the new development, one that included complete water, sewer, gas, paving, curbs, sidewalks, and landscaping in the selling price of lots. The plan featured four major boulevards — Yoakum, Audubon, Lovett, and Montrose — with esplanades that were landscaped with seven train-car loads of palm trees and 4,000 large shade trees.

Montrose was not planned just for the wealthy. Link provided a hierarchy of lot sizes and locations so that people of modest means could afford one. Houses were required to cost a minimum of $3,000. But to encourage others to think in grand terms, Link built a mansion for himself on Montrose Boulevard at a cost of $60,000. The neoclassical house, designed by architects Sanguinet, Staats & Barnes of Fort Worth, was faced with cream-colored, vitrified brick detailed with limestone from Carthage, Missouri, and enameled terra cotta tiles. The lavish interior included a 20-

J. W. Link House, now administration building, University of St. Thomas (Sanguinet, Staats & Barnes, 1912).

Paul Hester, 1980.

by 40-foot living room with high wood wainscoting, wood-beam ceilings, and fireplaces of English Caen stone. Five bedrooms filled the second floor, and a large ballroom was installed on the third. Link sold the house to oilman T. P. Lee for $90,000 in 1916, and Lee in turn sold it to the Basilian Fathers in 1946 to form part of the nascent campus of the University of St. Thomas, where it presently serves as the administration building. Other fine houses followed, and by 1925 Montrose was essentially built out. It continued to be a distinguished address up until World War II.

Although Montrose is still a distinctive neighborhood, little evidence remains of the stately homes that once lined the boulevard. All of the eight remaining houses have been converted to nonresidential uses. Among them are the Link House, the Walter W. Fondren House (Alfred C. Finn, 1923) at 3410 Montrose (now La Colombe d'Or), and the Westheimer House (Alfred C. Finn, 1919) at 3700 Montrose (now offices). Another Finn house at 3504 Montrose was razed in 1998 to make room for the awkward backside view of an addition to Annunciation Orthodox Church.

Deed restrictions that protected the exclusively residential character of Montrose expired in 1936, abetting a chain of dislocations. By then the automobile had become a primary determinant of the form of cities. Even before World War II new suburban developments lured people away from the inner city, and the unrestricted properties along Montrose Boulevard not far from downtown became more valuable as sites for gas stations, offices, and other commercial uses. Many houses were subdivided into duplexes or apartments for rent, then demolished to make room for a strip of purpose-built commercial buildings, apartment buildings, and cultural institutions. In the late 1940s, as a response to the increasing volume of vehicular traffic, Montrose Boulevard south of Westheimer was widened by removing its esplanade.

During the 1960s and 1970s, Montrose became more a state of mind than a location. It was Houston's version of Greenwich Village — albeit a "drive-in" version, according to a 1971 *Houston Chronicle* article. The relaxed attitude in the area, a reflection of the ethos of the Age of Aquarius, appealed to a wide range of people looking for or already experimenting with alternative lifestyles. The central axis for this action stretched out along Westheimer, which developed into a kind of free zone. Houses were converted into antique shops, topless joints, boutiques, bars, and restaurants and were frequently treated to decorative makeovers that reflected the anything-goes aesthetic of the hippie culture. The intersection of Montrose and Westheimer became an epicenter for students, dropouts, and runaways looking for the zeitgeist. The action didn't spread very far along Montrose Boulevard, but the big old homes in the neighborhood that weren't subdivided for apartments housed communes. Tension resulted: Westheimer nightlife did not mix well with longtime residents or young families seeking stability.

Montrose Boulevard managed to weather these changes reasonably well, in part because prestigious institutions gave it a solid anchor. It was a case in which the street's prevailing character was itself a primary asset and tended to attract restaurants and other kindred businesses whose personae were fashionably mixed and matched. Among the major north-south streets that slice through the residential fabric flanking US-59, Montrose Boulevard stands apart as an internal street with no direct connection to the freeway system. Advertising signs on buildings tend to be small and understated, and parking is not obvious. In the section of Montrose Boulevard that runs from the museums to Richmond Avenue, only a few buildings break the dominant character — the Goodyear Tire Store, a converted service station whose orientation is more about cars than people, is the most conspicuous example.

Montrose Boulevard, looking north, with Museum of Fine Arts, in foreground.

As a rule, other buildings are pulled close to the sidewalk, sometimes with intervening landscaping, and parking is either tucked in back or to the side. Some approaches are ingenious. The Campanile, a renovated church that houses a branch of the Houston Public Library and, in what was once the educational wing, a tail of small shops and restaurants, is a model pattern that addresses both the pedestrian and the car. It provides a token parking court up front while accommodating most of the parking behind in a lot and a tiered garage. Other buildings take a more ad hoc approach, relying on curbside parking and, in the case of the Chelsea Market, using fringe space under the elevated section of US-59. Even two chunky suburban-style buildings north of Richmond, the Kroger Grocery and the Walgreen Drug Store, both with large, front-loaded parking lots, are more companionable than might be expected. Other formulaic strip centers (such as a blocklong, mustard-yellow one at 3939 Montrose and an L-shaped model at 3407 Montrose) benefit from being lodged in the urban fabric rather than spaced out, as they would be in the suburbs.

CROSSINGS

Cross-streets offer major points of syncopation in the structure of a street. Each crossing brings another character into a conjunction that is highlighted at the corners. Like a tangential conversation, the crossings dissipate the singular focus of an avenue, connecting it with other places. A hierarchy develops: sometimes one street dominates, sometimes another. Still others, recognizing the potentials of a corner to unite rather than separate, treat their two faces more or less equally.

The southern portion of Montrose Boulevard is marked by four major street crossings and one freeway overpass. The first crossing, at Bissonnet, shows Houston's best example of the City Beautiful movement. Here, three museums are brought together: the

Lillie and Hugh Roy Cullen Sculpture Garden (Isamu Noguchi, designer, with Fuller & Sadao, 1986).

Museum of Fine Arts, with its modern neoclassical Brown Pavilion (Mies van der Rohe, 1974); the shiny-skinned, parallelogram-shaped Contemporary Arts Museum (Gunnar Birkerts & Associates, 1972); and the Lillie and Hugh Roy Cullen Sculpture Garden (Isamu Noguchi, 1986), a labyrinth of freestanding planes, hillocks, and free-formed landscaping. Also part of the crossing is the anomalous villa that Houston architect William T. Cannady built for his family in 1991, a house that is imposing enough to fit in with the neighboring museums.

The buildings are wildly divergent stylistically, though with the exception of the Cannady House, which is decorated down to a domestic scale, they all demonstrate variations on a minimalist aesthetic. The interaction among the museums is complex. The Brown Pavilion, opening up its interior as an extension of a narrow fringe of sidewalk, reinforces the gentle curve of Bissonnet, a move deflected by the razor-edged corners and blank sides of the Contemporary Arts Museum, whose shape, set into the orthogonal street grid, creates a background for a triangular patch of space facing the intersection. This small but prominently positioned scrap of real estate, once embellished with temporary sculptures, art installations, and banners, has been quieted down considerably by a landscaping plan with a pool and benches that creates a street-level plaza. Both buildings push their points of

Administration and Junior School Building (Carlos Jiménez, designer, with Kendall/Heaton Associates, 1994).

view almost to the paradigmatic—the MFAH's glass box registering clarity and openness and the CAM's metal box, whose entrance is a narrow slot at one of the vertices, an air of indifference and mystery. The sculpture garden does a good job of acknowledging each by giving the MFAH a large garden space and responding to the angularity of the CAM in its interior spatial divisioning.

The controlled character of this auspicious beginning to Montrose Boulevard is extended another block north by the Glassell School of Art (S. I. Morris Associates, 1978) on the east side of Montrose and the MFAH's Central Administration and Glassell Junior School Building (Carlos Jiménez with Kendall/Heaton Associates, 1994) on the west. The latter turns an appealing and elegant entrance façade to the boulevard, with well-composed windows that express the various functional volumes within. The Glassell School, by contrast, is a mall-like structure, with its main entrance opening onto the sculpture garden and its primary axis running parallel to Montrose. This configuration leaves a long, reflective, glass-block wall facing the street that is only interesting at night, when the interior is revealed. One block north, the picturesque, Regency-style Fourth Church of Christ Scientist (Wilbur Foster, 1940) and the brooding Holland House Masonic Lodge Number 1 (William McGinty, 1954) address each other in a cross-axial metaphysical dialogue.

Montrose Boulevard's other major intersections are far less distinguished. At Montrose and Richmond a gas station opens onto Richmond, and a convenience store and branch bank, both sited diagonally, are gathered and settled by the quiet of the five-story International Bank of Commerce Building. The Alabama crossing is populated by three gas stations, two facing onto Alabama and the other onto Montrose, and the stately Link Mansion (Saguinet & Staats, 1911), which gives the secluded campus of the University of St. Thomas behind it a Montrose Boulevard address. The Link Mansion, with its grand front porch, *porte cochere*, and blocky massing, is itself reminiscent of an old-style gas station, but with much more opulent scale, detailing, and material richness. The generous landscaped lawn, which formerly opened onto Montrose, was in 1988 privatized by wrapping it behind a perfunctory brick wall with metal bars, a wall that disfigures the character of the house and diminishes its street appeal.

Where the Richmond and Alabama crossings hint at the changing character of Montrose as it moves northward, the Westheimer intersection, where Montrose Boulevard once ended, is a resounding finale to the street's graciousness. Here the ragtag commercialism of Westheimer prevails, producing an intersection that includes a Taco Cabana drive-in restaurant with an apron parking lot, a convenience store and gas station, a pharmacy at the tail end of an inchoate strip of long, low buildings, and a newer strip center dominated by Blockbuster — the name is Dickensian — and an Eckerd Drugs that faces onto Westheimer.

Physically, the Westheimer-Montrose crossing resembles many other Houston intersections in older

Westheimer-Montrose intersection.

Gay Pride Parade, Westheimer-Montrose intersection.

suburban areas, except here little ironies spill out along Montrose, with stores such as Atomic Music and Extreme Skin Art and Condoms Galore sidling up to the Interfaith Ministries for Greater Houston. This intersection holds a symbolic cachet as the location of the sil-

Hester + Hardaway, 2000.

US-59 overpass bridging Montrose Boulevard.

ver disco ball that's raised above the street during the annual bacchanal of the Gay Pride parade. Just north of the intersection, a jazzy pylon marks the location of the flashy Montrose Townhouse Lofts (I. Phillips/Wild Design, 1997). Westheimer can be fascinatingly tawdry, especially at night, when it turns into a kind of street-wise costume party. But when it reaches Montrose, most of that character has been neutered by corporate symbols of the non-place urban realm. This is too bad, since properly configured as a people place and perhaps populated by institutions such as the Art Car Museum and a few kindred bars and restaurants, the intersection could become a lively meeting place for the cultures of the two streets.

As notable as the intersections is a cross-axis that appears in the form of the US-59 viaduct, a formidable intrusion whose gritty underside has been likened to a vast hypostyle hall. The viaduct segments Montrose, creating a shadowy underworld where, to the conster-nation of neighboring residents and business owners, vagrants often take up residence. All this will come to an end in the next few years when this section of US-59 is depressed below ground level. Like the success-ful effort by J. W. Link to get an existing railroad line re-located outside the boundaries of his development, lowering the freeway is an act of purification. The re-markable project was spearheaded by a coalition of neighborhood groups and civic associations who convinced the Texas Department of Transportation that this was a more reasonable solution than widening or double-decking the overburdened roadway. The scale and expense of the project is daunting, but when completed it will open new continuous vistas along Montrose Boulevard. The cross-axial gap that Montrose will soon cross, however, will remain, unless the bridge built to span US-59 can itself mend the rift, perhaps by becoming a contemporary version of the Ponte Vecchio.

NEW BUILDINGS

Many of the buildings that line Montrose Boulevard are nondescript, of the kind that establish an urban background. Others stand out as little urban experiments that have popped up over the years. Chelsea Market, which opened in 1985 on a burned-out block in the shadow of US-59, was an attempt by architect John Kirksey and partners Lance Goodwin and Norbert Choucroun to create a commercial development that both opened out onto the public street and contained a secluded pedestrian promenade within. As a typological prospect, it suggests an alternative to the auto-dominated strip centers that fill the city's commercial hinterlands. But it was never more than a segment of the length it would have needed to be to prove itself. People found it a perplexing anomaly; stores located

behind the exterior frontage or, even worse, on the second floor, went unnoticed. Despite winning several design awards, it was troubled almost from the beginning. By 1987 the center was 35 percent empty and fell into foreclosure. Not long after, it lost two of its bigger clients, Banana Republic and the upscale Anthony's restaurant. It was also troubled by mismanagement in the hands of Resolution Trust Corporation, which never seemed to understand what to do with the property. It's a good thing they didn't throw the baby out with the bathwater, though. Today, anchored by longtime tenant Butera's, a delicatessen that moved from a location closer to the museums, and the upscale Redwood Grill, the center seems to have found its metier. Main Street Theater occupies a back corner of the complex, and most of the in-between and upstairs spaces have become offices.

A little farther north at 4100 Montrose is the Campanile, Ray Bailey Architects' noteworthy conversion of the Central Church of Christ (William Ward Watkin, 1941, 1947), the first nonresidential building constructed on the boulevard following the lapse of deed restrictions. In 1986 the educational wing was made over into shops, restaurants, and offices, while the church itself became a branch of the Houston Public Library. The L-shaped plan of the complex neatly embraces a small front-court parking lot that is sometimes used for outdoor activities.

Several large apartment projects also attract notice, among them the twin towers of the Parc IV and V Condominiums at 3614 and 3600 Montrose (Jenkins Hoff Oberg Saxe, 1963, 1965). The 12-story buildings dwarf their neighbors and could have inflicted considerable damage to the street had they followed the present-day practice of garnishing upscale apartment buildings with garish, thematic decoration. Instead, they exude the studied simplicity and precision of the

Hester + Hardaway, 2000.

Montrose Boulevard, looking north toward Parc IV and Parc V apartment towers (Jenkins Hoff Oberg Saxe, 1963, 1965).

modern movement in clearly expressed modular construction of a white concrete frame and brick infill. The two buildings are well sited, with one holding the street edge and the other stepping back to create a front open space.

The Court at Museum Gate (Compendium, 1985), rendered in a somewhat overbearing postmodern idiom, is a 1980s period piece at 4004 Montrose. Although low-rise, it is bulky and overcoded in effect. The intricate plan densely fits 47 units and necessary parking onto a relatively small lot but smothers its exterior space within a formidable brick wrapper, giving it the look of a fortified enclave, partially relieved by exuberant landscaping on a narrow strip between the building and the sidewalk.

Nearby at 4801 Montrose was, until recently, a vividly painted, suburban ranch house that had been moved from a lot across the street to make space for Bell Park, a neighborhood-scaled garden respite with a pool and fountain. The house had marked the entrance to Gramercy Gables (F. Stanley Piper, 1928), a revivalist British Tudor-style residential village located in a landscaped 1.37-acre setting. Apartments are still there at the rear of the site, but where the house was is now empty land on which a 19-story high-rise apartment building will soon be erected. The Montrose-fronting section of Gramercy Gables was the subject of a battle between preservationists, who wanted to save the buildings, and the Finger Companies, which sees the land supporting some 280 loft-style units. In the context of Houston's weak preservation regulations, attempts to save the Montrose section of Gramercy Gables were too little too late. The new building will not be companionable to the surrounding residential neighborhood and may portend more of the same to come.

A similar case of disfiguring the sectional properties of the street occurred some 10 years ago, when the vertical scale of the Museum District was reversed by the construction of 5000 Montrose (Golemon & Rolfe, 1982), a hefty 22-story concrete apartment building that squeezed and dwarfed its neighbor, the once-fashionable Plaza Hotel (Joseph Finger, 1926). Prior to construction of this towering condominium, the Plaza Hotel, the Warwick Hotel, and two nearby church towers gave the area a more or less uniform vertical scale. The Finger Companies toyed with the idea of redeveloping the nine-story Plaza Hotel as an offset to the damage they were planning to do to Gramercy Gables but have abandoned the project as too costly.

MONTROSE SURVIVES

Within its urban frame, Montrose Boulevard is more artifactual than contrived. It represents a street that has evolved out of real events occurring in real time. There is an uncanny spatial composition there that is hard to explain. Against the prevailing building line, pockets of space and open lawns take on a distinct figural character that does not exist on streets where building lines and other homogenizing principles are scrupulously followed. Robert Maxwell, the former dean of Princeton's School of Architecture, sets out an argument for such places as having the quality of "sweet disorder and the carefully careless." "It is possible," Maxwell writes, "to see all cultural manifestation as a mechanism whose aim is to ensure a balance between control and inspiration, between order and disorder, in a dynamic system of change. Difficult as the attributes may seem to be, and in spite of the fact that at any one time they may be in opposition, they are both concerned positively with the same issue — the degree of control needed to assure and to structure an ever surprising future."

For architects working in terms of such an idea, the challenge is not to create everywhere the patterns of order for which their education prepares them too well. This has been tried by the planners and the architects of suburbs and model cities and has produced little beyond social and cultural entropy and boredom. The real challenge is to mediate between a stifling predetermined order and the disorder of individual narcissism—and through that to shepherd change. This is not a simple task, particularly in places such as Montrose, where incursions of seediness threaten stability. And when such incursions are successfully resisted, they make the area targets for profit-driven, large-scale development.

But Montrose, both boulevard and surrounding community, has a deserved reputation for self-serving activism. Here, battles have been joined over many issues, some of them quite remarkable. In 1990 a group of Montrose residents became frustrated that police were not doing enough to stem a rash of vandalism and car theft. They organized a march on the home of one of the suspected vandals, chanting, "Leave us alone" and carrying signs in English and Spanish. The demonstration was followed by the reinstitution of a citizens patrol. In another case, a neighborhood civic association carried on a three-year campaign to get large mounds of sand removed from under the US-59 overpass. The sand had been stored there for use on the highways in case of freezing weather. But it had become an eyesore and attraction for vagrants who took up residence under the viaduct.

Montrose Boulevard's prime location makes it ripe for plucking. Already, misguided visions of a much denser street of apartments, which in one version would create blocks of mid-rise apartments with shops beneath, dazzle some developers and architects. But urbanization doesn't necessarily mean bigger or require the higher densities of the 19th-century East Coast urban model. Neither does it mean the wholesale recasting of areas of the city into simulations of the New Urbanism, especially when the uprooting of a genuine urban past is a part of the bargain. For Houston, the best urbanization may be the sort that has evolved along Montrose. From Bissonnet to Westheimer, Montrose Boulevard could well be an example of what an unzoned city might be expected to look like when it is on its best behavior.

2002 UPDATE

Montrose Boulevard continues to evolve. The 19-story apartment building located on the former site of the Gramercy Gables apartments, which was still being planned when this article was written in 2000, is nearing completion. It may be the harbinger of what is to come because of the attractiveness of the Montrose area.

The ambitious Texas Department of Transportation project presently in the planning stages will see the freeway overpass that crosses Montrose dismantled and US-59 relocated in a below-grade channel.
Bruce C. Webb

"Lure of the Bungalow" by William F. Stern in *Cite* 16 (winter 1986) discusses the architecture and development of Montrose and other early streetcar suburbs in Houston.

Cite 8
WINTER
1984

Wielding the HACHet
at Allen Parkway Village

Diane Y. Ghirardo

The recent resolution of the Houston City Council (July 1984) to approve the Housing Authority of the City of Houston's (HACH) plan to demolish Allen Parkway Village caps at least seven years of determined efforts by a number of city agencies and Houstonians to clear away both the low-cost housing project and housing in the adjacent Fourth Ward. If the demolition program is successful, both black and white Houstonians will have been poorly served by their elected and appointed officials; taxpayers will shoulder entirely unnecessary burdens; and a few landlords and developers will be enriched at the expense of the rest of the community. The case of Allen Parkway Village (APV) raises at least two crucial questions for Houston:

• How does the community treat its least advantaged members?

• How are decisions made in Houston?

HISTORY

Allen Parkway Village was built during World War II as San Felipe Courts, wartime public housing for white defense workers. The land was acquired through eminent domain. As noted in the April 1942 issue of *Architectural Record*, design and structure of the complex were of special significance. The architects (MacKie and Kamrath, Claude E. Hooton, Eugene Werlin, and C.

A. Johnson) managed to fit 1,000 units into 37 acres of Houston's predominantly black Fourth Ward without sacrificing ventilation or variety in unit size. Federal guidelines at the time encouraged fireproof construction; the buildings are of reinforced-concrete frames,

Boundaries of Fourth Ward and Allen Parkway Village.

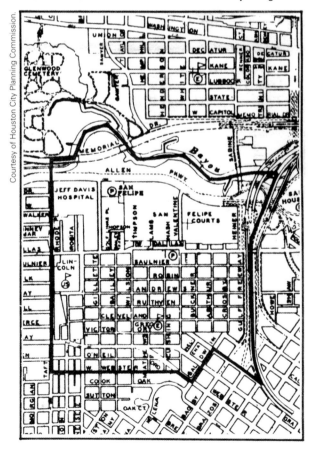

Courtesy of Houston City Planning Commission.

Allen Parkway Village, 1985 (Associated Architects of Houston, 1942).

with solid slab or pan-and-joist floors, cavity walls with brick exteriors, and hollow-tile plastered interiors. Referring to the solidity of construction, one Houston architect remarked, "If Houston ever undergoes nuclear attack, only Allen Parkway Village will survive."

A chain-link fence kept the white residents of San Felipe Courts at safe remove from the adjacent Fourth Ward. With the end of legal racial segregation in 1964, APV was desegregated, then became predominantly

black. By the late 1970s, as land values in downtown Houston soared, APV's strategic site between River Oaks, the central business district, and Buffalo Bayou made it attractive as a potential development site. HACH authorities began seeking demolition approval from the Department of Housing and Urban Development (HUD) in 1977 because, as J. L. Phillips, chairman of the HACH Board of Commissioners, wrote to Secretary Samuel Pierce in 1981: "Business leaders and developers have been approaching the authority for years to express an interest in the purchase of the land."[1] Phillips identified interest as "keen" but did not name developers. On the local scene, HACH pursued highly deceptive strategies to help ensure the sale of the project. Failure to maintain APV and attrition reduced the number of tenants by over one-third.[2] The Dallas Housing Authority pursued the same policy when it recently allowed Washington Place to deteriorate through lack of maintenance and failed to replace tenants when old ones moved, despite a critical shortage of low-cost housing.

Both in Dallas and Houston, the housing authorities advertised the supposedly adverse conditions of the two projects by leaving vacant and then boarding up the units that faced onto major public thoroughfares. Clearly this move was calculated to prompt the middle and upper classes who drive by on their way to and from work to view each project as an "eyesore"—and hence gain their implicit support for demolition.[3] But while the beneficiary of the destruction of Washington Place in Dallas was never in doubt (Baylor University Medical Center), the forces behind the decade-long struggle for the demolition of APV have operated largely under a cloak of secrecy.

Early plans to demolish APV stalled when HACH administrators were fired—the only time HUD had ever recommended such action anywhere in the United States.[4] With the appointment of Earl Phillips in August of 1982 as housing director, HACH proceeded with its program to demolish APV with even more vigor.

HACH currently maintains a policy of "constructive eviction": according to APV Resident Council President Lenwood Johnson, the authority refuses to allow families which have grown larger to move into larger quarters. When a family of four people is squeezed into a one-bedroom unit, the family eventually elects to leave, even if it means moving into substandard housing. For HACH and the Houston Department of Planning and Economic Development, destruction of APV is an essential precondition to the "urban renewal" of the Fourth Ward, a community of small, late-19th-century and early-20th-century clapboard cottages and shotgun houses which constitute Houston's oldest black community. For these agencies to complete their plans to demolish the Fourth Ward, APV must go first.

THE ACTORS

In the aftermath of a power struggle between HACH Director Earl Phillips and Planning and Development Director Efraím S. García over control of the area, Phillips had to settle for APV, while García retained control of the Fourth Ward.[5] Having worked closely with the Mexican-American community to accomplish the process for the rehabilitation of the Susan V. Clayton Homes low-cost housing project with the creation of the adjacent El Mercado del Sol on the eastern edge of downtown, García turned his energy toward relocating the blacks from the western edge of downtown rather than contemplating a renewal based on the Clayton/El Mercado example. His plan calls for Urban Development Action Grants (UDAG) to assist Fourth Ward families in their move out of the Fourth Ward, warning that if they fail to cooperate now, there will be no aid at all. For instance, García told me that if owners were to accept an offer from Hong Kong–based Allright Inc., which has already acquired property on Heiner Street along the eastern edge of the Fourth Ward, residents stand to receive nothing.[6]

This kind of thinly veiled economic blackmail evades the central issue of whether the residents should be moved at all, who will pick up the tab, and who will reap the profits. García is quick to label opponents of his proposal as "white do-gooders" and "outspoken blacks" who are not Fourth Ward residents.[7] The implication here (and he is not fully correct anyway) is that neither group has a right to participate in the fate of the Fourth Ward.

Steven V. Jarnigan is a real estate developer who represents a coalition of Fourth Ward property owners which informally dates back several years but has been most active in the past two years.[8] Jarnigan believes that recent tax increases in the area, artificially low rents, and the poor condition of the houses leave redevelopment as the only option. He expresses concern about the well-being of the tenants but finds building new housing the only option for them, and he insists that any development in the area will include 300–500 low-cost units (largely for the inoffensive elderly poor). But although he realizes that this will still leave several thousand people homeless with no low-cost housing elsewhere, he can see no viable alternative for Houston.[9]

Against the power and money represented by those who want to destroy APV and the Fourth Ward stand Lenwood Johnson, the president of the APV Resident Council; community activist Barry Klein; the Freedman's Town Association; the Fourth Ward Ministerial Alliance; Rice professor Dana Cuff and other faculty members from Rice University, the University of Houston, and Texas A&M; American Civil Liberties Union (ACLU) lawyer Stefan Presser; and a few architects from the area. Their financial and political resources are no match for those of their opponents, but even with meager funds and no staff support they have managed to challenge the data and conclusions of the HACH committee charged with evaluating whether APV should be renovated or demolished.[10] Despite the limited resources of this group, HACH has tried to silence opponents in several ways.

Lenwood Johnson is a soft-spoken, disabled, single parent who has lived in APV for only a few years, but it did not take him long to realize that the black community in the Fourth Ward was in serious danger. Soon after being elected president of the APV Resident Council, Johnson initiated a broad-based attempt to learn about the planned demolition of the APV. He

sought help from Fourth Ward ministers and residents but found little support for his view that "as APV goes, so goes the Fourth Ward." Events have proven the wisdom of Johnson's perception, and Fourth Ward activists are beginning to rally around the cause of the entire area. Raising some of the central concerns of APV residents and the larger black community, he began to attend HACH and City Council meetings. His efforts did not go unnoticed by HACH, which undertook a variety of objectionable actions designed to make it difficult for him to carry out his duties as president of the resident council and perhaps to intimidate him into silence.

HACH denied him use of the photocopying services available to all other resident council presidents on the grounds that he used it too much (never mind that he represented one-fourth of HACH's public housing stock). The lock in the APV community center was changed and he was denied a key, making it difficult to hold meetings. At an APV resident meeting which he was chairing, HACH Director of Housing Management Karen Moone instructed police to remove Johnson—they threw him to the floor—despite the fact that HACH had no right to intervene in tenant meetings. U.S. District Court Judge Norman Black affirmed this in a hearing on June 26, 1984.[11]

At a resident council election in June 1984, HACH Director Moone first invalidated a number of ballots and then, when Johnson won anyway, invalidated the entire election. Such intervention is not only unprecedented elsewhere, it threatens the rights of the tenants. On another occasion, according to Johnson, when Houston's resident council presidents met with Phillips at a dinner meeting in 1983, only Johnson did not receive a meal.

As petty as these actions seem, they are the strategies HACH is employing to humiliate and silence Johnson. Such behavior by HACH is more reminiscent of some two-bit totalitarian state than it is of a democratic institution in the United States; tactics which aim to stifle dissent threaten not just Johnson, but anyone who attempts to voice principled opposition to the policies of appointed or elected officials.

MAINTENANCE AND INFLATED REHABILITATION COSTS

As any homeowner knows, if you undertake no repairs on a structure for a decade, it will become dilapidated. Nothing has been done to APV for nearly a decade, and not surprisingly, it has become dilapidated. Beginning at least in 1977, HACH authorities failed to maintain APV in order to enhance the argument that it ought to be torn down; once they had made the proposal to Housing and Urban Development, HUD promptly denied HACH federal funds to repair a project which might be torn down at any time. HUD's grounds were, not unreasonably, that it would be a waste of taxpayer money.[12] Even by HACH's own wildly inflated figures, tearing down APV and moving the tenants is going to be more than twice as costly as rehabilitating

it. The cost of rehabilitating APV is a very troubling issue in the whole matter and cuts right to the heart of what is being hidden.

In the September 1983 HACH report, the total estimated cost of rehabilitation is set at $36.2 million, or $36,200 per unit. At the very same time, renovation of Clayton Homes is set at $14,546 per unit: units in much the same condition as APV. Elsewhere the job has been done for considerably less than $20,000 per unit. In San Antonio, for example, projects were modernized for between $15,358 and $18,181 per unit.[13] At Clayton Homes, HACH plans to do site work, modernize exteriors, and do interior remodeling; these are precisely the changes that are necessary at APV. Robert S. Means's annual publication, *Building Construction Cost Data*, the standard reference manual for cost estimators, lists the cost of *brand new* public housing (low-rise) at $42,900 per unit. In the HACH report of 1983, HACH lists the costs of utilities site work at $8.70 per square foot; Means gives a figure for this kind of project of $6.56 per square foot.[14] Among other expenses,

Allen Parkway Village, backyard gardens.

Paul Hester, 1985.

HACH lists $780,000 for security lighting. This will include, the report says, 10 high-pressure sodium fixtures per acre, plus building flood lamps and pavilion flood lamps. Given the amount of the site occupied by buildings, this figure appears ludicrous: lighting of this wattage (more appropriate for a parking lot) will light the project to a level comparable to high noon on the Fourth of July. HACH also claims that the façades need to be removed due to moisture penetration; however, close examination by architects reveals that cleaning and repointing the brick would be sufficient — *and* substantially cheaper.

Part of the cost for renovation derives directly from the HACH policy of not replacing tenants when they move; when an apartment is left unoccupied, sooner or later it will be vandalized. Initially, Phillips claimed that vacant units were not being filled because no one wanted to move into APV, and he denied that there was a waiting list.[15] When HACH decided to evict Indo-Chinese tenants who had bribed a housing official to find apartments at APV, however, Phillips based his action on the grounds that they had moved ahead of others on the waiting list.[16] A waiting list finally emerged, but only after legal action was initiated by the ACLU. The size of the list made it clear that, even with APV, Houston's need for low-cost housing is enormous.

THE DECISION-MAKING PROCESS IN HOUSTON

Houstonians ought to be upset about the way decisions are made in their community — especially when they have to pay the bill. The cards regarding APV that Houston officials hold have never been laid on the table. As the record shows, the entire campaign against APV and the Fourth Ward consists of misinformation, no information, crucial information withheld, concealed, or distorted, and opponents threatened and intimidated. Clearly a great deal of money for someone is riding on the fate of APV — which no doubt explains why it could not be placed fully on the public agenda.

Looked at in the cold light of day, Houston's largest and most solidly constructed public housing complex — paid for by taxpayers, structurally sound, and not a nest of crime and vice — will be demolished in order to allow potential developers full use of a site between River Oaks and the CBD, overlooking Buffalo Bayou, for expensive housing or office towers and a few hundred units of public housing for the low-income elderly and force taxpayers to subsidize a complete revamping of the road, sanitation, water, and lighting systems to "make the site attractive to developers."[17]

One proposal on the agenda is to create a tax-increment zone whereby taxes on Fourth Ward land would be frozen up for 40 years so that as development occurred, tax revenues over the base would be used for the infrastructure improvements *only in the zone itself.* Thus not only would the new Fourth Ward development *not* increase the tax base for Houston as a whole, it would ensure that taxpayers pick up increased general costs — even those generated by the zone itself (police, fire, administration) — in addition to the normal increases generated by inflation. Another problem with this kind of financing is that, unlike other bonds, voters need not be asked to approve it: it can be done by fiat. Developers cannot lose under the current "redevelopment" plans for the Fourth Ward and APV.

COST TO TAXPAYERS

At a minimum, then, through various levels of taxation, taxpayers will be paying for storm systems, sanitary systems, gas systems, underground electric systems, demolition of APV and the Fourth Ward, relocation costs for up to 12,000 people, and new low-cost housing and Section 8 housing subsidies for an indefinite period of time. Taxpayer dollars are being used to alleviate costs to developers and help current owners sell their property. Do Houston's taxpayers really want to subsidize the enrichment of developers — and then also bear the cost (through federal tax subsidies) of relocating and housing several thousand residents?

Aerial view, Fourth Ward, looking west from downtown before demolition of Allen Parkway Village.

Placing this issue on the public agenda hardly guarantees a just solution. As John Kenneth Galbraith noted in a recent article, prosperity and the achievement of middle-class status following the Depression and World War II seem to have led to less, rather than greater, concern for the well-being of the poor and disadvantaged. Although exactly what has fueled this tendency is not clear, that it is a real force in contemporary politics is increasingly apparent.[18] Nothing seems to have aroused Houston citizens as much as the prospect of having a low-cost project in their neighbor-

Aerial view, Fourth Ward, with new development on the Allen Parkway Village site.

hood, and in fact, for the past few years, they have successfully resisted such proposals.[19] This is known as the NIMBY effect: "not in my backyard," and that is about the only answer that Houston's neighborhoods have to the problem of where to house low-income families. By contrast, the Fourth Ward welcomes APV and is no doubt the only community in the city that would.

The important point, however, is that issues such as the fate of APV and the Fourth Ward never do come onto the public agenda. One or two City Council meetings in which a proposal sails through does not constitute an agenda. By public agenda, I refer to the presentation of diverse points of view, careful study of the long-term consequences of a decision, not only in that section of the community immediately affected but on the entire community in future years.

Placing matters on the public agenda demands *real* debate, not attempts to silence different points of view; it demands a press which resists mindlessly repeating official pronouncements; it demands committees to study the proposal which are not hand-picked to become involved in deciding issues which affect the community.

For a democracy to exist, citizens must participate in the decision-making process, but this cannot happen if they are ill informed about issues. HACH's deceptive report, its attempts to silence opponents, its failure to maintain APV, and its wildly lopsided distortion of renovation costs make it impossible for Houston's citizens to make responsible decisions now. Placing APV on the public agenda is the first of many steps that Houston must take toward the creation of a community which serves the interests of more than a few wealthy developers.

If we assess Houston by the way it treats its minorities in APV, the community emerges as seriously deficient. Blacks and Indo-Chinese in APV and the Fourth Ward will be forced out of their homes as well as their communities, with all that implies: displace-

ment anxieties, increased death rate among the elderly, and increased community problems. If APV were like Nickerson Gardens in Los Angeles, where 5,000 people live in a project which has a crime rate 12 times higher than other places in Los Angeles, then there might be reason to tear it down. But it is not.

There *are* other possibilities which would maintain the low-cost housing, permit tenants to become owners and to improve their property, ensure a fair return on their property to landlords (who have taken tax benefits for depreciation over the years, too), and spare the community. Among these are cooperative ownership with tenants allowed to share ownership with a public body, as has happened in St. Louis. Such programs gradually reduce public monies, allow tenants a stake in the community, and enable them to work to make their housing better. Jarnigan believes such programs are too advanced for Houston, but in fact there are no reasons why the city could not explore them and begin to blaze some trails. A community disrupted and dispersed is likely to have far more — and far more expensive — problems than one that is nurtured and helped to improve. Unless taxpayers blindly are willing to take on this enormous cost burden, someone will have to talk publicly about who pays and who reaps the profits in the Fourth Ward.

Notes

1. Robert L. Moore to Nancy Chisholm, letter of November 4, 1977. The name of the prospective buyer never appeared in correspondence between HACH and HUD and remains secret today. Documents do attest to the fact that there was such an individual, however. City Councilman Lance Lalor charged in 1981 that former Mayor Jim McConn was "in league with developers" to clear out the Fourth Ward and that he refused to spend funds for normal upkeep and improvements in the ward (*Houston Forward Times,* March 21, 1981). At the time of HACH's original proposal to HUD in 1977, APV was 95 percent occupied.

2. Karen M. Moone to Earl Phillips, "Occupancy Report for January 1984." Total units occupied numbered 608.

3. Public housing activists and HUD officials have found the same strategy and pursued it elsewhere as well.

4. HACH Director William A. McClellan and his financial director were fired in April 1982 for financial irregularities.

5. In September 1983 HACH submitted a proposal to redevelop APV and the Fourth Ward and to keep both projects under HACH control. In the meantime, García had been pursuing his own strategy with Fourth Ward landowners and developers. See Leigh Hermance, "Fourth Ward: A $100 Million Ghetto," *Houston City Magazine* 8 (May 1984): 106–111, 118–130, 137–145.

6. Steven V. Jarnigan of the Fourth Ward Property Owners Association expressed surprise when I related García's account of an offer from Allright Inc. some three or four months earlier: he said he had never heard of such an offer.

7. Hermance, "Fourth Ward," 119.

8. While some landlords pressured the HACH board to demolish APV and worked out the sweetheart deal with García that has the city and the federal government (read: taxpayers) paying a hefty sum of money to clear and improve the land, García has figured out a way to use federal and local tax dollars to facilitate sale of the property. García has been working closely with the property owners group, and when I asked him who would be picking up the tab and who would be making the profits, he flew into a rage and hung up on me.

9. Historically, new low-cost housing has proven too expensive for the former residents to return to, and there is no guarantee that things would be any different in the Fourth Ward. Property which currently sells for $5–$6 per square foot but has been revalued at $10–$12 will be sold at $20 per square foot—while adjacent areas sell for $39 per square foot, and just across the freeway, the figure often exceeds $700 per square foot. The best guess is that the eventual sales price will be a good deal higher, but still lower than adjacent areas. Despite the current economics of the situation, there is no question that things have arrived at this point because of the concerted efforts of a group of investors who have targeted the area for the next big development. Without this predatory kind of activity, the Fourth Ward and APV would not be in their current difficulties. If the argument is that current rents are "artificially low," it is equally true that current property taxes and values are "artificially high" because of speculative activity.

10. Johnson and Klein prepared a detailed critique and response to the September 1983 HACH report on APV and the Fourth Ward. Their November 1983 report challenged some of the fundamental premises and facts of the HACH report and proposed viable alternatives which would spare APV and the Fourth Ward.

11. *Johnson v. Housing Authority of the City of Houston,* Civil Action No. H-84-2682 (S.D.Tx., July 31, 1984). See also Janet Elliott, "Housing Authority Told Not to Meddle," Houston Post, June 27, 1984, 8B.

12. See, for example, the letter from Rogelio R. Santos of the HUD office to Earl Phillips on January 27, 1983, denying again a request to use funds allocated in 1979 for APV repairs.

13. Janet Elliott, "S.A. Chooses Facelifts for Housing Projects," *Houston Post,* November 14, 1983.

14. HACH figures for total costs are found in Housing Authority of the City of Houston, "Technical Report: Allen Parkway Village/Fourth Ward," September 1983, 6–10. For the Means figures see Robert Snow Means, *Building Construction Cost Data* 1984, vol. 42, Kingston, Maine, 1984.

15. Janet Elliott, "Vacancies Are Plentiful, but Renters Are Few for Allen Parkway," *Houston Post,* November 24, 1983.

16. Ira Perry, "Village Residents Staying," Houston Post, January 1, 1984. In both cases information came from HACH spokesperson Esther Delpolyi.

17. García, interview, September 21, 1984.

18. John Kenneth Galbraith, "The Affluent Society Reconsidered," *Los Angeles Times,* September 2, 1984.

19. Residents of Spring Branch, Westbury, and even Pasadena have stopped low-income projects in recent years.

2002 UPDATE

A decade after Ghirardo's insightful investigation of the APV saga, Brad Tyer in *Cite* 33 (fall 1995/winter 1996) accurately reported the swollen controversy: "Allen Parkway Village now symbolizes class issues, accountability issues, architectural and historical issues, administrative issues, and political issues."

Allen Parkway Village was listed in the National Register of Historic Places in 1988 as the San Felipe Courts Historic District. In 1994 then–HUD Secretary Henry Cisneros assured that no part of APV would be sold for commercial development. Although Lenwood Johnson and his supporters were skeptical, HACH has indeed held onto the property. However, a formal request for demolition was submitted in 1995, and in 1996 the entire project was depopulated by federal court order. Seventy percent of the complex was demolished the next year, leaving approximately 200 of the old San Felipe Courts apartments, which were re-

Paul Hester, 1984.

Shotgun houses, Robin Street, Fourth Ward, now demolished.

stored on the exterior and remodeled on the interiors. Construction of 500 new units which bear no resemblance to the original architecture began in 1999.

The Freedman's Town Historic District and the rest of Fourth Ward have been substantially destroyed in the past six years. Extensive new speculative row house construction has replaced many of the historic houses. HACH has built a two-and-a-half-block apartment complex and scattered-site housing in Freedman's Town. It also has created a "historic district" on several blocks of Andrews Street by moving houses from the rest of Fourth Ward. *Stephen Fox*

Along with zoning and public transportation issues, the fate of Fourth Ward and APV has been one of *Cite*'s most closely followed stories: "Proposed Historic District [Freedman's Town] Faces Opposition," *Cite* 7 (fall 1984); "A Fourth Ward Overview," *Cite* 8 (winter 1984); Dana Cuff, "News from Freedman's Town," *Cite* 10 (sum-

mer 1985); Lorenzo Thomas, "Architecture and Culture: the Fourth Ward," *Cite* 14 (summer 1986); Douglas Sprunt, "Fourth Ward Update: Houston Proud?" *Cite* 16 (winter 1986); Joel Warren Barna, "A Home of One's Own: Scattered Site Housing in Houston," *Cite* 22 (spring/summer 1989); Rives Taylor, "Fourth Ward and the Siege of Allen Parkway Village," *Cite* 25 (fall 1990) and *Cite* 26 (spring 1991); Stephen Fox, "Allen Parkway Village Update," *Cite* 26 (spring 1991); Curtis Lang, "A Depleted Legacy: Public Housing in Houston," *Cite* 33 (fall 1995/winter 1996); Brad Tyer, "Update: Allen Parkway Village," *Cite* 33 (fall 1995/winter 1996); Jacqueline Leavill, "Reassessing Priorities: 60 years of U.S. Pubic Housing," *Cite* 33 (fall 1995/winter 1996); Mitchell J. Shields, "Return to APV: Houston's Best-Known, Most Troubled Housing Project Reopens," *Cite* 46 (fall 1999/winter 2000).

Cite 19
WINTER
1987

Houston's Indo-Chinatown

THE FIRST GENERATION

Deborah Jensen Velders

As each work week ends, a transfusion begins: Houston slowly drains itself. By Sunday morning the process is nearly complete—the city utterly still, silent, and nearly empty. But just 10 or so blocks south of downtown in two areas east and west of Main Street, dense clusters of Indo-Chinese shops and restaurants begin to rouse, infusing the city with Asian sounds, smells, and movement. Entire families cruise through restaurants and shopping centers: children play, men talk, and new-wave teens loiter in pool halls or video shops. Women scour markets carefully for the week's groceries. Shoppers are mostly Vietnamese, but there are also Laotians, Filipinos, Indonesians, Malaysians, Thais, Cambodians, and Chinese.

An estimated 40,000–60,000 Vietnamese, 3,500 Cambodians, 1,100 Laotians, and 700 Thais live and work in Houston—four to six hundred times the number a decade ago. While this massive influx has injected new life into the city's decayed limbs, its adrenalin effect is countered somewhat by immigrant nostalgia. For many Indo-Chinese refugees their emotional and economic investments here are tenuous. Renovation and new construction are rare. Businesses set up shop in buildings catch as catch can, reflecting the Indo-Chinese struggle between present survival and future hope: returning to Vietnam. For some, a commitment to stay would be an admission of defeat.

The change came in 1975. Refugees had been trickling out of Saigon since the American troop withdrawal in 1973, but after Communist troops took the city in 1975, the trickle grew into a tidal wave. By late 1977 a third of America's half-million Indo-Chinese refugees settled in California. The next-largest group came to Texas.

On Houston's west side, a central corridor of Vietnamese businesses now extends southward from Drew Avenue to West Alabama, zigzagging between Main and Milam streets. Aged shopping centers, small businesses, and restaurants are clumped together in tight, pod-like formations, flourishing in the older, vacant buildings of Houston's commercial orphanage.

THE MILAM CENTER

The Milam Center, Trung Tâm Thuò`ng Mãi á Dông, is one of the largest and most popular shopping areas for Houston's Indo-Chinese community. The 64-year-old building, a recycled strip center, occupies a full city block at the corridor's north end. Neither renovated nor updated, the building's exterior is simply encrusted with layers of the center's past: a sweeping theater marquee with remnants of an outdoor clock, walls plastered with Vietnamese posters and painted advertisements, paint peeling away multiple layers of ice cream colors. Only the signboards—bright, dense, and heavily accented—reveal the center's current identity: Khai Thu's income tax service, Kim Hoan jewelry, Van Hu videotapes, Dr. Dung A. Nguyen, pharmacies, bookstores, restaurants, market, shoe stores, and gift shops. In this single block, social, commercial, and cultural threads are woven tightly together with a maximum use of space that is characteristically Asian.

Shops and restaurants face out toward the street on three sides, and interior shops open onto a central, bench-lined hallway that penetrates Milam Center from the north. The T-shaped hall has access doors to the center's east and west sides. Vietnamese Muzak floats through the hall and into the interior spaces. One entire side of the corridor is a long window, revealing

Hoa Binh (pronounced "Wah Been") Market. Just inside, huge slabs of meat and whole chickens hang, suspended over a steam table. The narrow aisles are crowded, and the shelves overstocked. Merchandise reflects the market's diverse patronage: clear jars of pickled papaya and sweet bananas from the Philippines, lotus nuts in syrup from mainland China, cans of ground bean sauce from Hong Kong, and French-Vietnamese coffee with chicory. Gigantic stalks of sugarcane lean against a front wall, and little jelly candies from Japan, shaped into delicate seashells, win the prize for clever packaging. Glittering Buddhist paraphernalia shares precious space with mystifying cookware. There are infinite varieties of tea and homey

Van Hu's Videotapes and Books, Milam Center.

Paul Hester, 1987.

Hoa Binh Market, Milam Center. The sign translates as "Welcome, customers."

trays of plastic-wrapped, sticky rice cakes. The latter sit on cartons of cigarettes below the roach spray. Hoa Binh Market could never be mistaken for Safeway.

Lan Thi Pham, a tiny, delicate woman of 36, is one of Hoa Binh Market's regular shoppers. She calculates the week's food budget and menu long before venturing out with her family to faraway Milam Center. Lan and her husband, Son Nguyen, live and work in southwest Houston, but most weekends, the family will shop in and around Milam Center, socializing and spending the day together. Like many Vietnamese refugees here, Lan and her husband work long hours, leaving little time for anything but the most immediate concerns of job, money, and security for their three children. Milam Center, both a commercial and social vortex, attracts Indo-Chinese from all areas of the city.

Lan and Son arrived in Houston on August 4, 1983, moving immediately with their three young children into a two-bedroom apartment on West Main Street with Lan's brother and two sisters. They came separately, each refugee sponsoring the next. Lan's elderly parents remained behind. Lan now works for Foley's, and her husband works as a mechanical engineer by day and an auto parts salesman at night. Both struggle with the isolation, exhaustion—and the language.

The terrifying escapes, long months of waiting, and painful assimilation are common experiences of uncommon terror shared by most of Houston's Indo-Chinese. In 1980, most of these were "boat people": 65 percent were Vietnamese, 21 percent Laotian, and 7 percent Cambodian. Frequently, initial escape attempts failed, and families had to repeat harrowing experiences several times before getting out. A single escape consumed several ounces of gold, often an entire family's savings. Over 30,000 died in the attempt, either from illness, pirate attacks, starvation, or boat sinkings. As Vietnamese priest Father Anthony Dao explains, many felt it would be "fresher to die at sea, rather than on land."

Chronicles of refugee experiences are found in the poetry and prose at the Milam Book Store on the center's west side. After browsing through the bookshelves there, one could walk across Drew Avenue, one block north to the Nam Thanh gift shop, then over on Milam Street to Saigon Dich-Vu Center, dining at the Saigon Cafeteria after a fitting at Chinh's Tailor. Traveling two blocks east along Dennis Avenue, a walker arriving at Thu Do Plaza on Main Street could take a self-defense class upstairs, pick up "beer to go" at the Yen Gift Shop, and plan a vacation in the travel agency downstairs. Milam Center is surrounded by small, satellite shopping centers and restaurants huddled within blocks of one another. Buildings, like abandoned mollusk shells, are reinhabited. Often single-story and constructed of brick or cinderblock, these buildings are frequently unified by nothing more than paint color or camperlike aluminum roofs. They offer compact, multifunctional containers for multipurpose stores containing multi-use products — Vietnamese one-stop shopping.

HOLY ROSARY CHURCH

At the south end of this Indo-Chinese business corridor, a chorus of Asian voices — high-pitched and slightly singsong — drifts faintly through the doors of a church out into the Sunday afternoon street. These are songs of devotion and worship, a traditional Roman Catholic mass. One non-Asian worshiper confesses that while he does not understand Vietnamese, he comes each Sunday for the high, sweet singing of the church choir.

Holy Rosary Church (Maurice J. Sullivan, 1933) is a large neo-Gothic edifice built of Texas limestone. The church holds masses in English, Latin, and Vietnamese. Each Sunday, Father Anthony Dao conducts two Vietnamese masses. In contrast to the gentle austerity of Holy Rosary's dimly lit interior, the incessant activity is startling: there is human traffic throughout the service — parents come and go with crying babies and restless children, teenagers scout for friends. Father Dao begins with a ritual plea for child control, asking parents to refrain from bringing infants. He is ignored. Families share every activity — shopping, eating, socializing, and worshiping together. Filial devotion is central to the Vietnamese culture.

Some hands move rapidly over rosary beads, while others are clasped to foreheads with rapid bowing, a strangely Buddhist gesture in this setting. The atmosphere is relaxed, comfortable, and tolerant of this Eastern intonation. The congregation is a cross section of Houston's Vietnamese population: young, affluent couples with infants, spike-haired teens, and elderly, withered women clothed in black pajamas. Many arms are folded across chests in a Vietnamese gesture of respect. There are surprising numbers of young men, reflecting the city's 5-to-2 ratio of Indo-Chinese men to women.

Father Anthony Dao is a tall, charismatic man of 36 with a quick, boyish grin and broad stride. One of Houston's 10 Vietnamese priests, he is known as the "spiritual advisor" of the Vietnamese community, widely respected for his extensive knowledge of both American culture and the Vietnamese experience. Like many of his parishioners, he was a refugee, escaping from Vietnam in 1978. Active in community and university affairs, Father Dao promotes complete assimilation for Houston's Indo-Chinese. Yet he admits that this social integration may take at least a full generation before the Indo-Chinese accept Houston — and Houston accepts them.

Father Dao credits Holy Rosary Church with the surrounding business expansion in downtown Houston. He notes that when Holy Rosary held the city's first Vietnamese mass in 1975, the parish had a largely social function for the Vietnamese — attracting non-Catholics and Catholics alike in their need for cultural and social contact in a strange new environment. He asserts that over a period of time, Holy Rosary's growing Vietnamese congregation catalyzed the introduction of surrounding businesses, catering to the new community of churchgoing immigrants.

The relationship between church and commerce seems ironic. Milam Center and Holy Rosary Church—at opposite ends of the Indo-Chinese corridor here—are like metaphors for the divergence of business and spiritual concerns in the Indo-Chinese culture, where commerce is valued least and education most. This hierarchical distinction stems from the role of Buddhist monks as highly respected teachers. Virtue is equated with wisdom. Later, this regard was transferred to priests and other spiritual leaders.

There is little doubt that Houston's Roman Catholic diocese is a well-organized and influential force within the Indo-Chinese community. Last June, Holy Rosary Church drew nearly 2,000 Southeast Asians to its Marian Year celebration. Processions of women in traditional Indo-Chinese dress were followed by rows of Western-suited elders, stumbling clumps of flower-festooned children in white gowns, Dominican nuns, and church dignitaries. A rainbow-colored votive statue of the Virgin Mary was held aloft while the silent, somber procession circled the city block, crowding into the parking lot. As high-pitched Vietnamese music blared through the speakers, people began to sing.

Father Dao calls the Vietnamese mixture of Confucianism, Buddhism, and Taoism an "art of living," explaining that religious fusions are common in Vietnamese indigenous religions: "Hoa Hao" (translated as "solidarity" or peaceful coexistence) and "Cao Dai" (meaning "high tower"—a combination of all religions). "Asians," he says, smiling, "are very religious. They accept religion, but not always governments."

VINATOWN AND VIETNAM PLAZA

Ten to 12 blocks east of Main Street, surrounded by vacant lots and boarded houses, a large, elegant structure of corrugated metal stands alone. This beautifully simple, rectangular building at 2501 St. Emanuel Street is adorned by a single sign, painted in saffron gold with red letters: "Buddhist Association for the Services of Humanity in America — Chu`a Dai Giác." Like Holy Rosary Church, the temple shares its neighborhood with Indo-Chinese shopping centers and businesses.

Several blocks north of the temple, Vinatown and Vietnam Plaza shopping centers lie in an area long considered Houston's Chinatown. Both are defined and bisected by freeways: Vinatown, south of I-45 and west of US-59, and Vietnam Plaza, north of I-45 and east of US-59.

The two-part Vinatown Center on Webster and Jackson streets is made from the same aesthetic dough as the nearby freeways. Design interest is limited to the lively play of Asian letters and words across bland concrete surfaces. Vinatown I includes Anh Hong Restaurant ("7 courses of beef"), Le Croissant D'Or French Bakery, and the enormous An Dong Supermarket. "Agent of Tai Ming Wah Rest Hong Kong White Lotus seed paste mooncake" is written over the entrance. Tape and record stores carry both American and Vietnamese popular music; beauty shop posters portray Asian models wearing western hairstyles.

Giao Ngoc Nguyen, 63, is owner and general contractor of the Vinatown Shopping Center. He is a slight, self-effacing man in white shirt, khaki pants, and generic gray spectacles. He smiles continually. Nguyen displays a 20-year-old construction license, newspaper articles, and photographs of massive, concrete housing projects in Saigon: Vinatown's aesthetic antecedents.

However, Nguyen's concerns are not aesthetic, but social. He employed Vietnamese refugees for the construction of Vinatown in 1981, and now, desperately seeking financial backers, he hopes to establish an economic base of Vietnamese self-reliance. He will begin with an Indo-Chinese credit union. He also dreams of constructing nearby housing projects for elderly Indo-Chinese—increasingly a problem in the community. Life in Houston, as elsewhere in America, has wrought drastic changes upon Indo-Chinese families. The elderly, traditionally revered in Vietnamese culture, are isolated by new lifestyles and language barriers. Entire families work, leaving older parents and grandparents alone. Television offers no solace, and the elderly are considered too old to learn English. Vinatown II houses the city's only Vietnamese Senior Citizen Association, to which elderly travel great distances for meals, conversation, and companionship. Unable to attain a tax exemption, the association is virtually helpless to provide more.

Surrounded by freeways and empty warehouses, five-year-old Vietnam Plaza occupies the former home of Finger Furniture. It is, according to a former manager, one of the only exclusively Vietnamese centers in the city. Across the street, an L -shaped, single-story, cement shopping strip is embellished with Chinese-red columns, pseudo-French green awnings, and a Tex-Mex plastic "tile" roof: an extraordinary polycultural statement.

Nhan Ngoc Luu, serious and intense, sits in an upstairs office of Vietnam Plaza at Jefferson Avenue and Hutchins Street. He speaks passionately of his commitment to freeing Vietnam from communist domination. Luu unlocks a nearby door, revealing another dingy office filled with a conference table, stained carpet, artificial cherry blossoms, and Vietnamese flags: three red bands across a brilliant yellow-gold. Grim black-and-white photographs of jungles and soldiers line the walls, and stacks of political literature cover the floor. The room, a quasi-political shrine, houses local meetings of the National United Front for the Liberation of Vietnam, a Washington, D.C.–based organization. A banner with "Tin Thong hoi cac anh" is draped across one wall. Luu points to the photographs of soldiers and translates, "We believe in them."

Resistance is the organization's monthly publication—a slick, eight-page newsletter printed entirely in English. On the back page, an explanation: "The National United Front for the Liberation of Vietnam (NUFRONLIV) was formed in 1980 by the Vietnamese people inside Vietnam and abroad to liberate their country from the Viet Cong and to build a free and democratic nation . . . To promote our just cause, your financial contributions are welcome."

In August 1985, Nhan Ngoc Luu quietly left Houston to return to Vietnam after more than 10 years. Knowing the dangers of the trip, he did not tell even his wife of the journey. As a Vietnamese refugee, he understood the risk of imprisonment or death. Luu walked through steamy, wet jungle for six days, traveling to a freedom-fighter campsite. As a supporter of the National United Front, he wanted to see the resistance effort himself. After two weeks in Vietnam, he returned to Houston more determined than ever, he says, to see his country free.

THE POLITICAL COMMUNITY

Three blocks east of Holy Rosary Church, 54-year-old Nam Nguyen sits behind a dusty glass storefront facing Fannin Street. It seems unlikely the store has been touched for 25 years. Nguyen is surrounded by tall, thick stacks of Vietnamese newspapers, a few chairs, and litter everywhere. The small, two-room office is hot and humid. Nguyen, a large, thick man dressed in brown slacks, white starched shirt, and a tie, twitches uncomfortably. He stares directly at his visitor—a strangely un-Vietnamese act—and explains that this office, which he personally finances, is a distribution center for the journalistic literature surrounding us. As if to illustrate his point, Indo-Chinese men come and go, exchanging stacks of newspapers.

Nguyen, considered a political spokesman for Houston's Vietnamese community, is articulate and emphatic about his country's current political situation. Concerned with the same adjustments as other Houston refugees, he also is obsessed with his vision of a free Vietnam — and his dream of someday returning. He hopes only to live long enough to help with the country's reconstruction efforts. Nguyen believes the issue of Vietnam's struggle is very much alive for the vast majority of Houston's Indo-Chinese population. Many still hope to return "home."

As a colonel in the Vietnamese army, Nguyen was responsible for 50,000 Communist prisoners during the war in Vietnam. He took part in the 1970–1973 Paris peace negotiations and helped formulate postwar prisoner agreements. Nguyen holds a French law degree; publishes and distributes a newspaper, Thô´ng Nhâ´t (translated as "Unity"); and is a former chairman of the Vietnamese Community Organization of Houston. As a shrimp fisherman in Seabrook between 1979 and 1981, he was involved in a famous battle with the Ku Klux Klan. After a long siege of harassment, that battle ended when the Vietnamese obtained a federal court injunction against the KKK in May 1981.

Nguyen's conversation is riddled with anti-Communist commentary. He explains that his country's economy has regressed some 30 years under the Communists, adding, "our families [are] still there, our friends [are] still there — in concentration camps." His voice crescendos: "*That* is why we fight to liberate my country."

When pressed for information about the estimated eight to 10 Indo-Chinese political groups in Houston, Mr. Nguyen gently explains that these are not actually "political," but *community* groups. He quietly adds that American laws prohibit certain political organizations. A small rodent runs across the room behind, as though signaling the interview's conclusion. Nguyen lumbers to his feet, and talks of his three children, ages 22, 10, and 6: "We ask them to learn two things. First, he has to believe in the United States, respect the law, and be fair. But also, he must know their father and mother and homeland is Vietnam. He must know that he has two countries. He cannot say, 'I do not recognize Vietnam.' He is a citizen of *two* countries."

A sense of transience prevails throughout Houston's Indo-Chinese community: urgency permeating conversation; businesses occupying buildings uneasily, like tight-fitting clothes; individuals waiting silently and working ferociously. Lan Thi Pham explains, "We do not know for how long we have *anything*."

In the interim, Houston is awakened, enlivened — and enriched.

Cite 3
SPRING
1983

Big Park, Little Plans

A HISTORY OF HERMANN PARK

Stephen Fox

Hermann Park with Sam Houston Monument and Reflecting Pool.

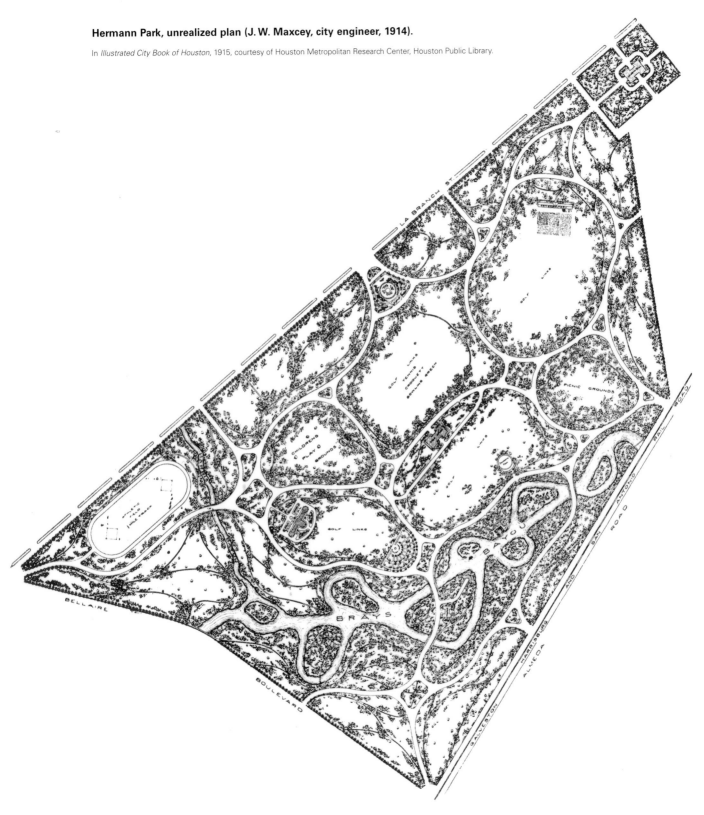

Hermann Park, unrealized plan (J. W. Maxcey, city engineer, 1914).

In *Illustrated City Book of Houston*, 1915, courtesy of Houston Metropolitan Research Center, Houston Public Library.

Hermann Park was one of the chief reasons Houston became involved in city planning during the second decade of the twentieth century. Not only was the park a focus of civic improvement and beautification, but the properties surrounding it — largely undeveloped when the park was acquired — seemed to present an exceptional opportunity for citizens concerned about Houston's future to achieve an example of integrated city planning. The history of Hermann Park's development exemplifies not only the challenges involved in realizing such projects, but also the equally difficult task of maintaining what already has been achieved.

In 1910 Mayor H. Baldwin Rice, a progressive reformer, appointed a three-member Board of Park Commissioners (Edwin B. Parker, an attorney, George H. Hermann, a real estate investor and industrialist, and William A. Wilson, a real estate developer) to advise on the acquisition, maintenance, and development of park property in Houston. They, in turn, retained Arthur Coleman Comey, a landscape architect from Cambridge, Massachusetts. Comey's report, published in 1913 as *Houston, Tentative Plans for Its Development*, recommended the acquisition of a major park within what he described as an inner park system to serve Houston and its area of projected expansion. Called Pines Park in his report, the park was to be located along Brays Bayou, across Main Street from the 277-acre Rice Institute (Cram, Goodhue & Ferguson, 1912). The location of Pines Park was not accidental, for most of the property shown on Comey's diagram was owned by George H. Hermann.

In May 1914 Hermann announced his intention of deeding to the City of Houston 285 acres of his property for a municipal park. The transfer was made in June. After Hermann's death in October 1914, his estate deeded several more acres to the City of Houston for the George H. Hermann Park. John W. Maxcey, the city engineer, produced the initial plan for developing this acreage, which extended from Almeda Road on the east to a line along the projected route of La Branch Street on the west, between what is now Hermann Drive on the north and Holcombe Boulevard on the south. Maxcey, who in 1899 had laid out Sam Houston Park, the city's first public park, worked closely with Hermann on the proposed design for Hermann Park.

According to Maxcey's plan, Brays Bayou was to be rechanneled extensively to create a series of wooded islands on either side of the existing channel. A curvilinear network of roads defined a series of oval-shaped meadows in the center of the park, and most of the remaining open space was devoted to a golf course. The main entrance was on the west side of the park, where a landscaped boulevard perpendicular to Main Street, opposite entrance 2 to the Rice campus, gave access to the park.

Maxcey's plan was never implemented. One reason was that in 1915, with the encouragement of Rice's successor, Mayor Ben Campbell, the City of Houston purchased from the Hermann Estate an additional 122 ½ acres between La Branch and Main Street, which increased the area of the park to 409 ½ acres. Rather than direct Maxcey to produce a revised plan, the Board of Park Commissioners retained another consultant, the celebrated St. Louis landscape architect and planner George E. Kessler. At the instigation of the oilman J. S. Cullinan, Kessler was appointed consulting landscape architect to the board in early 1915. His proposal for Hermann Park seems to have been presented the next year.

Kessler's plan relied upon the diagonal geometry resulting from the intersection of the newly extended Montrose Boulevard with the newly widened and paved Main Boulevard. He used this axis to generate an infrastructure for the improvements to be imposed upon the flat, wooded site. Where the two boulevards crossed, a landscaped elliptical island, the Sunken Garden, was located. Continuing southward into the park, Montrose Boulevard provided the axis around which different features were organized. In Kessler's only surviving drawing, a plan for the entrance quadrant dated 1916, the roadway broke into a series of circular drives around a traffic circle inscribed with a monument. This circle occurred where the axis of Montrose Boulevard was intersected by a line of vision projected along the principal axis of the Rice Institute campus. The roadway divided around the circle to encompass a shallow, rectangular reflecting pool flanked by walks and a music pavilion with its attendant seating area. Beyond these lay an irregularly configured lake called the Grand Basin, with pergolas, boat landings, and a large, arcaded Shelter House along its shores.

A city map of 1917 diagrammatically shows what must have been Kessler's general scheme of development. A central oval athletic field was bracketed by two other oval fields in a three-lobe configuration. The western lobe contained playground and picnic facilities, and the eastern lobe contained a swimming pool and bathhouse. A golf course lay southeast of this three-lobed group of open spaces.

That Kessler's proposal was more sophisticated than Maxcey's is not surprising. Kessler demonstrated a practical skill for reconciling the requirements of ceremony and informality in his design. The principal axis marked the ceremonial space of the park. Yet beyond the *allée* of trees flanking the reflecting basin, trees conformed to no fixed order in their location. The north and south embankments of the Grand Basin were part of the space of the axis. But the east and west shores (which were not) were eroded by canals and lagoons that broke down the sense of strict boundary and led to small-scale shaded dells.

The extent of the improvements undertaken during 1916 and 1917 is hard to ascertain, although the drives apparently were laid out, the rectangular reflecting basin was built, and the Shelter House in the southwest quadrant of the park was constructed. Along Main Boulevard double rows of evergreen live oaks were planted. Instrumental in the realization of these features of the Kessler plan were two Houstonians: Clarence L. Brock, general superintendent of city parks since 1912, and Herbert A. Kipp, consulting engineer to the Park Commissioners since 1915.

Several other projects contributed to the transformation of the Hermann Park–Rice Institute area. One was the development of a residential enclave by J. S. Cullinan called Shadyside. In February 1916 Cullinan purchased from the Hermann Estate nearly 37 acres along Main Street, north of the campus and west of the park. With the aid of Kessler and Kipp, he developed Shadyside as an elite neighborhood.

Before he died, George Hermann had promised the Houston Art League he would donate property for a museum building. In August 1916 the league acquired the triangular-shaped, three-acre lot between Main and Montrose, opposite the Sunken Garden, a joint gift of the Hermann Estate and Mr. and Mrs. J. S. Cullinan for the first building of what was to become the Museum of Fine Arts, Houston.

THE 1920s

The U.S. entry into World War I in April 1917 and the exhaustion by August 1917 of a bond issue voted in 1914 brought all park acquisition and civic improvement projects to a halt. Following the Armistice, the Progressive spirit of civic action that had been so active during the 1910s faltered. It was not until 1922, after the election of Mayor Oscar F. Holcombe, that park improvements and other planning programs obtained renewed public support. Holcombe recognized the political value of promoting measures aimed at achieving orderly urban growth and a more amenable urban environment. Consequently, he appointed the first City Planning Commission in 1922 and renewed the activity of the Board of Park Commissioners. Un-

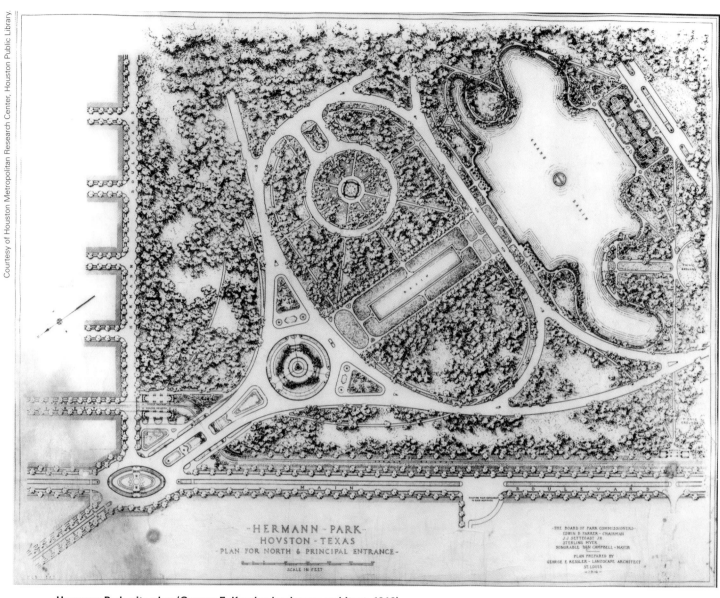

Hermann Park, site plan (George E. Kessler, landscape architect, 1916).

fortunately, this coincided with George Kessler's death in 1923. To replace Kessler, the Board of Park Commissioners, in 1923, and the City Planning Commission, in 1924, retained as their professional consultant the Kansas City landscape firm Hare & Hare.

S. Herbert Hare, the firm's junior partner, was in charge of the Houston work. Under Hare & Hare's guidance, Hermann Park and the rest of the Houston park system as envisioned by Comey and Kessler took shape. Between 1923 and 1933 Hermann Park gradually acquired not only improvements called for in the Kessler plan of 1916 but also a number of additions. Chiefly these were the inclusion of a zoo, the addition of a 133 ½-acre strip along the lower west side of the park, and the donation of the MacGregor Parkway along Brays Bayou to the east of Hermann Park.

In 1930 Hare & Hare produced a drawing depicting the extent of their park planning during the 1920s. The Houston Zoological Garden, opened in 1924, was located in what had been the central athletic oval on the south shore of the Grand Basin. Its layout was a miniature version of the park's, with a central axial pedestrian concourse flanked by open-air exhibits, all set in an informal network of curvilinear paths. Small buildings, finished with stucco and tile roofs, were built at intervals between 1924 and 1931 along the central concourse to provide enclosed exhibition space as well as quarters for the Museum of Natural History. An 18-hole golf course was constructed on the site specified by Kessler in 1922, following a design by the Houston stockbroker and golf enthusiast George V. Rotan and the engineer David M. Duller. On the site that Kessler designated a concert pavilion, the Miller Memorial Theater (William Ward Watkin, 1922), an austere Doric proscenium flanked by peristyles, was constructed. To provide better automobile circulation the theater grounds were linked by a short, curved drive to Caroline Street and Hermann Drive along the north boundary of the park. Another "improvement," also in-

Hermann Park, general plan (Hare & Hare, landscape architects, 1930).

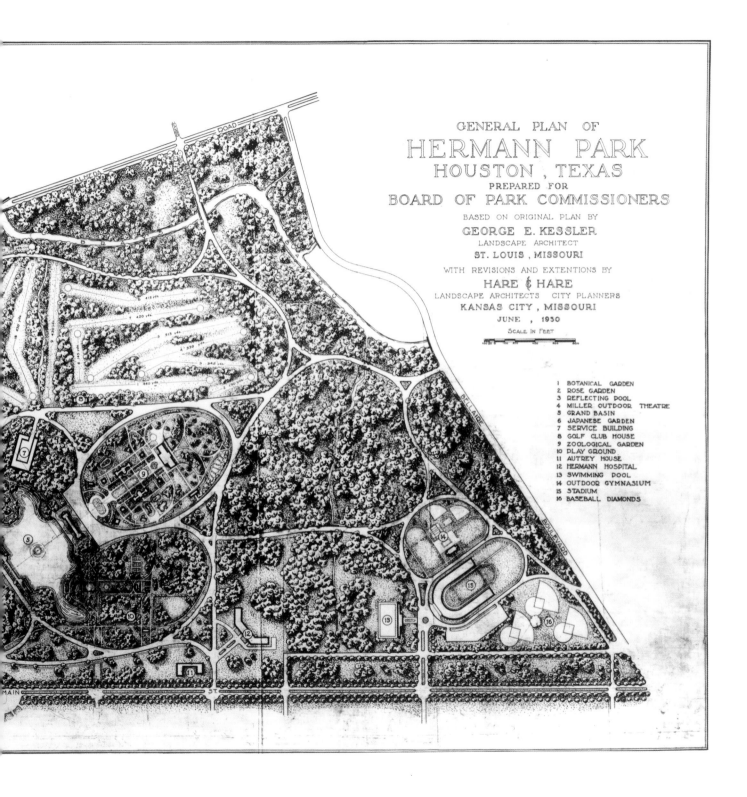

GENERAL PLAN OF
HERMANN PARK
HOUSTON, TEXAS
PREPARED FOR
BOARD OF PARK COMMISSIONERS
BASED ON ORIGINAL PLAN BY
GEORGE E. KESSLER
LANDSCAPE ARCHITECT
ST. LOUIS, MISSOURI
WITH REVISIONS AND EXTENTIONS BY
HARE & HARE
LANDSCAPE ARCHITECTS   CITY PLANNERS
KANSAS CITY, MISSOURI
JUNE, 1930
SCALE IN FEET

1   BOTANICAL GARDEN
2   ROSE GARDEN
3   REFLECTING POOL
4   MILLER OUTDOOR THEATRE
5   GRAND BASIN
6   JAPANESE GARDEN
7   SERVICE BUILDING
8   GOLF CLUB HOUSE
9   ZOOLOGICAL GARDEN
10 PLAY GROUND
11 AUTREY HOUSE
12 HERMANN HOSPITAL
13 SWIMMING POOL
14 OUTDOOR GYMNASIUM
15 STADIUM
16 BASEBALL DIAMONDS

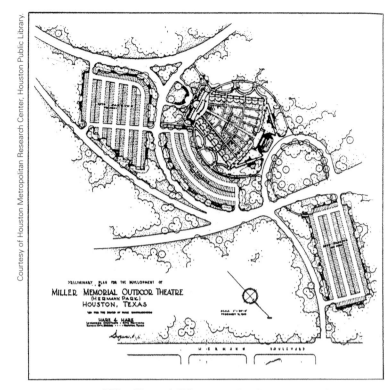

Miller Memorial Theater, redevelopment plan (Hare & Hare, landscape architects, 1940).

volving automobiles, was of short duration. This was the tourist-oriented Automobile Camp, opened early in 1922 and laid out by Clarence Brock to accommodate 150 vehicles. By the time Hare & Hare made their general plan drawing, it no longer existed.

Excavation of the Grand Basin began in 1925, but only about half of the 13-acre waterway called for in the Kessler plan was constructed initially. Between 1927 and 1931 the Parks Department repeatedly announced excavation of the remaining six and one-quarter acres, but this was not accomplished. A bronze equestrian statue of Sam Houston was installed in the monument circle on the Montrose axis in 1925. Modeled in bronze by Enrico F. Cerracchio after a painting by Seymour Thomas, the Sam Houston Monument, like the Miller Memorial Theater, was the result of private beneficence. Subsequent improvements included a botanical garden laid out along Hermann Drive, east of the main entrance, in 1927 according to plans of

Hare & Hare. A comfort station and the Hermann Park Clubhouse, a handsome Spanish colonial revival building designed by Arthur E. Nutter adjacent to the golf course, were completed in 1933.

With improvements suggested in the Kessler Plan under way, Hermann Park acquired two additional land tracts in 1923. Will C. Hogg, son of a former Texas governor who adopted civic planning as his foremost cause, purchased the 133½-acre Parker tract south of the Hermann Hospital site and sold it to the City of Houston at cost and on generous terms in January 1924. This brought the park's area to 545 acres. Hogg had already underwritten the War Mothers Memorial to Harris County men who died during World War I — 200 live oak trees planted along what is now North MacGregor Drive.

Similarly in April 1926 Peggy Stevens MacGregor, widow of real estate developer Henry F. MacGregor, donated 108 acres of wooded land on Brays Bayou, two and one-half miles east of Hermann Park, to the city as a memorial to her husband along with $150,000 to finance acquisition of property on both banks of the bayou between the two parks. During the early 1930s, bayou-side drives North and South MacGregor Ways were built to join Hermann and MacGregor Parks. Although not all the property on both sides of the bayou could be acquired, a sufficient amount was obtained to ensure implementation of the parkways.

Houston's expansion during the 1920s was phenomenal, but it caused problems. Automobile ownership increased year by year at a staggering rate, causing unforeseen transportation difficulties. One result was that the drives in Hermann Park were paved as well as the streets surrounding the park: Bellaire (now Holcombe), Almeda, and eight blocks of Hermann Drive. In 1916 Kessler could envision the park as the scene of leisurely "pleasure" drives in continuation of a well-developed 19th-century social custom. Ten years later, speeding and careless driving had effectively terminated this social ritual. When the location of the Sam Houston Monument was under consideration in 1925, the Board of Park Commissioners resolved that it should not be placed in the Sunken Garden, as this might at some point in the near future require removal to accommodate increased traffic. For this reason the esplanades on Main Boulevard north of the Sunken Garden, which Hare & Hare had landscaped in 1924 and 1925, were pulled up in 1928. Also in 1928 the Houston Electric Company substituted buses for the South End line trams.

THE 1930s

The Great Depression marked the end of the second epoch in Hermann Park's development. During the 1930s most improvements were incremental additions carried out under the supervision of Clarence L. Brock and Hare & Hare. In 1936 monuments commemorating the centennial of Texas independence from Mexico and the founding of Houston were dedicated in Hermann Park. One was a 50-foot-high granite obelisk, the Pioneer Memorial Shaft, donated by the San Jacinto Chapter of the Daughters of the Republic of Texas. The Pioneer Memorial was placed at the south end of the reflecting basin, between it and the Grand Basin. The Memorial Log House was situated on Outer Belt Drive behind the Zoological Garden. Another memorial was proposed in 1937 by the Central Lions Club of Houston — a standing bronze figure of George H. Hermann. A maquette was prepared by Julian Muench, and the landscape architects Fleming & Sheppard were retained to choose a site for the statue. Their choice was a location on axis with entrance 2 of the Rice Institute, at the western tip of the Grand Basin, once it was extended to its full size. The Lions Club must have been unable to secure the $15,000 to erect the statue, for it was never realized.

The correspondence of J. Robert Neal, a Houston banker and chairman of the Houston Board of Park Commissioners (1938–1940), indicates that by the late 1930s the Houston park system, not excluding Hermann Park, was suffering from poor maintenance. A series of confidential reports on the condition of city parks prepared by one of Neal's associates 1938 stated that despite a capable administrator (Brock) and an excellent consultant (Hare), the park system was inadequate. Miller Memorial Theater was described as being in "deplorable" condition, and vandalism had become so serious that repairs to park buildings and landscaping were inadvisable unless future protection could be guaranteed. Neal led the park board in a dramatic confrontation with the City Council in the summer of 1938. The council was unable to increase the Parks Department's appropriation and unwilling to assign fees charged for the use of the golf courses in Hermann and Memorial parks to the Parks Department rather than to the general revenue fund. Consequently, the Board of Park Commissioners recommended that the Zoological Garden be closed and all the animals sold to decrease expenses. The City Council assigned the golf fees to the Parks Department.

During Neal's tenure a number of requests were made for dedication of park property to non-park related uses. In 1938 a second golf course was proposed for the Hogg tract (a project Hogg opposed in 1925), the Houston Conservatory of Music asked for a three- or four-acre site along Main Boulevard, and the Houston Independent School District requested 50 acres for a public school stadium along Almeda Road. Following Hare's advice, all of these proposals were rejected. The last project to be implemented before World War II was the Houston Garden Center, a one-story pavilion containing a meeting and exhibition hall. Designed by William Ward Watkin in 1938, the Garden Center was not constructed until 1941. It was located on Hermann Drive, on axis with La Branch Street, at the east end of the Botanical Garden. In front of the south elevation Hare & Hare laid out the Rose Garden.

THE 1940s

In 1940 Oscar Holcombe, who was once again mayor of Houston, established the City Planning Commission on a permanent basis and created a Department of City Planning with Ralph Ellifrit, a member of the firm of Hare & Hare, as director. Ellifrit and Hare & Hare prepared two major city planning reports—a street and thoroughfare plan and a parks plan—released in 1942 and 1943, respectively. For Hermann Park the report recommended development of a recreation center and athletic fields and proposed that between 20 and 40 acres be acquired along Brays Bayou for this purpose. Acquisition of this property was to compensate for the pending loss of the Hogg tract, which occurred in 1943.

The previous year the trustees of the M. D. Anderson Foundation, a charitable trust established in 1936 by Monroe D. Anderson, a founding partner in the cotton-exporting firm Anderson, Clayton & Company, convinced the regents of the University of Texas to establish a cancer research institute and a dental school in Houston. They then persuaded the trustees of the Baylor University College of Medicine to transfer that institution from Dallas to Houston. In return, the foundation was to provide funds for construction of new buildings as well as building sites. The trustees of the M. D. Anderson Foundation, W. B. Bates, John H. Freeman, and H. M. Wilkins, considered the Hogg tract an ideal location, for it was adjacent to Hermann Hospital (Berlin & Swern and Alfred

C. Finn, 1925). Despite the opposition of Ralph Ellifrit, the City Council, under the successive administrations of mayors C. A. Pickett (1941–1943) and Otis Massey (1943–1947), supported this proposal, and in December 1943 a referendum in which 951 votes were cast confirmed the council's agreement to sell those 133½ acres to the M. D. Anderson Foundation for $400,000. Between 1945 and 1955 six hospitals and two medical schools were built on the Hogg tract, following a plan devised by H. A. Kipp.

Hermann Park, site plan, 1943.

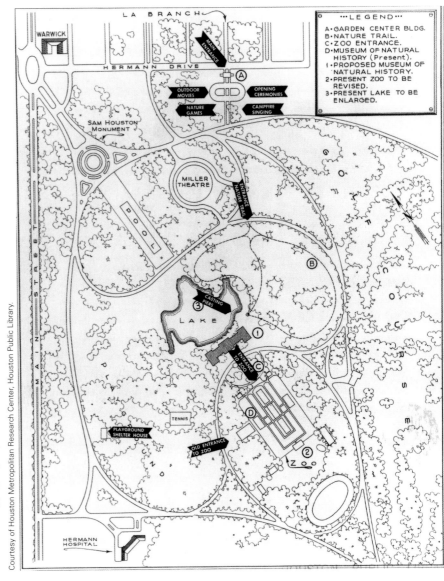

The development of the Hogg tract for the Texas Medical Center (as it was known after its 1946 dedication) was to accelerate the tempo of change around Hermann Park in the years following World War II. Other factors, however, were the demographic transformation of residential neighborhoods north of the park during the 1950s and a more gradual but no less surprising decline of the neighborhoods along the MacGregor Parkway during the 1960s. Yet at the same time, the Medical Center stimulated real estate development along Main Street and Bellaire Boulevard. Despite the institutional and commercial development occurring around Hermann Park, improvements within the park progressed at a slower pace. During the first term of Mayor Massey a city manager form of municipal government was adopted. Proceeding from this, the City Parks and Recreation Department was formed by consolidating two separate departments, and the landscape architect C. C. Pat Fleming was appointed to replace Clarence Brock as director of the new department in 1943. Throughout these changes, however, Hare & Hare remained as consulting landscape architects.

As early as 1943 priorities for postwar improvements to Hermann Park were formulated. Chief among these were an expansion of the zoo and provision for an adequately sized and equipped building for the Museum of Natural History. During 1945 and 1946 the Parks and Recreation Association, a group of citizens formed in 1919 to promote and support municipal recreation programs, proposed construction of a planetarium, an aquarium, and a new Miller Theater. Schematic plans for a number of these improvements were prepared: a large Museum of Natural History building was to be sited on the south shore of the Grand Basin, on axis with the entrance to the zoo. This would be flanked by the planetarium and aquarium. The Grand Basin was to be expanded from 13 to 20 acres, and the excavated soil was to be used to construct a ramped lawn where

10,000 people could sit in front of the new Miller Theater. As early as 1940 Hare & Hare had made plans for enlarging the seating lawn at Miller Theater and nearby parking. The "formal" north and south embankments of the Grand Basin were to be built.

Although a bond issue passed in 1944, it was not until Oscar Holcombe was re-elected in 1947 that Hare & Hare were commissioned to prepare plans for the expansion of the zoo. S. Herbert Hare recommended keeping the zoo in Hermann Park, expanding its area, and building habitats for animal exhibits rather than cages. In 1949 Hare & Hare was authorized to proceed with plans for the $800,000 expansion program. The loop drive bounding the southwest side of the zoo's oval site was moved farther to the southwest to increase the total area of the zoo. The axial arrangement of 1924 was preserved and developed much more carefully, with a sunken reflecting basin flanked by walkways, planting strips, and continuous, canopied passageways. A new Primate House terminated this formal concourse on the south. Beyond the central promenade, in the expanded southwestern and southeastern portions of the zoo, a network of curvilinear paths was developed, superseding those of the 1924 plan. The "new" zoo opened in 1950. Additions were gradually made according to the Hare & Hare plan of 1949 until the middle 1970s. In connection with the zoo expansion, the Grand Basin was reshaped, although it was not expanded in area.

During 1948 and 1949 Fannin Street was cut through Hermann Park between the westernmost drive and Main Boulevard. This provided a direct connection between downtown Houston and the Texas Medical Center and relieved traffic congestion on Main (which lost all but a narrow strip of its center medians in 1940). Subsequently, a connection was made between the Fannin Street extension and San Jacinto to ease traffic circulation further. An unfortunate effect of this traffic engineering was that the parkland between Fannin and

Main—now known as the Esplanade—became a residual corridor of greenery, making Fannin Hermann Park's effective west boundary. This was reinforced in 1967 when the Houston Federation of Garden Clubs adopted as a civic project construction of a high, landscaped berm along Fannin between the park's main entrance and Sunset Boulevard. Its purpose was to shield the park from the sight and sound of traffic along Fannin. Street improvements also included an extension of Hermann Drive east of Jackson to connect with Almeda Road. In order that this intersection occur at a right angle, Hermann Drive curved away from the park boundary at its northeast corner. The resulting triangle of land became the site of the Jewish Community Center, built between 1949 and 1950.

Hare & Hare proposed, during the design of the Fannin extension, that a museum be built in Shadyside on the estate of former governor William P. Hobby and his wife, Oveta Culp Hobby. This would incorporate a new Museum of Natural History, axially aligned with the Sunken Garden and Hermann Drive. At the same time they proposed a large fountain for the Sunken Garden. Because of its depressed, bowl-like configuration, the Sunken Garden had proved to be something of a traffic hazard, a problem that could be rectified by building above the curb line. None of these proposals was carried through, although the city did acquire an additional nine acres along Brays Bayou.

THE 1950s AND 1960s

No major work was done in Hermann Park during the 1950s except by the Harris County Flood District and the U.S. Army Corps of Engineers. A serious flood occurred on Brays Bayou in 1949, causing property owners in the South End of Houston to demand more effective flood control measures. In 1953 a $5 million program was announced to correct this problem on Brays Bayou; between 1956 and 1959 the channel was straightened and lined with concrete, and the banks were stripped of all vegetation, completely denuding the MacGregor Parkway.

Throughout the 1950s the Museum of Natural History struggled to secure a new building. In 1959 a four-acre site on Hermann Loop Drive was leased by the City of Houston to the Museum of Natural History, where, after a three-year fund drive, the first phase of the museum, including the Burke Baker Planetarium, was constructed between 1963 and 1964. A second phase, built between 1967 and 1969, added 8,000 square feet of exhibition and administrative space. Between 1967 and 1969 a new Miller Outdoor Theater, designed by Eugene Werlin & Associates, was constructed on the site of the old Doric proscenium. A high, bermed lawn provided amphitheater-type seating in front of the new stage and orchestra. The columns of the old theater were salvaged and grouped around a circular pool to form the Mecom-Rockwell Colonnade in 1968. Four years earlier, Mr. and Mrs. John W. Mecom had also donated the Mecom Fountain in the Sunken Garden, 16 years after Hare & Hare proposed a fountain for this area.

The protracted realization of facilities needed in Hermann Park since the 1940s underscored the lack of recognition and official support for the park, not unlike the neglect of many other public properties in Houston. Even though some improvements continued to result from private benefaction, it was clear by the 1950s that the Civic Art movement of the 1910s and 1920s was spent. And while a reversal of this negligent attitude occurred during the 1960s, good intentions were often accompanied by a lack of judgment and discrimination. This was evident in the Hermann Park Master Plan prepared for the City of Houston during 1971 and 1972 by two engineering firms, Lockwood, Andrews & Newnam and James Cummins Inc. Adopted in 1973 as the basis for subsequent park improvements, this new master plan departed considerably from Kessler and Hare & Hare's general plans. The reasoning for this de-

Hermann Park, aerial view, 1994.

parture was the need to accommodate growing numbers of people using park facilities, the number of automobiles entering the park, and another expansion of the zoo. South MacGregor Way was cut through the park in 1981, alongside the existing, two-lane North MacGregor Way. As with the Fannin extension, this effectively created a new boundary line separating the park from what became a linear greenway and bayou trail. Within the park, the historic infrastructure began to be eliminated in a piecemeal fashion to discourage through traffic. Thus Hermann Lake Drive and Zoo Circle became residual stretches of service alleys, leaving

Hermann Park, master plan (Hanna/Olin, Ltd., 1994).

HERMANN PARK

only Golf Course Drive to provide access to a 1,434-car parking lot between the zoo and the golf course. Hermann Park Clubhouse, the most architecturally distinguished older building within the park, was marked in the master plan for demolition, as was the Jewish Community Center, which was acquired by the City of Houston for use as the Hermann Regional Recreation Center.

Zoo service buildings spilled outside the enlarged oval of 1949, and the front gates were demolished and replaced by the intrusive Kipp Aquarium, built 1980–1982 with a bequest from Herbert A. Kipp. The Kipp Aquarium sits astride the main axis on the south shore of the Grand Basin, which was reshaped between 1981 and 1982. The master plan proposed that the Reflecting Basin be filled and that the formal promenade between the Sam Houston Monument and the Pioneer Memorial Shaft become an irregularly bounded, picturesque ramble. Parking and service facilities were to be spotted about the perimeter of the park, forming yet another barrier between it and the surrounding city.

Since 1973 additions and alterations not contemplated in the master plan have occurred. The Chinese Teahouse and Garden were constructed along Hermann Drive at the south end of Crawford Street. In 1980 the Cravens Walkway—a network of paths intertwined between berms, raised planting beds, and seating areas—was constructed in the esplanade south of Sunset Boulevard to the designs of Joel Brand & Associates. Between 1980 and 1981 the Hermann Hospital Estate sponsored construction of a memorial to George H. Hermann. Placed at the corner of Fannin Street and Outer Belt Drive, it consists of a standing bronze figure of Hermann set in a fountain display surrounded by a granite-paved court.

Hermann Park's history has been one of high hopes frustrated by a lack of popular understanding and support. It has received more attentive care than any other park in Houston, and it is one of the most intensively used parks in the city. Even so, Hermann Park has never compelled the sort of civic loyalty with which New Yorkers regard Central Park. It has failed to attain the symbolic importance of the Texas Medical Center or Rice University as a representative Houston place, although in terms of actual use it is perhaps more deserving of such recognition than either of its neighbors. It has been subjected to the sort of abusive exploitation that Americans seem to reserve for natural resources. Since the 1940s Hermann Park has decreased in acreage, either through deaccessioning of property or by routing of major thoroughfares. This diminished acreage has been expected to accommodate expanding activities and increasing use. However, the issue of how far various activities can expand without disrupting other activities or the general park setting has yet to be addressed. The issues of appropriate use, conservation, and preservation are only now beginning to crystallize. With the proposed formation of an ad hoc committee for Hermann Park under the sponsorship of the South Main Center Association, the opportunity exists to create a forum where such issues can be addressed and resolved. Hermann Park can no longer continue to be whittled away thoughtlessly, especially as its resources become more and more valuable to Houston.

Grand Basin renovated as McGovern Lake and boathouse, 2002.

2002 UPDATE

Hermann Park has received considerable attention since this article was written. After almost another full decade of negligence, Heart of the Park, a design competition sponsored by the Rice Design Alliance, Friends of Hermann Park, and Houston's Parks and Recreation Department in 1992, precipitated a renewal of activity in the park, leading to a number of improvements, the most important of which was a new master plan (1994) by landscape architect Laurie Olin of Philadelphia.

The park has been expanded to include Bayou Parkland (1999), an 80-acre area along Brays Bayou and Almeda Road transformed from an unused wasteland into adventurous wilderness trails. New and safe playgrounds including the Playground for All Children, funded by the Park People (1996), and new picnic areas have been installed. Among the most ambitious projects have been a $5.4 million renovation of Miller Outdoor Theater, including new concessions and restrooms available to all park users (Ray Bailey Architects, 2000) and a $3.7 million expansion and improvements of the former Grand Basin, renamed McGovern Lake for its benefactor John P. McGovern. Reopened in April 2001, McGovern Lake is now 7.9 acres with a fishing pier, boathouse, and nature walks. Construction began in late 2001 on the Heart of the Park, where a new reflection pool flanked by double rows of live oaks will terminate in the Molly Ann Smith Plaza. *Editors*

Cite has documented these changes throughout the past decade: Michael J. Kuchta, "Roundabout: Tanking Up Hermann Park," *Cite* 28 (spring 1992); "Heart of the Park Design Competition Winners Announced," *Cite* 29 (fall 1992/winter 1993); Olive Hershey, "For the People's Park," *Cite* 30 (spring/summer 1993); Barrie Scardino, "Doing the City's Work: Hermann Park Master Plan," *Cite* 32 (fall 1994/winter 1995); Jim Zook, "The State of the Park," *Cite* 43 (winter 1999); Mitchell J. Shields, "Parking Green: A Design Charrette Takes on Hermann Park's Biggest Problems," *Cite* 47 (spring 2000); and Mitchell J. Shields, "Cardiac Success: The Heart of the Hermann Park Gets Ready for Surgery," *Cite* 51 (summer 2001).

Cite 34
SPRING
1996

Loose Fit

THE HOUSTON MUSEUM DISTRICT

Peter C. Papademetriou

Museum District, looking south along Montrose Boulevard.

In the past five years, the area north of Hermann Park from Jackson Street to Montrose Boulevard has been the site of a succession of institutional initiatives that account for its designation as a "district." The coincidence of independent decisions has resulted in the relative proximity of a dozen or so similar institutions. In a city devoid of zoning this does not precisely constitute de facto zoning, but it certainly has resulted in a clearly identifiable zone. The Lawndale Art and Performance Center at 4912 South Main Street and the campus of the Menil Collection, west of Montrose four blocks, bordered by West Alabama on the north and Richmond Avenue on the south, are sufficiently close to be associated with this district. The perception of this area as the Museum District is intensified by the brief time span in which this growth has occurred; during the past three years and the next three years

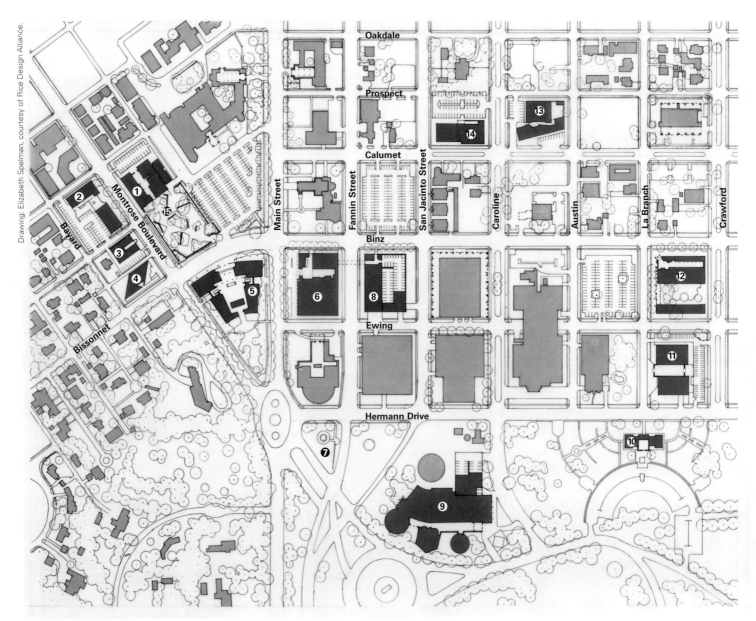

Principal public spaces, Houston Museum District.

1 Glassell school, MFAH

2 Administration and Junior School building, MFAH

3 Jung Institute

4 Contemporary Arts Museum

5 Museum of Fine Arts, Houston

6 Audrey Jones Beck Building, MFAH

7 Richard and Annette Bloch Plaza

8 Fannin service Building, MFAH

9 Houston Museum of Natural Science

10 Garden Center, Hermann Park

11 Museum of Health and Medical Science

12 Children's Museum of Houston

13 Houston Holocaust Museum

14 Clayton Geneological Library

15 Cullen Sculpture Garden, MFAH

PLACES OF THE CITY

coming, six new buildings, including the Beck Building of the Museum of Fine Arts, Houston, will have been completed.

MUSEUM OF FINE ARTS

The Museum of Fine Arts is the historical reason for this area's potential and a primary agent of its coherence. Yet there are some disturbing decisions that may well undercut the success of this fragile district, illustrating the lack of a vision that extends beyond the needs of separate institutions.

The Museum of Fine Arts (William Ward Watkin, 1924–1926) originally formed part of a 1920s ensemble adjacent to the Rice Institute that grouped it with the Hotel Warwick, Shadyside subdivision, and Hermann Park. Its front faced an oval sunken garden at the oblique intersection of Montrose and Main. As late as 1948, expansion plans reiterated this grouping, including a study by consultants Hare & Hare for additional museum facilities on the Cullinan estate within Shadyside, which borders the museum's original front yard. This all changed with a provocative master plan proposal from Kenneth Franzheim in 1952. Franzheim proposed recognizing Bissonnet Avenue's new presence in the city (resulting from a realignment through to Binz, east of South Main) by giving the museum a new "front door" and, more tellingly, by locating a one-way drive-through entry between Montrose and South Main. The Mies van der Rohe master plan of 1954 and eventual realization in Cullinan Hall (Mies van der Rohe, 1958) and expansion in the Brown Pavilion (Mies van der Rohe, 1974) pragmatically completed transferal of the front door to the Bissonnet side of the building; 1001 Bissonnet became the museum's address.

If expansion of museum facilities had been an issue in the mid-1950s when there were 4,000 objects in the collection, the collection's tripling to 12,000 works in 1970 and then more than doubling again to 27,000 works by 1992 heightened the difficulty of a managed expansion. Excluding the house museums at Bayou Bend and Rienzi, which contain important portions of the museum's collection in residential settings, a campus has essentially developed due to the exigencies of available properties near the original facility. The Alfred C. Glassell Jr. School of Art (S. I. Morris Associates, 1978) was the first obvious satellite to the campus, in part a means of gaining more internal space by pulling the museum school program out of the original building. Curiously, the school's entrance and its on-site parking face north, toward Bartlett Street, away from the museum itself.

Lillie and Hugh Roy Cullen Sculpture Garden (I. Noguchi, designer, with Fuller & Sadao, architects, 1986), with Brown Pavilion (Office of Mies van der Rohe, 1974) in background.

Hester + Hardaway, 1996.

Administration and Junior School Building (Carlos Jiménez, designer, with Kendall/Heaton Associates, 1994).

Funding initiatives to establish the museum school also set the stage for the Lillie and Hugh Roy Cullen Sculpture Garden (Isamu Noguchi, 1986). This loose chain of facilities along Montrose has resulted in a curious urban condition. The Cullen Garden's primary entrance is located mid-block, across the street from the front door of the Brown Pavilion, whose expansive, blocklong curving façade echoes the curve of the street. This implicit urban space is only half museum property, as is prominently noted by a sign identifying the entrance to a parking lot for the First Presbyterian Church.

ADMINISTRATION AND JUNIOR SCHOOL BUILDING

The most recently completed facility for the Museum of Fine Arts campus is the Administration and Junior School Building (Carlos Jiménez with Kendall/Heaton Associates, 1994), which is "out in left field," so to speak, across Montrose on the block bounded by Berthea and Bartlett. It is a taut composition that shows it conceptually belongs to a larger context through controlled adjustments in its form. The site Jiménez was given demanded clever corroboration with the other museum buildings to reappropriate a presence within the group. The education and administrative components are operationally separate, but both had to be housed in the new L-shaped building. The school was organized in a two-story wing facing Bartlett Street, making north light available to the studios. The administrative offices occupy the three-story block fronting on Montrose, where a barrel-vaulted, rounded metal roof gives added scale to the principal façade. The program areas are easily kept separate through this internal division. The two building blocks are interlocked on the third level, where the graphics and publications offices sit atop one end of the school block.

A mini-plaza softens the rear parking lot's relationship to the building. The front is set back from Montrose, effectively preserving a row of established live oak trees, and is more or less in line with the building setbacks of the Jung Center and Contemporary Arts Museum to the south, clearly tying the group together.

The Montrose entry of the Jiménez building is monumentalized by its external representation as a pure three-story element, set in from the exterior face of the block with an obliquely canted wall (behind which are service rooms). It is the precise placement of the entrance that knits Jiménez's design to context: facing east, the entrance is virtually centered perpendicular to the entrance face of the Glassell School, and its seemingly casually angled wall, something like 37 degrees, is rigorously constructed to align with the Montrose entrance to the Cullen Sculpture Garden and, by geometrical extension, with the center line of the garden's entrance across from the Museum of Fine Arts entrance on Bissonnet. Materially, the composition of anodized aluminum, limestone, standing-seam metal, and occasional sections of glass block refers to elements in the other campus buildings. The result is an elegantly proportioned, precisely detailed building that is visually interesting yet simple and clear in design, embracing complexity without being complicated.

BECK BUILDING

It is with the projected Audrey Jones Beck Building (Rafael Moneo with Kendall/Heaton Associates) and its associated Fannin Service Building that the substantial needs of the Museum of Fine Arts will be met. Currently still in design by Spanish architect Rafael Moneo (again with Kendall/Heaton Associates of Houston), the Beck Building reveals some fundamental repositioning of the museum's address, one more time.

The 185,000-square-foot facility will double the gallery capacity of the Museum of Fine Arts and pro-

Museum of Fine Arts, Houston, complex: Beck Building (Rafael Moneo with Kendall/Heaton Associates, 2000; center), Brown Pavilion (right), parking garage and visitors center (left).

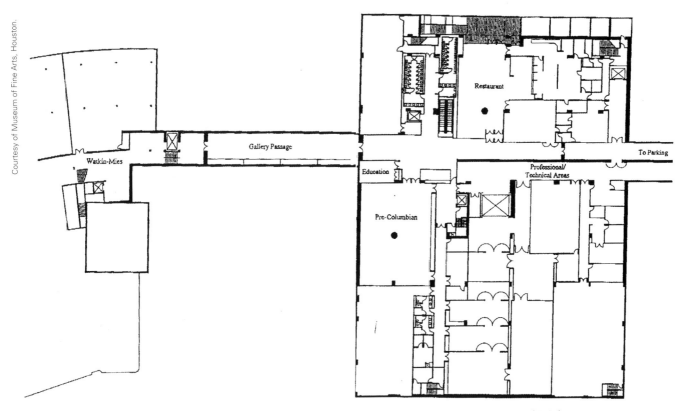

Plan illustrating connection of Beck Building and Brown Pavilion (left) and parking garage (right).

vide space for traveling exhibitions. The existing museum building will be renovated to house works from the permanent collection. Thus freed from the need to house everything, the Mies building can be restored to its original spatial intentions. The Beck Building, in turn, will provide spacious galleries for traveling exhibitions, particularly those of the "blockbuster" variety.

Moneo's design must be seen in light of the 1988–1990 master plan by Venturi, Scott Brown & Associates, a critical-needs assessment program as well as a study of physical form alternatives. Venturi clearly argued against a focus along South Main and warned, "Do not rely on underground tunnels for public access, and do not provide tunnel access under Main Street." Instead, the report pushed for reinforcement of the Bissonnet front through its extension across South Main along Binz. The proposed *parti* suggested an arcaded gallery, which would extend the Mies design

and be formally completed with the front of the Fannin Service Building in the next block. The report stressed the importance of extending without replicating the big sweep of the Mies façade along Bissonnet. An appendix expanded the argument against the tunnel, citing the problems of city utilities, the need for vertical elevator connections at each end, and the cost of basement space in Houston given the local groundwater conditions. "Underground pedestrian tunnels will be extremely difficult to make lively," it further observed. Of course, Venturi, Scott Brown & Associates was not given the job.

The Moneo proposal reflects clearly the museum board's view of how functional constraints of separated facilities must be resolved, but it seriously ignores, or at least devalues, the larger scale of the urban experience. Moneo's design, in a kind of good ol' boy inversion of the cosmopolitan urbanism his architecture has represented, gives precedence to humidity, heat, and drive-in ease in lieu of reinforcing the potential of the Bissonnet-Binz corridor.

The Beck Building's west elevation, along South Main, will be the principal façade, with the institution's name incised in huge letters, although the museum's published address will not change. Internally, public circulation centers on a three-story vertical atrium that parallels the Binz front, bookended by a three-section public stair and a pair of long escalators leading past a mezzanine level (where public access is primarily for scholars "by appointment") to the main gallery group on the second floor. It is these upper rooms that are illuminated by the cluster of lanterns that populate and characterize the building's roofscape.

The Binz façade features a moat that creates a light court for the new museum café on the lower level (dare we say basement?) from which it is possible to enter or exit the facility via an exterior stair parallel to the sidewalk. At this level a 23-foot-wide "underground gallery passage" (dare we say tunnel?) connects, under South Main, to the lower level of the Brown Pavilion. This subterranean spine extends completely through the Beck Building, under Fannin Street, and into the Fannin Service Building, which contains parking for 600 to 700 cars. This processional is essentially a linear, two-block underground trek to the existing museum. It has little lateral horizontal visual relief and no vertical extension to punctuate if not modulate the journey, let alone provide any sense of the world above.

Binz has been gratuitously recognized by a suspended canopy along the north face of the Beck Building, where one may enter the lobby through a set of double doors. Its dull south façade, directly facing the raised lobby of the Wyndham Warwick Hotel, comprises two fire exits and a loading dock. On the east (Fannin Street) side, Moneo set the building mass to approximate that of the existing museum—its lime-

stone cladding matches the original Watkin building and the stone base of the Mies pavilion.

In this way, a new urban spatial dialogue is established across South Main, but any urban experience is limited to the street corner, or effectively eliminated by the underground passage. There is no suggestion that a landscape theme will enhance whatever pedestrian experience there could have been and everything to suggest that this is an oh-by-the-way design to be visually enhanced by the foundation-planting school of landscape architecture.

CONTEMPORARY ARTS MUSEUM

Such is not the case with the modest program of rehabilitation, expansion, and exterior space enhancement of the Contemporary Arts Museum (Gunnar Birkets & Associates with Charles Tapley Associates, 1972). Architect William F. Stern, himself a collector of contemporary art, has opted for understated minimalist erasures to simplify the rabbit warren of lower-level spaces added over the years. William F. Stern & Associates devised a core of critical service spaces, including a long-needed elevator. Otherwise the lower level will provide a large space for mixed uses, including a projection room, and a gallery that enlarges the museum's downstairs exhibition space by nearly 50 percent. A cottage at 5201 Bayard Lane, rehabilitated by Stern, will provide offices and staff parking. The main gallery of the parallelogram museum remains essentially the same, with a new elevator concealed within what had been part of a triangular piece completing a solid-void mini-parallelogram in the entry vestibule. The Contemporary Arts Museum (CAM) has always had something of an address aberration: its Montrose Boulevard address was a slip-down-the-side-street (Bissonnet) front door marked only by a vertical slot between two metal wall planes. Stern has addressed this problem by proposing a triangular prismatic canopy projection into the exterior space over the entrance.

Hester + Hardaway, 1996.

Contemporary Arts Museum (Gunnar Birkets & Associates with Charles Tapley Associates, 1972).

The CAM's front yard has been at best a residual space activated only on occasion, such as Meg Webster's provocative environmental piece three years ago. The new CAM proposal developed in collaboration with Philadelphia landscape architect Laurie Olin, whose firm, the Olin Partnership Ltd., formerly Hanna/Olin, authored the visionary 1995 master plan for Hermann Park, injects a public space at the corner of Montrose and Bissonnet. Stern and Olin's plan appropriates the CAM lawn, injects a staggered row of Mexican sycamores along a reconfigured east-facing sidewalk, and unifies the ground plane with a band of granite gravel containing concrete benches, in turn shaded by the trees. A circular fountain 19 feet in diameter will add a measure of psychological cooling. The composition, a kind of Modernist collage, is completed by several revised elements. A serpentine, guitar-form parapet, high enough to serve as seating, bisects the lawn, which slopes ever so slightly downward from the sidewalk at its northeastern edge. Since the entry to the CAM is, in effect, halfway down the block, this plan will energize the corner, extending the museum's front door almost to the street. Such a commitment on the part of the Contemporary Arts Museum enhances the external life of the street as a means to amplify its own institutional presence.

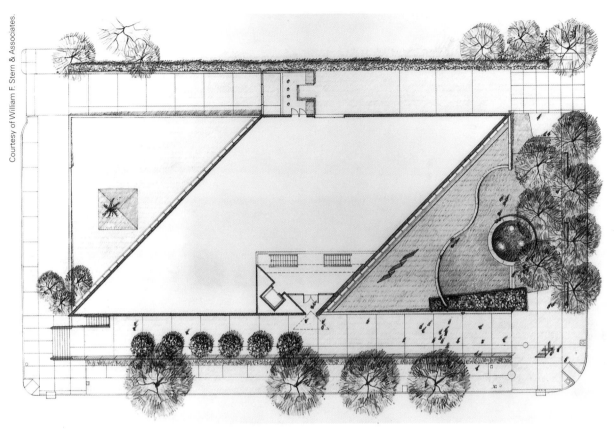

Contemporary Arts Museum, renovation plan (William F. Stern & Associates with Olin Partnership Ltd., landscape architect, 1996).

CHILDREN'S MUSEUM

Assuming that the vitality of this modest corner park may be seen as a contribution to Houston's cityscape, the question arises, What about the perception of the Bissonnet-Binz corridor as a public artery? This corridor is reinforced if the Children's Museum of Houston (Venturi, Scott Brown & Associates with Jackson & Ryan, 1992) is considered to anchor the eastern boundary of the Museum District. The Children's Museum set a precedent when its architects oriented the building to reinforce Binz as an approach.

While the Children's Museum has been the subject of lengthy review in *Cite*, its site plan was largely ignored. Venturi made a great point of the fact that today's buildings often require parking lots of a size equal to, or sometimes greater than, that of their own footprint. In his *Cite* review, Drexel Turner observes that the museum's west elevation, a low-tech metal-shed arcade populated by the now-famous "caryakids" and connecting the shop building on the south to the more figurative building on the north, creates a shielded edge to the interior courtyard. Turner's discussion of this arrangement was principally in terms of making the museum visually accessible "by the opportune placement of its parking lot, which intercepts the principal flow of traffic proceeding east from Main

Hester + Hardaway, 1996.

Hester + Hardaway, 1993.

Children's Museum of Houston, interior (Venturi, Scott Brown & Associates with Jackson & Ryan, architects, 1989–1992).

Children's Museum of Houston, exterior.

Street along Binz Avenue." In fact, the Children's Museum parking lot is a subtle urban landscape designed as an integral part of the building *parti*.

What is important is that this connection, the south side of Binz, establishes the visual position of the Children's Museum as an anchor to one part of the Museum District. However, the proposed Beck Building and Fannin Service Building of the Museum of Fine Arts do little to sustain this public domain by failing to enhance the potential of an occupiable urban streetscape. Even environmental realities fail to convince because

this pedestrian route would have been along north-facing elevations, where the buildings would comfortably shade the sidewalk. If the intervening city blocks were enhanced and sidewalks developed, the vista to the main entrance of the Children's Museum would visually connect the district's western point of origin at the CAM. With its placement, orientation, massing, and most assuredly its color scheme, the Children's Museum would be an appealing goal. The idea of street activity is extended even through the interior of the Children's Museum, whose central, streetlike arcade,

Museum of Health and Medical Sciences, Crawford Street elevation (Marilyn P. McCarnes, Architects, and Billy D. Tippit, Architects, 1996).

the Kids' Gallery, has been appropriated by activity and project areas, to the side of which "street" vendors such as a dairy bar and a museum shop have been added.

MEDICAL MUSEUM

Although it is a direct neighbor of the Children's Museum on the adjacent city block, the Museum of Health and Medical Science (Marilyn P. McCarnes, Architects, and Billy D. Tippit, Architects, 1995) vitiates any further urban design potential. When the Children's Museum established La Branch as a principal street, it extended the connection south to the Houston Garden Center, which lies on its axis as the termination of the vista. There are, however, three entries to the Museum of Health and Medical Science. The honorific entry is clearly on La Branch, with a gestural entry plaza grafted onto the sidewalk; parking and school bus drop-off are on the east side of the building, facing Crawford Street; and, curiously, the official address is 1515 Hermann Drive, the south side of the building, which is essentially a blank façade with car access into the basement parking area. The formal language of a pseudo-Classical architecture speaks of a visual hierarchy that reinforces this reading: front door on La Branch through a temple front that is woefully underachieving

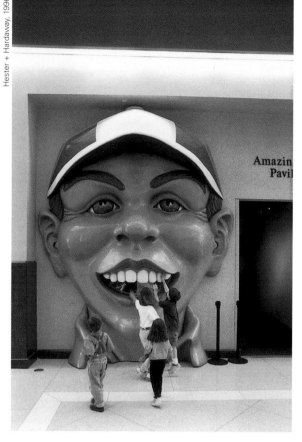

Amazing Body Pavilion, Museum of Health and Medical Sciences.

in contrast with that of the Children's Museum next door; side door, but actual entrance, on Crawford; and back door, garage entry, but building address, on Hermann Drive.

Externally, the building is a jogged cluster of two pavilions abutting a central spine; internally, the building's 28,000 square feet of public education areas are kept at grade, but administrative offices and the Harris County Medical Society offices are on the upper floor, joined through the central grand hall by a pair of glass vaulted tube-bridges between the two pavilions. The south pavilion contains the labyrinth-like Amazing Body Pavilion as well as a clear exercise in kiddie crowd control: gift shop, children's restrooms, a snack exchange (no preservatives, low-fat, no cholesterol, low sodium/sugar?), and a separate lobby for herding the li'l darlins back into buses.

The Amazing Body Pavilion features an incredible entrance element: an open-mouthed child's head that is a viewing window into the dental-and-mouth section. This glossy, colorful giant is made even more outstanding by contrast with the architectural sobriety of the grand hall, which separates the two sides of the building. The north side contains support functions as well as the Transparent Anatomical Mannequin Theatre and the Michael E. DeBakey Science Laboratory and Learning Center. The Grand Hall, which one envisions as primarily useful for receptions of the medical society, is so inherently empty that it is clearly not a space in which to linger: keep those little guys out of sight!

HOLOCAUST MUSEUM

Another new component of this cluster is the Houston Holocaust Museum, Education Center, and Memorial (Mark S. Mucasey, 1996). North and two blocks west of the other museums, at the corner of Calumet and Caroline, the Holocaust Museum is fortuitously sited across from the Houston Public Library's Clayton Library Center for Genealogical Research at 5300 Caroline, a complex that includes the renovated William L. Clayton House, designed in 1916 by architect Birdsall P. Briscoe. While the Clayton Library is not a museum, it is a publicly owned, accessible, and interesting component of the district.

The Holocaust Museum was initiated by Houston's Jewish community but expanded in program when Ralph Appelbaum Associates of New York, designers of the exhibition in the National Holocaust Museum in Washington, D.C., were brought in. What had been a renovation to an existing one-story building became a

Houston Holocaust Museum (Ralph Applebaum Associates, designer, with Mark S. Mucasey, architect, 1996).

Hester + Hardaway, 1996.

Holocaust Museum, Wall of Tears, Memorial Room (Murphy Mears Architects with artists Patricia and Robert Moss-Vreeland).

substantial addition to the same building. A national competition for a separate memorial room was won by artists Patricia and Robert Moss-Vreeland of Philadelphia in collaboration with Murphy Mears Architects of Houston. The Mucasey scheme had its entrance on Prospect Avenue, a reasonable connection to the siting of the existing building; fortunately, the insertion of and connection with a more distinctive exhibition hall made it logical for the entry to be at the conjunction of the two pieces, fronting on Caroline Street, which makes better sense in urban design terms. The final design comprised reworking of the existing building into an administrative center, support functions, multipurpose classrooms, a substantial gallery for changing exhibitions, and the library resource center (which will house materials from Holocaust survivors within the Houston community). The new building, whose wedge form is displaced on the site, contains an orientation auditorium, a permanent exhibition on the Holocaust, the memorial room, and an exterior garden. The Mucasey firm produced all documents for construction and interior finish; Appelbaum Associates controlled the exhibition design; Murphy Mears separately designed the memorial room in collaboration with the Moss-Vreelands. The construction documents bear a dedication to the memory of Mucasey's wife's grandparents, who were victims of the Holocaust.

Imagery indeed dominates form in the Holocaust Museum. The wedge-form roof seems to be a roadway to nowhere but is in fact a recollection of roads paved by the Nazis with Jewish gravestones; the displacement of forms reflects the displacement of European Jewish life; six vertical piers with wires between them recall both the Six Million (a second series down the interior hall leading to the resource center repeats the metaphor) and the death-camp fences; the conical form of the auditorium recalls the crematoria; the circulation arcade, which tapers to a point, suggests the trestle of a death train. The interior detailing is deliberately harsh: steel lintels and brick details, a 6-inch steel channel baseboard with exposed bolts.

The memorial room is a separate kind of architecture. The thickness of its walls emphasizes its isolation from the exhibition area; in fact, it appears as an object inserted within the space. Natural light dominates the interior volume, formed by Murphy Mears. The focus of the room is on the Wall of Tears, the memorial piece by the Moss-Vreelands. An intense space, it is also a place of hope.

Potentially, Caroline Street, an esplanaded boulevard built up with medical and residential buildings, could be enhanced as a connector between Hermann Park and the Holocaust Museum, and vice versa. The Clayton Library could expand public awareness by introducing an exhibition presenting a didactic explanation of its collections and their use; the Houston Public Library is always interested in increasing patronage of its branches and ought to budget promotion and marketing in this area.

MUSEUM OF NATURAL SCIENCE

Caroline Street has become an important entry point for the expanded Houston Museum of Natural Science (George Pierce – Abel B. Pierce and Staub, Rather & Howze, 1964). Transformed within the park from a street into an access road, Caroline serves public parking and the museum's east entrance court, regarded as the major entrance. Recent additions to the museum include extensions to the exhibition halls on two levels; a traveling exhibition hall on the third level (with a functioning Foucault pendulum through all three levels); collection storage and support spaces; a new entrance plaza and foyer; and the most dramatic expansion of all, the Cockrell Butterfly Center (Hoover Architects, 1995).

If the location of building entrances is a response to and recognition of external urban forces, then the design of the Houston Museum of Natural Science

Cockrell Butterfly Center, Houston Museum of Natural Science (Hoover Architects, 1995).

may be seen not as a deliberate urban strategy, but rather as a reactive condition. The new Cockrell Butterfly Center pavilion has the largest and most visible entry, but it is as far away from linkages to the larger Museum District as one could imagine. To be fair, the municipal water tank, reconstructed in 1991, that occupies a prime corner of the adjacent site was a barrier that designs for both the parking structure and the museum expansion had to work around, literally. Yet wayfinding at the site is as dislocating as it is disjointed, while the entry hall itself evokes a kind of shopping-mall experience. Destination informs the de-

cision of where to enter (Butterfly Center, IMAX theater, science exhibition halls, planetarium), but a new museumgoer, unsure of which entry leads where, will be at a loss. While the parking structure is a popular facility, one is confronted in its small at-grade lobby with signs on doors reading "NO ENTRY" and arrows pointing outside in order to get inside. On the exterior, no real signage program gets you around to the east entry from Hermann Park on the south or from the Museum of Fine Arts on the west. To find the "main entrance" on the east, you must bypass the Butterfly Center (if you haven't already tried to get in through the service door at the western corner of its pavilion). The only intervening and inviting set of steps, up to the old planetarium, is roped off; only a low barrier of chain fence directs you around.

The Cockrell Butterfly Center is a great addition to the vocabulary of Hermann Park structures and to the experience of nature. Being able to move up through its glass interior is one of the more satisfying spatial experiences within the museum, and the tropical world of live butterflies fluttering by is simply wonderful. The transparent, tapered, and segmented conical form stands in marked contrast to the other beads on a string — the IMAX theater and the planetarium, both inherently solid, closed forms. The Cockrell pavilion works architecturally, as a shimmering solid during the day and as a glimmering beacon at night.

There is an alternative pedestrian route, for the adventuresome, from the Contemporary Arts Museum and the Museum of Fine Arts to the Museum of Natural Science. This is one marked by water features and round markers: the Mecom Fountain, at the intersection of South Main and Montrose; the rounded south façade of the Wyndham Warwick Hotel, ringed by a line of fountains; the Bloch Cancer Survivors Plaza with its wrought-iron frou-frou domed gazebo and small fountain, for better or worse a stopover destination on the path to the science museum; and the circularized colonnade of the original Miller Outdoor Theater (William Ward Watkin, architect, 1923), now resituated around a lighted fountain with an abundant water spray. This streetscape with residual landforms (parklets) results from the engineering of roadways sorting out traffic on Fannin and San Jacinto. The aforementioned water tank could be an element in a conscious continuation of this theme, although camouflage appears to have been the main response to its presence. The towerlike butterfly center is the visual anchor that completes this progression from art to science.

IS THERE A DISTRICT IN ALL THIS?

Laurie Olin was engaged to address the issue in the Houston Museum District Study Draft Summary Document, submitted in April 1995. Where the study is clear is in its recognition of the obvious clusters, the recommendation of incremental improvements such as "a gradual repair and relocation of sidewalks along with additional street tree planting . . . installation of a comprehensive system of signage . . . new street furniture . . . [to] provide a range of basic facilities along the streets to sustain a visitor." The report goes on to suggest that "the area streets . . . should become vital places full of life and activity in their own right." This is expanded into a concept for a Primary Street, featuring a canopy structure "that would provide shade and weather protection for market vendors [and] could contain utilities such as electricity, and possibly drainage." In addition, the study advocates a program of public art, as well as a schedule of specially designed everyday items such as manholes, parking meters, trash cans, and so forth. There is talk of a shuttle bus among the museums, extending north up South Main to include the Lawndale Center and up Montrose to include the Menil Collection campus.

My own analogy for the most appropriate strategy came through my old pair of Bugle Boy jeans. Not intended to give a precise contour to a form that has become, shall we say, somewhat less defined in time, the cut is what Bugle Boy calls "Loose Fit." This casual model may be the best analogy for the Houston situation: enough has already been done ad hoc to mitigate any rigorous cohesion that might have resulted from a strategy arising from consensus, if the institutions had actually anticipated the opportunities their separate actions would generate. The perceived relationship between the museum groups requires substantial physical intervention to make it all clear—which seems unnecessary. Yes, reinforce the principal corridors, particularly with a tree-planting program, and clarify them as arteries; develop a system of consistent signage; and provide some street amenities for pausing and resting. Maybe some people will actually walk between the clusters, but the proposal should work for those in cars as well as the few brave souls on foot. Perhaps it's enough to know what the options are, and where they are, to achieve a sense of a district. In fact, in program, content, and intent the museums appeal to diverse audiences. The likelihood of combining visits is probably remote. As for street activities, cultural geographer J. B. Jackson once observed, "Street life in America is a sign of poverty." Oh, there may be occasions when the dozen city blocks involved could sustain a festival-type atmosphere, but Houstonians don't need a heavily tailored infrastructure to perceive a sense of identity for the area—just a loose fit. The pity is some of the seams, as currently laid out, might ultimately be a bit crooked.

2002 UPDATE

The Audrey Jones Beck Building of the Museum of Fine Arts, Houston, was completed in 2001, and, as Papademetriou predicted, the tunnel system is its most frequently used entrance. The tunnel section between the new and old museum buildings was transformed by James Turrell's vivid and ever-changing light sculpture, "The Light Inside," giving the museum visitor a magical trip rather than a monotonous trek. Urbanistically, however, the issue of collective space versus private precinct is a question still unresolved.
Editors

Museum buildings in Houston have been the subject of several *Cite* reviews: Stephen Fox, "A Clapboard Treasure House: The Menil Museum," *Cite* 1 (August 1982); Peter J. Holliday, "Lillie and Hugh Roy Cullen Sculpture Garden," *Cite* 10 (summer 1985); "Romancing the Stone: The Cullen Sculpture Garden," *Cite* 15 (fall 1986); Geoffrey Brune, "I-Maxing Out: Addition to the Houston Museum of Natural History," *Cite* 25 (fall 1990); Patrick Peters, "A Temple for Tots: Children's Museum of Houston," *Cite* 26 (spring 1991); Stephen Fox, "Administration and Junior School Building, MFAH," *Cite* 30 (spring/summer 1993); Drexel Turner, "Little Caesar's Palace: The Children's Museum of Houston," *Cite* 30 (spring/summer 1993); Lynn M. Herbert, "Seeing Was Believing: Installations of Jermayne MacAgy and James Johnson Sweeney," *Cite* 40 (winter 1997–1998); Fares el Dahdah, "Shedding Light on the Beck," *Cite* 47 (spring 2000).

Cite 34
SPRING
1996

The Twombly Gallery
and the Making of Place

William F. Stern

The 1995 completion of the Twombly Gallery in an early-20th-century Montrose neighborhood continues a contemporary pattern of building that was established with the Rothko Chapel in 1971. Like the Rothko, the Twombly Gallery is the result of an unusual three-way collaboration among artist, architect, and patron.

For the 1987 opening of the Menil Collection, the collection's founder, Dominique de Menil, with the Menil's first director, Walter Hopps, and its current director, Paul Winkler, had hoped to mount an exhibition of paintings and drawings by the American artist Cy Twombly. Not until 1989, however, was such an exhibition presented. The Menil Collection already owned works by Twombly, and for the exhibition these were augmented by paintings and drawings from the Dia Art Foundation and private collections. The Dia Art Foundation, founded by Dominique de Menil's daughter Fariha (Philippa) and her husband, Heiner Friedrich, owned Twombly paintings and drawings collected in the 1970s and additional pieces purchased for Dia in 1980. At the time of the Twombly exhibition in Houston, discussion began about collaboration between Dia and the Menil for a permanent Twombly installation in Houston, with a smaller installation in New York. In fall 1990, Paul Winkler, Dominique de Menil, and the Friedrichs visited Twombly at his home in Rome to so-

licit his support for the project. Twombly was receptive, producing a conceptual sketch that would later become the basis for the Twombly Gallery plan. He also offered to give works he owned to both spaces. The Dia and Menil representatives agreed that a new building would be constructed in Houston for a major installation of Twombly's paintings, drawings, and sculpture drawn from the Menil and Dia collections, along with more than 35 works donated by the artist himself. The Menil took title of six paintings from Dia and in so doing helped the foundation purchase a building on West 22nd Street in New York across the street from the foundation's existing four-story loft building. When renovated, the new building will be used for single-artist installations drawn from Dia's collection, with part of one floor designated for a permanent installation of works by Twombly. With this determined, in November 1991 the Renzo Piano Building Workshop in Genoa began to develop a design for the Twombly Gallery in Houston.

UNIVERSITY OF ST. THOMAS
Thirty-five years earlier, in the mid-1950s, John and Dominique de Menil came to the neighborhood that would eventually house their extensive collection of art through their association with the University of St.

Thomas, a Catholic liberal arts university founded by priests of the Order of St. Basil. The Menils' architectural influence would first be felt when they were asked by the university to assist in the selection of an architect for new buildings. Among those recommended, Philip Johnson, who had designed the Menil House in River Oaks in 1950, received the commission to draw a master plan for the St. Thomas campus. The Menils underwrote the costs of the master plan and soon became actively involved in helping to form a new art department for the university. Fashioning his plan after Thomas Jefferson's academic village at the University of Virginia, Johnson proposed a series of two-story block buildings laid out around an elongated court, interconnected by a U-shaped covered walkway.

The design, a boldly modern composition of exposed black steel frames inset with panels of dusty-colored brick and floor-to-ceiling glass, demonstrated Johnson's allegiance to the International Style of Mies van der Rohe. Without upsetting the balance and scale of the older neighborhood, these buildings stood comfortably among the picturesque bungalows, frame houses, and live oaks, setting a pattern that would be adopted by a succession of architects.

At the time of the St. Thomas master plan, the area surrounding the campus was in decline. The Montrose subdivision and its adjoining neighborhoods had been developed in the teens on open farmland by entrepreneurs intent upon providing modest middle-class housing. With its tree-lined streets and parklike land-

Menil neighborhood map.

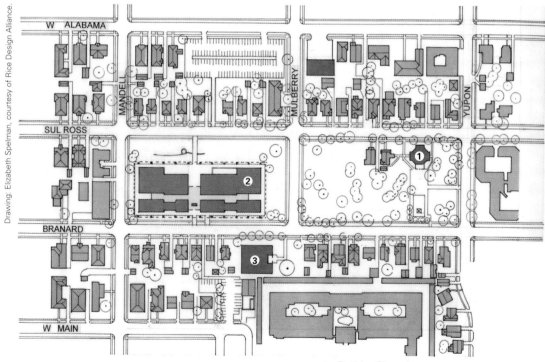

Drawing: Elizabeth Spelman, courtesy of Rice Design Alliance.

1 Rothko Chapel
2 Menil Collection
3 Twombly Gallery

The Menil Collection and neighborhood of bungalows along Branard Street.

scape, Montrose was typical of America's first suburbs. Restricted for residential use and planned with uniform building setbacks, the neighborhood matured during the 1920s into a harmonious pattern of one-story Craftsman bungalows and larger two-story houses set among graceful live oaks. After World War II, as a younger generation sought housing in newer suburbs, the planning restrictions in Montrose and many of its surrounding neighborhoods lapsed, leaving the area vulnerable to apartment construction and small-scale commercial development. Paradoxically, the loss of the restrictions and the uniformity they maintained set in motion an unusual transformation of the neighborhood that continues to this day.

During the 1950s and 1960s the Menils began to acquire property west of the St. Thomas campus, at first for the future expansion of the University of St. Thomas and later for the building of what would become one of Houston's richest cultural enclaves. In retrospect, their activity in this neighborhood can also be seen as the first and most comprehensive program of historical preservation in a city that cared little about its building past. The majority of the bungalows and houses acquired

by the Menils in this period were saved. When new buildings were proposed, older houses were often moved to new sites rather than destroyed. Over the years, these houses have been rented at modest rates to artists, scholars, and non-profit organizations. Among the organizations leasing houses are the Da Camera chamber music society, Writers in the Schools, Texas Accountants and Lawyers for the Arts, and Inprint Inc., the fund-raising and promotional arm of the University of Houston creative writing program. The bungalows and frame houses acquired a particular distinction and the neighborhood was unified when the architect Howard Barnstone suggested painting all the houses a medium gray with white trim. Another Menil property, Richmond Hall, located on Richmond one block south of the Menil Collection, has been used as a supplementary exhibition space for the Menil and most recently for Houston's annual FotoFest.

ROTHKO CHAPEL

The trio of cultural buildings constructed within the neighborhood between 1971 and 1995 shows similar patterns of site planning and general relationship to

Rothko Chapel (Howard Barnstone and Eugene Aubry, 1971) with *Broken Obelisk* (Barnett Newman, 1970) in foreground.

The Menil Collection (Renzo Piano with Richard Fitzgerald & Associates, 1987).

their surrounding neighborhood. The first, an ecumenical chapel designed to house commissioned paintings by the great American abstract painter Mark Rothko, was built by John and Dominique de Menil to the west of the University of St. Thomas between Sul Ross and Branard. Based on plans by Philip Johnson, who had earlier been retained to design the chapel (then intended for the south end of the St. Thomas mall), the completed building was designed by Howard Barnstone and Eugene Aubry. Like the Twombly Gallery, the Rothko Chapel is turned away from the street in favor of a self-contained site plan. Backing up closely to Sul Ross on the north, this centrally planned, octagonal building faces a rectangular reflecting pool on axis with Barnett Newman's *Broken Obelisk* and is screened from Branard Street to the south by a dense stand of bamboo (see neighborhood plan). The main approach to the entrance is from a side street, Yupon, along a walkway that enters at mid-block and leads to a paved plaza between the building and the reflecting pool. This unconventional relationship of building to street effectively allows the Rothko to stand both comfortably and independently among its residential neighbors at the edge of the University of St. Thomas campus.

MENIL COLLECTION

The much larger building for the Menil Collection (Renzo Piano, 1987) built to house the de Menil art collection, follows a similar pattern of siting to produce a compatible relationship with the smaller surrounding houses. Occupying an entire block, the rectangular building is asymmetrically positioned on the site. By

Cy Twombly Gallery (Renzo Piano/Building Workshop, Genoa, with Richard Fitzgerald & Associates, 1992–1994).

adjoining Branard on the south and Mandell on the west, the building leaves a wide expanse of lawn to the north along Sul Ross and a narrower space on the east that joins with park space across Mulberry Street. The building's main entrance, from Sul Ross, and the secondary entrance, from Branard, are placed slightly off center, further diminishing symmetrical formality. While the use of gray-stained cypress siding and white steel structure help relate the Menil to the neighboring bungalows, it is the asymmetrical siting that moderates the impact of the greater building mass on the residential neighborhood.

NEW NEIGHBOR: THE TWOMBLY

The Twombly Gallery, located across the street from the Menil on Branard, strategically aligns with the 1920s bungalows to either side. Unlike the bungalows, with their eccentrically articulated gabled front porches, the gallery turns a blank wall to the street, and its entrance is rotated 90 degrees to the east, facing a

grassy plaza anchored by a single mature live oak. Like the siting of the Rothko Chapel a block down the street, this maneuver effectively mitigates the formal impact of the entrance. By establishing the movement from street to building entrance through the private space of a pocket park, the experience becomes relaxed and intimate. As the termination of Mulberry Street, this space is also linked to the two open spaces on either side of Mulberry, enhancing the parklike setting. Both the Rothko Chapel and the Twombly Gallery are monumental masonry buildings, barely penetrated by windows or doors, but because the formal relationship to the street is played down, their mass does not disturb the delicate and informal fabric of the residential neighborhood. Although the Twombly Gallery displaced one small house (which was moved intact to an empty lot a few houses east on Branard), this late-20th-century building is perfectly at home with the Craftsman bungalows, not through architectural style but through compatible scale and thoughtful site relationships.

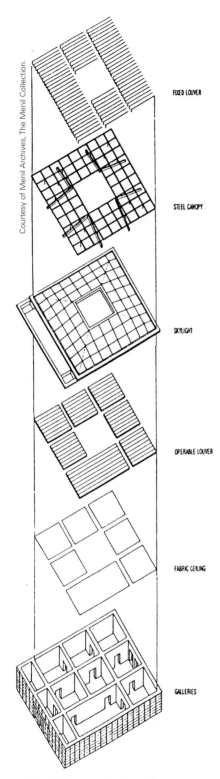

FIXED LOUVER

STEEL CANOPY

SKYLIGHT

OPERABLE LOUVER

FABRIC CEILING

GALLERIES

Cy Twombly Gallery, roof schematic.

The Rothko Chapel and the Twombly Gallery also share certain internal planning strategies, particularly their simplicity and directness of plan. A single gallery space, the Rothko Chapel is centrally planned and is entered through a foyer that serves as a threshold where visitors can pause before moving left or right into the ethereal volume occupied by Rothko's panels of color, which are installed on four opposing walls of the octagonal room. At the Menil Collection the visitor also arrives into a receiving area, larger in scale than the more intimate Rothko foyer and open to the outside. Through the simple idea of a centrally planned foyer with a transepting hallway that extends the length of the building and contains galleries on one side and a restricted service zone on the other, Piano assured a clarity of organization that makes the experience of the Menil building relaxed and unencumbered. The wide, graceful hallway, open on either end to the outside light, connects the museum interior to the lush greenery of Houston and the neighborhood beyond.

The conceptual plan of the Twombly Gallery that originated from the sketch drawn by Cy Twombly during the early planning discussions shows a rectangular block containing five connected galleries. Piano significantly elaborated Twombly's concept by laying out galleries within a plan based on a nine-square grid, adding at one end of the building block a narrower rectangular volume for the entry vestibule. Where the foyer of the Rothko is substantially closed, the foyer of the Twombly Gallery, like that of the Menil Collection, opens to the outside through a wall of glass and glass doors framed by a poured-concrete portal. On the opposite side of the building, the required second means of egress has been treated like the entrance, opening through an identically framed glass wall to the outside. The vestibule might be compared to the porch of a Greek or Roman temple, framed by a tripartite portal with perfectly proportioned poured-concrete columns and lintel standing in for an ordered Classical structure.

Hester + Hardaway, 1996.

Cy Twombly Gallery, interior.

Although born and raised in Virginia, Twombly has spent the past 40 years in Italy, and many of his paintings make reference to the ancient world. Italian architect Renzo Piano has subtly incorporated references to that world into the building, respecting as well the intentions behind the Twombly sketch that generated the plan.

The entry foyer leads to eight separate galleries laid out within the geometry of the nine-square grid. Taking advantage of the multiple combinations inherent in that geometry, Piano designed one of the outer galleries as a double square to accommodate larger and longer paintings. All of the galleries save the center one open on two sides to adjacent galleries, allowing uninterrupted circulation in either direction. Portal openings between galleries align but are not necessarily centered, creating variations in wall lengths to ac-commodate paintings of different horizontal dimensions. In the middle gallery facing west, on the opposite side from the foyer, the space is brightly illuminated through windows and glass doors, producing a sensation so dramatic that in moving into this gallery it is as if one has actually stepped outside. This transitional space compares to the Menil Collection, where one is constantly brought to the outside. And like the Menil, the logic of the plan and the clear sequence of spaces provides for an easily perceived path between galleries, with subtle variations giving each a slightly different spatial quality.

NATURAL LIGHT
Beyond these planning and spatial continuities, what most closely unites the Rothko Chapel, the Menil Collection, and the Twombly Gallery is the use of overhead

Rothko Chapel, interior.

The Menil Collection, interior.

natural light as a means of illuminating spaces. From the Rothko to the Twombly Gallery one encounters a drive to achieve perfect natural lighting, and while the effect in each case is different, the results are equally astonishing.

The paintings and interior of the Rothko Chapel are illuminated from a roof-mounted pyramidal skylight centrally positioned over the chapel space. After the initial installation, it became apparent that too much direct sunlight came through the unprotected glass, and a cloth scrim was soon added underneath the glass pyramid. Later, a concave baffle replaced the scrim beneath the skylight allowing light to drift in softly along the edges, delicately washing the paintings.

The experience with natural light at the Rothko Chapel served as a lesson for the Menil Collection. Acknowledging overhead illumination as an ideal, though difficult to control, light source, Renzo Piano designed a system that would accept natural light and at the same time diffuse the light as it entered the galleries. Ranks of ferroconcrete baffles, suspended beneath coated skylights, are angled to filter sunlight from the north, providing a cool white glow that reflects into the galleries, most strongly illuminating the south walls. This light is supplemented by the expanse of glass openings at the entrance and either end of the wide hallway, by narrow slit windows along the perimeter walls, and by light from an interior atrium on the east end of the building. The overall effect is a remarkable use of daylight to gently illuminate the art and, in Piano's words, "bring life to the space."

Working with a single-artist gallery, Piano was confronted with an even more specific program of natural light for the design of the Twombly Gallery. To achieve the appropriate levels and desired quality of light, the architect designed a roof system that filters light in stages through four screens placed over the outer galleries, with opaque flat roofs covering the center gallery and the entry vestibule. The uppermost layer of this intriguing filtration system is manifested on the outside by a bright white steel canopy, supporting a mesh of fixed aluminum louvers that appears to float over the building mass. While lighter and more delicate, the light-filtering louvered canopy makes friendly reference to the white concrete baffles of the Menil Collection across the street. But unlike the Menil, where the curved baffles are exposed beneath the skylights, the louvered canopy of the Twombly Gallery is intentionally obscured on the inside. Beneath the canopy, a double-glazed, clear-glass hipped roof seals the interior from the outside elements. Barely visible from the outside, the glass roof has a nickel coating to filter ultraviolet light in the range most harmful to art objects. Beneath the glass roof and inside the building, operable louvers supported by a steel frame provide the third layer of protection. Mechanically controlled and operated with a light-sensitive photoelectric cell, the louvers automatically adjust their apertures according to changes in daylight. Directly below the mechanically controlled louvers, a stretched cotton scrim fabricated by a Galveston sail maker forms a ceiling and provides the final layer of Piano's light-filtering sandwich. For night lighting, custom-designed fixtures attached to light tracks suspended from the steel frame discreetly poke through the cloth.

This technological tour de force produces light virtually without shadow, a condition so rarely experienced that the initial sensation is a kind of dizziness. The perfectly even natural light is different from the Menil's light, which varies subtly, or the Rothko's, which changes in intensity from top to bottom. As light filters through the sailcloth it takes on a warm tonality, filling the space with a lantern-like glow that quietly varies when outside conditions shift from clear to cloudy. The light softly reflects from the crisp plaster walls, providing near perfect illumination for Twombly's paintings, particularly those with pale backgrounds and intricate markings that weave in and out of the surface. These paintings, subtle in content and delicately expressed, are seen at their best in the airy, shadowless light that filters into the galleries. Appropriately, paintings more vibrant in color and thicker in surface are displayed in the gallery on the opposite side of the entrance, where filtered light is mixed with daylight coming through windows and doors. Only the center gallery and the archive room next to the entrance, both intended for the display of more delicate works on paper, receive no daylight. Selected galleries in the Menil Collection are also closed to outside light and provided with controlled, often dramatic, artificial lighting. It is no exaggeration to claim that the lighting of the Twombly Gallery, particularly under natural conditions, is as beautiful and unusual as can be hoped for in any space intended for the exhibition of art.

CULTURAL ENCLAVE

While the Rothko, the Menil Collection, and the Twombly Gallery share essential qualities, the three buildings are articulated as individual works of architecture, each building like a member of a family in a shared precinct. Whereas a campus of museum buildings singular in style, material, and character would have dominated the neighborhood, each of these structures is a separate work, invested with the inventive spirit of modern architecture. Relating the Rothko Chapel to the University of St. Thomas, architects Barnstone and Aubry adopted the same light-colored, iron-spotted brick that Johnson had selected in the 1950s for the new buildings of the University of St. Thomas. While separate from the campus, the Rothko

Cy Twombly Gallery, entrance, with The Menil Collection museum in background.

Chapel might appear to the stranger to be a part of the university. Renzo Piano's building for the Menil Collection in some ways harks back to Johnson's St. Thomas buildings. Both architects utilized an exposed steel frame structure with in-fill panels, brick at St. Thomas and horizontal cypress siding at the Menil. Whereas Johnson was clearly influenced by the work of Mies van der Rohe, Piano, as architectural historian Reyner Banham has observed, seems to have taken as his point of departure the work of California architect Craig Ellwood and others who participated in the Case Study Houses program of the 1940s and 1950s. But Piano goes far beyond Johnson, whose 1950s design seems almost imitative of Mies van der Rohe's buildings at Chicago's Illinois Institute of Technology. For the Menil Collection Piano designed an exceptionally innovative work of architecture whose elegantly detailed steel frame, painted white, embraces the gray-stained cypress panels and supports the white ferroconcrete sun baffles, consciously joining the Menil to the neighboring bungalows by echoing their painted gray clapboard and white trim.

The Twombly Gallery and the Menil Collection are composed of simple boxlike forms, exquisitely put together with precise detailing and richness of material. But in the Twombly Gallery, Piano departed from the expression of the articulated frame, designing a building dominated by mass and weight. The building is essentially a concrete-block structure with concealed-perimeter poured-concrete columns and concealed interior steel columns. The outer wall is made up of a double concrete block wall comprising an interior 8-inch-thick block and a custom-cast 6-inch block on the outside. Concrete block walls are often clad with another facing material such as brick or stone, but Piano realized that concrete block could emulate the richness of stone without disguising its materiality. Both color and profile were customized for the precast outer blocks. While stone varies in color, the process of precasting yields a uniform light sandy color, giving the building a singular resonance. Departing from the flatness and perceived thinness of stone cladding, Piano expressed the thickness of the facing blocks with a 3/4-inch joint, producing a finely scaled rectangular grid derived from the dimensions of the block's face, 34 inches wide by 17 inches tall. The white, louvered metal canopy, hovering over the block, provides a counterpoint to the heaviness of the masonry structure and suggests the chamber within. By carrying the masonry materials into the foyer and adjacent side rooms, the inside and outside are brought together at the entrance. The purity of the exterior is reiterated inside, where the 15-foot-high rooms are finished with plaster walls that meet natural oak plank floors. Rooms fold into one another through the wide, square portal openings in the thick walls. While monolithic in form, the building is graciously proportioned and never overwhelming in scale, fulfilling Twombly's desire for a building that would be a timeless expression of architecture.

The collaboration that brought about the Twombly Gallery fulfills an intention articulated 40 years earlier, when John and Dominique de Menil began planning the University of St. Thomas campus to promote art and architecture as a source of cultural and civic enrichment. Taken together, the St. Thomas campus, the Rothko Chapel, the Menil Collection, and the Twombly Gallery in their neighborhood of historic bungalows and modest houses form a place of lasting significance, reminding us that a city at its best is an evolving work of art. While privately planned and funded, this enclave is a vital center of Houston's public realm.

UPDATE 2002

In 1997 a fourth building, designed for the display of two 13th-century Cypriot Byzantine frescoes, was added to the Menil arts district. Designed by John and Dominique de Menil's youngest son, architect François de Menil, the Byzantine Fresco Chapel adopts a similarly discreet siting strategy as the Twombly Gallery with an unassuming stone and concrete building set back from Yupon Street in deference to the surrounding neighborhood. The intimate interior of the chapel receives diffused natural light from above, washing the peripheral walls. But unlike the naturally lit spaces of the Rothko Chapel, the Menil Collection, or the Twombly Gallery, the frescoes themselves are illuminated solely by artificial means.

Richmond Hall was renovated in 1998 for the installation of a fluorescent light sculpture by artist Dan Flavin. In 2000 the Rothko Chapel was renovated to correct foundation and air-conditioning inadequacies. For better climate control of the chapel, the foyer was isolated with glass entry walls, diminishing the uninterrupted experience of moving from space to space. A redesigned light baffle beneath the central skylight better controls and distributes the light.

Following the death of Mrs. de Menil in 1997, the Menil Foundation has maintained her commitment to the lasting preservation of the neighborhood.

William F. Stern

Cite 34
SPRING
1996

Neighborhood of Make-Believe

THE HOUSTON THEATER DISTRICT

Drexel Turner

It is a strange thing, the like of which, I think will occur to one hardly anywhere else than in Texas, to hear teamsters with their cattle staked around them on the prairie humming airs from *Don Giovanni.*
FREDERICK LAW OLMSTED,
New York Daily Times, April 24, 1854

When Frederick Law Olmsted, then a 32-year-old journalist, visited Houston on the return leg of his journey through Texas in spring 1854, he observed that the town of not yet 5,000 showed "many agreeable signs of . . . wealth accumulated, in homelike, retired residences, its large and good hotel, its well supplied shops, and its shaded streets." Among its cultural as-

Hester + Hardaway, 1996.

Jones Hall Plaza and Alley Theater (Ulrich Franzen, 1968).

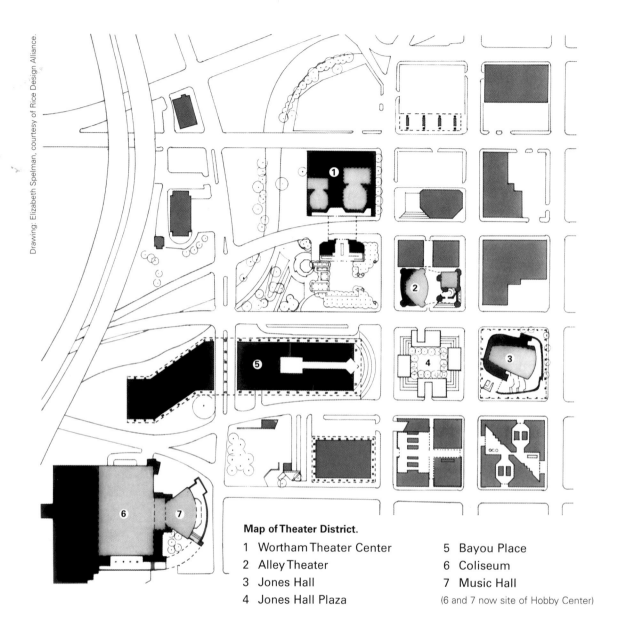

Map of Theater District.

1 Wortham Theater Center
2 Alley Theater
3 Jones Hall
4 Jones Hall Plaza

5 Bayou Place
6 Coliseum
7 Music Hall

(6 and 7 now site of Hobby Center)

sets he counted "several neat churches, a theatre (within the walls of a steam saw-mill), and a most remarkable number of showy bar-rooms and gambling saloons."[1] Today prim churches have been reborn as suburban tabernacles the size of sports arenas; the showy barrooms have swelled, multiplied, and migrated to the outside-the-Loop forum of Richmond Avenue; and the converted sawmill has given way, on the south side of the downtown bend in Buffalo Bayou, to what is said to be the second greatest concentration of theater and performing arts seats in the United States — 10,501 by actual count.

Houston's Theater District is a conspicuous, if still somewhat disjointed, sign of wealth accumulated and invested on behalf of an audience no longer primarily composed of cattle. After a false start in 1890 when the Sweeney & Coombs Opera House opened on the west side of Courthouse Square, the city's performing arts organizations have tended to gravitate toward the right angle in the bayou, which, at the turn of the century, also included a farmer's market, a small hotel with an open courtyard (the Brazos Court), and several breweries (Magnolia, American) that flourished until Prohibition intervened.

The Houston Symphony offered its first concert on June 21, 1913, in the original Majestic, later Palace, Theater on Texas Avenue (Mauran & Russell, 1911), a vaudeville house that was first bridged over, then eventually swallowed up by the expansion of the Houston Chronicle Building. In 1931 the symphony moved to the budget Beaux Arts luxe of the all-purpose City Auditorium (Mauran, Russell & Crowell, 1913), a hall so adaptable that it was converted into a school for the more than 500 children of servicemen stationed at Camp Logan during World War I. In the early 1950s my parents watched the touring company of "South Pacific" in un-air-conditioned comfort in the auditorium, which was also the site of Friday night wrestling matches.

Majestic Theater (Mauran & Russell, 1911).

City Auditorium (Mauran, Russell & Crowell, 1913); site now occupied by Jones Hall.

Sam Houston Coliseum and Music Hall (Alfred C. Finn, 1937); site now occupied by Hobby Center.

The symphony next moved to the air-conditioned Music Hall (Alfred C. Finn, 1937), a Public Works Administration project with a face only a commissar could love. Built in tandem with the Sam Houston Coliseum, it shared a connecting proscenium with the Coliseum as a concession to theatrical Calvinism. The Music Hall was remodeled in 1955 with the addition of a fan-shaped lobby, wedge-shaped auxiliary seating areas on either side, and a one-way stage by Hermon Lloyd & W. B. Morgan. So improved, it persisted as the city's venue of choice or default through most of my childhood. My parents eventually took me there to see a road company performance of "My Fair Lady" complete with revolving sets; on other nights, Leopold Stokowski presided over the Houston Symphony in his post-Philadelphia diminuendo. Next door, the Coliseum served up rodeos, revivals, wrestling matches, and, on the Fourth of July 1962 — as Tom Wolfe relates in *The Right Stuff* — 30 barbecued animals to the seven Mercury astronauts and a thundering horde of "5,000 businessmen, politicians and their better halves, fresh from the horrors of downtown in July."[2] Also on the menu was the fan-dancing of sexagenarian Sally Rand, then regularly engaged in stretching the envelope of occupational age discrimination at the Stork Club on Texas Avenue.

JONES HALL

The 3,000-seat Jesse H. Jones Hall, shoehorned onto the former site of the City Auditorium in travertine-clad splendor by Caudill Rowlett Scott, replaced the Music Hall as the city's premiere venue in 1966. The construction cost of $6.6 million was contributed by Houston Endowment Inc., the philanthropic heir to Jones's fortune, which included considerable real estate holdings in the immediate vicinity. Jones Hall took in the Houston Symphony, the Houston Grand Opera (which had

Jesse H. Jones Hall (Caudill Rowlett Scott, 1966).

Albert Thomas Convention Center, remodeled as Bayou Place (Caudill Rowlett Scott, 1967).

produced its inaugural season in the Music Hall in 1955), the Houston Ballet Foundation, and the Society for the Performing Arts (SPA), a nonprofit presenter formed to fill the gap left by the death of the impresaria Edna B. Saunders.

The functional characteristics of Jones Hall were determined by the theater consultant George Izenour; its design, otherwise the work of Charles E. Lawrence of Caudill Rowlett Scott, was schematically not unlike Le Corbusier's hall for the Palace of Assembly at Chandigarh (1956). Like its contemporary the Astrodome, Jones Hall was a variable-configuration novelty, although, unlike the Dome, variation was achieved by "stopping down" the size of the interior to a mere 1,800 seats for greater intimacy by means of an elaborately counterweighted, though rarely used, movable ceiling.

ALBERT THOMAS CONVENTION CENTER

As an accessory to Jones Hall and the aesthetically challenged Albert Thomas Convention Center one block west (Caudill Rowlett Scott, 1968), the city also built a three-level, 1,750-car underground parking garage lodged beneath the convention center and a residual one-block "plaza" separating Jones Hall and the convention center. Jones Hall Plaza (also designed by CRS) featured an awkward truncated pyramid mounted on some sides by backward-sloping steps and topped with lollipop-sized trees in a not very convincing attempt to disguise two double-lane entrance ramps to the parking below. The convention center followed a footprint promulgated by the econometricians of the now-defunct Stanford Research Institute in 1962 as part of a comprehensive plan for the Houston Civic Center. It spread over three city blocks at a cost of $12 million with the grace of a centipedal box-culvert, enveloping more than 200,000 square feet of clear-spanned exhibition space together with a lobby that doubled in its promoters' dreams as the National Space Hall of Fame.

Not only was the convention center too small to be viable the day it opened, it was sufficiently hemmed in to preclude expansion except by spanning Buffalo Bayou, as the farmers market that once occupied part of its site had managed to do. Albert Thomas was vacated upon completion of the George R. Brown Convention Center on the east side of downtown in 1987, only later to become the unlikely object of one of the most costly preservation efforts ever contemplated within the city limits.

ALLEY THEATER

The Alley Theatre (Ulrich Franzen & Associates with MacKie & Kamrath, 1969), a small but accomplished repertory company formed in 1947, for years made do in a converted electric fan factory on Berry Street. In 1968 the Alley moved downtown into striking if improbably castellated new quarters on the north side of Jones Hall Plaza. The Ford Foundation provided two-thirds of the $3 million construction cost as part of a program to support regional theater. The Alley's inner workings, as those of Jones Hall, were masterminded by George Izenour. Its special features included a lighting system controlled by an analog digital computer using "stapled cards rather than the hole-punch variety" and ergonomically accommodating chairs spe-

cially designed in the Electro-Mechanical Laboratory of the Yale School of Drama. The 800-seat main theater was conceived as a "multi-space" stage with caliper-like extensions embracing the sides of the fan-shaped seating area, a peripheral detail appropriated by Nina Vance, the Alley's founder and director, from the runways of Japanese Noh drama.[3] When plans were first published, the building was described as "programmed to attract pedestrians during non-theater hours. An arcade running through the building will house stores, an inexpensive restaurant, and a cafe. The large-scale elements of the building (the castle turrets) having been placed on the side of the freeway, serve to attract the attention of the approaching motorist from a considerable distance. In addition, a drive-in box office has been provided."[4]

The Alley also included a smaller, 300-seat arena stage in the basement replicating the Berry Street location sans columns. But the shops and eating places failed to materialize as promised. Whereas the Berry Street location had managed a marquee of sorts, Franzen made no such undignified provision, even though Jones Hall was endowed with a demure backlit signboard ("PDQ Bach . . . Tonite . . . 8 p.m. . . . Don't Fuguet!"). The Alley management soon took to slipcovering the southeast ramparts with banners advertising events ("Greater Tuna — Limited Engagement — Dolphin Friendly") and the names and trademarks of patrons, corporate and otherwise.

WORTHAM CENTER

By the mid-1970s, Jones Hall could no longer satisfy the demand for performance dates generated by the symphony, opera, ballet, and SPA. A Lyric Theater Foundation was chartered to break the seatjam, beginning with a campaign to spread the news that the city's theatrical resources compared unfavorably with those of Newark, New Jersey. Philip Johnson, whose experience included the design of the New York State

Gus S. Wortham Center (Morris*Aubry Architects, 1987).

Theater in Lincoln Center (1964) for the New York City Opera and the New York City Ballet, prepared an initial scheme in 1978 for a two-theater complex. His generic proposal, tentatively following the Alley's cue, was a jumble of robust, round-cornered towers with intermittent boxes for lobbies and auditoriums. The estimated $100 million estimate, however, precipitated a case of sticker shock that purportedly cost the architects the commission.

As ultimately configured (and built for $72 million) according to the plans of Morris*Aubry Architects (1979–1987), the Wortham Theater Center disposes its two houses, the 2,225-seat Brown Theater and the 1,102-seat Cullen Theater, side by side on the block farther from Jones Hall Plaza, with the stage loading docks backing onto Preston Avenue along the north side of the block. The Siamese twin arrangement of the two houses is achieved at the expense of a second full side stage and deep enough backstage for the opera house. The block itself is almost completely filled by the stage and audience areas, causing the ceremonial entrance and principal lobby to be forced over Prairie Avenue and onto the block closer to Jones Hall Plaza.

The entrance to the lobby is marked by a supercolossal, round-arched opening on the scale of that of Paul Bonatz's Stuttgart train station (1928) but derived, according to the architects, from the 11th-century Benedictine abbey church at Tewkesbury, Gloucestershire. This dominant glazed aperture stares across the leftover part of the site into the sidewall and loading docks of the former Albert Thomas Convention Center. The formidable bulk of the theater block is solidly clad in dark brown brick except for a few slit windows serving offices along the backstage side and granite trim-work around the base. The brick veneer extends across the bridge and onto the main entrance face, pausing for an occasional large window. A freestanding, low-riding, backlit signboard is planted on the east side of the plaza in lieu of a marquee, while a phalanx of six large, copper-colored, immobile metal balls keeps stretch limos at bay. By virtue of its somewhat sheltered sidewise orientation, the plaza provided a serviceable setting for trill seekers to take in the free outdoor simulcast of last fall's production of "La Cenerentola" with Cecilia Bartoli, but it is seldom so happily engaged.

The Wortham has proved an undoubted boon to the operation of the Houston Grand Opera and the Houston Ballet, as well as the Society for the Performing Arts and Da Camera, a more recently formed chamber music and recital presenter. But its architectural and urbanistic qualities remain problematic, as Ann Holmes and Stephen Fox have pointed out.[5] One can rationalize its deficiencies, as Carl Cunningham attempted in the *Houston Post* by observing that "the world is full of great-big, chunky-looking, utilitarian opera houses. That's the nature of the beast."[6] But to arrive at this consolation, one must ignore instances such as Adler and Sullivan's Chicago Auditorium, wrapped in a thick skin of hotel rooms and offices (1886–1889); William B. Tuthill's Carnegie Hall, mingled with the studios and offices of Henry J. Hardenbergh's companion tower (1891, 1894); and J. C. Cady's original Metropolitan Opera House (1883), which contained both commercial space and an apartment hotel.

Nevertheless, several small projects should contribute some street life to the district. The rebirth of the small Lancaster (née Auditorium) Hotel at the corner connecting Jones Hall and the Alley and the conversion last year of the Hogg Building, another block away, to residential apartments already suggest that the neighborhood is able to reward entrepreneurship.

JONES HALL PLAZA

Jones Hall Plaza, another less-than-ideal multipurpose fixture of the district, shows occasional signs of life. Bereft as it is, the plaza was the site that Central Houston Inc.—a special-purpose downtown improvement association—fixed on for its Thursday-evening block parties for lonely urban professionals (Single Female Accountant seeks Single/Divorced Male Arbitrageur to enjoy cndllt spprs, smmr cruises, Wll St Jrnl—no hostile takeovers, shared modems or debit cards). This feat of matchmaking also brought the portable-toilet industry to the district on a regular basis. The plaza proved no less compatible with the installation in October 1987 of luminaria—intricately contrived displays of nightlighting produced by the Italian Ministry of Tourism and Performing Arts. This special effect was one-upped in December 1995 by the thin fringe of snow manufactured across the street for the filming of "Evening Star," Larry McMurtry's sequel to "Terms of Endearment," in which the colonnade of Jones Hall was made to simulate a wintry Lincoln Center.[7]

Plazas are not something most Americans—let alone Houstonians—take to gladly. As Paige Rense, editor of *Architectural Digest*, observed, there should "be a law requiring that the person who invented concrete pedestrian plazas get his [or her] head examined. Walking across those expanses of hot, glaring concrete is one of the most alienating things imaginable."[8] Jones Hall Plaza—riven by parking ramps, exposed on all four sides to traffic, and irradiated by the Texas sun—is more incorrigible but arguably still this side of hopeless. With adequate funding, ramps could be relocated, and below-grade trees could be gouged from the recesses of the garage. Water features might be introduced as well, adding blue noise to muffle the sounds of traffic. The stubby ventilation shafts that presently stake out the four corners of the plaza could also be moved offsite with some creative rerouting of ducts and fans.

Plan recommendations for Buffalo Bayou as an amenity corridor in downtown Houston (Dennis Frenchman et al., 1987).

SESQUICENTENNIAL PARK

The bayou edge of the Theater District has already been altered by the partial development of Sesquicentennial Park, a two-phase, public-private project orchestrated by Central Houston Inc. following a design won in a competition (sponsored by the Rice Design Alliance) by TeamHOU (Guy Hagstette, John Lemr, and Robert Liner with David Calkins) in 1986.[9] The second phase, now under construction, includes the landscaping of a slender strip along the west wall of the Wortham Theater Center and the entire block immediately to the north of the Wortham. Mel Chin and Dean Ruck have been selected to provide additional embellishments through the art-in-public-places program of the Cultural Arts Council of Houston/Harris County.

In May 1996 Mayor Lanier endorsed the plans of the Houston Music Hall Foundation to redevelop the site of the Music Hall and Coliseum at a cost of $60 million, to include a 2,700-seat theater and a smaller 700-seat hall.[10] The original plan had been to partition the site between a reconstituted Music Hall and a gambling casino that would replace the Coliseum — a pairing that recalls Charles Garnier's Theater and Casino at Monte Carlo (1878–1882). The Texas Legislature, however, declined to pass enabling legislation, and all bets were put on hold long enough to discourage potential investors. In the latest scenario, Theater under the Stars (TUTS), a nonprofit musical theater company that began operation in Miller Outdoor Theater in Hermann Park in 1968, will be the primary tenant, with the Society for the Performing Arts' Broadway Series, produced in association with Pace Entertainment, accounting for a substantial portion of the remaining dates. The smaller hall is to be used for children's programming and emerging companies. As luck would have it, a plaza also figures into the scheme, "possibly in the form of a grassy park," to set the complex back from Bagby Street and the not-so-grassy Tranquility Park on the other side of Bagby (Charles Tapley Associates, 1979), which spreads across yet another city-owned underground parking garage. Funds are being raised, and a short list of prospective architects has been settled on, though not made public. The city expects to contribute approximately $1 million each year toward the project, a commitment that can be used to secure construction bonds.

The directors of the Music Hall Foundation have been afforded the opportunity to retain an architect of national or international distinction for a pair of theaters that will occupy a place of pride within the greater civic center at the edge of Buffalo Bayou Park, one of Houston's most appreciable, if freeway-scarred, legacies of the City Beautiful movement. But the problem is more than one of sifting through the right set of résumés — crucial as that will be. For although the site does offer sufficient room to accommodate all elements of the program without bridging streets or scrimping on wings, it is also four blocks removed from the main cluster of theaters around Jones Hall Plaza. This estrangement is compounded by the disposition of the ex-Albert Thomas Convention Center, the tail end of which effectively forecloses any direct communication between the proximate north edge of the Music Hall site and the rest of the Theater District via the bayou walk.

PROPHECY

The bayou could in fact become the thread that gives a connective and scenic fluency to the district. Such a strategy would require demolishing the west block of Albert Thomas and the section spanning Bagby, as earlier proposed by both Dennis Frenchman and Michael Graves.[11] The opening so gained could be redeveloped as a series of broad steps ascending from the bayou walk to the foyer of the new Music Hall. The theater and casino at Monte Carlo are approached from below in somewhat the same manner. This maneuver could be reinforced by developing an ampler loggia/sheltered

promenade along the north side of Albert Thomas, extending the original arcade out into the zone once reserved for loading docks. A bayou walk ascension to the new Music Hall would also provide a merciful exemption from the compulsion to produce a plaza of any kind; any residual inclination for public hospitality could be satisfied by the development of a congenial indoor space for casual assembly, comparable to Garnier's atrium at Monte Carlo or the winter garden the architects of the Wortham considered at one point.

Before World War II, downtown Houston accounted for almost all the city's tall buildings, specialty retailing, and nonresidential hotels as well as its major performing halls. Today downtown enjoys a monopoly only of halls. If, as Jane Jacobs maintains, "the natural neighbors of halls are restaurants, bars, florist shops, studios, music shops, all sorts of interesting places," it is also the case that these cannot flourish on theatrical traffic alone without special nurturing, even subsidies, in the nine-to-five downtown of a spread-out city such as Houston has become.[12] Nor do the parking arrangements help much. "Even with the big-draw performance centers grouped together," Bruce Webb observed, "patrons slip in invisibly from underground parking lots and leave the same way, as though they were being delivered like city utilities in hidden conduits."[13]

Realizing that more intensive cultivation is necessary to convert the district to a "full-service entertainment complex," a nonprofit coalition of Theater District interests sought to have the last Texas Legislature approve a rental-car tax that could be used in part for such a purpose. House Bill 2447, sponsored to that effect in the 74th session by Houston Representative Garnet Coleman, did not pass. Inasmuch as this particular "vehicle" is now viewed as a potential means of financing a share of the recently proposed $625 million in new or improved sports arenas essential to retain the city's Major League bragging rights, other options may have to be explored.[14] Last year, the Theater District's resident companies drew in excess of 1.5 million paying customers, more than the Astros and the Oilers combined. None is threatening to leave Houston any time soon nor asking for heroic efforts to double season ticket sales or add more luxury boxes to shore up bottom lines. But neither are they just whistling "Don Giovanni" when it comes to the need for relatively modest levels of investment to help make the district's artificial turf user-friendly and economically fertile. In seeking to extend and actively promote the range of experiences the district offers, its proponents have come to the same realization Charles Moore did several decades ago in observing the workings of Disneyland: "You have to pay for the public life," whether you buy your tickets at an outer gate or not.[15]

Notes

1. Frederick Law Olmsted, *A Journey Through Texas; or, a Saddle-Trip on the Southwestern Frontier* (New York: Dix, Edwards, 1857), 361.

2. Tom Wolfe, *The Right Stuff* (New York: Farrar, Straus, and Giroux, 1979), 298.

3. William C. Young, "Alley Theatre, Houston, Texas, Opened November 28, 1968," in *Documents of American Theater History,* vol. 2: *Famous American Playhouses, 1900–71* (Chicago: American Library Association, 1973), 160–161.

4. "Alley: A Director's Dream," *Progressive Architecture,* October 1967, 172.

5. Ann Holmes, "A Crazy Salad of Disappointment," *Houston Chronicle,* July 21, 1983; Stephen Fox, "Report on the Wortham," *Cite* 8 (winter 1984). An appreciative account of the Lyric Theater Foundation's fund-raising success recently appeared in a Canadian newspaper: Robert Crew, "If They Can Do It: How Houston Put It All Together to Build an Opera/Ballet House," *Toronto Star,* January 27, 1996.

6. Carl Cunningham, "Wortham Theater: Time and Needed Funds Are Running Short," *Houston Post,* August 17, 1983.

7. Bruce C. Webb, "Illuminations of the Ephemeral City," *Cite* 19 (winter 1987); Bruce Westbrook, "Snow in Houston? Wintry Movie Scene Shot Near Jones Hall," *Houston Chronicle,* December 13, 1995.

8. Paige Rense, quoted in Lisa Taylor, ed., *Urban Open Spaces* (New York: Rizzoli/Cooper-Hewitt Museum, 1979), 30.

9. John Pastier, "The Houston Sesquicentennial Park Design Competition," *Cite* 18 (fall 1986).

10. Julie Mason, "Downtown Arts Facility Proposed: Both Music Hall, Coliseum Would Go," *Houston Chronicle,* May 21, 1996. The alternative of building a new hall for the Houston Symphony and turning Jones Hall over to TUTS and Pace was raised in a subsequent letter to the editor of the *Chronicle* by a symphony musician. Such a hall would be better suited to the needs of an orchestra and less expensive. Robert Deutsch, "New Hall for Symphony," *Houston Chronicle,* May 26, 1996.

11. "Bayou Place Theater, Houston, Texas, 1992," in Karen Nichols, Lisa Burke, and Patrick Burke, eds., *Michael Graves: Buildings and Projects, 1990–94* (New York: Rizzoli, 1995), 210–213. Dennis Frenchman et al., "Plan Recommendation to Reinforce Bayou Amenity Corridor," in Central Houston Civic Improvement Inc., *Design Plan for Downtown Houston* (1987), 14.

12. Jane Jacobs, quoted in Alexander Garvin, *The American City: What Works, What Doesn't* (New York: McGraw-Hill, 1995), 86.

13. Webb, "Illuminations," 28.

14. John Williams, "Stadiums May Put Bite on Public," *Houston Chronicle,* May 21, 1996.

15. Charles Moore, "You Have to Pay for the Public Life," *Perspecta: The Yale Architectural Journal 9/10* (1965): 57–97.

Hester + Hardaway, 2002.

Hobby Center (Robert A. M. Stern with Morris Architects, 2002).

Bayou Place (Gensler & Associates, 1998) conversion of the Albert Thomas Convention Center.

two performance halls, the largest of which seats 2,600 people in a setting Stern fashioned after early-20th-century Broadway theaters. The added halls boost the Theater District's seat count to 12,948 for live performances, which, city promoters are proud to point out, ranks second only to New York City in the number of theater seats in a concentrated area.

In 1998 the vacant Albert Thomas Convention Center, described by Turner as "aesthetically challenged," was extensively remodeled into a successful entertainment complex, Bayou Place, containing a film center, a live theater, and several restaurants and bars. Jones Hall Plaza, a congenitally empty public space built over the underground Civic Center parking garage, was extensively renovated by Mark Wamble of Bricker + Cannady Architects in 2000. The plaza was outfitted with shade canopies, an outdoor stage, food concessions, and lavatories.

Growing theater crowds, together with fans from the new downtown baseball stadium a short distance to the east, have encouraged a number of new restaurants and bars in the district, resulting in nightlife the likes of which hasn't been seen downtown for many years. Despite the completion of the first phase of Buffalo Bayou Park, the hoped-for bayou thread that Turner suggested might give "connective fluency" to the district hasn't materialized. Buildings such as the new Hobby Center, with its bulky parking garage located along the bayou edge, continue to ignore the potential for addressing this urban amenity. *Editors*

Other *Cite* articles on buildings in the Theater District include: Stephen Fox, "A Report on the Wortham Center," *Cite* 5 (winter 1984); Mitchell J. Shields, "A Plaza To Come To: Jones Plaza to Be Reborn," *Cite* 45 (summer 1999); Mitchell J. Shields, "Jones Plaza Makeover Begins," *Cite* 49 (fall 2000).

2002 UPDATE

Houston's Theater District has continued to grow with the notable addition of the Hobby Center for the Performing Arts designed by New York architect Robert A. M. Stern in association with Morris Architects of Houston. The new theater opened in the spring of 2002 and replaced the Music Hall, a Depression-era theater that occupied the same site. The Hobby Center contains

Cite 35
FALL
1996

Houston's Academic Enclaves

Richard Ingersoll

The four major university campuses in Houston — Rice University, University of Houston, Texas Southern University, and University of St. Thomas — occupy sizable swaths of the city, each only three or four miles from downtown. The Rice campus is about half the size of the entire downtown area, while the combined campuses of UH and TSU, which are nearly adjacent to each other, are almost the same size as downtown. The universities are comparable in size to pre-industrial city-states and set the example for the first ring of neo-feudal enclaves in the city. At all four campuses, recent planning decisions and architectural additions encourage a stiffening of the university enclave, reinforcing boundaries, and in some cases closing public through-streets in order to assert the autonomy of the campus as a landscape while reducing the possibilities of casual interactions with the city.

RICE UNIVERSITY

Rice University, the most prestigious and oldest college in the city, possesses one of the most admired campuses in the country. As a small, extremely selective institution, its student population of about 4,000 students is close to Plato's recommendation of 5,020 citizens as the size of his ideal *polis*. Rice has followed a course of slow growth and fairly coordinated expansions since the first general plan (1910) by Cram, Goodhue & Ferguson. The two initial Mediterranean-style buildings designed by Ralph Adams Cram and the accompanying landscape of oak-lined axes established a commanding language of narrow, brick-faced, arcaded volumes arranged in courtyards and connected by tree-lined paths — a lexicon that has rarely been contradicted in successive building campaigns.

In 1983 Cesar Pelli, who had already been engaged as the architect of Herring Hall, built to house the graduate school of administration, was asked to produce a new master plan to update the original, and in it he specifically insisted that the new additions conform to the original language. Although Pelli's plan was only a set of recommendations, it has been followed fairly assiduously in the siting and massing of subsequent new buildings including Mechanical Engineering (1985); Pelli's addition to the Rice Memorial Center (1987); Ricardo Bofill's Alice Pratt Brown Hall for the Shepherd School of Music (1991); Cambridge Seven Associates' biosciences and bioengineering building, George R. Brown Hall (1991); Thomas Beeby's James A. Baker Institute for Public Policy (under construction); and John Outram's Computational Engineering Building (under

Rice University, Lovett Hall with Academic Court (Cram, Goodhue & Ferguson, 1912).

construction). The only additions that were not anticipated in Pelli's plan are Antoine Predock's Center for Nanoscale Science (under construction), set adjacent to the Space Science Building, and the new police department headquarters (1992) across from the Media Center, an anonymous tilt-up building that guards the only campus entrance open after 2 a.m.

Most of the new commissions at Rice involved the selection of an internationally known architect, a practice that began with the addition to the School of Architecture by Stirling & Wilford (1981). The Board of Governors' building and grounds committee from 1979 to 1994 was presided over with charming determina-

tion by Josephine Abercrombie, whose own real estate interests included an unbuilt project by Cesar Pelli and the development of Cinco Ranch. The taste for historicist details found in the Bofill, Beeby, Outram, and Cambridge Seven projects can be traced as much to Abercrombie's personal postmodernist inclinations as to the inherently conservative nature of the campus plan.

In addition to Pelli's plan, Rice is guided by a general landscaping plan, prepared by Stuart Dawson of Sasaki Associates in 1990 in anticipation of the Economic Summit of Industrialized Nations. Like Pelli's plan, the landscaping suggestions sensibly build on the existing patterns of tree-lined axes, strengthening the courts and

James A. Baker Institute for Public Policy, Rice University (Hammond Beeby & Babka and Morris Architects, 1997).

Computational Engineering Building, Rice University (John Outram Associates with Kendall/Heaton Associates, 1996).

Center for Nanoscale Science and Technology, Rice University (Antoine Predock and Brooks Coronado Associates, 1997).

edges, and projecting to the eventual greening of the vast stadium parking lot. Additional gates and thickened perimeter hedges are among the suggestions being acted upon. Dawson's planting scheme subtly strengthens the primacy of the inner loop road and emphasizes the intersections of the three secondary cross-axes of the original plan, both of which instill a superb system of orientation. One of the recommendations in Pelli's plan that has yet to be fulfilled is the tracing of an outer loop road just inside the hedges for services such as food delivery.

Another idea that could be easily acted upon would be to provide articulated bike paths like those at Stanford University, an improvement that could become a model to extend to the surrounding neighborhoods. While two of the new buildings on campus will include showers as an incentive to those who brave pedaling to work in 100-degree weather, there is currently no plan for bike paths or bike parking, and neither Rice nor any of the city's universities has cooperated with the various municipally backed plans for city bike paths that have attracted federal funding during the past three years. Likewise Rice could be much more involved in the city's public transportation programs.

Since 1988, Dean Currie, Rice's vice president for finance and ad-

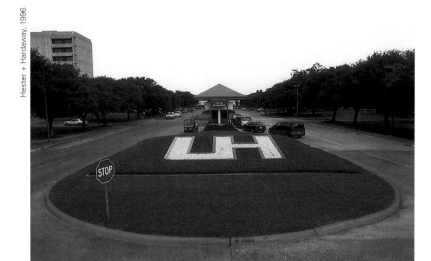

University of Houston, entrance 1.

ministration, has been the pivotal player in negotiations among Abercrombie's committee, the donors (who of course have a significant say in determining the architectural products), the celebrity architects, the local support architects, and the institutions that must be served. Rice's planning succeeded because both clients and consultants were educated about the needs, traditions, and goals of the campus. Currie maintains that it is Rice's desire to hire the best possible architects to represent the specific moment of architectural discourse, while encouraging use of the existing campus language, in the hope that the architectural results will "elicit strong criticism while contributing to a coherently great collection of buildings." This strategy of balance has produced a very subtle kind of growth in which nondescript buildings such as Mechanical Engineering or overly expressive designs such as Bofill's and Outram's are subsumed in an overall context, a consequence of the formal power of the landscaping and the unifying texture of St. Joe brick. The recently unveiled drawing for Predock's Center for Nanoscale Science, which displays very subtle asymmetries in the placement of the fenestration but almost obsequiously reiterates the ty-

pological and material palette of the other Rice buildings, is a case in point of the strength of the campus's conventionality in disciplining the most nonconformist of architects. Rice has been expanding in an organic and seemingly inevitable manner that forces both stodgy and avant-garde architects to be deferential.

UNIVERSITY OF HOUSTON

By contrast, the University of Houston is a much larger, public institution that is currently suffering from state budget cuts and using most of its building funds for deferred maintenance. UH is by definition less selective than Rice in its enrollment, with a student body at the main campus about eight times the size of Rice's, one of the largest in the country. Aside from its central campus it has branches downtown (currently undergoing an impressive expansion of 600,000 square feet), at Clear Lake City, and in Victoria. Due to the lack of strong orientation patterns and the absence of formal landscape devices, the diversity of buildings on the UH campus tends to be exaggerated, and architects have further accentuated this with their mismatched choices of volumes, cladding, and fenestra-

University of Houston, aerial view ca. 1955.

tion, making the campus appear as exogenous as a world's fair. To the same degree that Rice displays a concerted aristocratic cohesion, UH conveys the open, awkward, and inharmonious tendencies of democracy.

The initial plan for the Settegast-Taub donation of 110 acres of land, prepared in 1937 by Hare & Hare, seems to have emulated the organization of the Rice plan. The administration building, the Ezekiel Cullen Building, was placed at the head of an entry axis, followed by a loop road lined with parallel buildings. A minor cross-axis on the south was left for a courtyard of student residential halls. Unfortunately, the primary axis of the plan was directed in the short, east-west dimension of the site, and the subsequent growth was forced along an informal lateral axis to the north. In 1966, when the campus was replanned by Caudill Rowlett Scott, roadways through the campus were eliminated and some of the implied cross-axes of the original plan were blocked, confounding any clear axial orientation. Automobiles currently must skirt the perimeter of the campus and are only allowed to penetrate it at the edges.

A persistent ambiguity plagues UH. Is the campus entrance located at the original site, off Calhoun Road, or is it to be approached from Cullen Boulevard, which is closer to downtown? The construction of the Gulf Freeway in 1952 created a strong attraction to Cullen Boulevard and the northern side of the campus, where Philip Johnson's Architecture Building (1987), a smug simulacrum of C. N. Ledoux's 18th-century design for a House of Education, now greets freeway motorists, its redundant *tempietto* competing with billboards for cheap motels and vasectomy reversals. SWA's Kevin Shanley was asked in the mid-eighties to improve the freeway approach to Cullen Boulevard with a significant threshold. The resulting split obelisk, whose elements on either side of the road are joined at the top by laser beams, appears like a stranded relic of postmodern carnival ephemera, attempting to establish an axial order that refuses to congeal.

In 1992 Gerald D. Hines commissioned the Houston architectural firm of Kendall/Heaton to develop a new plan for the campus. This most recent UH plan foresees the closing of Cullen Boulevard between Holman and Wheeler avenues, the closing of Calhoun Road, and the shifting of emphasis to the original entry axis, which will soon feed into a new freeway extension of Texas 35. By closing these streets the campus will add about 30 percent more bulk to its already formidable enclave, but the problem of internal orientation and circulation will probably be aggravated: the perimeter loop for automobiles will be enlarged rather than shrunk, making the connection to the center ever more unclear. Instead of dreaming of reinventing Rice with its clear axis, UH needs remedial, adaptive strategies to tie its landscape together. One example can be found at the University of Caracas, where a variety of buildings in different modern styles are linked by freestanding porticoes that extend from the perimeter parking lots to the central spaces. These shaded paths

Hester + Hardaway, 1996

University of Houston from the Gulf Freeway, with Gerald D. Hines College of Architecture building prominent in background.

create much-needed orientation as well as social spaces; some of them are even fitted with blackboards to be used as teaching areas. As at Rice, a combination of bicycle paths and bus stops could also give a new order to the campus, making it more accessible to the rest of the city.

In 1994 UH made national news with the announcement of a $50 million donation by Rebecca and John Moores. This type of windfall is one of the reasons why the campus does not evolve in an orderly manner. In this case the patrons specified that the money had to be spent on sports facilities, at a time when endowments were needed for educational buildings and the clarification of the center of the campus. Later the package was reassembled to redistribute some of the donation toward the construction of a new concert hall and music school. HOK Sports has already completed the Athletics/Alumni Center, with a 120-yard indoor football field simulating the conditions of the Astrodome, an indoor track and field, and, positioned triumphantly at the entry, a Cougars Hall of Fame.

The façade of the enormous complex has been slathered with a tawdry postmodern portal that greatly detracts from the purity of the building's semi-elliptical shed roof, whose beauty can still be appreciated from the rear elevation. It also houses the alumni center, and attached to it is a new baseball diamond. Mary Miss, the artist commissioned to create a sculptural enhancement to this project at the intersection of Cullen and Elgin, has designed a casually arranged collection of chairs in different scales set against an ivy-covered backdrop, a vision inspired by Houston backyards. The randomness of her project echoes the democratic incoherence of the campus and offers a contextual suggestion to campus planners as to how to perceive their inchoate collection of buildings.

Across Cullen Boulevard (the part that will remain open), Houston architect Barry Moore with The Mathes Group has designed the new building for the

Athletics/Alumni Center, University of Houston (HOK Sports Facilities Group, architects, 1995).

John and Rebecca Moores School of Music, University of Houston (The Mathes Group, 1997).

Moores School of Music, which will have a Baroque-scale opera theater that seats 800 (under construction). The building will be approached from the northern parking lots along a shaded entry court with amphitheater steps. Its façades will carry very low-relief pilasters reminiscent of the limestone pilasters on the Ezekiel Cullen Building. Some interior decoration will be designed by Frank Stella. Neither the athletic center nor the music school counteracts the tendency for each building to have its own style and volumetric

Texas Southern University, central mall with clock tower.

character. The music building promises to establish a more coherent arts courtyard with the Wortham Theater and the Blaffer Gallery, but there is no corresponding landscape improvement to enhance the idea.

The probable demolition of one of the only buildings on the campus that has an endearing style, the limestone-clad Technology Annex, and the possible demolition of Jeppesen Stadium to make room for a professional-size replacement seem unnecessary sacrifices to the idea of an ever-bigger future. Bruce Webb, dean of UH's School of Architecture, offers a much more sensible direction of development, noting that since UH owns the equivalent of 16 blocks on both sides of the approach from the split obelisks to the northern parking lots on Cullen Boulevard, it might be time to consider developing this site as a sort of academic new town, comparable in scale to the Rice Village, providing a mix of residential and commercial buildings for the substantial community of 35,000 who use the campus and have housing, shopping, and other commercial needs. Such a project would generate a strong focus of orientation and would ultimately enhance the flowing, democratic nature of the campus.

TEXAS SOUTHERN UNIVERSITY

Two blocks west of UH lies Texas Southern University, founded as a state-funded institution in 1947, before desegregation, as a college "for Negroes" on the model of Tuskegee Institute. It currently has a student population of 10,233, of whom 79 percent are African American. Although "for Negroes" was dropped from its name, the institution still strives to provide higher education for the minority that has been most excluded from other local universities. Rice, which has a 22 percent minority enrollment among undergraduates, is the social inverse of TSU.

The TSU campus is clustered on either side of a six-block stretch of Wheeler Avenue originally open to vehicles. Closed to traffic in the 1970s, this walk creates a strong pedestrian spine for the TSU campus. The major buildings were designed by the Houston architect John S. Chase, including the Martin Luther King Humanities Building (1969); the Ernest Sterling Student Center (1976); the Robert J. Terry Library (1958), which contains the Barbara Jordan Archive; and the Thurgood Marshall School of Law (1976). These buildings are all on an axis lined by plane trees. The Greek fraternity system is particularly important at TSU, and

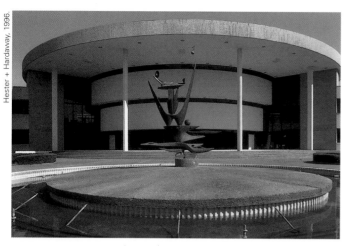

Martin Luther King Humanities Center, Texas Southern University (John S. Chase, 1969) with "African Queen Mother" sculpture (Carroll Sims, 1968) in foreground.

Fraternity Walk, Texas Southern University.

since there are no fraternity houses, members have claimed these trees along the Wheeler as their meeting places, painting the trunks with the fraternities' colors and symbols. While this is not very healthy for the trees, it has created an exceptionally colorful street scene. A paved plaza in the center of the campus is shaped by the tall columns of Mack H. Hannah Hall (Lamar Q. Cato, 1950), one of the earliest buildings on the campus and by far the handsomest with its Texas limestone façade. Hannah Hall contains an auditorium and administrative offices. This was the site of Houston's only race riot during the 1960s.

Since the adoption of a master plan in 1978, TSU has torn down about 350 buildings in the adjacent neighborhood, isolating the perimeters of the campus. Half of the student housing has been demolished as substandard and has not been replaced. Cuney Homes, the second-largest public housing complex in Houston, forms the northern border of the campus and is currently undergoing rehabilitation. The campus is in fact permeable along this shared edge, and the easy access between Cuney Homes and TSU represents what other institutions would consider a dangerous al-

ternative to the enclosed enclave. As always, the best defense is the presence of responsible people.

TSU is directly on the itinerary of one of the four projected public bike routes in Houston, the Columbia Tap Rail-to-Trail. The potential site, which is currently awaiting public funding, would use the abandoned Houston & Columbia rail line right-of-way that runs from the beginning of State Highway 288 downtown through Third Ward to Brays Bayou, where it links up with another bike trail. TSU, midway on the route, could become a key player in facilitating this alternative form of transportation and could supply articulated local bike paths, safe bike racks, and showers. As the poorest of Houston's universities, TSU has the least potential to make major changes by constructing buildings and the greatest potential to change things through landscape intervention.

UNIVERSITY OF ST. THOMAS

The University of St. Thomas, the smallest of Houston's university campuses, has half as many students as Rice and the lowest tuition of any private college in town. Founded in 1946 by Roman Catholic priests of the Basilian order, the school had the good fortune to be patronized by Dominique and John de Menil, who engaged their favored architect of the time, Philip Johnson, to create one of the best works of his career, a diminutive Modernist version of Jefferson's arcade-lined lawn at the University of Virginia, rendered with spindly black steel for the columns of the two-level colonnades and St. Joe brick cladding for the attached boxy volumes. For three decades this colonnade extended on the north into emptiness as a mysterious grid without attached volumes, evoking the stunning beauty of a Sol Lewitt sculpture. Only recently has a new academic building been hitched to the walkway to complete the symmetry of the court.

Construction is currently under way on what promises to be one of the silliest works of Philip Johnson's long career, a chapel that terminates the arcaded axis and cuts the court off definitively from the surroundings. The chapel is a rectangular box topped with a

University of St. Thomas, Academic Court showing Jones Hall and Strake Hall (Philip Johnson with Bolton & Barnstone, 1958–1959).

golden dome intersected by a diagonal wall that carries carillon bells. It will be entered through outward-folding flaps reminiscent of the gap at the bottom of a monk's robe. In both scale and style this frivolous design promises to overwhelm the subtle order of the original buildings, almost as if the architect were seeking revenge on himself—a perverse privilege that could only be granted to someone of Johnson's status.

The campus of St. Thomas was surreptitiously woven into the surrounding neighborhood, integrating

Welder Hall, University of St. Thomas (Philip Johnson with Bolton & Barnstone, 1958–1959).

Chapel of St. Basil, University of St. Thomas (Philip Johnson, Ritchie & Fiore with John Manley and Merriman Holt Architects, 1997).

existing wood-framed houses with its boxy brick volumes. Unlike other campus enclaves it was truly permeable, and until recently one could drive through it on city cross-streets. The 1996 additions and street closings will prevent this promiscuity. Partly because of declining enrollments and the need to better market the school, and partly because of the initiative of Stanley Williams, the local developer of a neighboring commercial center who thought the school grounds needed more cohesion, St. Thomas hired SWA's Kevin Shanley in the late 1980s to come up with a solution for defining the campus's edges, resulting in new yellow brick fences and enclosed parking lots that demonstrate the connection of the Link House (Sanguinet & Staats, 1911) on Montrose Boulevard with the 11 city blocks that make up the campus. Since then the campus planners have closed Mt. Vernon Street, one of three cross-streets that continued the city's grid through the campus. Slowly the borders are hardening, destroying what was once a pleasant ambiguity between university and neighborhood.

The university campuses in Houston are extremely important, both to the cultural quality of life of the city and as examples of planning that the city (the world's most famously unplanned one) is unwilling to pursue. As a client for architecture, Rice offers an extremely important process of educating both the clients and the architects about the qualities that have worked and new conditions that are emerging. But Rice represents a poor model as a participant in the city, having from the start closed itself off and insulated itself from all contact with auxiliary urban functions. The other three universities, which at times have shown a better integration with the city fabric, are now pursuing analogous isolating strategies without considering permeable alternatives. While planning bureaucrats will usually argue that defensive structure is necessary for public safety because of the threat of crime, it can be shown that the presence of people, not walls, is the best deterrent to crime.

While the universities have served as the model for enclaves for other institutions, they should now seriously consider reversing that isolationist tendency for the health of the city's fabric and the survival of urban values. The best place to start is with a new attitude to public transportation and nonpolluting forms of transportation. It is here that all four campuses, blessed with young, intelligent, and idealistic populations, could shed their neo-feudal attitudes and produce a sustainable model of urbanity for the rest of the city to follow.

Building reviews and other articles about Houston's university campuses have appeared in *Cite* as follows: Peter C. Papademetriou, "Pelli Crams Old Ideas into Rice's Future," *Cite* 5 (winter 1984); William F. Stern, "Robert R. Herring Hall [Rice]," *Cite* 9 (spring 1985); Drexel Turner, "W(h)ither the Rice Museum?" *Cite* 15 (fall 1986); "Music Mall: Ricardo Bofill's Building for the Shepherd School of Music [Rice]," *Cite* 21 (fall 1988); Stephen Fox, "Biomass: Cambridge Seven's Addition to the Rice Campus," *Cite* 22 (spring/summer 1989); Gerald Moorehead, "Scenes from the Mall: Philip Houston's University of St. Thomas Chapel," *Cite* 27 (fall 1981); Drexel Turner, "Slouching Towards Byzantium: About Face at the Rice Library," *Cite* 28 (spring 1992); Drexel Turner, "Stirling Example: Rice School of Architecture," *Cite* 29 (fall 1992 / winter 1993); Terrance Doody, "Is Rice a City?" *Cite* 35 (fall 1996); Phillip Lopate, "Halls of Lively [UH]," *Cite* 35 (fall 1996); Alvia Wardlaw, "Heart of Third Ward: Texas Southern University," *Cite* 35 (fall 1996); Karl Killian, "Flashback to the Sixties: University of St. Thomas," *Cite* 35 (fall 1996); Stephen Fox, "Campus Idea," *Cite* 35 (fall 1996); Barrie Scardino, "Stella Studio Houston and the Moores School of Music [UH]," *Cite* 37 (spring 1997); Gerald Moorehead, "Making Connections: Dell Butcher Hall [Rice]," *Cite* 48 (summer 2000). See also Mark A. Hewitt's "Much Ledoux about Nothing?" in this volume.

BUILDINGS OF THE CITY

Hester + Hardaway, 1997.

Introduction

WILLIAM F. STERN

Perhaps the strongest impetus behind the founding of *Cite* was the almost complete absence of consistent architectural criticism and commentary from the local press. By 1982, the year *Cite* began publication, Houston featured prominently among American cities as a leader in new building. Celebrated architects from Philip Johnson to Cesar Pelli were leaving their mark in Houston with buildings that had caught the attention of the national press, recognizing Houston as something of a mecca for a bold, new form of commercial architecture. In 1976 Ada Louise Huxtable, the *New York Times* architectural critic, remarked on this unprecedented wave of building, suggesting that in Houston one could witness the future direction of architecture in America. By the 1980s newspapers in most cities of comparable size employed full-time architectural critics, even in places where growth was nothing like the building boom in Houston. The two daily papers, the *Houston Chronicle* and the *Houston Post*, regularly presented design features on home decorating and furnishings, but in-depth reviews of new buildings were rare. At the *Chronicle*, that writing was left to the fine arts editor, who also covered ballet, opera, and theater, leaving little time or space for architectural reviews. What news there was about new buildings was likely to be found in the business or real estate sections.

Cite's first issue, published in August 1982, presented a mix of articles about architecture and the city of Houston intended to place the discussion of Houston buildings in a larger social, cultural, and urban context. From the beginning, the publication viewed architecture as a very direct part of the city's formation, demonstrating how buildings give shape to what was, and still is, a young, unruly city looking for a sense of itself. Comprehensive reviews of individual buildings, along with shorter design reviews, photo essays, neighborhood tour guides, exhibition reviews, book reviews, and interviews with noted architects have formed a running commentary on Houston's architecture during an expansive period of building activity. *Cite* has examined many of the buildings that have had a significant architectural impact on making the city and in so doing has chronicled much of Houston's architectural legacy in articles that also reveal the city's experience with the major movements in American architecture.

By 1980 Houston's very image as the booming American city was keenly associated with its recently built crop of sleek modern skyscrapers. Savvy commercial interests creatively combined with skilled architectural expertise to produce the latest versions of America's most powerful building type. To give a critical framework to this outpouring of high-rise construction, the spring/summer 1984 issue of *Cite* was devoted to the phenomenon of tall buildings in Houston. In that issue's lead article, John Kaliski reviewed the architectural competition for the new Southwest Center, presenting not only the winning scheme by Chicagoan Helmut Jahn but critiques of the two runners-up as well. Kaliski used the competition as an opportunity to talk about some of the latest directions in high-rise design.

Balancing Kaliski's view of the future skyscraper, Stephen Fox in his retrospective article "Scraping the Houston Sky: 1894–1976" traced the development of tall buildings in Houston from the earliest structures in the 19th century through the Modernist era of the post–World War II years and into the mid-1970s, just as an economic boom would flood downtown and new regional commercial centers like the Galleria with an array of impressive skyscrapers. In his carefully researched survey, Fox set Houston's historically important tall buildings within a national context. The issue also included an illustrated essay that reflected on skyscrapers that never were or had yet to become. Ironically, Helmut Jahn's Southwest Center was fated to become an unbuilt dream itself, falling victim to the 1984 recession that seriously curtailed high-rise construction in the city.

Among the architects who predominated the Houston skyscraper scene at that time was Philip Johnson. Indeed, no other architect in modern times has had a greater presence and influence in Houston than Johnson. Beginning in 1950 with a house for the Menil family and culminating with a series of high-rise office buildings commissioned by developer Gerald Hines, Johnson's career was nurtured by Texas patrons. Mark Hewitt in "Much Ledoux about Nothing?" previewed Johnson's latest visitation upon the city, a new building for the College of Architecture at the University of Houston. As curious as Johnson's seemingly Xeroxed design (which closely followed a visionary scheme for a building in Claude-Nicolas Ledoux's 18th-century plan for the ideal city of Chaux) was Hewitt's explanation of how Johnson, late in his career, received the commission. As he points out, the choice had more to do with the image the university hoped to project than the wishes of faculty members who had sought a competition. Johnson with partner John Burgee responded to the university's charge, delivering a building that was indeed more image than substance, providing the University of Houston with distinctive signage by way of an "octastyle Doric temple crowning the building" easily seen from the nearby Gulf Freeway. Three years after the building's completion, it was once again the subject of a review, this time by John Kaliski (*Cite* 14, summer 1986). Less accepting of Johnson's historical premise, Kaliski confirmed much of what Hewitt anticipated, taking the architects to task for contradictions in plan resolution and a general lack of detail and craftsmanship.

Documenting the influence of Frank Lloyd Wright, Kaliski's article "The Wright Stuff: Houston's Natural House" was one of several articles that featured Houston in the 1950s in *Cite*'s fall 1984 issue. "The Wright Stuff" portrayed Houston in the boom years following World War II as a city that wholeheartedly embraced the new and modern. Two distinct schools emerged: one influenced by the work and teachings of Frank Lloyd Wright and the other as influenced by the work of Mies van der Rohe. "The Wright Stuff" reviews the work of the "master's" foremost followers in Houston, MacKie & Kamrath, along with a discussion of work by Bailey Swenson,

Herb Greene, Bruce Goff, and Wright's only contribution to the architecture of Houston, the Thaxton House. *Cite*'s fascination with Houston's architecture at mid-century, a subject *Cite*'s editors would return to again in subsequent issues, derived as much from the architecture itself as its desire to portray the vitality and innovative spirit of the work at a time when Houston was on the cusp of becoming one of America's economic and cultural centers.

Cite regularly has visited the lives and careers of Houston's key architectural figures, including memorial essays on William W. Caudill (fall 1983), Hugo Neuhaus (winter 1987), Sally Walsh (spring 1992), and Donald Barthelme (fall 1996). "Howard Barnstone (1923–1987)" chronicles the life of Houston's most celebrated modern architect. Stephen Fox, who worked as Barnstone's research assistant on *The Architecture of John F. Staub: Houston and the South*, reviews Barnstone's career overall in this extended memorial. Fox shows how Barnstone, who came to Houston in the 1940s after studying architecture at Yale, combined influences of Mies van der Rohe and Philip Johnson in his own stunning array of steel-frame houses, which he designed with his partner Preston Bolton. Barnstone produced an equally distinguished body of work in the 1960s realized in a modern, expressionistic language executed in a variety of materials from wood frame to reinforced concrete. Throughout his career, Barnstone's work demonstrated an almost magical combination of space, light, and proportion.

Houses and housing have been frequent subjects in *Cite*, since residences, whether single- or multi-family, make up the majority of Houston's building inventory. Moreover, the house often exercises the most progressive thinking in architecture and historically has been an incubator for architectural innovation. While *Cite* occasionally has reviewed individual houses, more attention has been paid to residential architecture as a collective phenomenon, seeking to explore the broader social and historical issues of urban form. This was exactly the approach Peter Waldman took in "Recent Housing in Houston: A Romantic Urbanism." Coinciding with the commercial building expansion of the 1970s and early 1980s, a spate of inner-city housing developments had brought an innovative typology of automobile-oriented townhouses to Houston's older suburban neighborhoods. The work of young architects in concert with a group of adventuresome developers, these housing enclaves pointed to a new direction for the future of Houston's urban housing form. Waldman reflects on these new housing trends by looking back at several historic housing models, which in their time projected a visionary image of what Houston might become.

Stephen Fox in "Framing the New: Mies van der Rohe and Houston Architecture" expands upon Ludwig Mies van der Rohe's influence on Houston's architectural scene in the 1950s, 1960s, and early 1970s. Fox relates the story of how a group of young architects including Howard Barnstone, Hugo Neuhaus, Burdette Keeland, and Anderson Todd, many of whom were teaching at the University of Houston or Rice University, were captivated when John and Dominique de Menil retained Philip Johnson, Mies's acolyte, to design their home. Though the house lacked the structural purity and rationale of the Mies's Farnsworth House, its interior spaces exhibited the "expansive, lofty proportions" associated with the German master's work. The completion of the Menil House marked the beginning of what would be an outpouring of Miesian-influenced work by the array of those young, talented Houston architects, Philip Johnson at the University of St. Thomas, and, later, the nationally well-regarded firm of Skidmore, Owings & Merrill. Mies van der Rohe himself was brought to Houston through the influence of his admirers — Anderson Todd, Preston Bolton, and Hugo Neuhaus — to design two additions to the Museum of Fine Arts: Cullinan Hall (1958) and the Brown Pavilion (1974). Fox describes how Houston, through the leadership of a handful of cultural patrons, became a leading proponent of modern architecture in America.

A photograph on the cover of Cite's fall 1989 issue caught the reflection of an architectural detail mirrored in the glass façade of the Conoco Headquarters Building, a suburban office complex completed in 1985. While the three-story structures of this complex are not nearly as visible as the more glamorous downtown skyscrapers, the new Conoco Headquarters is a superlative work of architecture by the renowned firm of Kevin Roche John Dinkeloo and Associates. The Conoco Headquarters, as described in the article "Floating City," set a standard for the suburban office building in Houston with a complex of structures that was as sensitive to its site as it was to the workplace. As author of the article, I was fascinated with the building as a phenomenon of Houston's most recent suburban growth, miles beyond the center city, as part of a cluster of buildings whose location along I-10 had become known as the Energy Corridor. With its annexation laws, forgiving geography, and consequently ever-expanding city limits, Houston was fast defining a new kind of suburban city. The Conoco Headquarters would come to represent the ideal for its business environment and the model for a city on wheels.

"Diamond in the Round: The Astrodome Turns 25" by Bruce C. Webb and "Fair or Foul" by James Zook tell the tale of two cities: Houston in the 1960s and Houston in the 1990s. Webb's article about the making of the Astrodome, on the occasion of its 25th anniversary, portrayed a city itching to get into the big league with a baseball venue unlike anything else in the country. Under the guidance of the legendary Judge Roy Hofheinz, the city built what was touted as the eighth wonder of the world — the first domed, air-conditioned stadium in the country, easily visible for miles around in a field on the outskirts of town. Less a work of great architecture, the building was a spectacular engineering feat, especially for environmental control of air-conditioning on a grand scale that helped to establish Houston as the air-conditioning capital of the world. But by the early 1990s the Astrodome no longer fit the needs of a modern sports franchise.

Threatened with the loss of the city's Major League baseball team, the Houston Sports Authority, prodded by Astros franchise owner Drayton McLane Jr., pulled up stakes for a move downtown.

While the Astrodome, built on cheap land surrounded by acres of parking asphalt, symbolized a city moving inexorably outward into an endless coastal plain, the new stadium was planned as a catalyst for revitalization in the city's downtown core. Initially called the Ballpark at Union Station (now Minute Maid Park), the new stadium was strategically sited in an area ripe for development on the east side of downtown, and it incorporated as its grand entrance Houston's historic Union Station (Warren & Wetmore, 1911). The years between the building of the Astrodome and the design for the new downtown ballpark had not been kind to progressive modern architecture, which had become overwhelmed by a stylistic neo-traditional fashion favoring a historicist approach. Unlike the Astrodome, whose design looked to the future, the Ballpark at Union Station looked backward, taking its cues from the adjacent rail terminal building and the romance with baseball parks from the beginning of the 20th century to evoke the nostalgia of an era gone by. Designed solely for baseball, the stadium is an open-air affair, protected in rainy weather or when the temperatures soar with a sliding retractable roof, a hulking form looming awkwardly over the stadium and its downtown neighborhood. The two authors reveal the force of personalities and dynamics that produce these kinds of grand civic projects, both symbols of the city's perceived image and its aspirations at two distinct times in its recent history.

Preservation has never been an easy sell in Houston, the only major city in the United States without an effective preservation ordinance. Regulations of the sort entailed in landmark designation have more often than not been viewed as anathema by the dominating development forces that build the city. But when preservation is deemed good for business, those forces can often be reversed. Such was the good fortune for the Rice Hotel, where the same sort of cooperative revitalization efforts that brought the Ballpark at Union Station to its downtown home were applied to restoring the 1913 hotel as a residential apartment house. Bruce C. Webb in "Deconstructing the Rice" thoughtfully reviews the history of the Rice Hotel. He analyzes the financing mechanisms between the city and the developer and concludes with a balanced critique of the finished renovation, which converted a 1,000-room hotel to 312 rental loft apartments with a new adjoining parking garage. A fold-out page in *Cite* neatly illustrated the renovation with a vertical section through the building keyed to brief descriptions of the restoration components. This kind of article, the story of a noteworthy older building and the struggle to save it, represents *Cite*'s advocacy for preserving Houston's legacy of historic buildings.

The individuality of American cities is derived as much from their architecture as from differences in age, topography, climate, and planning regulations. While there is duplication of form and building types throughout the country, every American city contains certain buildings that are absolutely particular to its place. The Houston buildings reviewed, referred to, and described in the pages of *Cite* are those that most set this city apart from others. These buildings supply the information we need to read the history of our place. They stand as symbols of the aspirations of the people who built them and underscore the contribution that Houston has made to the larger history of American architecture.

Cite 6
SPRING /
SUMMER
1984

Scraping the Houston Sky 1894–1976

Stephen Fox

The skyscraper is a building type that underwent its initial phases of development in New York and Chicago in the last three decades of the 19th century. Its distinguishing characteristic was the height achieved by piling floors of habitable, rentable space on top of one another. Two technological developments contributed to the formation of this building type: the steam-powered passenger elevator and structural framing in high-strength, low-density, non-combustible metals. The passenger elevator made it possible to transport people vertically beyond a height that stairs ceased to be practical. Skeletal steel framing (and eventually steel-reinforced concrete) made it possible to construct buildings higher than was practical with masonry bearing walls. Technical developments in foundation design, artificial illumination, and mechanical ventilation contributed to the practicability of the tall building. The construction of tall buildings was a response to the burgeoning growth of American cities after the Civil War, accommodating greater numbers of people in existing urban centers and providing space from which to conduct efficiently the centralization of American business enterprise.[1]

Tall office buildings were first built in Texas during the 1890s.[2] Fort Worth, Dallas, and San Antonio already had tall office buildings by the time Houston's first sky-scraper, the six-story Binz Building, was constructed at Main and Texas in 1894–1895. Just after the Civil War, two four-story buildings had been built in Houston: the Capitol Hotel (1883) was five stories high and had a passenger elevator, as did the five-story Kiam Building (1894). Therefore, the Binz Building (demolished 1950–1951) did not dramatically alter the profile of Houston's skyline, but it was noticed. When *American Architect and Building News* illustrated the Binz Building in 1894, it became the first Houston building published in a national architectural journal.

Designed by Olle J. Lorehn, a young architect new to Houston, the Binz Building was decorated with Italian Renaissance ornament. Although it possessed an interior frame of cast iron and steel, its exterior walls were of load-bearing brick. It was not until after the turn of the century that Houston's first steel-framed skyscraper was constructed, the eight-story First National Bank Building of 1903–1905.[3] However, the First National Bank Building retained its superiority for even fewer years than had the Binz Building.

HOUSTON'S FIRST SKYLINE

Between 1908 and 1913 a construction boom endowed downtown Houston with a respectable skyline of buildings ranging from seven to 17 stories in height.

Binz Building (Lorehn & Fritz, 1895), Houston's first skyscraper, now demolished.

First National Bank Building (Sanguinet & Staats, 1905, 1909), Houston's first steel-frame skyscraper.

The Beaconsfield (A. C. Pigg, 1911).

Main Street with S. F. Carter Building (foreground) and Hotel Bender (background).

Main Street, looking north from Capitol Avenue, 1913, showing the newly completed Rice Hotel (Mauran, Russell & Crowell, 1913) and the Binz Building (right).

BUILDINGS OF THE CITY

These tall buildings adhered to the planimetric, volumetric, and architectural conventions introduced in the Binz Building. In plan, they comprised U or L shapes to facilitate illumination and ventilation. They were slab-sided, rising straight from the sidewalk to the overhanging cornices. Elevations were divided into base, shaft, and attic zones, with architectural decoration (usually of classical derivation) reserved only for the street sides; the party-wall sides were left unadorned.

In addition to offices, retail stores, hotels, and hospitals came to occupy tall buildings, as did flats. By 1913 Houston had three high-rise apartment buildings, the Savoy Apartments, the now-demolished Rossonian (both seven stories), and the Beaconsfield (eight stories). As Houston's commercial district expanded, residential neighborhoods were transformed. When the 15-story S. F. Carter Building and the 10-story Hotel Bender were built at either end of the 800 block of Main Street between 1910 and 1911, a two-story wooden house, set in its own little garden, was left sandwiched in between.

Out-of-town architects dominated design of Houston's first skyscrapers. Two firms — Sanguinet & Staats of Fort Worth and Mauran, Russell & Garden of St. Louis (Mauran, Russell & Crowell after 1911) — were especially prolific. Sanguinet & Staats opened a Houston office in 1903; D. H. Burnham & Co. of Chicago, Jarvis Hunt of Chicago, and Warren & Wetmore of New York each designed one tall building in Houston.

The names of many early Houston skyscrapers (Binz, Paul, Stewart, Scanlan, Settegast, Carter, Bender, Rice, Cotton) commemorated their owners. One entrepreneur, however, Jesse H. Jones, refused to comply with this practice. Instead, he named his buildings for major tenants. Jones shrewdly understood the skyscraper to be an economic phenomenon. Jones was intimately involved with the design of his buildings, which were planned to incorporate a number of profitable uses, to be expandable, and to be con-

structed and maintained as efficiently as possible. With the exception of the Rice Hotel, all of Jones's early buildings were built with structural frames of reinforced concrete, making them among the tallest concrete buildings in the United States during the early 1900s and, more to the point perhaps, cheaper to erect than steel-framed buildings.[4]

THE SOARING TWENTIES

Sanguinet & Staat's Carter Building, for only a few months the tallest building in Texas, remained the tallest in Houston from 1911 until 1926. After 1913 the pace of tall building in Houston slowed. During 1917 and 1918 it halted altogether and resumed only slowly in the early 1920s. But as Houston expanded to become the largest city in Texas by 1930, another surge of tall-building construction dramatically changed the appearance of the city. This was marked not only by a general increase in the height of tall buildings but also by striking compositional and stylistic developments. In addition, tall buildings began to define new suburban subcenters. Such developments stemmed from a mythology of the skyscraper that Rem Koolhaas described as "delirious."[5] This romantic notion saw the skyscraper as a symbol of a new era, an icon of glamour and an impending modern, urban civilization.

Despite these trends, Houston skyscrapers of the 1920s still adhered to the use of U- or L-shaped plans, tripartite compositional divisions, and the custom of architecturally ornamenting only the street fronts of a building, irrespective of its height. The perpetuation of these tendencies derived in part from a much greater reliance on local architects than in the previous decade. Sanguinet & Staats (whose Houston office became Sanguinet, Staats, Hedrick & Gottlieb, then Hedrick & Gottlieb) and Alfred C. Finn (a former Sanguinet & Staats draftsman who became Jesse Jones's architect) were Houston's chief skyscraper architects during the 1920s, with Joseph Finger and James Ruskin Bailey

Niels Esperson Building (John Eberson, 1927).

suburban skyscrapers were generally limited to eight to 11 stories. Tall buildings constructed for professional or commercial tenants, a development of the 1920s, resulted locally in the 16-story Cotton Exchange Building (1923–1924) and the 21-story Medical Arts Building (1924–1926), Houston's only neo-Gothic skyscraper, both by Sanguinet, Staats, Hedrick & Gottlieb.[6] In the near-downtown area, tall-building construction remained an acceptable way to induce changes in existing land use, site coverage, and height patterns. But the two tall residential hotels built near the Museum of Fine Arts in the middle 1920s, 2½ miles south of downtown, drew criticism for encroaching on newly developed neighborhoods of single-family housing. The 1929 Report of the City Planning Commission singled out Joseph Finger's eight-story Plaza Apartment Hotel on Montrose (1924–1926) as an example of the environmental consequences of Houston's lack of height control and zoning ordinances.

It was just such legal strictures that led to the shaping of a distinctive formal type for the 1920s skyscraper. The New York Zoning Law of 1916 established formulas for height control, mandating that as a building rose it step back in plateau-like stages from the street line. The result was a tiered profile that architects often capped with an elaborate crown. By the mid-1920s, the setback had become the architectural symbol of the modern skyscraper.

The first two setback skyscrapers built locally were the 32-story Niels Esperson Building (John Eberson, Chicago, 1924–1927) and the 22-story Petroleum Building (Alfred C. Bossom, New York, 1925–1927). The Esperson Building was an ebullient production that terminated in a steel-framed, terra cotta–clad tholos memorializing the eponymous Niels Esperson. The massing and decoration of the Petroleum Building were derived from Bossom's proposition that the Meso-American stepped pyramids of Central America represented the most valid precedent for shaping the

distant runners-up. Sanguinet, Staats, Hedrick & Gottlieb were the most accomplished. Their work was especially evident on the east side of downtown, where they participated with the entrepreneur Ross S. Sterling in defining a new corridor of high-rise development along Texas Avenue. Finn (and Jesse Jones) concentrated on the Main Street corridor, which they continued to expand up the street.

New downtown buildings typically ranged from 16 to 22 stories, with two taller than 30 stories, while modern American setback. The last skyscrapers completed in Houston before the Depression incorporated what, in the late 1920s, became the canonic modern style of the setback skyscraper — Art Déco, which eclipsed both classical decoration and neo-Gothic detail for exteriors of tall buildings.

Jesse Jones's Gulf Building (1929–1931), at 450 feet the tallest of Houston's 1920s skyscrapers, summed up the extravagant skyscraper euphoria of the late 1920s. Although the design (a collaboration of Alfred C. Finn with New York architects Kenneth Franzheim and J. E. R. Carpenter) was based on Eliel Saarinen's Chicago Tribune Building project (1922), its stepped profile evoked Manhattan, skyscraper capital of the world, and promised to transform Houston magically into the New York of the South. The Gulf Building also exemplified what might be called the urbane skyscraper of its era. Its six-story base, which extended from Main Street through the block to Travis, contained the specialty store Sakowitz Brothers, several small shops, a compact elevator lobby, and the majestic banking hall of the National Bank of Commerce. The setback tower of the Gulf Building was freestanding, square in plan, with four architectural façades rather than two. Atop its four-story crown were mounted an observation deck and the Jesse H. Jones Aeronautical Beacon. At night the towers of the Gulf and Niels Esperson Buildings were brilliantly illuminated, highlighting their role as the twin *stadtkröne* of the Houston skyline.

DOWNS AND UPS

The Great Depression abruptly halted Houston's race for the sky, quashing such "delirious" proposals as a 20-story City Hall (1929) modeled on the Los Angeles City Hall; a 21-story First Christian Church skyscraper (1929); and a deluxe, 18-story apartment tower (1931) to have been built alongside the residential enclave of Shadyside. The only one of these exotic visions actually built was Jefferson Davis Hospital (Joseph Finger

Paul Hester, 1980.

Gulf Building (Alfred C. Finn, Kenneth Franzheim, and J. E. R. Carpenter, 1929).

and Alfred C. Finn, designed 1931, built 1936–1938). This 12-story, freestanding setback skyscraper was cruciform in plan and, like the 1920s commercial skyscrapers, finished on all four sides.

Although the Depression proved temporary, none of the tall buildings built between 1934 and 1942 competed in height with those of the 1920s. Most were additions or annexes to existing tall buildings. The highest buildings constructed in the 1930s were all 10 stories: the Federal Office Building (Louis A. Simon, 1936–1938), Houston City Hall (Joseph Finger, 1937–1939), and the YMCA Building (Kenneth Franzheim, 1938–1941). While the YMCA retained a 1920s flavor with its picturesque setback massing and Renaissance detail, the Federal Office Building and City Hall were more typical of the 1930s architecture. The City Hall was a blocky, stepped mass accentuated by a smooth limestone skin, vertical channels containing the window bays, and panels and screens of modernistic ornament, the 1930s successor to the 1920s Art Déco. Finger exchanged the previous decade's model (the Los Angeles City Hall) for a more up-to-date reference, Holabird and Root's modernistic Racine County Courthouse in Racine, Wisconsin, of 1932.

American skyscrapers of the first half of the 20th century did not reflect the technological developments that made their construction, maintenance, and inhabitation possible.[7] The introduction of air-conditioning in the early 1930s, although widely heralded, did not exercise any radical effect on the design of tall buildings.[8] The nine-story Humble (now Main) Building (Clinton & Russell, New York,

Houston City Hall (Joseph Finger, 1939).

Hester + Hardaway, 2002.

1919–1921) became in 1932 the first local office building equipped with central air-conditioning. Its annex, the 17-story Humble Tower (John F. Staub and Kenneth Franzheim, 1934–1936) was the first local skyscraper built with a central air-conditioning system, a fact revealed only by the handsome neo-classical penthouse with which Franzheim capped the building to conceal the system's cooling tower. The most visible architectural concession to technological development among Houston skyscrapers involved the automobile. A limited number of buildings — three downtown and the two hotels near the Museum of Fine Arts — contained built-in parking in miniscule (but stylistically harmonious) garages.

Kenneth Franzheim, who moved his office from New York to Houston in 1937, embraced both the car and cool air in one of his most urbane buildings, the now-demolished Oil and Gas Building (1937–1939). The small, seven-story, L-shaped building contained a double-level attached garage, a Conoco service station (Continental Oil was the chief tenant), a ground-floor shopping arcade, street trees along three sides of the building, a setback level with extensive terraces occupied by the Ramada Club, and a crowning modernistic penthouse concealing the air-conditioning equipment.

In *Lions Club Book of Houston*, 1928, courtesy of Houston Metropolitan Research Center, Houston Public Library.

View looking north from Hermann Park, 1927, toward downtown Warwick Hotel (Brickey & Brickey, 1924–1926) and Museum of Fine Arts, Houston (far left — William Ward Watkin, 1924, 1926).

Preliminary scheme for the McCarthy Center (Hedrick & Lindsley, 1945). The central building became the Shamrock Hotel (Wyatt C. Hedrick, 1949), now demolished.

with at the Prudential Building (now the University of Texas Health Science Center), which occupied a 27½-acre site containing gardens, tennis courts, a swimming pool, and parking lots. Franzheim composed the Prudential Building as a series of stepped slabs, also on the Rockefeller Center model. This architecture was stodgy, but it met the ground confidently and put on a good show up top, where the company's name and insignia, the Rock of Gibraltar, were featured in a spec-

THE END OF AN ERA

A postwar building boom that ran its course between 1945 and 1951 concluded, rather than superseded, the "delirious" era of the skyscraper that began in the 1920s. It was the last gasp of the urbane, setback skyscraper tradition in Houston. Its monuments were the 23-story City National Bank Building (Hedrick & Lindsley, 1945–1949), the 16-story Hermann Professional Building (Kenneth Franzheim and Hedrick & Lindsley, 1947–1949), and the 18-story Prudential Building (Kenneth Franzheim, 1950–1952).

Among the most interesting postwar skyscrapers were those that defined a new Houston subcenter along South Main Street. Glenn H. McCarthy, builder of the Shamrock Hotel (Hedrick & Lindsley, 1949), envisioned a suburban skyscraper city based on the model of Rockefeller Center in New York (1930–1940) to be called McCarthy Center. Franzheim mixed modernistic details and massing with historical ornament at the Hermann Professional Building, as had Hedrick & Lindsley at the Shamrock. Historical quotations were dispensed

Prudential Building (Kenneth Franzheim, 1952).

tacular, Texas-sized neon display. The Prudential Building was the first tall office building constructed outside downtown Houston. All these museum–medical center area buildings were freestanding, but the Shamrock still preserved a distinction between its main façade and its massive rear elevation, which abutted the one- and two-story houses of Braeswood.

Although Kenneth Franzheim replaced Alfred C. Finn as Houston's principal skyscraper architect during the late 1940s, his firm's work began to show a loss of direction. In attempting to come to terms with modern (rather than modernistic) architecture, Franzheim's buildings became less convincing urbanistically and only marginally more up to date. The urbane formulas prevailed at the aggressively green 21-story Texas National Bank Building (1952–1955) and the 24-story Bank of the Southwest Building (1953–1956), but the magic was gone. Despite the fact that the Bank of the Southwest Building was faced with Houston's first all-aluminum curtain wall, that its underground passageways to the Commerce Building and the Ten-Ten Garage inaugurated the downtown tunnel system, and that Florence Knoll designed its immense banking hall (with a mural by Rufino Tamayo), the impact of the new was still too weak to compensate for the exhaustion of the old. Franzheim's last tall building in Houston was a tactful, appropriate, but no longer assured 16-story annex (1958–1960) to Warren & Wetmore's grandiloquent Texas Company Building (1915).

THE FORWARD LOOK: MODERN ARCHITECTURE ARRIVES

During the 1950s most new office construction occurred outside the central business district, which underwent a period of stagnation that provoked considerable alarm. The modernist counterparts of Franzheim's buildings typically were small, occupying less than full-block sites, and therefore conforming (by necessity rather than design) to tradition: U or L plans, small lob-bies, retail shops and services on the ground floor entered directly from the street, even the despised distinction between front and back. As an ideal form the preferred alternative to the setback was the slab, with blank end-walls bracketing long expanses of gridded glass, aluminum, and porcelain-enameled curtain wall, floating above ranks of exposed structural columns at the ground-floor level. The image, derived from Le Corbusier's tall-building designs of the late 1920s and 1930s, filtered through his design for the Secretariat of the United Nations in New York (1947, executed by Harrison & Abramowitz in 1950) and Lever House (SOM, 1950–1952) also in New York. Paradoxically, America's modern tall buildings in the 1950s were as dependent on the late 1920s as were their old-fashioned modernistic competitors.

Hermon Lloyd and W. B. Morgan produced Houston's first modern skyscraper, the 21-story Melrose Building (1949–1953), but they approached the Corbusian model more closely with The Mayfair (1953–1956), a 16-story apartment building near the Prudential Building. The Lever House *parti* (a horizontally aligned slab floating on structural columns, atop which a vertical slab was positioned) was omnipresent locally. But it lent itself to considerable variation, ranging from the doctrinaire, the 18-story Medical Towers (SOM, 1954–1957) Houston, for which Golemon & Rolfe were architects of record;[9] to the clunky, the 16-story Memorial Professional Building (Wirtz, Calhoun, Tungate & Jackson, 1955–1958, now demolished), faced with a garish turquoise-and-gold anodized aluminum curtain wall; to the chunky, the 11-story World Trade Center (Wilson, Morris, Crain & Anderson, 1959–1962), where the *parti* was adhered to, but the proportions were somewhat off. In recognition of Houston's priorities, the floating horizontal bases of the Medical Towers and the Memorial Professional Building were filled with parked cars. Disregarding the Lever House formula was the five-story Gibraltar Building (Greacen & Brogniez and

Night view, Gibraltar Building (Greacen & Brogniez and J. V. Neuhaus III, 1960).

J. V. Neuhaus III, 1957–1959). Houston's first all-glass curtain wall, it was sheathed on three of its four sides in heat-absorbing, solar gray glass, a debt to Le Corbusier, who had proposed such an all-glass curtain wall with his *mur neutralisant* (1929).

The changes these modern buildings made to the appearance of Houston in the 1950s were slight, where the skyline still peaked at the Gulf and Niels Es-

person Buildings. In contrast, Dallas had the Republic National Bank Building (Harrison & Abramowitz, 1954), the Statler Hilton Hotel (William B. Tabler, 1955), and Southland Center (Welton Becket & Associates, 1958) — the biggest and most conspicuous of a group of modern towers exhibiting the forward look in modern architecture. Houston had no concentration of new tall buildings; most were dispersed along the Main

Street corridor. South of downtown, Houston's skyline was dominated by Franzheim's and Hedrick's postwar setbacks.

THE TOWER IN THE PLAZA

This trend reversed suddenly in the late 1950s. Between 1958 and 1960 five significant new skyscrapers were announced: the 32-story First City National Bank Building (SOM, New York, with Wilson, Morris, Crain & Anderson, 1958–1961); the 44-story Humble Building (Welton Becket & Associates with Golemon & Rolfe and George Pierce–Abel B. Pierce, 1958–1963); the 33-story Tennessee (now Tenneco) Building (SOM, San Francisco, 1960–1963); Cullen Center (Welton Becket & Associates, 1960–1963), a six-block urban renewal–style planned development; the 28-story Sheraton-Lincoln Hotel (Kenneth Bentsen Associates, 1960–1962); and the 21-story Southwest Tower (Kenneth Bentsen Associates, 1960–1963, now demolished). These buildings provided downtown Houston with a sharp, clean-lined, classic modern skyline that made Dallas look dowdy by comparison. At 600 feet, the Humble Building topped the Gulf Building and was, for one year, the tallest building west of the Mississippi.

Corporations constructed these buildings for their own occupancy. Almost all occupied full-block sites, and those that didn't (Bentsen's two buildings) were set back from the property lines. This permitted conformance to the newest model for emulation, New York's Seagram Building (Ludwig Mies van der Rohe and Philip Johnson, 1958), which was set back from the sidewalk to make room for an open, paved plaza from which the building rose as an isolated tower. The image of the tower in the plaza governed Houston's newest high-rises. All were based on square or rectangular plans constituted by a repeating module determining the internal partitioning systems, the hung, acoustical ceilings, panels of fluorescent lighting fixtures, and even in some cases, the furniture layouts.

Central elevator and service cores permitted a uniform depth of leasable space on all sides of the buildings and helped to reduce the number of internal columns required. Such thorough rationalism made modern architecture economically very attractive. Nationally prominent architectural firms brought to Houston's new high-rises a level of currency and quality not experienced since the early part of the century. Moreover, the practice of having Houston architects associate with the imported firms raised local standards of tall-building design considerably.

Courtesy of Houston Metropolitan Research Center, Houston Public Library.

Tennessee Building, also known as Tenneco and now El Paso Building (Skidmore, Owings & Merrill, 1963).

In most of these buildings an externalized structural frame (what Skidmore, Owings & Merrill called an "exoskeleton") doubled as a *brise-soleil* (literally a sun-break, another invention of Le Corbusier). Such structural detail rendered the architecture "truthful," environmentally responsive (therefore "regional"), more interesting visually, and more dignified than the flat, flashy curtain walls of the 1950s. The grid remained, but the scale was more monumental. External finishes, whether of glass and porcelain enamel, anodized aluminum, marble, or precast concrete, were monotone and sober. The creation of ground-level plazas finished with elegant pacing, planting, and fountains seemed to represent a tasteful, enlightened alternative to the crowding of drug stores, beauty parlors, coffee shops, and shoe repair stands up to the sidewalk. Such services were tucked discreetly into the basement if their presences were deemed necessary.

The tall office buildings of the 1960s possessed as strong a type form as those of the late 1920s and the 1930s. Individually, those built in Houston were exemplary, and their effect on the skyline was exhilarating. But for urbanity they substituted rational planning and good taste. Collectively, these buildings, isolated in their plazas, tended to erode rather than relieve the fabric of downtown Houston, which, under the impact of retail flight and the economics of speculation, slowly came unraveled. For although implicitly dependent on the existing fabric to provide a dense, contrasting "cityscape," new high-rises tended to go up amidst blocks of land cleared of earlier development for asphalt-topped parking lots, awaiting the day when tall office buildings would be built upon them as well. Instead of "cleaning up" downtown Houston, these lithe, graceful, modern towers participated in its cleaning-out.[10]

THE RISE OF SUBURBAN SKYLINES

Complementing the reshaping of the downtown skyline was a suburban high-rise boom that began in the mid-1960s. Emerging as nodes of tall-building development were Sharpstown Center in Frank W. Sharp's 6,500-acre Sharpstown, 9½ miles southwest of downtown; Greenway Plaza, at the western terminus of the Richmond Avenue office building corridor; and the Post Oak–Westheimer intersection, 5½ miles west of downtown. Predicated upon access by private automobile, each of these sites adjoined a part of the regional freeway network then under construction. Each was conceived as an internally focused development, marrying the planning and design techniques of modern architecture and urbanism to the economies of speculative real estate development.

Of these, the two most cohesive were Greenway, a 41-acre office and residential park begun in 1963 but sold in 1967 to Kenneth Schnitzer's Century Properties, and the Galleria Post Oak at Post Oak and Westheimer on a site purchased in 1964 by Gerald D. Hines Interests. Schnitzer doubled the size of Greenway Plaza by buying out an entire restricted subdivision that adjoined it to the west and retained Lloyd, Morgan & Jones to replan the tract. They adopted the tower-in-the-park strategy first proposed by Le Corbusier, arranging a series of 11-, 21-, and 31-story office buildings built between 1968 and 1973 atop a landscaped podium containing a parking garage and a retail concourse. Hines retained Hellmuth, Obata & Kassabaum of St. Louis and Neuhaus & Taylor to plan the Galleria as a three-level, enclosed shopping mall to which were attached two office towers of 22 and 25 stories, a 22-story hotel, and Neiman-Marcus. The Houston Galleria was opened in stages between 1969 and 1973.

NEW DIRECTIONS

By the end of the decade Century Properties (now Century Development) and Gerald D. Hines Interests had emerged as the two major developers of high-rises in Houston. Both began planning their first major downtown buildings in 1965: Century the 28-story Houston Natural Gas Building by Lloyd, Morgan &

Greenway Plaza (Century Development; Lloyd, Morgan & Jones, 1969–1973).

Post Oak Tower at Galleria (Gerald D. Hines Interests, Neuhaus & Taylor, 1969).

One Shell Plaza (Skidmore, Owings & Merrill and
Wilson, Morris, Crain & Anderson, 1970).

Pennzoil Place (Johnson/Burgee with S. I. Morris Associates, 1976).

Jones (completed 1967) and Hines the 50-story, 715-foot tall One Shell Plaza (SOM, Chicago and Wilson, Morris, Crain & Anderson, 1971). These marked the course for the immediate future in Houston: new tall buildings would be built by developers rather than by corporations for their own use.

One Shell Plaza closed out the 1960s architecturally as it introduced the 1970s entrepreneurially. It was the perfect tall office building: economically determined, optimally planned, structurally innovative, and architecturally pure in its glistening mantle of travertine.[11] Slightly boring but prestigious nevertheless, One

Shell Plaza established Smith Street as downtown's new avenue of skyscrapers and sired two progeny by the same architects: the adjacent 26-story Two Shell Plaza and the 50-story One Shell Square in New Orleans. Gerald Hines approached real estate development with the acumen of Jesse Jones; he keenly understood the economic nature of the tall building and how to exploit it for maximum profit. He also discovered that the name-recognition value of designer architecture figured importantly in attracting both project financing and prime corporate tenants. Hines thereby became the first real estate developer since Herbert

Greenwall and William Zeckendorf to be acclaimed a patron of architecture.[12] In Houston his example was instrumental in maintaining the generally high standards of high-rise architecture achieved in the early 1960s.

THE SHAPES OF THINGS TO COME

By 1970 the most critical architectural problem confronting the design of tall office buildings in Houston seemed to be the avoidance of repetition. Philip Johnson and John Burgee's Pennzoil Place (1970–1976) and Post Oak Central (1973–1976), both with S. I. Morris Associates for Hines, resolved that problem decisively and opened the present era in Houston's skyscraper history. Pennzoil, although clad in a Seagram-like curtain wall, broke every rule that made One Shell Plaza the perfect office building. Every rule but one—it was immensely successful financially. That was the point of the tall building in the first place, and in Houston it still is.

Notes

1. On the history of the skyscraper see Francisco Mujica, *History of the Skyscraper* (New York: DaCapo Press, 1979; first published 1929); Alfred C. Bossom, *Building to the Skies: The Romance of the Skyscraper* (London: The Studio Limited, 1934); Carl W. Condit, *American Building Art: The Twentieth Century* (New York: Oxford University Press, 1960); Winston Weisman, "A New View of Skyscraper History," in Edgar Kaufmann Jr., editor, *The Rise of an American Architecture* (New York: Metropolitan Museum of Art and Praeger Publishers, 1970), 113–160; Paul Goldberger, *The Skyscraper* (New York: Alfred A. Knopf, 1982); Jeffrey Karl Ochsner, "Tall Buildings: Houston as a Case in Point," *Texas Architect* 32 (May/June 1982): 38–45; John Pastier, "The Cardboard Skyscrapers of Texas, 1911–1932," *Texas Architect* 32 (May/June 1982): 55–57.

2. Willard B. Robinson and Todd Webb, *Texas Public Buildings of the Nineteenth Century* (Austin: University of Texas Press for the Amon Carter Museum of Western Art, 1974), 111–113.

3. Designed by Sanguinet & Staats and expanded in 1908–1909 and again in 1922–1925, the First National Bank Building may have been the first steel-framed skyscraper in Texas, inasmuch as Dallas's first steel-framed skyscraper, the 14-story

Praetorian Building by C. W. Bulger and Son, was not built until 1909.

4. Condit, *American Building Art,* 156–159. Jones's first downtown building was the nine-story, concrete-framed Bristol Hotel Annex of 1908–1909 (demolished 1953). This was followed by a series of other 10-story, concrete-framed buildings: the Houston Chronicle Building and the original Texas Company, now Bankers Mortgage (Mauran & Russell, 1909–1910) and the Foster and Gulf (now Houston Bar Center) buildings, both by Alfred C. Finn (all extant but refaced). According to his biographer, Jones had wanted Houston to remain a "ten-story city" but built higher than that after the S. F. Carter Building was constructed. See Bascom N. Timmons, *Jesse H. Jones, The Man and Statesman* (New York: Henry Holt & Company, 1956), 77–83.

5. Rem Koolhaas, *Delirious New York: A Retroactive Manifesto for Manhattan* (New York: Oxford University Press, 1978). See also Diana Agrest, "Architectural Anagrams: The Symbolic Performance of Skyscrapers," *Oppositions 11* (winter 1977): 26–51.

6. The first specialized medical professional building in the United States is said to have been the 19-story Medical Arts Building (Barglebaugh & Whitson, 1923). The tallest concrete-framed building in the world at the time of its completion, it was demolished in 1978.

7. Condit, *American Building Art,* 178.

8. The first air-conditioning system in Houston was installed by Dixie Heating & Ventilating Company in the banking hall of the Second National Bank in the S. F. Carter Building in 1922. Two years later, a Dixie system was installed in the cafeteria and coffee shop of the Rice Hotel. See "Air Engineering," 9, and "Air Cooling Everywhere," 10–11, in *Houston* 4 (August 1933). This issue also contains an advertisement, 9, for the Dixie Company, listing its installations in Texas, Louisiana, Florida, Alabama, and Tennessee, most of which were in movie theaters.

   Reyner Banham identified the 21-story Milam Building in San Antonio (George Willis, 1928) as the first centrally air-conditioned tall office building in the world, as well as the tallest concrete-framed building in the world at the time of its completion. See Reyner Banham, *The Architecture of the Well-Tempered Environment* (Chicago: The University of Chicago Press, 1969), 178–179.

9. The Medical Towers was the first Houston building to win a *Progressive Architecture* Design Awards citation (1954) and the first tall Houston building to win an AIA Award of Merit (1957). The only other tall Houston buildings to receive AIA

Honor Awards have been the Tenneco Building (1969) and Pennzoil Place (1976).

10. Because Houston had no planning controls, all sites, in theory, were eligible for high-rise construction. Those who paid high prices for underdeveloped property were encouraged by taxing policy to demolish existing structures (often low-rise, retail buildings leased to merchants facing increased rents coupled with a disappearing clientele), thereby allowing sites to revert to an unimproved status, lowering taxes to a minimum, but generating income by using the cleared sites for surface parking.

11. At One Shell Plaza, SOM structural engineer Fazlur Khan devised what he called a "framed-tube" structural system, combining it with the use of lightweight concrete to achieve significant reductions in construction cost. The building's designer, Bruce Graham, articulated the structural properties of the external wall tube by rippling its surfaces where the structural loads were greatest. At the time of its completion, One Shell Plaza was the tallest concrete building in the world. See Gene Dallaire's interview with Joseph P. Colaco, "The Quiet Revolution in Skyscraper Design," *Civil Engineering/ASCE* 53 (May 1983): 54–59.

12. Paul Goldberger, "High Design at a Profit," *New York Times Magazine* (November 14, 1976): 76–79.

Paul Hester

Downtown Houston skyscrapers, 1984.

2002 UPDATE

From 1976, the year Fox ends this skyscraper history, until 1984, Houston's downtown experienced a boom in new skyscraper construction beginning with the completion of Pennzoil Place (Johnson / Burgee Architects and S. I. Morris Associates, 1976) and followed by First International Plaza (Skidmore, Owings & Merrill and 3D/International, 1980). Texas Commerce Tower (I. M. Pei & Partners and 3D/International, 1981) still is Houston's tallest building. Four Allen Center (Lloyd Jones Brewer & Associates, 1983); Allied Bank Plaza (Skidmore, Owings & Merrill and Lloyd Jones Brewer & Associates, 1983); RepublicBank (Johnson / Burgee Architects and Kendall/Heaton Associates, 1983); 1600 Smith Building (Morris*Aubry, 1984); and finally, Heritage Plaza (M. Nasr & Partners, 1987) were constructed before building in downtown Houston came to an abrupt halt.

While Houston is building once again, it has recently seen the demolition of several tall buildings discussed by Fox, among them the Shamrock Hotel in 1999 and Jeff Davis Hospital in 2000. Houston's newest skyscraper, 1500 Louisiana Street, was designed by Cesar Pelli in 2002 and reviewed in *Cite* 55 (fall 2002). *Editors*

Cite often has reviewed Houston skyscrapers: John Kaliski, "Great from Afar, Far from Great: Helmut Jahn's Southwest Center," *Cite* 6 (spring / summer 1984); Joel Warren Barna, "The Texas Commerce Tower," *Cite* 19 (winter 1987); Richard Ingersoll, "The Last Skyscraper: Heritage Plaza," *Cite* 19 (winter 1987); Joel Warren Barna, "Never Mind the Bollards: Houston Industries Plaza," *Cite* 37 (spring 1997); Kevin Alter, "SOM in Houston," *Cite* 40 (winter 1997–1998); Mitchell J. Shields, "Class of 2000," *Cite* 46 (fall 1999/winter 2000); Lisa Gray, "Photo Developments: Paul Hester's Skyscrapers before September 11," *Cite* 52 (fall 2001); William F. Stern, "1500 Louisiana Street: Building a 21st-Century Skyline," *Cite* 55 (fall 2002).

Paul Hester, 2002.

1500 Louisiana Street Building (Cesar Pelli and Associates with Kendall/Heaton Associates, 2002).

Cite 4
FALL
1983

Much Ledoux about Nothing?

NEW COLLEGE OF ARCHITECTURE
FOR THE UNIVERSITY OF HOUSTON

Mark A. Hewitt

Philip Johnson may be the last architect of the Enlightenment.

PETER EISENMAN

Houston has been good to Philip Johnson. And Philip Johnson, in the course of a long, distinguished, and controversial career, has given this city a group of illustrious buildings that, along with a few monuments like the Astrodome, represents a substantial part of its contribution to contemporary architecture.

In the 1950s, as a late bridegroom, Johnson entered the Houston architectural scene with the refined,

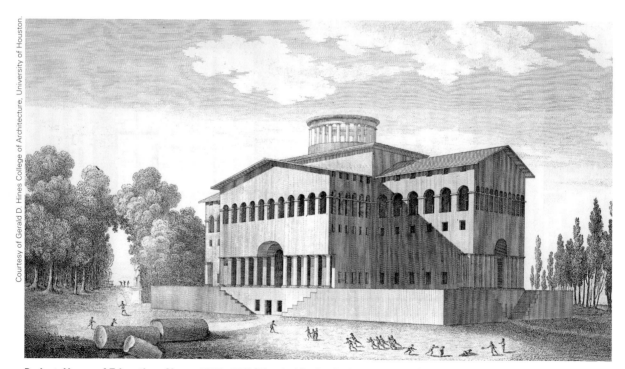

Project: House of Education, Chaux, 1773–1779 (Claude-Nicolas Ledoux, architect).

Courtesy of Gerald D. Hines College of Architecture, University of Houston.

Miesian University of St. Thomas campus — still one of the highlights of any architectural tour of the city. In the early 1970s, when his prestige was reportedly flagging, he founded a hugely successful comeback on the merits of two Houston office tower complexes: Post Oak Central, near the Galleria, and the renowned Pennzoil Place downtown. Both proved to be national trendsetters, with more offspring, it seems, than the Seagram Building. Johnson's relationship with the city continues today, as the Transco Tower soars above the Galleria and the RepublicBank Center rises above Jones Hall Plaza, dwarfing Johnson's 10-year-old Pennzoil towers.

The unveiling of a new Philip Johnson design in Houston, then, is bound to be greeted with lively anticipation and treated as an event. But when the 76-year-old architect, through collaborators John Burgee and Eugene Aubry of Morris*Aubry Architects, presented his design for the $18 million University of Houston College of Architecture on May 23, 1983, reactions at the university and in the local architectural community were cool. The building is modeled self-consciously after Claude-Nicholas Ledoux's House of Education for the ideal town of Chaux, designed between 1773 and 1779. Though it raised eyebrows and stirred controversy in this conservative town, its impact and even

Drawing: Patrick Lopez, courtesy of University of Houston.

Gerald D. Hines College of Architecture, University of Houston, perspective, south elevation (Johnson/Burgee Architects and Morris*Aubry Architects, 1986).

the presence of its prestigious architect were undercut by a sense of disappointment in the process that the university followed in selecting an architect and arriving at a building program. "It's a lost opportunity," said one UH College of Architecture faculty member, "both for the campus and for the department."

That lost opportunity stemmed from the college's intention, supported by a large portion of the architecture faculty, to hold an open design competition for the building more than a year ago. A fund was set up in the spring of 1982 and a professional advisor, Roger Schluntz, retained. A small faculty committee worked with the Facilities Planning Department of the university to develop a program. Participation in this process was unenthusiastic, partly because (according to Peter Wood, associate professor of architecture at the college and assistant dean) the college had witnessed several aborted attempts to plan and build a new facility over the years. Dean William Jenkins and the faculty also considered a competition limited to 10 local architects during the fall of 1982, but it too was rejected by the university administration.

In spite of the clear imperative to replace the college's makeshift, overcrowded, and often squalid facilities, many were skeptical that state or private funding could be obtained even if an architect were retained to design the new building. But both state and university politics resulted in scrapping the idea of a competition altogether. The university administration decided to expedite the architect selection process in anticipation of state funding before last fall's gubernatorial election.

Johnson had been proposed early as an alternative to a design competition (apparently without serious faculty objections), and it was known that he was eager to have the commission, which would be his first school of architecture building. Moreover, he had the support of Burdette Keeland, an influential senior faculty member, who could sway the Board of Regents.

The project was given its first significant boost when the Texas Legislature allocated $25 million for the construction of a College of Business Administration and a College of Architecture in May 1982. Though much of the fund was earmarked for the business school, it gave the architects something to work with, and it set the political wheels rolling at a more urgent pace.

Arguments were advanced at a university level for a local firm with international credentials, and the pattern of recent building on the campus suggested that a local office with strong political connections stood a good chance of winning the job. Hiring a Houston firm — especially one with the dubious distinction of having designed one or more of the university's lackluster recent buildings — would not have served the interests of the architecture faculty, administration, or students.

Recently the College of Architecture has been expanding programs, hiring new faculty, and attracting a broader range of students. The school needed the kind of prestige that a new building by a well-known architect could provide. And the example of Houston's other architecture school on Main Street loomed large. "We had visiting critics coming to the school," said Peter Wood, "who, when asked what buildings around town they wanted to see, would always mention the Stirling [School of Architecture] building at Rice."

Late in the fall of 1982, with options narrowing and time running short, Dean Jenkins joined with Keeland to recommend the selection of Johnson/Burgee in joint venture with Morris*Aubry. The compromise worked. The university administration approved the choice, and shortly after the start of the new year, Johnson/Burgee began design and programming meetings with the university's Department of Facilities Planning. Preliminary design for the building was complete by early spring of this year.

The haste with which the programming and schematic design process was carried out, and the fact that it was so largely under the control of Facilities Planning, also irritated some architecture faculty members. William F. Stern, an assistant professor, felt that all faculty and students should have been consulted in programming the new building and in choosing its architect. "The university has not acted in the public interest," he said.

Nevertheless, with the allocation by the state Legislature of funds for the building, its approval on June 6 by the Board of Regents, and the architects' confidence that it will have "noble presence" on the campus, the College of Architecture faculty and students can rest assured that their much-needed facility is a reality at last.

However, the questions of the aesthetic and pragmatic merits of the building as presented in the schematic design in late May, and of its relationship to the architecture of the campus, its precedents, and other works by Johnson, are issues that far outweigh administrative machinations within the university and the College of Architecture.

With a characteristic blend of mischievousness and aplomb, Johnson has presented Houston with another provocative architectural idea. It is a campus *propylaea*, massive and grand in stature, that goes beyond any of his recent works in its fastidious use of precedent. The selection of the Ledoux House of Education is ingenious and apt—Johnson has always been brilliantly concise in his choice of models. It is also not in the least surprising. In September 1950, when he published art-historical analysis of his own epochal Glass House in *The Architectural Review*, he featured Ledoux's spherical Maison des Gardes Agricoles at Maupertuis as a model, with the caption: "The cubic, 'absolute' form of my glass house and the separation of functional units into two absolute shapes rather than a major and a minor massing of parts comes directly from Ledoux, the eighteenth-century father of modern architecture."

In Johnson's earlier works, Schinkel and Ledoux were his spiritual and philosophical masters; and Mies was the father/inventor of his chosen idiom. Today, the postmodern PJ can unabashedly re-do Ledoux and reshuffle Schinkel with only a wink at Mies.

As ideal, absolute form, Johnson's design is praiseworthy. Its elements are strong in conception and relevant in their applicability to an architectural school. The atrium and simple massing bring to mind numerous fine examples of university buildings in this country, from John Galen Howard's Hearst Mining Hall at Berkeley to Henry Hornbostel's architecture building at Carnegie Mellon University and many of the early buildings at Stanford. The octastyle Doric temple crowning the building acts as a simple sign. Had the building been clad with fossilated limestone, as originally intended, instead of brick, its monumentality would have been enhanced. Like nearly all Johnson buildings, this one has a blunt conceptual clarity that can border on the clichéd or on the sublime. But unfortunately, like many of his more recent postmodern works, the University of Houston College of Architecture fails to make the step from image to pragmatic architectural reality, from Ledoux's paradigm to a building sustaining the needs of a growing architectural school in the 1980s.

Johnson's love of the witty, the clever, the brilliant abstractness of an architectural idea—the same qualities that brought power and resonance to works like Pennzoil, the Glass House, and the Kline Tower at Yale—now stands in the way of his ability to make the difficult translation of traditional forms to the present day. He has chosen not to confront the problems of detail and ornament, dichotomies between compositional systems in plan and in three dimensions, and construction problems that preoccupy many of his younger colleagues. He does not know Ledoux and Schinkel as intimately as he does Mies. His latest works have a slapdash quality that belies the seriousness and care that were hallmarks of early Johnson buildings.

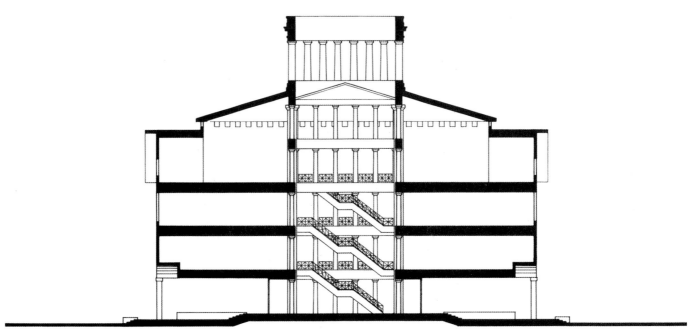

Hines College of Architecture, section. Courtesy of University of Houston.

An acute self-analyst, Johnson spelled out what are undoubtedly the strongest aspects of his architecture in a talk at Columbia entitled "What Makes Me Tick" (1975). Calling himself a "functional eclectic," he outlined three themes central to his work: the Footprint, the Aspect of the Cave, and the Building as Sculpture.

Of the first he remarked, "It is with the richness of processionals that I try to imagine architecture," and indeed, his best buildings are generally marked by a diagrammatic clarity of circulation and sensitivity to the ritual of movement. There is a succinct atmospheric character to many of the best Johnson interiors, like that of the Port Chester synagogue, which testifies to his concern with the second of his themes. But of the three, he is most consistently brilliant as a manipulator of sculptural form and massing, as his Houston skyscrapers show. Simplicity, purity, powerful directness — the traits that distinguished the Glass House — are ever present in a Johnson design. Yet he cannot stomach the complex, the idiosyncratic, the "messy" in his sculptural manipulation.

The University of Houston College of Architecture building displays some of the concerns in Johnson's triad. As the architects point out, it takes advantage of its position in the newly revised campus to bring visitors through its atrium, though one wonders whether the Serlian main entrances are large enough in relation to the building mass to be inviting. But why, on the long axis of the building, do we find a fire stair and a loading dock framed with arches that signal a secondary cross-axis penetrating the building? Will the atrium itself, grand in size, receive enough light from the square skylight, shaded by the temple six stories above, or will it literally be a cavelike space?

Light is also a major problem in the studio spaces, especially on the second floor, where relatively small, square windows light a room that is more than 50 feet deep at its center. The fenestration patterns on the outside, clearly meant to replicate those of the 18th-century model, bear little relation to the lighting needs of offices and other spaces inside. Moreover, for a designer known for his adept handling of massing, this building has a clumsy, ungainly quality that the original

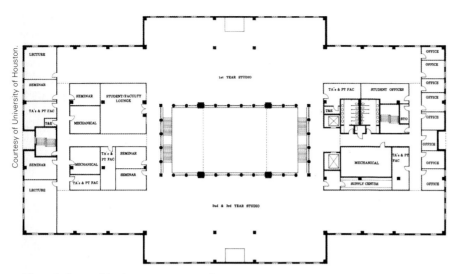

Hines College of Architecture, second floor plan.

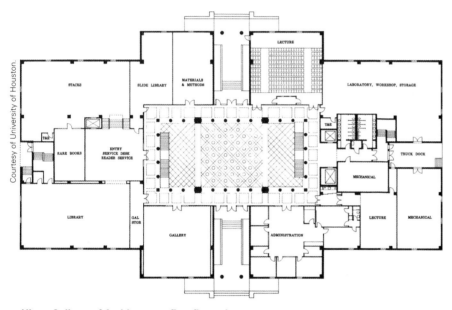

Hines College of Architecture, first floor plan.

avoids through careful balancing of simple bands of fenestration and loggias with larger massing elements. And Ledoux, had he built his building, would certainly have enriched it with the kind of spare, careful classical detail found in the other buildings at the Salt Works. Details of the Houston building are cartoonishly abstract.

But what is most disconcerting about the design of the new College of Architecture is the listlessness of its plan. By treating the zone between the outside walls and the atrium as loft space and allowing the complex program to run riot within, the architect has avoided the resolution of inherent tensions between the rigid, idealized formality of the model and the builtin complex asymmetries of the program elements. Looking at the result makes one appreciate Schinkel's

Hines College of Architecture, University of Houston.

protean genius as a planner in buildings like the Neus Schauspielhaus and the Altes Museum in Berlin and lament the fact that Johnson has not learned more from his artistic heroes.

Are these comparisons with Ledoux and Schinkel (and even with Johnson's former self) unfair? Are the building's weaknesses small in comparison to the visual and functional amenities it provides for a campus that has had few distinguished buildings to its credit in recent years? Perhaps. Opinions on the design have ranged from downright raves (by no less a luminary than Howard Barnstone) to outright condemnations. Johnson is no stranger to controversy and impassioned criticism. Perhaps improvements will be made between now and the completed construction documents. But in any event, the University of Houston College of Architecture will have a lavish new building and a powerful architectural drawing card—both long overdue.

2002 UPDATE

As Mark Hewitt predicted almost 20 years ago, Philip Johnson's architecture building, visible as it is from many vantage points around the university, has become a landmark. While major donors to the university and other privileged groups enjoy gala balls and banquets in the atrium of the UH architecture building, many of those who use the building daily remain unconvinced. *Editors*

Other articles concerning this building and activities within it include: "Johnson-Burgee and the UH College of Architecture," *Cite* 3 (spring 1983); "UH Architecture Building to Be Dedicated," *Cite* 12 (winter 1985–1986); John Kaliski, "Master Johnson's House of Education," *Cite* 14 (summer 1986); and Bruce C. Webb, "Atrium Art," *Cite* 47 (spring 2000).

Cite 7
FALL
1984

The Wright Stuff

HOUSTON'S NATURAL HOUSE

John Kaliski

A perusal of decorator and lifestyle magazines from the 1930s through the 1950s suggests that the obsessive focus of the American home shifted from the matriarchal interior with its all-electric kitchen to the patriarchial exterior patio and requisite barbecue pit. This reorientation of the home reflects a nascent back-to-nature movement, yet, more important, it is related to a systematic quest carried on in the popular press for a natural American domestic order.

Somewhat simplistically, we now believe that the post–World War II family was not only buffeted by the mental anguish of war-related separations but also by the rigidity of corporate life in a homogenized, mass-production society. Other neuroses were related to the new threat of nuclear holocaust and, worst of all, the belief in Communist infiltration and the inevitable destruction of the American way of life.

While millions of Levittown-like Cape Cod, Colonial, and Cinderella cottages continued to be built across the country, a new, authentic American style — the "organic" — was defined not as "form follows function" but as "comfort and performance and beauty."[1] For every glass or "modern" house designed by Mies van der Rohe, Marcel Breuer, Philip Johnson, or their followers, thousands of organic houses peppered the expanding landscape. By the end of the

1950s the organic style had reached a peak of fevered popular acceptance.

The casual house of the late 1940s through the early 1960s was an escape from the pressures of this new, unstable world. On another level, the organically styled house was a reaffirmation of the American pioneer spirit, a perennial attempt to get back to the land and define a personal backyard frontier. In countless houses throughout the rapidly spreading suburbs, Dad grilled sirloin, Mom and Sis washed dishes in the kitchen, and Davy Crockett Jr. slashed away at spirits in his backyard fort.

In Houston the look and feel of entire subdivisions and sections of the city were affected by this style. Such neighborhoods as Riverside Terrace and Timber Crest are filled with architect-designed, organically styled houses. North and South MacGregor Ways from MacGregor Park west to Hermann Park are, in parts, dominated by the postwar natural style. Even staid River Oaks boasts an organic-style oasis.

Large developers as well as builders were influenced by organic architecture. Many houses in Tanglewood or Sharpstown display detailing that suggests an organic stylistic tradition that rests squarely on the works and writings in the 1930s and 1940s of Frank Lloyd Wright. In his Usonian houses of this period,

Mitchell House with plan (MacKie & Kamrath, 1963).

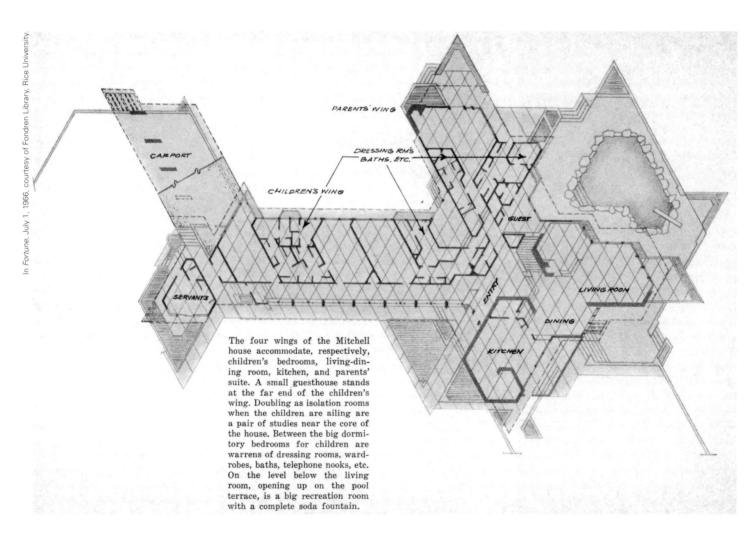

The four wings of the Mitchell house accommodate, respectively, children's bedrooms, living-dining room, kitchen, and parents' suite. A small guesthouse stands at the far end of the children's wing. Doubling as isolation rooms when the children are ailing are a pair of studies near the core of the house. Between the big dormitory bedrooms for children are warrens of dressing rooms, wardrobes, baths, telephone nooks, etc. On the level below the living room, opening up on the pool terrace, is a big recreation room with a complete soda fountain.

Wright developed the servantless, self-sufficient single-family house. This type of house emphasized the horizontal relation between the line of the horizon and the lines of the house. These houses made use of local materials and simple detailing. The automobile was accommodated in a carport, a word Wright claimed he invented. Family life was centered around a living-dining-kitchen-hearth space. This "work area" looked out onto the all-important backyard garden. In short, Wright played a crucial role in the development of the 1950s dream house.

MACKIE & KAMRATH

Frank Lloyd Wright's ideas are prolifically expressed throughout Houston in the built work of the firm of MacKie & Kamrath. Formed in 1937 by Frederick J. MacKie and Karl Kamrath, this architecture firm's early work expressed a variety of eclectic styles. But by the outbreak of World War II the firm was beginning to experiment more frequently with Wrightian forms. This new direction in their work did not become emblematic, however, until June 1946. At this point Kamrath, like many young architects, made a pilgrimage to Taliesin, Wright's home and studio school located near Spring Green, Wisconsin.

Kamrath showed the great master his office's organic style work and felt encouraged by Wright's response to them. Wright told Kamrath, "Karl, anybody that builds buildings ought to be here."[2] Though he regretted his ultimate decision not to stay at Taliesin to work directly with Wright, Kamrath did return to Houston inspired. After this direct encounter with Wright, MacKie & Kamrath worked exclusively in the master's manner and became the city's most direct link to organic ideology for almost 20 years.

Residential buildings by MacKie & Kamrath are scattered throughout Houston. The most concentrated group of their organic houses of the 1950s is found nestled on Tiel Way in a corner of River Oaks. Here, almost an entire neighborhood of MacKie & Kamrath's organic houses is hidden under an umbrella of trees, where they designed six houses and many others are heavily influenced by the MacKie & Kamrath work.

The first and perhaps strongest impression that marks the houses of MacKie & Kamrath is the overwhelming horizontality of the masses. From low garden walls that lead the eye up driveways, to low-pitched, hipped roofs that stretch well beyond the brick or redwood siding, the design emphasis is always low and in the direction of the horizon. Often all that is presented to view from the street is a shadowed carport.

Entry to these houses is deep within cool shadows under overhangs or down paths mysteriously hidden from view. At 8 Tiel Way a squat, vertical mass contrasts with the dominant horizontality. Here the vertical mass encloses a great, central hearth around which the family gathers. For Wright the hearth was a seat of paternal authority. As Kamrath designed this house for himself, one suspects that the hearth was meant to serve the same purpose. The Wrightian details on Tiel Way houses extend even to the garden wall lamps. At 54 Tiel Way, Wright's signature red square becomes a simple lamp box that marks the corner of the house.

MacKie & Kamrath's largest and most meticulous organic house was begun in 1958, though was not completed until 1963. Designed for Houston oilman and Woodlands developer George Mitchell, his wife, and 10 children, no expense was spared to create finely crafted exteriors and interiors.[3] To keep the scale of the 12,500-square-foot house from overwhelming its neighbors, not only was the roofline kept low, but the tennis court was sunk into the ground. Because 10 children can quickly wear down linoleum floors running to and from the refrigerator, the decision was made to use onyx floors as a durable substitute in the kitchen. Despite the huge scale of the house, only the dominant hipped roof of the house is visible from the street, and even it seems to disappear into heavy landscaping.

The plan of the Mitchell House is organized on a Wrightian diamond grid made up of joined equilateral triangles. Halls and galleries spin out from a 170-ton chimney wall. Galleries, which provide access to the four living/sleeping wings of the house, stretch up to 300 feet into the wooded landscape. The exterior detailing of the Mitchell House makes broad use of regional materials, especially Austin limestone. Inside, coved lighting with triangular incandescent fixtures and plaster ceilings stripped with thin wood slats are a MacKie & Kamrath homage to Wright.

Townsend House (Wylie W. Vale, 1955).

HOUSTON SCHOOL OF WRIGHT

While MacKie & Kamrath were the closest imitators of Wright working in Houston, the organic style appealed to many other local architects. Some of these designers flirted only briefly with organic notions of design before moving on to other work for which they are better known today.

John F. Staub, Houston's most famous eclectic architect, was not averse to experimenting with a watered-down organic modernism. The Fay House (1950, in Kemah, Texas) and the Sacks House, built the same year, are low-swept ranch houses that gently hug their hillocks.[4] Both houses realize an organic ideal by accentuating the means of construction in a decorative manner. In this regard the exposed ceiling rafters of the Fay living area are of particular interest.

O'Neil Ford, the dean of Texas regional architects, tried his hands at the organic in Houston when he designed the Garth House (1956, at 63 Briar Hollow Lane). This flat-roofed house is sited at the end of a cul-de-sac and addresses the street with several eye-level concrete panel screens that allow the viewer just a glimpse through glass-walled rooms to the shaded wood beyond.

Howard Barnstone, who achieved wide publicity during the 1950s for his brick, steel, and glass houses that helped push the ideas of modern architecture to a more forgiving stance, also made a foray into the organic early in his career. Barnstone described the Bloxsom House (1952, at 22 East Shady Lane) as his "Frank Lloyd Wright house." The use of weathered wood siding and a low, hipped roof with overhangs is a departure from Barnstone's usual aesthetic devices.

Among Houston architects better known for their organic work, Wylie W. Vale must be included. His Townsend House (1955, at 3723 Knollwood) in River Oaks features a giant stone chimney, which is only one of several rectangular wood-and-stone masses that overlap or intersect horizontal roof slabs. The master bathroom of this house featured turquoise mosaic tiles that matched the opera-singing Mrs. Townsend's eyes.[5] Another local architect, David D. Red, designed his own house (1951, at 1802 Sunset Boulevard) in Southampton. This house, formed of triangular elements in plan,

Paul Hester, 1984.

Penguin Arms Apartments with interior (Arthur Moss, 1950).

has a prow-shaped room with strip windows that speed the movement of the eye in a horizontal direction around the corner site. A triangular shed roof precariously ties the one-story prow to a two-story bedroom wing. Originally this inclined roof boasted a grass surface—a literal organic roof.

Perhaps the most startling domestic organic structure in Houston is a multiple-unit apartment complex located at 2902 Revere Street, the Penguin Arms Apartments (1950) designed by Arthur Moss. Labeled "googie architecture" by an imaginary Professor Thrugg in Los Angeles, this apartment building is an authentic Houston example of organic expressionism.[6] Giant, inverted triangular trusses float precariously over glass-corner windows that bulge out from the force of the visual load. The structure seems rather poised for take-off, or imploding even as one views it.

The materials of Penguin Arms run the gamut of the organic palette. The juxtaposition of the angled-out glass set in redwood trim, rubble walls, and green rolled tar paper siding gives the impression of an abandoned semipermanent encampment set amidst a stone ruin. The effect is not unlike an exaggerated, populist version of a Frank Lloyd Wright's desert architecture.

Paul Hester, 1984.

The 1950s work of Bailey A. Swenson is more difficult to place within the organic camp. The eclectic nature of this architect's work during the period is a combination of influences from Art Déco to the Arts and Architecture California Case Study houses of the late 1940s. Unlike either of these precedents, which tended to contain a single volume within the confines of a box, Swenson always stretches and erodes, then ruptures the box with secondary volumes.

Proler House (Bailey Swenson, 1948).

The primary components of Swenson's compositions are manifest in the design of the Proler House (1948, at 4216 Fernwood). There, a long brick wing races to the west yet is anchored to its corner site by a slightly rotated, two-story, boxy wing. The rotated angle of this box acknowledges the intersection of two streets. Where the two main pieces of the composition intersect, the slab roof of the western wing cuts across a vertical slab of plate glass at the corner of the box and demarcates the entrance.

In Swenson's Daniel House (1950, at 4505 North Roseneath) vertical and horizontal strip windows are placed at the corners of a cubical two-story pavilion beneath a low-pitched roof. The resulting box visually disintegrates and at the same time appears to split the long hipped roof of the brick, one-story wing.

Swenson's architecture during this period is not just an undisciplined, formal, compositional exercise. It is an attempt to resolve two types of architecture: the organic, which demanded fealty to a vision of the horizon, and the International, which reveled in the manipulation of the box. Swenson worked with both ideas at the same time. The work that resulted is uniquely inventive, even when it appears awkward. Unfortunately for the present-day aficionado of Swenson's architecture, the work is generally neglected and at times appears to be in an advanced state of decay.

There were several organic houses built in this city to the designs of nationally recognized architects. In each of these houses the strength of the architectural statement transcends the purely aesthetic motivation that guided most Houston designers. An examination of four houses designed by different architects reveals that ideology rather than fashion generated the work.

The Reed House (1960, at 111 Carnarvon Drive) was designed by one of Frank Lloyd Wright's most talented disciples, Alden B. Dow. Many of the compositional devices previously described are present in this house; the hipped-roof forms, the subtle overlapping of verticals and horizontals, and the low, brick garden walls defining outdoor rooms. What is unusual in this design is a classicizing tendency. Dow restrains the typical robust organic asymmetry for a staidness of massing and detail that is Japanese in effect.

Despite this calm, the house is also a celebration of the automobile. A huge auto-court (possibly the largest domestic carport in Houston) is accentuated by wonderfully perverse upward-turning roof eaves. Springing up from the brick walls like 1950s tail fins, these eaves and the planning of the house seem inspired by an infatuation with the automobile. Both as potent symbol of suburban freedom and as prime generator of the plan, the automobile is crucial to an understanding of Dow's design.

Like the Reed House, the Lyne House (1957, at 3605 Meriburr) uses the automobile as a prime design consideration. This house, designed by Herb Greene after an apprenticeship with Oklahoma architect Bruce Goff, also features a remarkable carport as an introduction to the rest of the house. Terminating a short gravel drive, the carport sweeps like a giant bird wing to form

Paul Hester, 1984.

Lyne House (Herb Greene, 1957).

a huge entrance overhang. The (originally) self-supporting hyperbolic form of the carport then melds into the roof, which covers a triangular floor plan. Like a giant, but lopsided, mushroom the house hovers over the forest floor.

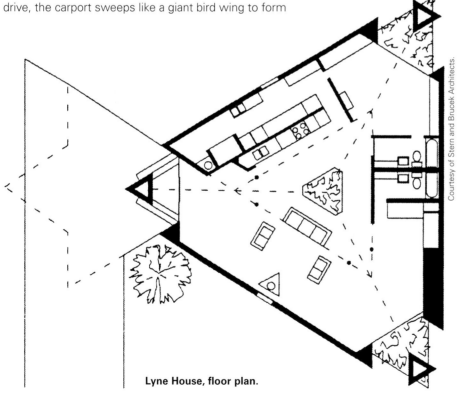

Courtesy of Stern and Brucek Architects.

Lyne House, floor plan.

Durst House (Bruce Goff, 1958).

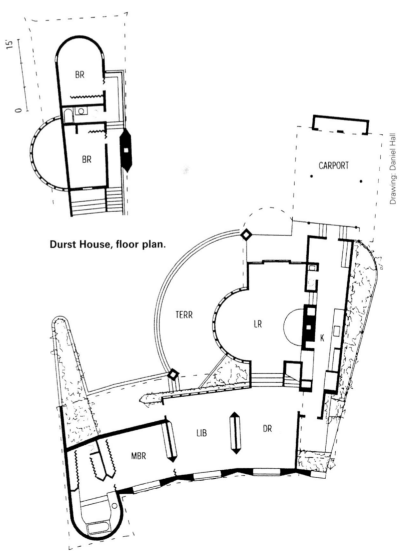

Durst House, floor plan.

Frank Lotz Miller.

One of America's most original architects, Bruce Goff designed one house in Houston, the Durst House (1958, at 323 Tynebrook Lane).[7] Goff, with Herb Greene as supervising architect, generated the design of this house from the round cul-de-sac adjacent to the site. The site-specific plan, landscaping, and articulation of the massing and details constantly refer to this circle. Greeting the viewer from the roundabout are three giant, circular windows popping like eyes out of the brick front façade. This façade's gentle curve has a radius terminating in the center of the cul-de-sac. Segments of circles also appear in plan, in the apses completing the wings of the house, the bay of the living room, and the backyard terrace.

Two stories above the carport of the Durst House a great overhanging roof floats above a strip window; as in Greene's Lyne House, the roof resembles a fragile but protective bird wing. Goff's design is notable for the integration of the plan with the site and is the best example of an organic design process of any house examined to this point.

Durst House, garden terrace.

THE MASTER HIMSELF

While MacKie & Kamrath worked as if they had a mirror to Wright's work, their designs were a shadowed resonance when compared to the master's projects. Wright's Thaxton House (1955, at 12020 Tall Oaks Road) is based on the same diamond grid of equilateral triangles as MacKie & Kamrath's Mitchell House. Unlike the Mitchell House, Wright's design always rigorously conforms to the hexagonal grid. Even beds accommodate the geometry of the house with oblique configurations.

As in any Wright design, a demanding, ritualized use of the house is suggested by the plan. From the street all that appears to the visitor is a low, horizontally banded concrete block wall that is suddenly terminated by a huge pylon of block that conceals the maid's room and marks the entrance path. Supported by this pylon is the carport, under which natural light takes on a mysterious quality. Filtered through a wood screen, the light spills onto a short path that parallels the screen to the front door. From the entrance, the axis of movement continues along an interior glass wall that opens onto an outdoor room designed to serve as both a porch and a pergola. To the other side of the axis, deep within the shadows of the house, is the living room. The axis terminates at the center of the house—the dining room table. From this table the house radiates in different directions to the kitchen, the living area, the bedrooms, and the garden. The table is just a step or two from the kitchen as well as from the garden pool. The family is symbolically gathered at this center even when they are apart. The table becomes the source of familiar sustenance as well as authority. A social hierarchy within the family, as well as an order between man and nature, is suggested by the configuration of the plan.

The Thaxton House is detailed with a module and panelized construction methods that were developed for Wright's earlier Usonian houses. Much of the furniture is built-in, and every joint and square foot of the house is studied. When asked once what his detailing grid was, Wright replied that it was a 16th of an inch. The ruthless level of integration that permeates the detailing of this house reflects his comment.

One particularly beautiful element of the house is the pool, which is set directly against the exterior wall of the master bedroom and bath. This placement allows for a reflection of western light onto the ceilings of the adjacent rooms and permits the owner to wake up in the morning, pass through the master bathroom, and dive directly into the water for a refreshing morning swim.

The use of the organic style in architecture was not limited to domestic architecture in Houston during the 1950s. Corporate office parks, schools, churches, a museum, and eventually even a skyscraper were built. This work constitutes an unseen treasure, ignored in the bustle of expansion. By the mid-1960s taste had moved onward, and today Karl Kamrath is the only remaining link to a rich tradition and ideology that extend back to the attempt to define an American architecture after the Philadelphia Centennial in 1876.

To explain the popularity of the organic style one must recognize what this architecture symbolized for the popular press. In such articles as Elizabeth Gordon's "The Threat to the Next America," a McCarthy-like stance was taken. This argument outlined a battle of the styles and its relations to conflicting national ideologies: Communist, European-influenced Internationalism versus red-blooded, American organicism. Gordon wrote with paranoia: "There is a well-established movement in modern architecture, decorating, and furnishings, which is promoting the mystical idea that 'less is more' . . . They are promoting unlivability, stripped-down emptiness, lack of storage space, and therefore lack of possessions."[8] In an atmosphere of red-baiting, Frank Lloyd Wright and organic-inspired architecture were held up as a fortress of individual self-expression and the fruit of American democracy.

The organic house glorified the particular nature of the American landscape. It projected a reassuring hierarchical image of the American family that provided psychic comfort in times of psychic disintegration. The family, mother, and apple pie were intertwined and protected as surely as the roof provided shelter or the hearth warmth. The organic house was where Americans imagined themselves alone on the frontier, steeped in the Jeffersonian values of mythic American individuality. But, conveniently, the organic house also embraced and celebrated the automobile.

The best organic architecture transcends, however, the passions of the moment and projects a stronger living unity. Deeper emotional concerns than correct fashion direct the mind and eye of the true organic architect. Ultimately, organic architecture was not a style for these designers, but an attitude. For Frank Lloyd Wright it was a struggle to integrate natural law with structure, life with architecture, and the ideal of the organic whole with immortality. He wrote: "After death we experience true freedom. Without that, we would not be true individuals. The sense of continuity is the soul of organic architecture, and it is equally essential to the individual."[9]

Notes

1. Elizabeth Gordon, "The Threat to the Next America," *House Beautiful* 95 (April 1953), 131.
2. Karl Kamrath "Organic Architecture," October 26, 1983, lecture at the University of Houston College of Architecture.
3. For more information on the Mitchell House see Walter McQuade, "Good Living in Houston: At Home beside the Bayou," *Fortune* 74 (July 1966), 110–115.
4. For more information on the Staub houses see Howard Barnstone, *The Architecture of John F. Staub: Houston and the South* (Austin: University of Texas Press, 1979), 272–273, 329.
5. "The $250,000 House," *Fortune* 52 (October 1955), 141.
6. "Googie Architecture," *House and Home* 1 (February 1952), 86–88.
7. For more information on the Durst House see "Goff on Goff," *Progressive Architecture* 43, December 1962, 116. See also "Autobiography in the Continuous Present: An Interview with Bruce Goff," *Cite* 3 (spring 1983), 7.
8. Gordon, "Threat to the Next America," 126.
9. Frank Lloyd Wright, *House and Home* (May 15, 1959), 95.

Cite has revisited the influence of Frank Lloyd Wright on Houston architecture several times: Gerald Moorhead, "Wright Face: The Work of MacKie & Kamrath," *Cite* 21 (fall 1988); Robert Morris, "Do the Wright Thing: The W. L. Thaxton Jr. House," *Cite* 26 (spring 1991); and S. Reagan Miller, "The School of Frank Lloyd Wright," *Cite* 40 (winter 1997–1998).

Howard Barnstone (1923–1987)

Stephen Fox

Henri Cartier-Bresson. Courtesy of Houston Metropolitan Research Center, Houston Public Library.

Howard Barnstone, 1962.

One sometimes has the feeling that at least half of the people who live in Houston got here by accident. The pattern recurs: a chance visit, an unanticipated invitation to remain on what seems to be a short-term basis, and then opportunities arise, connections are made, and without ever quite making the commitment to stay, it becomes "us" and "our" rather than "they" and "their." This was a story that Howard Barnstone, who died on April 29 at the age of 64, loved to tell. It was the summer of 1948. Having completed two years of architectural study at Yale, preceded by two years' service in the U.S. Navy, two years before that at Yale College, and two earlier years at Amherst College, he had come to Houston, the young graduate and registered architect (you could take the Connecticut licensing exam in those days without serving an apprenticeship as long as you had a professional degree), to visit a distant relative. One afternoon this aunt drove him out to the University of Houston so that he might look around the architecture department, begun the year before as a division of the College of Engineering. He met and conversed with one of the faculty members, who concluded their chat by proposing that Barnstone teach at Houston. Barnstone accepted, thinking it might be amusing to spend a couple of years in Texas before he returned to Maine, the state where he was born and where he intended to start a practice. The previous eight years of his life had been divided into two-year segments; two years in Houston would round out the decade.

Barnstone never made it back to Maine. He soon had a host of promising students at the University of Houston — Burdette Keeland, William R. Jenkins, Kenneth Bentsen, Harwood Taylor — and his first job, a small house in Beaumont. During the spring semester of that academic year the American Institute of Architects held its annual convention in Houston. Frank Lloyd Wright came to accept the institute's Gold Medal and to bestow his opinions, the most memorable being his pronouncements on the Shamrock Hotel, which had its fabled opening the week after the AIA convention. It was that spring as well that two other new Houstonians, the French immigrants Dominique Schlumberger and John de Menil, embarked on an architectural project that was to prove pivotal in Barnstone's life: commissioning Philip Johnson, then director of the department of architecture at the Museum of Modern Art, to design their house in Briarwood. Although it may well seem that light years separated the Shamrock Hotel and the Menil House, it was in the space between them that the history of modern Houston was to be made, a history with which Barnstone's life was intertwined.

BARNSTONE AND MIES

Howard Barnstone once remarked that the Menil House was a source of almost obsessive fascination to him and his students during its construction in 1949 and 1950. They would haunt the building site after hours to inspect its progress, drawn there out of reverence for the first built example of modern architecture many of them had ever seen. The north side of the Menil House was all wall, the south side all glass, the roof awesomely flat and edged by that fabulous Miesian fascia, not merely a construction detail but an

Paul Hester, 1987.

Rosenthal House (Bolton & Barnstone, 1954).

icon of modernity. Yet despite its impact, Barnstone initially resisted in his own architecture the influence of Ludwig Mies van der Rohe, whose work was the source of Philip Johnson's inspiration. That first house in Beaumont, the Hartman House (1949), and its successors, the Herbert Blum House in Beaumont (1952), the Bloxsom House in Houston (1952), and even Barnstone's earliest houses with Preston M. Bolton, his partner from 1952 until 1961, the Hardison and Rottersmann houses (1953 and 1954), were "contemporary" rather than "modern" in design, to employ the critical distinction of the period. But Hugo V. Neuhaus Jr.'s recommendation that Mr. and Mrs. de Menil retain Barnstone to correct some problems they were experiencing with air-conditioning ducts and the awesomely flat roof brought Barnstone into irresistible contact with the Johnson house. "I learned more in six months about detailing and water-proofing and, by osmosis, proportions than from four years of graduate studies in architecture at Yale," Barnstone later remarked of the experience.[1] He succumbed to the impact of Mies, hesitantly at first, in his and Bolton's house for his cousin Evelyn Rosenthal (1954) and then unabashedly

Farfel House (Bolton & Barnstone, 1957).

in their Lawrence Blum House in Beaumont (1954), the first of the canonical series of Bolton & Barnstone houses: Gordon (1955), Moustier (1956), Farfel (1957), Hosen (1957), Smithers (1958), Owsley (1961), Cook (1959), Winterbotham (1960), and Challinor (1961).

These houses were conceived as structural cages, with the frames (almost always of steel, although on occasion of wood) expressed externally. They exhibited geometric precision and, in the contrast to their delicately modulated framing members and interstitial wall panels (of brick, or wood weather-board, and glass), a sure sense of proportion. Ostensibly "Miesian," they

Winterbotham House (Bolton & Barnstone, 1960).

betrayed a debt not only to Philip Johnson (most evident in the Farfel, Smithers, and Cook houses) but to Charles Eames's Case Study House in Santa Monica (1949), of which the Gordon House, with its double-volume living and dining room, was an elaborated, more conventionally formal rendition. Colin Rowe's suggestion of a Palladian permutation proved especially appealing to Barnstone, who used the term to characterize the Moustier, Owsley, Winterbotham, and Challinor houses.

Yet identification of influences can be misleading if it causes one to overlook the most startling aspect of Bolton & Barnstone's work: the wide range of their often idiosyncratic adaptation of conventional domestic programs to the requirements of the regular Miesian container. Their internal planning diagrams were exceedingly quirky, possessing none of the measure and clarity of Philip Johnson's domestic plans, although their aim was the same: to create those high, static, limpid volumes that seemed, paradoxically, to expand to infinity, thanks to the hypnotic effect of walls of glass. In Bolton & Barnstone's houses, these spaces were likely to be experienced along with much more compact enclosures, sometimes rather constricted in feeling, but more often intimate, a sensation that Barnstone became adept at producing.

Mark A. Hewitt has written about this episode in Houston's architectural history ("Neoclassicism and Modern Architecture — Houston Style," Cite 7, fall 1984), and more recently it has been acknowledged in critiques of Renzo Piano and Richard Fitzgerald and Partners' Menil Collection museum, most insistently by Reyner Banham, who positioned Houston alongside Chicago and Los Angeles as a place where a distinctive local school of steel-framed modern architecture developed in the 1950s.[2] What is most intriguing about this episode—and especially Barnstone's part in it—is how it differed from the IIT school of Chicago and the Case Study school of Los Angeles. The idea of Baukunst, whether as a theoretically conceived discipline (Chicago) or an ingenious pragmatic (Los Angeles), seems to have been far less compelling in Barnstone's case than the cultivated humanist project of Mr. and Mrs. de Menil, which promoted a "spiritual" (rather than critical materialist) awareness of modernism. Modern art and architecture, by virtue of the nature of their challenge to the provincialism and illiberality of the Houston establishment, acquired a sign status; it was not protest that they registered, but superiority.

The classical precision, rhythmic proportions, and patrician reserve of the Mies-inspired pavilion made it the optimal modernist building type to represent this attitude. Colin Rowe, in 1957, had discerned in such buildings as the Moustier House a significance quite different than that to be deduced from modern architecture of the 1920s: an aristocratic inclination, a fascination with "correct" forms of architectural conduct.[3] Henry-Russell Hitchcock, who, when in 1959 he admired Bolton & Barnstone's "distinctly personal" development of the "now classic model" in their Gordon House, then proceeded to cite the Greek Revival movement as the last episode in architectural history in which "individuality in the handling of a stringent and widely accepted mode of design counted for so much," implicitly acknowledged the invidious distinction being claimed in Houston: authentic confrontation with the conditions of the present and the sanction of history.[4]

The discipline of Mies, even that of the Miesian image, imposed a semblance of consistency on this period, not only in Barnstone's architecture but, as Hewitt discerned, on vanguard architecture in Houston. After 1960 this consistency evaporated. Barnstone wrote of Mies and Wright as "the Academy" and of the inexorability of change: air-conditioning freed architecture from climatic responsibility; the car was the new datum of urban and architectural order.[5]

BARNSTONE AND RUDOLPH

During the 1960s the two trends most readily visible in the work of Howard Barnstone & Partners (as his practice was known from 1961 to 1966, following the dissolution of Bolton & Barnstone) and of Howard Barnstone and Eugene Aubry (his partnership from 1966 to 1969 with Eugene Aubry, a former student who began working for him in 1959) were constructional expression and a neo-vernacular. Both can be seen in the work of the architect who supplanted Mies as the new cultural hero of the architectural vanguard, Paul Rudolph. Less obvious were a concerted exploration of spatial variety and intimacy, and the domestication of the automobile.

The Bolton & Barnstone projects completed by Howard Barnstone & Partners exhibited these tendencies. The Wing House (1962), inspired by Philip Johnson's house for Sylvie Schlumberger Boissonnas (1956), was loosely configured, strung out along a series of passageways defined by load-bearing brick piers and articulated wood joinery. The Hogg Memorial Building at the Child Guidance Center (1961) retained the characteristic boxlike shape and externalized structural frame of the earlier work, but its bays were infilled with arched windows outlined with brick surrounds. The Mermel House (1961) was intriguing in its development of programmatically varied shapes configured around a series of distinct garden spaces and a motor court. There, so many of the qualities that would distinguish Barnstone's subsequent work were present: the combination of privacy and intimacy with spatial expansiveness and extensive glazing, the integration of the car, and carefully proportioned yet discreetly anonymous street elevations.

At Howard Barnstone & Partners' Vassar Place Apartments (1965) these attributes informed the design of a small apartment enclave. Barnstone took full advantage of a strategically located and configured site to create a complex sequence of inwardly focused interior and exterior spaces. Barnstone & Aubry's Levin House in Galveston (1968) and Kempner House (1969) were further extensions of this idea, as were Guinan Hall at the University of St. Thomas (1971) and the adjacent Rothko Chapel (1971), in which intimacy, spatial fulfillment, and discreet anonymity were incorporated into a public building to produce an atmosphere of profound solemnity and silence. The Barnhart Bay House at Kemah (1968) and the Bell House (1968) admitted in their allusion to vernacular house types the possibility of influence by historical models. Abandonment of the

Kempner House (Howard Barnstone & Eugene Aubry, 1969).

Paul Hester, 1987.

Paul Hester, 1987.

Bell House (Howard Barnstone and Eugene Aubry, 1968).

steel frame in house design in favor of wood stud construction (conditioned by economic considerations) made it possible to inflect buildings to their sites and to shape internal volumes, rather than slot them into an armature of structural bays.

BARNSTONE AND THE NEW BRUTALISM

The more evident tendency in the work of the Barnstone office during the 1960s was that of the "New Brutalism," in part because it obtained expression in public buildings rather than houses: Piney Point Elementary School (1964), the Galveston County Publishing Company Building in Galveston (1965), and the Center for the Retarded (1966). These buildings were the opposite of the Miesian houses. Built of reinforced concrete, they emphasized, even exaggerated, particularities of program and construction. Here the big-scaled structural pieces dominated, rather than framed, infilled bays of concrete block (or brick) and glass. Barnstone later was prone to recount — without amusement — the time that Louis I. Kahn (who had begun teaching at Yale when Barnstone was a student) showed up unannounced at his office to give him a critique of the "brutality" of the Center for the Retarded.

Yet despite its aggressive, forbidding aspect from Allen Parkway, onto which it backs, the Center for the Retarded is not bereft of the sense of delight that animates so much of Barnstone's work. The rear of the complex is visible, but the entrance is hidden, requiring one to follow a circuitous.path in order to discover the center. Cars are wended all through the complex, as are pedestrians, in intimate walkways sheltered beneath awesomely scaled concrete pieces.

Howard Barnstone & Partners designed two houses encompassed by the Brutalist tendency. One, for Barnstone's stepmother, Marti Franco, was a concrete-framed, stone-faced tower house, on the beach at Puerto Vallarta, Jalisco. The other, Barnstone's most assured project of the 1960s, was the Maher House

Frank Lotz Miller.

Galveston County Publishing Company Building (Howard Barnstone & Eugene Aubry, 1965).

Paul Hester, 1987.

Center for the Retarded (Howard Barnstone & Eugene Aubry, 1966).

Paul Hester, 1987.

Maher House (Howard Barnstone & Partners, 1964).

(1964) in River Oaks. This was of steel-framed construction, and it was epic. The living and dining rooms were contained in a 55-by-30-foot pavilion, carried one story above grade on brick piers that supported the walls — 18-foot-high steel trusses infilled with glass. Inside, one side was surrounded by space and the other by canopies of trees growing in profusion along Buffalo Bayou. Barnstone simply described the house as a "p-a-l-a-c-e." But rather than Versailles, it was a modern Escorial. For like the Galveston County Publishing Company Building and the Center for the Re-

tarded, the Maher House possessed an almost privational sense of austerity. It was this attribute that imbued it with authentic grandeur. Where Barnstone tempered austerity, it was not with luxury but with wit. Cars lived with the family. They descended ramps beneath the main entrance, drove through the bedrooms, and came to rest underneath the living and dining room pavilion. In the amply dimensioned reception hall, the door to the powder room was discreetly differentiated from other doors by its material and finish: brushed stainless steel.

Two projects exemplified the delight, spontaneity, and anti-pretentious expediency that were characteristic of Barnstone & Aubry's work. One was the design of executive offices on the 44th floor of 277 Park Avenue in New York for Schlumberger Ltd. (1966). The other, one of the partnership's last projects, was the corrugated iron-sheathed Art Barn (subsequently known as the Rice Museum, 1969) for Mr. and Mrs. de Menil on the campus of Rice University. The Schlumberger Ltd. offices were where the Wiggle Wall, as C. Ray Smith called it in *Progressive Architecture*, originated: steel-framed glass partitions circling the core in irregularly angled configurations, generating a sense of spatial buoyancy animated by constantly changing internal vistas, an otherworld cobbled together with the most expedient means to yield "a sensation of magic" — one of Barnstone's favorite expressions.

HISTORIAN AND AUTHOR

It is melodramatic but not inaccurate to say that 1969 was the end of Howard Barnstone's first life. The year before he had been elected to fellowship in the American Institute of Architects. In 1966 his book *The Galveston That Was*, with photographs by Henri Cartier-Bresson and Ezra Stoller, was published by Macmillan, the result of four years' work under the sponsorship of John de Menil and James Johnson Sweeney. But these achievements masked a personal crisis of catastrophic proportions. During 1969 Barnstone underwent intensive electroshock therapy to treat a manic-depressive psychosis — the tragedy of Barnstone's life. It not only brought about the dissolution of his partnership with Aubry, but the breakup of his marriage, and, professionally and financially, near-calamity. A resurgence of this condition in 1985 caused another episode of extreme uncontrolled behavior followed by a year and a half of depression, which Barnstone escaped in the end by taking an overdose of sleeping pills.

In 1970 he was faced with the necessity of starting over again. Electroshock therapy left him dazed, it impaired his memory, and it did not eradicate his manic-depressive condition. Friends supported him with minor commissions — a guesthouse for Mr. and Mrs. de Menil (1970) and a small office building for Albert B. Fay (1970), both rather tentative, nondescript works. In spite of emotional oscillations that did not entirely abate until correct doses of lithium were determined in the late 1970s, Barnstone resisted the crippling effects of internal turmoil and a widely disseminated reputation for craziness to rebuild his practice. In this he was aided by a succession of talented young assistants (among them Anthony E. Frederick, Hossein Oskouie, Jim Powers, Theodore B. Gupton, Roger Dobbins, Edward Rogers, and Rudolph Colby) and professional collaborators (Anthony Disunno, Robert T. Jackson, Doug Michels, and Carlos Jiménez). Barnstone had the ability to design through his associates, to mold and shape by instruction, criticism, and humor (sometimes gentle, other times caustic). But in turn his assistants learned from him, absorbing his inclinations, attitudes, and prejudices to the extent that they carried into their own careers as much of Barnstone as Barnstone had extracted from them during their apprenticeships. This makes the attribution of credit for ideas difficult. What is not ambiguous is the consistent look and feel of Barnstone's buildings, their combination of diminutive scale and spatial expansiveness, of proportional grace with wit and charm, however diverse they appear formally.

The built works of the 1970s were not numerous, but they were varied — in location, program, size, and appearance. Marti's, the specialty store for his stepmother in Nuevo Laredo, Tamaulipas (1972), the three 16-foot-wide Graustark Family Townhouses (1973), alterations and additions to the Herzog House (1974), the Riboud House in Carefree, Arizona (1976), additions to the Robert Barnstone House in Austin (1976), the Encinal condominium apartments in Austin (1979), and the Schlumberger-Doll Research Center in Ridgefield, Connecticut (1980), represented particular responses to existing conditions, developed with ingenuity and tact. Spatial sensation was a common attribute of these buildings, whether it was achieved by complex configurations or the seductive effect of glazed openings. The graying of Do-ville, Barnstone's surreal chromatic unification of the bungalows and apartment houses assembled by Mr. and Mrs. de Menil in the vicinity of the Rothko Chapel (1974), was a telling example of his instinct for making memorable places. He achieved this not by architectural exhibitionism but by sly subtlety, subverting the conventionality of an ordinary 1920s neighborhood with nothing more than a coat of paint, imposing an obvious visual order that paradoxically revealed the wide range of individual variations present.

BARNSTONE AND POSTMODERNISM

Between 1974 and 1979 Barnstone produced another book, *The Architecture of John F Staub: Houston and the South*, on the work of Houston's preeminent eclectic architect. Its publication coincided with Barnstone's decision to declare himself a postmodernist. In arriving at this decision he was influenced by the example of Philip Johnson. It was not the intrinsic merit of Johnson's work that appealed to Barnstone but his conceptual audacity: Johnson ventured new experiments rather than reworking old formulas. Beginning with alterations to the O'Conor House (1981), Barnstone's postmodern series included the Bramlett House (1982), the De Saligny condominium apartments in Austin (1983, with Robert T. Jackson), the Houssiere House (1983), and the opulent, Mediterranean-style Peterkin House (1983). Barnstone's eclectic detail was not especially satisfactory. It tended to be improvised in design, and it was invariably executed in stucco, giving even the most expensive houses a sketchy, makeshift aspect. One had to experience the interiors

to be reassured that Barnstone had not sacrificed his abilities in anxious conformance to fashion. Invariably they were "Pompeiian," his term for the sensuous manipulation of relationships between inside and outside, of light, space, planting, and water: high, white, serenely lit rooms, expanding outward through glass to appropriate the out-of-doors, inducing that haptic sensation, as one moved through them, of what he called the "divine float."

The last buildings Barnstone's office produced indicate that he had begun to pull away from this not-too-successful foray into eclecticism. It was perhaps through contact with younger Houston architects who rejected the allure of postmodern eclecticism that Barnstone reconsidered his own direction. He was intrigued alike by the austere, elemental buildings of Carlos Jiménez and the abstruse, almost mystical complexity of Ben Nicholson's exploratory work. His final building project, the Schlumberger Austin Systems Center in Austin (1987, with Robert T. Jackson), was his homage to Mark Mack and Andrew Batey's Holt House in Corpus Christi. Design development and production of the Austin Systems Center began just before the outbreak of Barnstone's manic episode, which complicated the execution of the design, as is apparent externally. But inside the Schlumberger Wiggle Wall was reintroduced as part of a continuous circuit of indoor and outdoor promenades, counterbalancing in its horizontal and vertical expansiveness the intimacy of individual offices. Both kinds of spaces are contoured to the idiosyncrasies of the site, so that human artifice complements and underscores natural conditions, as it does also with the filtering of skylight into the "Broad Way," Barnstone's name for the internal promenade.

SENSATION OF MAGIC

In the course of his 39-year career Howard Barnstone demonstrated an ability to make spaces that seemed peculiarly receptive to human occupation and buildings

De Saligny Condominiums, Austin (Howard Barnstone and Robert T. Jackson, 1983).

that occupied their sites with authority rather than arrogance. Like many American architects trained in the 1940s, he seemed to conceive of himself as the young rebel, contemptuous of orthodoxy, eager to demonstrate the superiority of personal vision to conventional wisdom. He rebelled against the orthodoxy of his youth by engaging the scandalous proposition that architecture came and went in styles. His work seemed to do this. But not at the expense of continuity and an internal coherence rooted in the experience of occupying architecture.

Contempt for common sense and received opinion compelled Barnstone to operate at a level of extreme subjectivity. He cultivated an insightful sense of space, light, and proportion, an instinctive feel for place that he could reproduce in buildings. He almost never spoke directly about these abilities, preferring to discuss his work in terms of style, personalities, or social

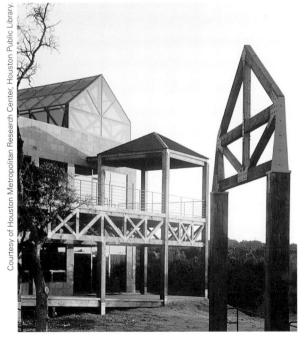

Schlumberger Austin Systems Center (Howard Barnstone and Robert T. Jackson, 1987).

circumstances. "The magic and success of architecture in our time will come from the genius of the architect," a statement made to Nory Miller in an interview published in 1977, was about as close as he came to articulating what, in his experience, was essential for making great buildings.[6] In trusting his own genius, Barnstone defined a personal sensibility (what John Kaliski aptly called his "nutty magic") that was sufficiently profound and intense to involve all who were around him.

Houston without Howard Barnstone seems as inconceivable as Houston without the Shamrock Hotel. Each embodied a provocation too outrageous simply to cease to exist. Yet such a state of affairs has come to pass. It is odd how vulnerable a large city can seem to the death of a single person. Yet Houston, especially Houston architecture, is diminished without Howard Barnstone. He takes from it a spirit of free inquiry, of courageous individuality, and of mischievous delight that were always too rare. He leaves in his place a body of work that perpetuates his vision of how life ought to be lived, a vision that these buildings will enable us to share as long as they remain.

Notes

1. Howard Barnstone, "Obit: John de Menil," *Architecture Plus* 1 (August 1973), 71.

2. Reyner Banham, "In the Neighborhood of Art," *Art in America* 75 (June 1987), 126.

3. Colin Rowe, "Neo-'Classicism' and Modern Architecture I," in *The Mathematics of the Ideal Villa and Other Essays* (Cambridge: MIT Press, 1976), 120–134.

4. Henry-Russell Hitchcock, introduction to exhibition catalogue, *Ten Years of Houston Architecture* (Houston: Contemporary Arts Museum, 1959).

5. Esther McCoy, "Young Architects in the United States: 1963," *Zodiac* 13 (1964), 167, 186.

6. Nory Miller, "Lone Stars — Howard Barnstone and Karl Kamrath," *Inland Architect* 21 (July 1977), 16.

Cite 9
SPRING
1985

Recent Housing in Houston

A ROMANTIC URBANISM

Peter D. Waldman

There are differences between conventions of style and conventions of urbanity. Recent housing projects in Houston give ample evidence of this concern for image over understanding the potentials of building type. Housing is not a collection of individual house types. Rather, it is the stuff of cities. This fabric permits urban decorum to exist. Housing has a long history as the systematic, not romantic, resolution of tight dimensions and high densities. In London, one dwells in a terrace house fronting a square. In Paris, one dwells in an apartment facing a boulevard. In Rome, even the pope dwells in the *poché* between institution and urban garden.

HOUSE TOWN

It is rumored that until recently Houston was "House Town," where, with rare exception, one moved out of the brilliant sun and into one of a dozen or so imported house types.

Paul Hester, 1985.

Isabella Court, interior courtyard (W. D. Bordeaux, 1928).

Gerald Moorhead, 1990.

Graustark Family Townhouses (Howard Barnstone, 1973).

Three notable exceptions are Isabella Court (W. D. Bordeaux, architect, 1928), Graustark Family Townhouses (Howard Barnstone, 1973), and Lovett Square (William T. Cannady and Associates, 1978). Isabella Court is an apartment block organized around an interior court with an elaborate promenade that encourages social interaction. Though the architecture is Miami-Moorish in style, ultimately issues of style are transcended by a real understanding of the court-block type. The ground-level commercial activity reinforces the vitality of the street, while private functions are clearly zoned to upper floors. At Isabella Court the difficulty in recognizing when one unit ends and another begins is an aspect of anonymity crucial to the success of good housing.

In the early 1970s, the Graustark Family Townhouses established the premier model for small infill projects in Houston. They are sophisticated and rigorous solutions to a dimensionally constrained problem. In this case the realm of the automobile (i.e., the garage) and the architectural promenade (i.e., the entrance) are distinct but mutually reinforcing. The restrained linear progression in plan is played against a skillful generosity in section. Issues of style do not enter into these restrained spaces between two-party walls.

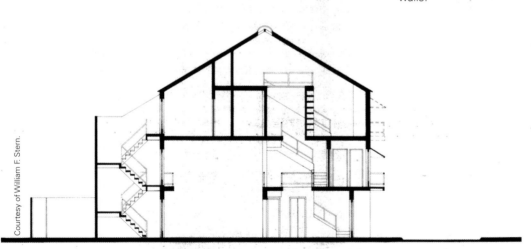

Courtesy of William F. Stern.

Graustark Family Townhouses section.

Rick Gardner, 1985.

Lovett Square (William T. Cannady & Associates, 1978).

The third precedent, Lovett Square, is the best model in Houston for an aggregation of townhouse units in a block configuration. Raised above a parking platform, the townhouses look inward to a private streetscape that consists of a subtle sequence in pedestrian circulation spaces from the sidewalk to the front door. Roof terraces reinforce a three-dimensional development of increasingly private zones while taking advantage of the rich, reflective lighting possibilities of the Houston sun. Lovett Square establishes its vitality not from the exploration of image through style but through the conscious development of a communal space through the inventive use of systematically resolved units. There is a modesty to all these precedents, which recommends them as examples for potential development of an urban fabric in Houston.

In contrast to these examples, the endless apartment complexes and townhouse blocks that compose much of the recent growth within and outside Loop 610 are conceived as big houses, not housing, monumentalized by mansard roofs, colonnades, statuary, and endless fountain views. The result of recent residential development at several scales seems to establish an imaginary, stylistic city. Simultaneously neo-Georgian or neo-Colonial, often country French, with an occasional Cape Cod of note amidst ranchburgers and bungalows galore, a potpourri of Northern house types characterizes Houston houses, which have rarely been missionary and certainly not visionary.

Houston does not have a strong tradition of housing. Consequently, it lacks the kind of indigenous housing stock evident in the row houses of Baltimore and Philadelphia, the brownstones of New York, or the triple-deckers of industrial New England. The shotgun house at a certain scale does provide the city with a model of housing conventions giving dignity, for example, to the Fourth Ward. In addition, San Felipe Courts—antithetically renamed, in suburban lingo,

Allen Parkway Village — is another model for the spatial conventions of in-between space, making the precinct potentially one of the most urban residential districts in town.

What is it then about convention and repetition, housing and urbanity, that distinguishes Houston from other cities in the South and the West? Charleston, Savannah, New Orleans, Cincinnati, St. Louis, and San Francisco have whole districts composed of elegantly repetitive, anonymous housing stock. They have developed conventional responses to aggregation to one another, to the street, and to the district. The most striking characteristic of housing in these cities is the modesty of individual intervention.

These units typically do not draw attention to themselves but add to the coherence of the street and the block. The crucial question, however, is the relevance of these conventions. What do 18th- and 19th-century urban conventions have to tell us about dwelling in Houston, the city of today if not tomorrow?

Ultimately, the difference between "house" and "housing" centers on issues of density and convention. A house is spatially and socially isolated; the boundaries of a house and its garden are identifiable, and the character of both shelter and precinct is individual. Housing is literally attached, serial, and often overlapping, and its character is generic. Housing does not emphasize the inventions of style or scale, but rather values the conventions of modesty and social decorum.

Urban housing traditionally has provided both a porch for commission and a garden for refuge. Yet in Houston, the garden takes the form of the sheltering shade of endless live oak trees. Here, porches are transposed (i.e., change location but not form) in townhouses from the street level to the *piano nobile* or to the rear overlooking a mandatory room-size pool. Though necessitated by the pragmatic issue of parking automobiles at ground level, this kind of inversion of convention is one of either a witty sophistication or a misunderstanding of social conventions within urban settings.

The live oaks establish an urban porch, the civic loggia, as seen along Main Street between Rice University and the Museum of Fine Arts, Houston along North and South Boulevards, and along Sunset, rivaling the incessant brownstone stoops of New York, the marble thresholds of Georgian London, and the consecutive façades, courts, and gardens of 17th-century French hotels.

Along with the expansion of the city through the 1970s came a corresponding increase in density in inner-city neighborhoods. Within the Loop, particularly around the cultural institutions of the city, a number of townhouses recently have been constructed and a consistent pattern unique to Houston has emerged. What is marketed, however, is house, not housing. Avoiding the opportunities of seriality by developing small infill projects, each of which has stylistic rather than strategic identification, these projects forfeit the fabric of the city for the flavor of style. Little is thus achieved except stimulating an even more diminished vision of urban life than that of the Arts and Crafts bungalow, which has been given renewed life at great cost in Houston. Small, ever-so-witty dollhouse townhouses perched on parking plinths are the new urban convention of these romantic urbanists. Fortunately, these projects are scattered through an established neighborhood whose live oaks mask their presence. What one increasingly sees is one opaque garage door after another where neglected bungalow porches once served important functions.

NEW VISIONS

Curiously, much of this romantic urbanism is the work of young architects who would have been, in previous generations, critical of stylistic superficiality. However, three extreme positions deserve closer investigation.

These sensibilities are represented by the recent Houston work of three firms: Arquitectonica, Makeover-Levy Associates, and William F. Stern & Associates.

The Stern position is that of the romantic pragmatist. In this firm, architecture is conceived from the inside out. The Arquitectonica position is that of the romantic polemicist. Their work is conceived from the outside in. The Makeover-Levy position is not romantic; rather it is modest in terms of image and programmatically innovative. As such, its stand becomes the most provocative in the field of housing in Houston at this moment.

Early works of Stern — the Colquitt, Albans, Vassar, and Wroxton townhouses — exhibit a commitment to the romanticism of House Town, the imaginary city described earlier. While spatially quite generous and inventive in the interior, their exterior configurations, orientations, and appearances range dramatically from contemporary barn structures to cool visions of the International style, from neo-Palladian porches to the robustness of Richardsonian Romanesque. Somehow all of the above sit with equal composure above the articulated plinths of parking garages. The innovative significance of these early projects lies in their sections. Major living areas are on the *piano nobile*, secondary bedrooms below, and studio lofts above. These "Great Rooms" effectively stretch very modest houses in terms of square footage into very grand refuges indeed. These early works are diminished only by a qualitative meanness in arrival from ground to grand hall and by that superficial picturesqueness of exterior expression that marks much of the residential construction in Houston.

The early works of Arquitectonica in Houston presents the opposite idea. Their first townhouse project, located on Haddon at McDuffie, consists of 10 units facing the same street and spanning two blocks. It achieves a sense of continuity and urban decorum rare in Houston. Yet unlike the early Stern projects, these

Paul Hester, 1985.

**Vassar Townhouses, interior
(William F. Stern & Associates, 1983).**

units find their conceptual strength externally in deliberately ambiguous façades that stretch in their blatant whiteness across two blocks. The firm's Miami origins serve them well, heightening their sensitivity to sun and color. They know how to master shadow as well as reflection and make places in their façades for dwelling in the limbo between house and community. Their projects are certainly not of two-dimensional significance. However, in the Haddon project the interiors are configured so tightly that the tragedy of the dollhouse is

Haddon Townhouses (Arquitectonica, 1983).

Mandell Townhouses (Arquitectonica, 1985).

achieved internally in their work while an urban expansiveness is reserved for the exteriors.

Later projects, in particular four units on Mandell, exhibit a reversed sensibility. Here a wall of idiosyncratic invention, not systematic repetition, engages the street. All commitment to the idea of seriality breaks down, and the exception becomes the rule. On the other hand, the undesigned rear elevation exhibits the systematic fenestration that the values of the idiosyncratic front deny. The façades are romantic, not in nostalgia for the past as is true of most of Houston's romantic architects, but rather in their willful, skillful composition. The dimensional width of the units is exceptionally generous, giving breathing room for some of the arbitrary spatial gymnastics.

Finally, Arlington Court by Stern and Hyde Park Village by Makeover-Levy deserve attention. Both projects involve half-block aggregations of 18 residential units. Their urban conventions and programmatic postures present crucial issues that must be debated.

Arlington Court, at the corner of Arlington and East 14th Street in Houston Heights, makes a strong contribution to Houston's urbanity in the spirit of Lovett Square. Arlington Court is more than the sum of its 18 parts. More like the linear configuration of a streetscape or a mews than a court, it establishes an architectural promenade from gatehouse to pavilion. A streetscape is achieved by the syncopated undulation of four unit types. This streetscape is framed by two tower units, which successfully define the precinct but allude to a full-block solution applied to a half-block site. As a consequence, a diminished urban scale is applied to this mini-block. As with other romantic urban work, an open-ended modesty, a block waiting for com-

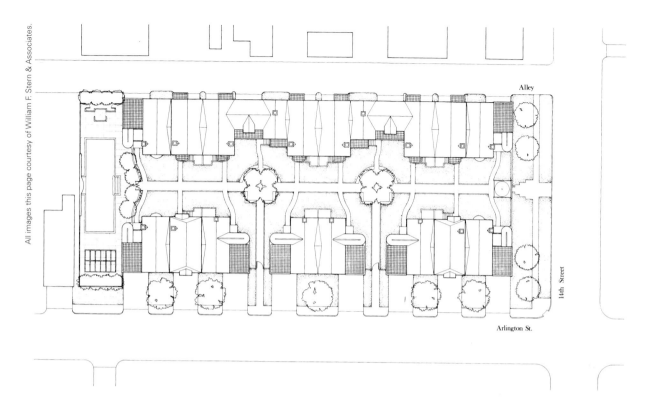

Alley

14th Street

Arlington St.

Arlington Court, site plan and models (William F. Stern & Associates, 1985).

  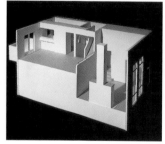 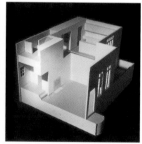

pletion, is not yet evident in this internally resolved project from "dollhouse" to "miniature block." The tendency seems to diminish the scale of the city into suburban isolation rather than urban intensification. The streetscape at Arlington Court is hierarchical and relaxed, axial as well as picturesque. The units themselves reveal these kinds of strategic polarities. The plan appears axially symmetric, but large stair halls pull out of the sheltering volume and establish side vestibules in a most

civilized and relaxed manner. The massing is romantic: part Norman keep, part 19th-century Glasgow. There is a dominant Northern flavor to these massive volumes. No longer mere signs of stylistic pastiche, their taut skins and precise voids apologetically coexist on the same surface or bulge out to capture light.

From their appearance one would hardly know that the sun shines brilliantly in Houston, that deep shadows are as welcome as protective walls. A critical eval-

Paul Hester, 1985.

Arlington Court.

uation of Arlington Court must deal with several para-
doxes in this important project. It is deliberately rational in its hierarchic plan, but it is also deliberately romantic in its vertical appearance. The rational is
combined with the picturesque so systematically that
the picturesque stair towers that work so well on the
14th Street elevators become devalued by repetition at
every entry condition. Exceptions to the rule of convention must be selective. Finally, the number of unit
types seems to belie the opportunity for seriality
achieved so well in Lovett Square, where the space between units modulates although the units remain constant. What is important about this latest project by
William F. Stern & Associates is its ability to achieve

this level of coherence and order in a part of the city so
ripe for rational development. Together with the more
maturely developed Lovett Square, this project provides the basis for debate between the romantic urbanists of Houston in the 1980s and the rational urbanists of the International style.

Projected for a revitalized Montrose Boulevard,
with a misleading and conjunctive name, Hyde Park Village by Makeover-Levy Associates is a radical departure
from recent housing in Houston. Yet this intervention
is radical because it demonstrates a common sense unusual for Houston. The project is visionary because the
architects understand cities and are not afraid of them.
The scheme, which is to commence construction

shortly, sets an urban precedent for Houston, combining housing units with commercial development. The lower levels contain retail lofts with mezzanines on the street fronts and double-garage levels in back. The third-floor plaza establishes the entry level for duplex units that have separate roof gardens. The image of this project is sober, repetitive, systematic—all those fine words that have helped to establish livable cities and sensible dwellings in the past. Housing for profit is built differently from a single-family house when the serial scale of structural

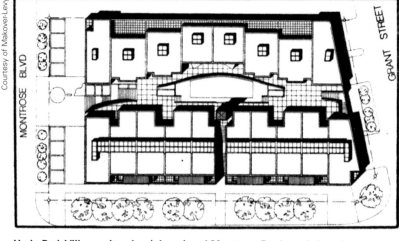

Hyde Park Village, site plan (above) and Montrose Boulevard elevation (below) (Makover-Levy Associates, 1985).

bays establishes the dominant organizational pattern. Hyde Park has only two basic unit types. Repetition is the rule, establishing a dominant core; only the corner units are modified to respond to the pressures of the site. The streetside units are aggregated differently than the inner-block units, and the resultant space is not picturesque for its own sake. Shadows will be cast, and façades will reflect light with sensitivity to its Southwestern context so rare among romantic urbanists. Neither imported nor abstracted, Hyde Park proj-

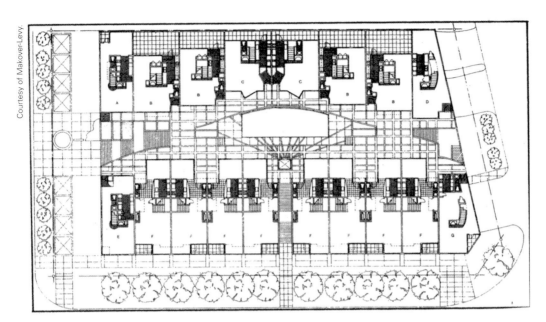

Hyde Park Village, third-floor plan.

ects the vital ambiguity seen in Isabella Court: one cannot tell where one unit ends and another begins. There are giant orders and intimate places, neither recall nor affectation. Urban housing in this new Houston prototype is not about dwelling in isolation, not about the myth of suburbia. Rather, one lives above a store in a community of neighbors and underneath a canopy of paradise constructed by one's own labor.

Ultimately, the landscape treated as human refuge is not recalled from the past but is a promise of Houston's future: on the roof in the light of day. The Garden City has a new vision of paradise now raised a bit closer to tomorrow.

An architecture of convention is the program of recent housing in Houston. The degree to which a commitment is made to dwelling in this city, without the nostalgia for imaginary ones, will determine its vitality as well as our own self-respect. Those who build the gleaming reflections of tomorrow in the Galleria and Greenway Plaza have provided places of work and play for a city without nostalgia or guilt. It is curious that those who built the dwelling places for the same citizens of this Radiant City do not have the same vision and modesty to project the same faith in the future. The fabric is beginning to be woven; but before young architects get too excited about leaving their mark on this city, they should modestly look back to Isabella Court, the Graustark Family Townhouses, and Lovett Square to measure the immense strength of quiet maturity.

2002 UPDATE

In *Cite* 49 (fall 2000) a group of articles including "The Houston Townhouse: Architects versus the Market" by Stephen Fox and "Building the Better Townhouse: Thoughts on an Urban Style" by Danny Samuels addressed the explosion of housing development in those same inner-city neighborhoods Waldman had written about 15 years earlier. Clearly, the historic vision of urban place-making, hinted at in the 1980s, had been overwhelmed by the economic realities of unregulated development in the 1990s. *Editors*

Other *Cite* articles on housing include: John Kaliski, "Diagrams of Ritual and Experience: Learning from the Park Regency," *Cite* 3 (spring 1983); Mark A. Hewitt, "The Stuff of Dreams: New Housing outside the Loop," *Cite* 10 (summer 1985); Jan O'Brien, "Wuppie Housing: New Housing in West University Place," *Cite* 16 (winter 1986); William F. Stern, "The Lure of the Bungalow," *Cite* 16 (winter 1986); Mark Wamble, "Five Houses: Domesticity and the Contingent City," *Cite* 29 (fall 1992/winter 1993); Drexel Turner, "Powers of Tin," *Cite* 31 (winter/spring 1994); Joel Warren Barna, "Glendower Court and Melanie Court: How Many Houses Does It Take to Make a Neighborhood?" *Cite* 33 (fall 1995/winter 1996); Curtis Lang, "A Depleted Legacy: Public Housing in Houston," *Cite* 33 (fall 1995/winter 1996); Keith Neu and Drexel Turner, "Houston's Drive-in Apartments," *Cite* 38 (summer 1997); Stephen Fox, "Modern Home Craft: The Houses of Katherine B. and Harry L. Mott," *Cite* 42 (summer/fall 1998); Nonya Grenader and Stephen Fox, "Rooms with a View: In Praise of the Vanishing Garden Apartment," *Cite* 45 (summer 1999); Stephen Fox, "Home/Work," *Cite* 53 (spring 2002); Margaret Culbertson, "Some Assembly Required," *Cite* 54 (summer 2002); Nonya Grenader, "The (small) House," *Cite* 54 (summer 2002); Keith Krumwiede, "Super Model Homes," *Cite* 54 (summer 2002); Danny Marc Samuels, "Three Bedrooms, $86K, Really," *Cite* 54 (summer 2002).

Cite 45
SUMMER
1999

Framing the New

MIES VAN DER ROHE
AND HOUSTON ARCHITECTURE

Stephen Fox

The Houston architecture of Mies van der Rohe and those whom he influenced represents an attitude toward building that now seems immeasurably distant. But in the 1950s, Mies's integration of construction, architecture, and the poetics of spatial experience proved so compelling that a generation of young Houston architects committed itself to his discipline. In a way that is not stylistically explicit, their architecture resonates with Houston history, suggesting narratives that involve such significant personages as Mies, Philip Johnson, and Dominique and John de Menil; the divergent preoccupations and motivations of Houston's Miesian architects and their clients; and competition among local modernists for cultural hegemony. When compared to Chicago or Los Angeles, where, as the British architectural historian and critic Reyner Banham noted, Miesian architecture also exerted special influence, what distinguishes Houston's "school" of Miesian architecture is this exploration of the place of history in modern life.[1]

THE PROPHETS:
JOHN AND DOMINIQUE DE MENIL

It was John de Menil and his wife, Dominique Schlumberger, who brought Miesian architecture to Houston, although they did not bring Mies himself. During World War II, Mr. and Mrs. de Menil became acquainted in

Photo: Maurice Miller and Caroline Valenta of the *Houston Post*, courtesy of Menil Archives, The Menil Collection.

Dominique de Menil and Philip Johnson, November 1949.

New York with the French Dominican priest Marie-Alain Couturier. Father Couturier introduced them to their vocation as collectors, and through him they met modern artists. One was the sculptor Mary Callery. When asked to recommend an architect to design a house in Houston for the Menils' expanding family, Callery suggested her friend Ludwig Mies van der Rohe. James Johnson Sweeney later implied that the Menils found this suggestion a bit intimidating. Callery's second recommendation was another close friend, Philip Johnson, whose Glass House in New Canaan was then under construction. The Menils took this suggestion to heart, and in the spring of 1949 they commissioned Johnson to design their Houston house.[2]

By the standards of Houston in 1950, the Menil House was without precedent.[3] The discipline of Johnson's mentor, Mies, was reflected in the house's slab-sided composition, flat roof, elongated fascia, and glass walls. The house's carefully studied proportions, apparent in the expansive, lofty feel of its interior spaces, were similarly Miesian. Johnson incorporated an internal courtyard, which Mrs. de Menil filled with lush tropical vegetation. James Johnson Sweeney later ascribed this to her "nostalgia," as he called it, for

Hester + Hardaway, 1999.

Menil House (Philip Johnson, 1950).

Menil House, floor plan.

a house in Caracas in which the Menils had lived briefly in the 1940s. As one passed through the opaque exterior plane into the house's transparent interior, the courtyard afforded a surreal contrast. This contrast induced an intense sensual and emotional reaction that the house's reticent wall planes and flat roof did not forecast.

The Menil House lacks the exquisite clarity of Johnson's Glass House and other Miesian houses Johnson designed in the late 1940s and early 1950s. The floor plan suggests Johnson's struggle to organize the varied spaces required by a family with five children into a one-story configuration. Remarking its "modernity" in terms of American domesticity of the 1950s, the house dispensed with a formal dining room in favor of a "play room." A three-car "carport" was incorporated in the body of the house. Perhaps for reasons of economy, the structural design of the house was not as rigorous as in Johnson's publicized early houses. The Menil House is of brick cavity wall construction. Steel beams are used to span major spaces, but the joists, decking, and fascia are wood.

Nonetheless, the architectural detailing of the house is tectonic. In major rooms, a panelized division of the wall surface was applied, particularly to the detailing of doorways. Panelization implied that the design was based on a modular planning grid, rationally and economically regulating all aspects of construction, as Mies customarily did with his buildings. At the Menil House, where no planning module is evident, this practice seems to have been followed for aesthetic reasons. Crisp, right-angled millwork makes door frames, especially those with inset transom panels, stand out, imbuing wall surfaces with a plasticity not apparent in photographs, as moldings would do in a classically detailed interior.

Compensating for the house's awkwardness in plan are its spatial serenity and amplitude. Johnson achieved these attributes with a 10-foot-6-inch ceiling height that prevails throughout the house and with the big scale of glazed openings (the wood-framed sliding glass door in the living room is 10 feet 1 inch wide). Johnson also opened vistas through the house that underscore his quest for "freedom and order," the subject of a polemic he published with Peter Blake in 1948.[4]

For Johnson, freedom and order were embodied in

the modern architecture of Mies van der Rohe. Johnson adopted and adapted the architecture that Mies invented with great skill. In doing so, he was bound to observe certain limits beyond which his architecture would cease to be Miesian. Johnson demonstrated the way in which young American modernists—without, perhaps, quite understanding what they were doing—formularized the visions of the masters of modern architecture into competing stylistic alternatives. Dominique and John de Menil, in their persistent curiosity and disinclination to subscribe to one formula or another, implicitly challenged this reductive approach. They seem to have been attracted to Mies's architecture because it provided spaces that were clearly defined yet liberating, authoritative yet uninsistent. For them, such architecture represented a beginning rather than an end.

HOUSTON'S OWN: HUGO NEUHAUS, HOWARD BARNSTONE, BURDETTE KEELAND

In Houston, the Menil House was unquestionably a beginning. The "School of Mies" that developed in the city by the mid-1950s stemmed from Philip Johnson and his work for the Menils. Hugo V. Neuhaus Jr., a young Houston architect who had been a classmate of Johnson's at the Harvard Graduate School of Design in the early 1940s, supervised construction of the Menil House. The impact of Johnson's Miesian modernism on Neuhaus was immediate. The house Neuhaus designed for his family in the Homewoods section of River Oaks, completed in 1950, was his refined and perfected version of the Menil House: a garden pavilion of serene, glass-walled spaces carefully adjusted to its site and made to seem luxurious because of Neuhaus's orchestration of views, day lighting, and proportion.[5]

In such details as the lattice screening of the pool house, Neuhaus made nostalgic connections to the kind of traditional screening devices he would have known from the Houston houses of his childhood. Rather than dismissing such connections, as modernists impatient with the past were inclined to do, Neuhaus made modern architecture that engaged the past. Unlike the Menil House, which was not published in the national press until 1963, the Neuhaus House secured national recognition through publication almost immediately.

Neuhaus continued to draw on the past in the small, courtyard-centered house he designed for Nina J. Cullinan in the Tall Timbers section of River Oaks in 1953. There, Neuhaus finished the exterior walls with pale pink stucco, the same material and color that Birdsall Briscoe and John Staub had used on their River Oaks houses of the 1920s. With exquisite delicacy, Neuhaus used the most rigorous of modern architectural alternatives to evoke personal memories and resonances. The proposition that Neuhaus ventured with the Cullinan house—that modernism could engage history dialectically—expanded upon the eclectic scheme of furnishing pursued by the Menils, who had

Paul Hester, 1981.

Cullinan House (Cowell & Neuhaus, 1953).

Cullinan House, internal courtyard.

Gordon House, interior (Bolton & Barnstone, 1955).

filled their house with a mixture of European antiques and upholstered pieces designed not by Johnson or another modernist, but by the flamboyant couturier Charles James. The resulting combination of shapes and textures was unusual in the context of postwar American modernism, which tended toward all-modern furnishings for modern houses.

It was through association with Neuhaus's modern yet subtly nuanced houses as much as with the Menil House that Miesian architecture acquired the identity it would assume in Houston in the 1950s as the patrician style of modernism. This class-specific terminology is not how Neuhaus or the Menils would have described such architecture. Yet it is how the architect Howard Barnstone, at least in retrospect, characterized it. Barnstone and his partner Preston M. Bolton became the most publicized young architects in Houston during the 1950s on the basis of their flat-roofed, slab-sided, glass-walled houses in the Mies-Johnson style. Their first important house, the Gerald S. Gordon House in Braeswood of 1955, was steel-framed with interiors by the Knoll Planning Unit and landscaping by the San Francisco landscape architect Thomas D. Church. Barn-

stone, however, maintained that the Gordon House was as Eamesian as it was Miesian. Analysis reveals the extent to which Barnstone Miesianized the Eames Case Study House in his spatial organization of the Gordon House. The Gordon House formalized and stabilized the Eames's whimsy, positioning Miesian architecture in Houston as a defender of standards and forms, albeit modern forms.

As an architecture instructor at the University of Houston, Barnstone exercised persuasive influence on his students, several of whom had become colleagues by the mid-1950s. Burdette Keeland, an early UH alumnus, produced his first steel-framed Miesian buildings at the same time Bolton & Barnstone did. What is intriguing about Keeland's architectural career is the extent to which his tectonically and spatially rigorous buildings were integrated into the mainstream building economy of 1950s Houston.

Keeland collaborated with Harwood Taylor on the photographic studio and apartments built for Fred Winchell on Richmond Avenue in 1954. The site was a former residential lot on what had become a busy street. Keeland and Taylor used steel frame construction to create a pair of cages—one two stories high, the other a pavilion—separated by a gridded garden designed by the landscape architects Bishop & Walker. What seems so remarkable about the photographic studio, which for 30 years was the interior designer Sally Walsh's house, is its generosity of scale and sense of calm. Keeland manipulated planar walls, big openings, controlled views, and the admission of natu-ral light to compose an unusually serene space within the armature of the structural frame.

For the Houston Home Builders Association's 1955 Parade of Homes in the subdivision of Meyerland, Kee-land designed a steel-framed Miesian courtyard house for the builder Buck King. The Parade of Homes House was Houston's nearest equivalent to the steel-framed houses that the Eameses, Pierre Koenig, and Craig Ell-wood built in Los Angeles as part of *Arts and Architec-ture* magazine's Case Study program. Keeland con-densed the courtyard plan into a compact, but not confining, interior organization. The complete exposure of the house's steel-frame structure and insulated panel roof deck, and its use of hard red paving brick (associated more with Caudill Rowlett Scott rather than Philip Johnson), gave it a tectonic character that was rigorous yet appropriate to a domestic setting. The tec-tonic detailing of the house was so refined—the dry-wall panels appear to be set in individual frames—that the exposure of construction is not abrasive. The inte-gration of the courtyard into patterns of use meant that it functioned as the center of the house rather than as a sealed landscape installation viewed from within.

Parade of Homes House (Burdette Keeland, 1955).

Paul Winchell.

Parade of Homes House, floor plan.

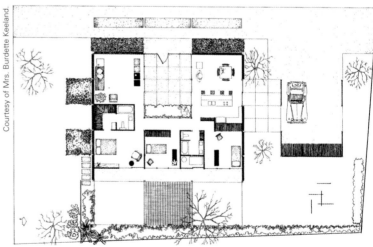

Courtesy of Mrs. Burdette Keeland.

Keeland's Spring Branch Savings and Loan Association Building of 1956, designed with Clyde Jackson, brought the authority of Miesian architecture to the Long Point Road suburban strip. Through Keeland's buildings, Miesian architecture began to address the suburbanizing city as well as Houston's elite residential suburbs. By the end of the 1950s, the influence of Mies was visible at the City of Houston's Garden Villas Park Recreation Center of 1959 by William R. Jenkins, a UH alumnus; the South Park National Bank complex of 1960 on Martin Luther King by Kenneth Bentsen, also a UH alumnus; and the Willowbend Medical Clinic of 1961 by Wilson, Morris, Crain & Anderson.

UNIVERSITY OF ST. THOMAS

The prestige of Miesian architecture in Houston was confirmed by two important projects. The first came in 1956, when Mr. and Mrs. de Menil prevailed upon Houston's newest college, the University of St. Thomas, a small Roman Catholic liberal arts school, to retain Philip Johnson to prepare a master plan for its new campus on a three-block site in Montrose. It was typical of John de Menil's largesse and enthusiasm that he proposed to pay Philip Johnson's fees for the master plan and the design of the first building to be built. John de Menil assured the university's somewhat apprehensive trustees that Johnson worked fast, could build cheaply, and was not dogmatic. He also emphasized an argument advanced by Father Couturier: the Catholic Church had once called on the greatest architects and artists to carry out its building programs, and it must continue to do so in the 20th century. That meant embracing modernism, because the greatest artists and architects of the 20th century were modernists.[6]

When the University of St. Thomas's first two buildings, Strake Hall and Jones Hall, were published in the American architectural press in 1959, they seemed to confirm Johnson's role as Mies's primary

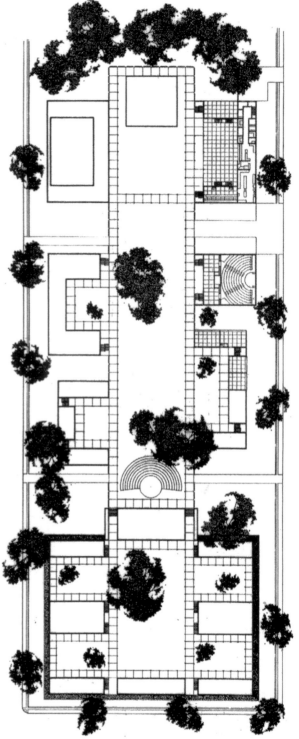

Master Plan, University of St. Thomas (Philip Johnson, 1957).

structural frame, Ford and his collaborators emphasized the horizontally aligned concrete floor and roof slabs, recessing the structural columns so that the buildings appeared to float above their site. The double-level system of walkways used in the dormitory group at Trinity was made independent of the buildings, so that the walkways, too, appeared floating rather than grounded as at St. Thomas.

Strake Hall and Jones Hall, University of St. Thomas (Philip Johnson Associates with Bolton & Barnstone, 1958).

American interpreter, although Johnson himself drew attention to an unexpected historical reference implicit in the master plan: Thomas Jefferson's master plan for the University of Virginia of 1817, where walkways connect a series of pavilions lining a central lawn. Johnson described the walkways as analogous to a monastic cloister enframing a space of community. "Formal" was the word that Johnson chose to characterize this space, a word that in the 1950s was most often used in modernist discourse as a term of opprobrium.[7]

Johnson's descriptive terminology encoded layers of reaction to the modern architectural scene of the late 1950s in the United States. Comparing his master plan to the most famous university campus plan carried out in Texas in the 1950s — at Trinity University in San Antonio — clarifies Johnson's polemical use of "formal." Trinity, designed by O'Neil Ford of San Antonio with the planner Sam B. Zisman and the San Francisco modernist William W. Wurster, was anti-formalist. Its buildings were organized with respect to its sloping site rather than to enframe space. As at St. Thomas, the architecture of Trinity's buildings was constituted by their construction. But instead of emphasizing the

Jones Hall, interior.

At St. Thomas, Johnson employed Mies's architectural approach as an urbanizing architecture. He used it to shape a sequence of clearly demarcated outdoor spaces and to sympathetically relate a new institutional complex to its setting, a neighborhood of substantial 1910-era houses set on landscaped lots. Following Mies's example, Johnson emphasized the integration of structure into architecture, in contrast to Ford's deliberate exposure at Trinity of the process of construction.[8]

In stylistically undemonstrative ways, Johnson explored at the University of St. Thomas the problematic relation of history and modernity. Dominique and John de Menil also pursued this exploration when, in 1959, they arranged for Jermayne MacAgy to become head of St. Thomas's art department. In the second-floor gallery of Jones Hall, as well as in occasional installations in the double-volume space of Johnson's third campus building, Welder Hall (now floored over), MacAgy repeatedly challenged the stability of categorical definitions and conventional expectations in order to entice Houstonians to engage works of art. In the context of such exploration, the virtue of Johnson's Miesian architecture was its autonomy. It achieved its fulfillment in framing human activities rather than in trying to compete with them.[9]

CULLINAN HALL

The second project to confirm the prestige of Miesian architecture in Houston proved even more momentous than the University of St. Thomas. This was the master plan for completing the Museum of Fine Arts, which was produced by Mies van der Rohe in 1954. Hugo Neuhaus's client, Nina Cullinan, presented the museum with funds to build a new gallery for traveling exhibitions. Cullinan required the museum to commission an architect of international stature to design the addition as part of a master plan. The museum's ad hoc building committee—whose members included Neuhaus, Preston Bolton, and Anderson Todd, a young architecture instructor at Rice—recommended Mies.

The first phase of Mies's master plan, Cullinan Hall, opened in October 1958. It was an awesome demonstration of the rigor of his architecture. What it also exhibited, although it was accomplished in such an undemonstrative way that Mies made it seem almost commonsensical, was an abiding regard for maintaining continuity between the new and the existing. Mies's addition extended the original museum's geometry and patterns of circulation, architecturally engaging the history-modernity dialectic with exceptional subtlety and precision.[10]

Mies incorporated an extraordinary, spiritually moving spatial experience in the 30-foot-high, glass-walled interior of Cullinan Hall. With Cullinan Hall, Mies revealed to Houstonians that modernism was not simply an exercise in rejecting the past or imposing obvious systems of constructional and visual order. Rather, it was about creating spaces of discovery with simple means yet profound imagination. Cullinan Hall radically externalized the ideal space of the art museum, which was no longer represented as a temple of art but as an art agora.

As had happened with Philip Johnson and the Menil House, the connections Mies made while working for the Museum of Fine Arts extended his influence in Houston. The effect of working with Mies on Cullinan Hall transformed Anderson Todd into a Miesian architect of exceptional rigor and poetic skill, as the house he completed for his family in 1961 demonstrates. David Haid, a young Canadian architect who worked on Cullinan Hall in Mies's office, came to Houston in 1960 and for two years was a design associate of Hugo Neuhaus, working on such projects as the Letzerich Ranch House near Friendswood and the McAllen State Bank Building in McAllen of 1961.

By the early 1960s, the Miesian modernism that Dominique and John de Menil and Philip Johnson had introduced in 1950 emerged as the representational style of modern Houston. The first high-modern skyscraper in downtown Houston, the First City National Bank Building (Gordon Bunshaft of Skidmore, Owings & Merrill, 1961) projected its Miesian frame 32 stories above Main Street alongside a 30-foot-high glass and aluminum pavilion. The 33-story Tenneco Building of 1963, by Charles Edward Bassett of Skidmore, Owings & Merrill, affirmed in even more rigorous and monumental terms the prestige of Mies's architecture.

Cullinan Hall, Museum of Fine Arts, Houston (Mies van der Rohe with Staub, Rather & Howze, 1958).

AFTER MIES

The modern architecture of Mies van der Rohe was interpreted by Philip Johnson, Skidmore, Owings & Merrill, and Houston's cohort of young Miesian architects represented a protest against the suburbanizing impulse that its advocates saw embodied in Frank Lloyd Wright's architecture and other modern trends current in the early 1950s. Yet as most of the Houston Miesian buildings demonstrate, they too were implicated in this trend. Suburbanization was the dominant theme of American — and Houstonian — city development in the 1950s. No single modern architectural tendency, nor all

of them combined, was capable of arresting what was a pervasive phenomenon. This is what makes the University of St. Thomas so intriguing as a demonstration of a potential Miesian urbanism. Johnson's university campus fit its neighborhood context; it was not totalizing. Preston Bolton's most important project, 5000 Longmont Drive (1961), is another example of Mies's urban potential. Five Thousand Longmont is a street of courtyard houses that shape urban space. The similarity of this street-wall of courtyard houses to Mexican urbanism seems to have encouraged the decoration of façades with framed openings in place of the tectonic rigor and spatial subtlety with which Johnson shaped space at St. Thomas.

The suburbanizing imperative is evident in the vicissitudes of Miesian architecture in Houston in the 1960s. Harwood Taylor and his partner, J. Victor Neuhaus III (Hugo Neuhaus's cousin), developed a more formally assertive architecture out of Miesian design for their early 1960s office buildings in the West Alabama and Richmond Avenue corridors. Wilson, Morris, Crain & Anderson and George Pierce–Abel B. Pierce derived the pavilion organization of their own studio building from Miesian architecture.

These buildings did not explore the full range of tectonic and spatial attributes of Miesian architecture. Since the language of architectural detail that modulated and lent resonance to Houston's Miesian buildings of the 1950s derived from tectonics, the result of this diminution was buildings and spaces that seemed

Brown Pavilion, Museum of Fine Arts, Houston (Office of Ludwig Mies van der Rohe, 1974).

bland or were decorated with materials and shapes meant to add "warmth" and interest. Because of the increasing pervasiveness of systems of pre-engineered building components, curtain walls, partition systems, and ceiling and lighting grids could be ordered from catalogues. As a result, the kind of individual design of architectural components that Keeland and Taylor had produced for the Winchell Studio became the exclusive province of such firms as Skidmore, Owings & Merrill, whose top-of-the-market clients were willing to pay a premium for prestige design.

During the 1960s some Houston architectural firms continued to adhere to Mies's discipline. Anderson Todd's firm, Todd Tackett Lacy, produced such refined buildings as the City of Houston Fire Station 59 on South Post Oak in 1969. Todd's Suit House of 1970 near Rice University is another variation of the courtyard house. Its planar wall engages the curvature of the street in a subtle play, spatializing the curve. Hugo Neuhaus and his partner during the 1960s, Magruder Wingfield Jr., produced such intense designs as the Rice Hotel Laundry near the Houston Ship Channel and a courtyard house in River Oaks for Mr. and Mrs. Louis Letzerich that, like Anderson Todd's Suit House, is an intelligent model for a compact but spacious urban house. Wilson, Morris, Crain & Anderson were responsible for a series of steel-framed demonstration houses off Stella Link and one of Houston's most notable Miesian buildings, the pavilion of the Bank of Houston on Main Street of 1967.

BROWN PAVILION

The last building to be completed to Mies van der Rohe's design was the Brown Pavilion of the Museum of Fine Arts, which opened in 1974, five years after Mies's death. By the time of its completion, 20 years after Mies had proposed it, the Brown Pavilion seemed out of step, especially given the postmodern critique of modernism then in the ascendant.[11] But 25 years

after the Brown Pavilion's completion, it is its virtues that stand out. The rigor of the steel and glass construction of the principal exhibition hall, Upper Brown Gallery, its amazing spatial breadth, and the urbanistic responsiveness of Mies's design to the curvature of Bissonnet Avenue, which the Brown Pavilion faces, seem so obvious that the effort required to integrate these attributes into a single design remains inconspicuous. Mies achieved classic precision in his treatment of the Brown Pavilion's surfaces, but it is the sense of spatial liberation that the Upper Brown Gallery contains, rather than its architectural surfaces, that is the addition's most important characteristic.

MENIL COLLECTION

The extraordinary identification of Miesian architecture with exalted spaces and ingenious tectonics reappeared in Renzo Piano's Menil Collection (1987). Reyner Banham praised the Menil Collection museum, in part, because he saw it as being in the tradition of the Case Study houses in Los Angeles. One need not go as far afield as Los Angeles to see that Piano also paid tribute to the Menil House in his design. The museum's interior proportions, its courtyards, and its elegant linearity are even more fully appreciated when one understands how embedded they are in the vision of modern architecture and culture that took shape at the Menil House.

Architectural reflections of the University of St. Thomas and Mies's additions to the Museum of Fine Arts can also be discerned in Piano's use of encircling ambulatories and exposed steel framing. Like Hugo Neuhaus's early houses, Piano's rigorous architecture contains echoes that resonate with the architectural inclinations of Dominique and John de Menil. The Menils remained true not to a Miesian style but to the essential experiences that Johnson's Miesian architecture of the 1950s embodied. In the Menil Collection, Piano reincarnated those essential experiences because they

Todd House (Anderson Todd and Iris G. Todd, 1994).

HOUSTON SENSIBILITIES INVERTED AND TRANSFORMED

Miesian architecture in Houston represents more than a local chapter in the dissemination of modern architecture in the United States. By virtue of its association with certain personalities and settings, it acquired strong local connotations. It was the patrician style of modernism, which appealed because of its composure, containment, and restraint. In its effort to formalize and stabilize, Miesian architecture in Houston was positioned as a conservative antidote to the spatial dissolution of the suburbanizing city. Yet it concealed a surreal experience of spatial liberation that charged it with an energy that its architectural elements did not expressively portray.

The implicit urbanism of the University of St. Thomas seems to lead to the urbanism of the Menil Collection neighborhood; the Mexican-Miesian urbanism of Preston Bolton's 5000 Longmont suggested the possibility of strong-form, modern urban space based on the courtyard house typology. The attributes of Houston's Miesian buildings — their serenity, amplitude, and what Anderson Todd describes as their "generosity" — represent a set of values that were not characteristic of what Houston was becoming but what it might be. These paradoxical associations culminate in Miesian architecture's dialectical engagement with history, suggesting that Miesian architecture functioned as a critical inversion of mainstream Houston, spatializing a forum for staging alternative presents where value was not restricted to financial calculation and where speculation involved the imagination. It framed the new and offered the possibility of a transformation in awareness and sensibility.

were profoundly relevant to building a public art museum in contemporary Houston. Piano, Mrs. de Menil, Walter Hopps, and Paul Winkler achieved in this building what it seems so difficult to achieve in American architecture, implicated as it is in a cycle of fashion that insists on novelty and change: They developed and clarified an idea with which Mrs. de Menil had become involved 40 years earlier.

The same can be observed of Anderson Todd and of the small courtyard house in Southampton that he and his wife and partner, Iris G. Todd, completed in 1994.[12] Anderson Todd insists that the house's architecture does not represent a Miesian style but a Miesian practice. This involves an exploration of limits in planning and construction, one embedded in the use of a planning module and vertical dimensions based on standardized material lengths. The purpose of this exploration is to achieve a sensation of the illimitable by challenging material limits with the rigorous, inventive resolution of problems of design and building. In this respect, the Todd House reveals what is most compelling about Mies van der Rohe's modern architecture, and about 20th-century modern architecture in general, when it is practiced with conviction and imagination.

Notes

1. Mark A. Hewitt, "Neoclassicism and Modern Architecture—Houston Style," *Cite* 7 (fall 1984), 12–15; Reyner Banham, "In the Neighborhood of Art," Art in America 75 (June 1987), 126–127.

2. James Johnson Sweeney, "Collectors' Home: In the John de Menils' House a Great Ranging Art Collection," *Vogue* 147 (April 1, 1966), 184–191. Frank D. Welch documents Johnson's contribution to Houston's Miesian movement in *Philip Johnson and Texas* (Austin: University of Texas Press, 2000).

3. Kathleen Bland, "Glass House Builder Expands on Ideas," *Houston Post,* January 11, 1950.

4. Peter Blake and Philip C. Johnson, "Architectural Freedom and Order," *Magazine of Art* 41 (October 1948), 228–231: "Architects like Mies van der Rohe believe that they are coming close to creating an objective architecture—a large-scale unhampered environment, whose orderly spaciousness is full of the air and the open freedom necessary for human development."

5. "Roman House," *House + Home* 2 (July 1952), 68–73. The text of the article implicitly contrasted Neuhaus's house to spatial arrangements associated with the contemporary ranch houses, stating, "This house does not ramble, for Neuhaus felt that large rambling plans could easily dissipate themselves in formless confusion." It is intriguing to note that the article ends by observing, "While the special needs and problems of this plan called for a very special solution, architect Neuhaus has demonstrated one way of merging the entirely modern esthetic developed by men like Mies van der Rohe, with the classical formality that gave the Roman house its characteristic elegance. This successful blend of modernity with tradition gives his house a sense of style that has been lacking in much modern work in the past."

6. Report on Meeting of Building Committee with Mr. and Mrs. de Menil, typescript, July 20, 1956, University of St. Thomas Archives.

7. "First Units in the Fabric of a Closed Campus," *Architectural Record* 126 (September 1959), 180. What went without saying because it was so evident at the time was Johnson's dependence on Mies's buildings at the Illinois Institute of Technology in Chicago, especially Alumni Memorial Hall (1946). The University of St. Thomas campus design was Johnson's last undiluted example of Miesian design.

8. Kevin Alter performed a comparative analysis of Ford's and Johnson's architectural articulation of construction in his paper "O'Neil Ford at Trinity University," delivered at the annual meeting of the Society of Architectural Historians, Houston, April 16, 1999.

9. "Two Ways of Looking at Art in Houston: I. The Museum of Fine Arts; II. The Gallery of Fine Arts, University of St. Thomas," *Interiors* 123 (November 1963), 92–98.

10. Celeste Marie Adams, "The Museum of Fine Arts, Houston: An Architectural History, 1924–1986," *Bulletin of The Museum of Fine Arts, Houston* 15, nos. 1 and 2 (1992), 66–96.

11. Peter C. Papademetriou, "Varied Reflections in Houston," *Progressive Architecture* 56 (March 1975), 52–57. When *Progressive Architecture* published Papademetriou's comparative critique of the Brown Pavilion and the Contemporary Arts Museum, the editors treated the article as though it were exclusively about the CAM building, evidence of how passé Mies seemed in the mid-1970s.

12. Frank Welch, "At Home with Anderson Todd," Cite 34 (spring 1996), 48–49.

2002 UPDATE

Many buildings of this modernist period are now threatened or have been demolished. An exception is the Menil House. After the death of Dominique de Menil in 1997, her house was bequeathed to the Menil Foundation. The foundation has confirmed its commitment to the preservation and conservation of the Menil House. *Editors*

Cite 23
FALL
1989

Floating City

CONOCO'S CORPORATE HEADQUARTERS
BY KEVIN ROCHE

William F. Stern

During the recent period of intense building activity in downtown and suburban Houston, an elegant, albeit unassuming, office building joined the ranks of corporate Houston without fanfare. In 1985 Conoco Inc. moved its headquarters toward the city's western edge, leaving a multistory office tower in Greenway Plaza for a series of three-story pavilions set in a park along the Katy Freeway (I-10). Conoco's new 1.2 million-square-foot building was designed by Kevin Roche of Kevin Roche John Dinkeloo Associates, the architectural firm whose reputation was established in the mid-1960s by the Ford Foundation Building in New York City.[1] It is a commentary on our time that Conoco, a building whose design innovatively addresses the requirements of a contemporary working environment, is far less celebrated than the more prominently displayed, stylish tall buildings of Houston.

Conoco is perhaps the best example in Houston of the office campus, a building type that has become popular in the outer limits of America's corporate suburbs. Conoco and its neighbors, Shell, Exxon, and Amoco, are part of a new kind of suburb defined by Robert Fishman in *Bourgeois Utopias* as the "technoburb." The traditional suburb, as found in the 19th- and early-20th-century American city, was an extension of the urban center, a place for living and recreation linked closely to the workplace of the center city. The technoburb, a development of the late 20th century, with its massive shopping malls, housing tracts, and office parks built along the freeways, loops, and interstates that surround the older city, exists independently of the center city. The technoburb is so detached and self-sufficient that its population need never venture to the city center. Because of the concentration of oil-related service companies along this stretch of I-10 near Highway 6, the technoburb around Conoco is known as the Energy Corridor. Conoco's three-story complex, built in a 62-acre park, represents an alternative to the self-contained, multistory office building. Indeed, if Conoco had chosen to build an office tower, its height would almost have equaled that of the 64-story Transco Tower adjoining Houston's Galleria. By moving farther from the center of the city Conoco was able to spread the building components out, making a completely self-contained environment, a workplace in the garden of the technoburb.

In 1979, Roche Dinkeloo Associates was awarded the commission for Conoco Inc.'s Houston headquarters. Using an approach he had developed a few years earlier at the Union Carbide corporate headquarters in Danbury, Connecticut, Roche began by interviewing representative groups of employees from all ranks of

Conoco Building, pavilion over man-made lake (Kevin Roche John Dinkeloo Associates, 1985).

Union Carbide Headquarters, Danbury, Connecticut (Kevin Roche John Dinkeloo Associates, 1982).

morale; moreover, time and money (up to $2 million annually) were consumed in altering offices whenever promotions or personnel shifts occurred.

Employees felt cramped and compartmentalized in the impersonal surroundings of Conoco's high-rise quarters and shut off from the world in its many interior offices. What the employees wanted was an office environment more akin to the living rooms or libraries of their homes. They also expressed a strong preference for covered parking, with easy access to individual offices. Clearly many of these desires could more readily be realized in a building unconstrained by its site, a site that would permit the dispersal of office functions over several acres.

Conoco's white concrete maze of buildings is approached by automobile from the freeway feeder. Although Conoco closely borders the Katy Freeway, it would be easy to drive by and only barely notice the 16 buildings that make up the complex. This is accomplished by Roche's strategic placement of an undulating grass berm, which shields the buildings from the noise and view of the busy interstate. Passing through Conoco's security gates, one is scarcely conscious of the 18-wheelers and Suburbans speeding along eight lanes of freeway only a few yards away. From that moment, one enters the serenity of a lush green park of trees and grass, and of buildings meandering over a still lagoon.

Kevin Roche has for some time been intrigued with the idea of the superhighway as an organizer of and distributor for the great distances to be traveled in

Conoco, plan.

the company. From these interviews he ascertained what was currently unsatisfactory and what employees wanted in the workplace: for instance, they disliked waiting for elevators. He also learned that, as at Union Carbide, disparities in office size and proximity to outside windows fostered jealousy and affected the technoburb. In describing the relationship of the highway to the building at Union Carbide, Roche remarked: "The front door . . . is the act of arrival by automobile. You drive from home on a highway system. You get off the public highway onto a private highway system, which goes straight into the garage, and for an employee is the first act of entry."[2]

At Union Carbide the highway literally enters either side of the building, terminating with parking garages at the center. At Conoco the highway is also terminated by parking, contained this time within two outdoor covered areas for 1,500 cars on the east and west sides of the complex. Roche further extends the metaphor of the superhighway as distributor with an elevated and enclosed second-level pedestrian walkway, nearly a third of a mile long, linking the two employee parking areas. Access from the ground-level parking to the walkway is by escalator. From this main avenue, and on the same level, a secondary system of interior as well as protected outdoor walkways links the adjoining three-story buildings. From both central and secondary distributors the journey to the ground or third levels is only one story. At Conoco, Roche has devised a clear and efficient system of circulation, one that gives employees easy access from the automobile to their offices. Beneath the raised east-west walkway a street for visitor, executive, and service vehicles penetrates the center of the complex, with guest and executive parking under the main building, next to the visitor entrance.

The three-level Conoco complex is composed of 16 buildings arranged in five groups, with an additional service structure at the center. A 60-foot-wide bay with double corridors is the regulating module for each building. In keeping with the employees' desire for views to the outside, offices face outward to the garden; storage, toilets, and service facilities are situated in the middle of the 60-foot bay, between the corridors. Roche also established a standard office size, de-

signing a universal office module of 12 by 16 feet to achieve a more democratic distribution of personnel. The exception is a series of double-module offices for top executives in the central building. Each office is separated from the corridor by a 5-foot-3-inch-high storage wall for files, shelving, and closets, with mullionless glass to the ceiling above the storage wall allowing daylight into the corridors and interior service rooms. In an effort to satisfy individual tastes, employees are given a choice of three basic office styles—traditional, transitional, and contemporary. The drawback of the democratic office, however, is a uniformity that tends to be disorienting and repetitious. This problem

Conoco, two-story atrium connecting three adjoining buildings.

Paul Hester, 1989.

Paul Hester, 1989.

Conoco, pedestrian bridges.

might have been addressed through shifts of interior finishes and decor as well as a bolder selection of art.

Functionally, Conoco's 2,300 employees work in buildings divided between the "upstream" business of exploration and production, occupying the western half of the campus, and the "downstream" business of refining, marketing, and transportation in the east. Between these two, a central service building, larger than a football field, provides executive and visitor parking, third-floor executive offices, basement mechanical services, loading docks, a fitness center, a computer center, employee cafeterias, a credit union, and a travel agency. The multitude of services and amenities was located intentionally in the central building so employees would have little need to leave the grounds during the workday. The overall layout and positioning of building groups surrounding the center was determined compositionally rather than in response to programmatic requirements. The 15 adjoining buildings, arranged in five groups, vary in size from 33,000 to 100,000 square feet. The three buildings of each group form a pinwheel; a pair of two-story atrium spaces at right angles to each other extend from the pinwheel's center.

A single elevator serving the three buildings sits at the juncture of the atrium spaces, but most employees prefer to use the stairs in the naturally lit wells at the ends of the buildings. On each floor, near the stairwell, a conference room pokes out from the building's end with a semi-octagonal glass bay. The three buildings of each grouping define an irregular pattern of outdoor courtyard spaces laced in and around the lagoon.

In discussing the outdoor space, Roche has remarked: "In Conoco . . . we do not have the central community space; instead we turn the idea inside out and create a park into which the whole building is placed. It is a campus and will have the same felicitous effect on the occupants as if they were working in a well-planned university campus."[3] The community space Roche refers to was first introduced in his work at the Ford Foundation and became a prominent element of many designs to follow. In such programmatically diverse buildings as the additions to the Metropolitan Museum in New York City and the corporate headquarters for General Foods in Rye, New York, Roche has used the indoor communal space as a primary organizer. At Conoco, Roche realized the site's potential for year-round green by placing the communal space outside, surrounding an informally designed lake with an indigenous garden of willows, oaks, and pines. Carolina jasmine and fig ivy climb the columns and trellises of the ground-floor arcade. Even though the grounds are easily accessible and are popular for picnicking, walking, jogging, and occasionally fishing, it is from the inside looking out that one most effectively experiences the calm of this idealized landscape.

In making the garden, Roche turned Houston's semitropical climate to his advantage. Going further, he ingeniously adapted the complex of buildings to the extremes of sunlight and heat in Houston. Giving strength and drama to Conoco is an awning system made from a translucent fiberglass sandwich panel supported by an aluminum frame, which projects 13 feet outward from the face of the wall to screen the offices from the relentless summer sun. Controlling levels of natural light and providing protection from the sun has been an ongoing concern in the work of Roche Dinkeloo. The awning canopy that distinguishes the Conoco building was introduced as a screening device in earlier, similar work, most notably at Richardson-Vicks (1974), Kentucky Power Company (1978), and more recently Union Carbide (1982). But the Conoco awning is perhaps the most expressive and developed use of this device. Whereas the awning at Union Car-

Conoco, awning-covered outdoor walkway connects buildings at the second level.

bide projects above each level, Conoco's white, translucent awning extends only from the roof parapet, giving the appearance of a great eave gracefully hovering over and sheltering the structure below. Like the overhanging eaves of a Frank Lloyd Wright Prairie house, the awning draws the building into the landscape. In combination with silver reflective glass, the 13-foot projection adequately screens the east, west, and south façades on the second and third levels. The north face is unscreened, as direct sunlight to this exposure is minimal. To shade the ground level, a ¾-mile elevated outdoor walkway runs beneath the awning, serving also to connect the complex at the second level.

Conoco, covered employee parking.

Responding to the employees' desire for covered parking, the canopy design is repeated for the outdoor parking in what is surely the finest architectural solution in Houston for disguising the endless sea of automobiles and asphalt. From the parking area the canopy climbs over the escalators at either end of the complex, running the length of the second-level central walkway. The expression of the awning is synthesized with the structural expression that defines the character of building at Conoco. Hefty poured-concrete columns support precast concrete beams, framing members, and wall panels and a poured-concrete floor. The translucent white of the awning is reiterated in the milky white of the concrete, rendering a bright cohesiveness against the surrounding garden.

As Houston continues to grow outward, it is likely that the office campus will be a choice for the corporation seeking consolidation of its operations under one roof. Where land values are lower, this building type is a viable alternative as well to the multistory office building. As the technoburb matures, communities with the assets and planning sophistication of the traditional suburb will become increasingly needed. In many ways Conoco points to future possibilities for the workplace and office buildings in the technoburb. Take away the steel security fence that surrounds the Conoco grounds, and one might imagine a series of similar buildings, loosely connected to make an ex-

traordinary landscaped park on the scale of the 18th-century French gardens. Conoco emphatically reaches a new plateau for office design in Houston. Kevin Roche at the Conoco headquarters has dignified the office community by considering and responding to the aspirations of the employees. Moreover, he has intelligently resolved the conflict between the imposition of man-made structure and nature's opposing forces. What was formerly dull, empty land along a noisy freeway is now a peaceful park with a series of handsome structures straddling a lake, within a sculpted landscape of grass and trees.

Notes

1. Kevin Roche and John Dinkeloo had previously been partners in the office of Eero Saarinen & Associates in Bloomfield Hills, Michigan. From 1950 to 1961, the year of Saarinen's premature death at the age of 51, they were closely associated with Saarinen projects. In 1961 Roche and Dinkeloo opened their office in Hamden, Connecticut, outside New Haven. Until his death in 1981, John Dinkeloo was actively involved in all projects. Kevin Roche, principal designer for the firm, has continued the practice under the name Kevin Roche John Dinkeloo Associates.

2. Francesco Dal Co, *Kevin Roche* (New York: Rizzoli, 1985), 64. These remarks are taken from a conversation between Roche and Dal Co that makes up the majority of the text of the monograph.

3. Ibid., 58.

2002 UPDATE

Since the completion of Conoco, the idea of the campus-like office complex has continued to be explored. BMC Software built a series of sleek office towers outside Beltway 8 in the 83-acre City West Place office park, including its corporate headquarters (Keating Mann Jernigan Rotett and Ziegler Cooper, 1993). But unlike Conoco and BMC, the majority of more recent suburban office developments have been speculative without consideration for sensitive land planning.
William F. Stern

Cite 24
SPRING
1990

Diamond in the Round

THE ASTRODOME TURNS 25

Bruce C. Webb

Paul Hester, 1990.

Astrodome, view from the upper stands.

When its turnstiles opened for business in the spring of 1965, the Astrodome seemed like a shrine to all those Texas jokes founded on outrageous hyperbole and insufferable boasting. Hearing its promoters tell it, the Dome was like nothing else on earth; to find suitable comparisons you had to travel to the ancient world, recalling the great (or most colossal) monuments from antiquity.

EIGHTH WORLD WONDER

"Not since the seven wonders of the world has man allowed his imagination to soar, to conceive and to construct such wonder," trumpeted the official press pamphlet, which then went on to equate the Astrodome with the Tomb of Mausolus, the Hanging Gardens of Babylon, and the Colossus of Rhodes. A commemorative booklet sold to the public on opening day put it in the form of a more complicated metaphor, calling the Dome "the Taj

Project for the Paris Opera, perspective (Etienne-Louis Boullée, 1781).

Mahal of all stadia." Anxious letter writers to the local papers, inquiring how the Dome fared when compared with, say, the Colosseum or Piazza San Pietro in Rome (or some other large structure, past or present, in another city), were reassured, usually by the use of the reader's example as a kind of measuring stick to explain just how much space would be left over if it were placed inside the Dome.

Almost overnight, a barely imaginable part of the country took on recognizable form as the Dome quickly became the nation's number three man-made tourist attraction behind the Golden Gate Bridge and Mount Rushmore National Memorial, according to a U.S. Department of Commerce poll of travel agents. And unlike some of its rivals — Walt Disney World (number six) and the Gateway Arch in St. Louis (number seven) — the Dome was a practical idea. Forty-eight thousand people could sit inside on comfortable, theater-style seats to watch a baseball game. In a little less than three hours, a simple realignment of the lower stands (which rotate 35 degrees on motorized steel rails) could reset the stadium for 53,000 football fans. There would also be rodeos, concerts, religious rallies (Billy Graham's 10-day crusade in 1965 attracted a flock of 380,194), demolition derbies, tractor pulls, soccer games, circuses, tennis matches (Billy Jean King defeated Bobby Riggs in "The Battle of the Sexes" in 1973), daredevil exhibitions, prizefights, political rallies, bullfights, basketball games (though not bridge or chess matches), and two feature-length movies — Robert Altman's *Brewster McCloud* (an Icarus-under-glass fable) and *The Bad News Bears in Breaking Training* (the world Little League championship, with fences pulled way in). And all of them taking place in a nearly perfect thermal environment. In the spirit of the air-conditioning mania of the 1960s, when places were being defined in terms of the amount of chilled air pumped into them on a hot day, the Astrodome was the biggest place in town. It also was a curiously appropriate symbol of the city of Houston and its location in the steamy, semitropical Gulf Coast. In the words of Jim Murray, a sportswriter for the *Los Angeles Times*, the Dome was a "monument to the unliveability of East Texas." But maybe Texas's climate wasn't an error in the Grand Scheme of Creation; it was just a bigger challenge to human ingenuity.

The Dome was like some chimerical island plopped down in a vast field on the far south edge of the city, offering a tantalizing glimpse of the brave new world Houstonians were creating for themselves. Although a downtown site had been investigated, it was bypassed in favor of the open prairie (leaving to New Orleans the distinction of being the first American city to install such an extraterrestrial presence alongside downtown). In that first year, the most spirited contest enacted there was a war of lexical attrition between visiting sports scribes from around the country trying to outdo one another in lavishing figures of speech. There was also some journalistic debunking by out-of-town writers who'd had their fill of hearing about the Dome. Jim Murray continued to be unimpressed, even by the

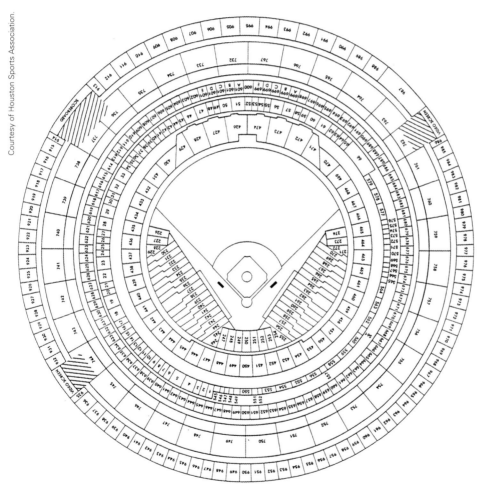

Courtesy of Houston Sports Association.

Astrodome, general plan (Hermon Lloyd and W. B. Morgan and Wilson, Morris, Crain & Anderson, 1960–1965).

Astrodome Ground-blazing, January 3, 1962.

sheer engineering of the Dome: "Hoisting a roof is a theoretical problem well within the reach of the average Purdue sophomore. But Texans being Texans, the problem was keeping it all from blowing away until they had it all tacked down. They told everyone in town to shut up for a day or two until this was accomplished."

COLT .45S

For a city seeking to plant itself in the national consciousness, nothing seems to work so well as acquiring a major-league sports team. A city's participation in professional sports portrays something about the city as a social formation in much the same way a picture postcard of the city's monuments or most splendid views represents the city as a place. Reported on national television and radio and covered on a daily basis in the newspapers, a sports team—how it deports

itself, what it calls itself, where it plays its games, the peculiarities of its fans—presents a distilled picture of the city it represents to the world. In extreme situations (consider Green Bay, Wisconsin) a sports team may be the only thing most people associate with a city.

It is probably one of the great American myths that there is anything even approaching fealty between a sports team and its city. But at some point in their development, most cities seem to feel an acute need for professional sports and set out to do something about it. How else to explain the way Jacksonville, Florida, collectively prostrated itself at the feet of Houston Oilers owner Bud Adams in a bidding war with the Houston Sports Association, the prize being a perennially mediocre NFL franchise? But a city seeking a franchise faces a chicken-and-egg dilemma: the baseball establishment says, "Get a first-class stadium and we'll talk about a team"; the city says, "Give us a team and then we'll build a stadium." Take the case of St. Petersburg, Florida, which is putting the finishing touches on a new, tilted-dome stadium with no tenant but with which the city hopes to lure a Major League baseball team down from the north; or San Antonio, which is engaged in an equally speculative maneuver involving the construction of a domed stadium on its east side.

Houston in the late 1950s was feeling similarly deprived and in need of the reassuring presence of a professional baseball team. When the city made its pitch to the National League's board of directors in 1960, a model of a proposed covered stadium was brought along to propitiate those skeptics who questioned the feasibility of playing in the mosquito-infested heat and humidity of a rainy Gulf Coast summer. When the National League awarded Houston one of two expansion franchises for the 1962 season—the other going to the New York Metropolitans, who were to occupy the Polo Grounds until Shea Stadium could be built—the Houston Sports Association devised a $22 million, tax-supported bond issue, hastily erecting a temporary 33,000-seat stadium next to a rapidly expanding hole in the ground where the Domed Stadium would be built. The name settled on for the new franchise was the Colt .45s, and the team was framed in a Texas-style mixture of Wild West mythology and gun fetishism. Parking-lot attendants at Colt Stadium, attired in orange 10-gallon hats, blue neckerchiefs, and white overalls, directed cars into one of several parking sections, each marked with a sign proclaiming it "Wyatt Earp" or "Matt Dillon" territory, or the domain of some other legendary hero of the television Wild West. Ushers in modish cowgirl outfits were called "Triggerettes," and there was a "Six Shooters Club" for kids. The "Fast Draw Club," a bar designed to look like the Long Branch Saloon of the "Gunsmoke" series, was a members-only club for adults, since Houston's laws at the time forbade serving liquor by the drink except in clubs.

Set against the relatively serene character of baseball's traditional venues, all this manufactured hoop-la captured national attention. But it wasn't ultimately the kind of image you wanted to have working for you when you were trying to build the 21st-century city ahead of schedule.

In the days before cities could set public relations firms to work on their image problems, Nathaniel Hawthorne wrote "all towns should be made capable of purification by fire or decay within each half century." It's an idea that would appear strange to modern Houstonians, who seek to purify their city by building instead. What the Houston Sports Association and its

visionary leader, former mayor and county judge Roy Hofheinz, had in mind was to build a sports stadium so novel and so audacious it would make people forget there ever was an old Houston. (The old Houston had partaken of baseball in Buffalo Stadium, a 12,000-seat outpost of the St. Louis Cardinals on the east side of town.) Hofheinz's sources were practical ones: he formulated the idea for a covered stadium from his experience trying to get an enclosed shopping mall built in 1959 on a site at Weslayan and Bissonnet, coupled with his recollections of a visit to the Colosseum in Rome, which he later discovered had had a velarium, or canopy, that could be erected over the arena to shade and protect it from the elements. A further catalytic ingredient was a series of fruitful meetings with R. Buckminster Fuller, the protean inventor of the geodesic dome. Hofheinz with his impossible dream and Fuller with his bag of impossible solutions were probably made for each other, according to Edgar Ray in his biography of Hofheinz, *The Grand Huckster*.[1] Fuller, who once asserted the cost-effectiveness of covering a sizable portion of New York City with one of his domes, convinced Hofheinz that it was possible to cover a space of any size and control the climate inside, provided you didn't run out of money. That was the kind of challenge that appealed to Hofheinz.

ASTRODOMANIA

During construction of the Dome, Houston was also refashioning its image from "Bayou City" to "Space City," drawing on the recent relocation of the NASA Manned Spacecraft Center to nearby Clear Lake City and the city's association with the Great Society adventure in outer space (even the police department had adopted an orbiting cosmos for its uniform patch, and the local counterculture newspaper appeared under a *Space City* masthead). Hofheinz, not to be included out, decided to capitalize on this new image by changing the name of Houston's team to the Astros.

The stadium, still officially the Harris County Domed Stadium, became known as the Astrodome. (In discarding the old Colt .45 appellation, the Houston Sports Association also rid itself of a sticky problem with the Colt Firearms Company over royalties from profits made on the novelties sold at the stadium that used the name.) When fans arrived at the Domed Stadium for opening day in April 1965, they were treated to a whole new scenario: the female ushers were now "Spacettes" and outfitted in gold lamé miniskirts and blue space boots. "Blast Off Girls" worked the counter at the "Countdown Cafe," and the groundskeepers, wearing specially designed astronaut suits and bubble helmets, were called "Earthmen."

The landscape inside the Dome was a circus world, fusing elements of shopping-center kitsch with modern rationalism. Around the playing field, tiers of seats in five vivid colors terraced up from field level to upper deck under a lattice-and-Lucite sky. In the topmost reaches of the stadium Hofheinz had his designers create a girdle of private Sky Boxes for the elite expense-account crowd. The boxes were like private party rooms in a fantasy hotel, with a ball game going on outside the window some 10 stories below. Each was equipped with bathroom, bar, and television, furnished and decorated in a different motif, and given a name such as "Captain's Cabin," "Imperial Orient," "Spanish Galleon," or "Egyptian Autumn." Out in center field was the famous scoreboard, a 60-by-300-foot mural of electronic pyrotechnics that celebrated the home team's successes and rudely taunted the opposition. Before a computerized Diamond-vision scoreboard was installed in 1983, the Astrodome scoreboard was surprisingly low-tech: like the apparitions created by the Wizard of Oz, many of the displays were produced by a man sitting inside the scoreboard, back-projecting slides (or silhouettes of his own clapping hands) onto a perforated screen to create the illusion that they were produced by exotic electronic technology. But the effect was like combining real live baseball with the responsive persona of an electronic pinball machine: an Astros homer would set off a chain reaction of lighted displays that included charging bulls, fireworks over a lighted Dome, a gun-toting cowboy, and a waving Lone Star flag.

There was usually so much going on in the vast space that it was easy to forget about the Dome itself. Being in the Dome was a condition sensed first by the skin, the thermal delight of leaving an overheated day for the near-perfect conditions inside: 74 degrees, with a slight breeze blowing out of the air-conditioning ducts. The sensation that you were actually inside was momentary; then it slipped just outside of consciousness, returning when, for example, the pall of cigarette smoke that built up inside before the city banned smoking would gather in the upper reaches, then slowly descend, creating atmospheric conditions like Pittsburgh in the 1940s. Or when a well-hit high fly ball would direct the spectators' view upward and set them to wondering if it would hit the lattice framework or that frightening little bridge that crawled along the inner surface of the Dome, connecting to the gondola high above the center of the field.

During that agonizing first year it became apparent that putting the Dome up was a simpler engineering feat than solving some of the problems it created. The Dome design settled on a lamella frame with diamond-shaped bracing, within which 4,596 Lucite skylights were inserted to admit the sunlight needed to nourish the grass on the field. The builders of the Dome might have done well to consult that 18th-century designer of hyper-realities, Etienne Boullée, rather than their engineering manuals. Boullée wrote: "When light enters a temple directly, art is pitted against nature . . . the light is reflected in those places where it falls directly and hurts the eyes."[2] The skylights in the Dome acted like lenses, making the sunlight dazzle the ballplayers when they were tracking down fly balls. Undaunted, Hofheinz had the skylights painted out. But without sunlight, the grass on the field died, a problem solved

Astrodome, interior during construction, 1964.

first by painting the brown stubble green. Then they discovered Astroturf.

ASTROTURF

God only knows what the Monsanto Chemical Company was doing when it concocted this plastic grass — the tactile equivalent of scratch-and-sniff food books or freeze-dried ice cream. Coming like carpet in 15-foot rolls that zipped together to cover the ground, it looked from a distance like a too-perfect, retouched fashion photograph. Up close it had all the pastoral charm of a green Brillo pad — or "concrete with fringe," as it became known to the National Football League players who pitted flesh and bone against its unyielding, prickly surfaces. Carpeting the Astrodome completed the work of creating the artificial world. Soon the stuff was as ubiquitous as kudzu, and every ballpark looked like a billiard table.

Baseball has always lacked the neo-gladiatorial festivity of football, with its nearly nonstop action and a supporting cast of cheerleaders, marching bands, and precision cloneette drill teams to fill in the empty spots. For all the historical appeal and strategic maneuverings of the game, baseball is a comparatively aus-

tere spectator sport, riddled with in-between time, pauses, and endless waiting for something to happen. While a football team is always playing against both the other team and the clock, baseball creates its own time existentially, precisely the kind of game to exist in the temporal limbo of the Dome. To bring it into the television-shortened attention spans of the 1960s and to attract a following for the new and painfully marginal franchise, Hofheinz reconstituted the stadium as a kind of theme park, with the ball game as simply one of its attractions.

But like a fairground after the carnival has gone, the Astrodome today has lost some of the color of the early years, the victim of changing attitudes and economic pressures. As a concession to the Houston Oilers 10,000 seats were added, but then the football team threatened to move to a more capacious stadium with greater revenue-producing potential in Jacksonville. The new seats perfected the arena configuration by filling in the 300-foot gap formerly occupied by the electronic scoreboard and television screen in center field — preempting the cyclopean eye that had invested the green-carpeted Dome with the ambience of an enormous living room. Promises of a new, more spectacular, higher-tech replacement, which included hints of laser displays designed by film impresario George Lucas, have so far proved unfulfilled.

A DOME FOR ALL GAMES

History will probably remember the Dome for another, more insidious achievement: it is a kind of idealized typological harbinger of the modern, multipurpose stadium, roofed or not. It represented a milestone not only in the denaturing of two national sports (to say nothing of the rodeo), but also in the standardization of sports stadiums and a purification of the idiosyncrasies that had distinguished one baseball park from another. Traditional baseball parks were formed by shoehorning the field and stands into a preexisting urban context, with the result that each had its own circumstantial and nearly always asymmetrical configuration. Unlike football, which is played on a field of prescribed dimensions, baseball is played on a field with a strictly regulated infield and an outfield of no fixed dimensions. Of the baseball parks built between 1909 and 1923, only one was perfectly symmetrical, and no two were alike.[3] Students of the game have always been attentive to the subtleties of selecting a lineup and strategies for playing each field. Setting the Astrodome in the center of a wide-open prairie allowed the designers to realize a Platonically multipurpose stadium. But in catering to several tenants, its economies of shape yielded a universal configuration expressive of neither the genius loci nor the genius baseball. Today nearly every stadium subscribes to more or less the same doughnut configuration, creating a situation about which baseball player Richie Hebner confessed: "When I stand at home plate in Philadelphia, I don't honestly know if I'm in Pittsburgh, Cincinnati, St. Louis, or Philly. They all look alike." For spectators the multipurpose ring stadium involves compromises that reduce the immediacy of experience found in single-purpose stadiums, baseball as well as football.

Television has shifted the emphasis of spectator sports from stadium crowds to a vicarious, electronically fed audience. Baseball, with its natural intervals, fits neatly into the commercial scheduling pattern. But football has had to invent artificial gaps — the two-minute warning, commercial time-outs — that interrupt the natural flow of the game and can only be understood in terms of the way television measures time. Spectators often find themselves missing more by seeing the game live than by watching it on television, particularly with the advent of multiple camera angles, instant replays, and interpretive commentaries: hence the odd sight of fans lugging portable television sets into the stadium. Presently more than 500 television monitors are permanently mounted throughout the Astrodome, some of them installed to compensate for impaired sightlines. Television's domination has made the game into a media event staged for the home viewer, and Nielsen ratings count for more than the gate. Perhaps the Astrodome is closest to the final iteration of the stadium, which may well be the non-place realm of the television studio. (Ironically, Channel 13's studios are housed in a pint-sized version of the Astrodome.)

But if the symmetrical, multipurpose, look-alike stadium-in-the-round has become the rule in the latter part of the 20th century, the Dome was still at one point a true and authentic symbol of Houston, portraying in its form and enterprise three of the things for which Houston was becoming known: audacity and entrepreneurship, a suburban concept of space, and air-conditioning. The entrepreneurship was purely a matter of private and individual, rather than civic, will, reinforcing the belief that a good businessman was worth a hundred city politicians when it came to getting something done. The sense of space was not the Renaissance idea of space, considered architecturally integral with buildings. Rather it was space in the exploded, suburban sense of separating things from one another. Beginning on the outside, the Dome sits like a giant oil storage tank, estranged from whatever context it might have had by acres of concentric parking lanes, and tenuously linked with the various satellite enterprises of its domain: exhibit halls, amusement park, hotel. Unlike Boullée's schematic design of 1781 for an ideal opera house surrounded by a circle of heroically scaled columns holding up an exterior ambulatory, the Dome on the outside is pure marketplace technology, presenting the blind face of a shopping center punctuated by giant mechanical air chillers and diminutive entrance pavilions. In a reversal of Leo Marx's "machine in the garden" characterization of early-20th-century domestic architecture, the Dome reserves its paradisiacal pleasures for the inside, using its engineered container to create not architectural space but its suburban equivalent: air.

COLD AIR

It was the air-conditioning that had everyone talking—6,600 tons of it. It was a part of that magnificent Houston vision before the energy crises, when it seemed that the whole city, or at least as much of the city as anyone cared about, would be set under glass and air-conditioned. Even when the place wasn't closed in like the Galleria, the Astrodome's street version, cold air could still be blown around, as it was on the lines of people waiting to get on the rides at the Astro World amusement park next door.

Roland Barthes in his essay on the Eiffel Tower claims the tower to be the absolute embodiment of a monument. "In order to satisfy the oneiric function by which it becomes a monument," Barthes writes, "the tower has to escape reason . . . [It] must become totally and utterly useless."[4] By Barthes's definition the Dome fails entirely to become a monument: its entire *raison d'être* is to be for something. But one might claim for it a special case of momentary monumental-

ity, fulfilling the obligations of irrationality and uselessness for a short time before the original, practical claims of its makers appear fulfilled and the sense of the monumental passes over to a sense of normality. One no longer sees it as extraordinary. One of the more distressing features of life in the latter part of the 20th century is a penchant for disguising extraordinary realities by investing them with fictional contents, leading to the conclusion that most of life is a sham. In the case of the Dome, the inelegance of its "architecture" leads one to conclude that its designers must have considered it to be nearly invisible, or at best merely a circumstance judged solely on the basis of what it did rather than what it looked like. But for a short time there is an overwhelming feeling of the sheer extravagance of effort it takes to make a place that somehow dwarfs the sense of its contents. It appears as a pure phenomenon. As David Brinkley ventured on the evening news when the Dome first opened, "Baseball here is almost incidental." You can still recover the feeling from time to time, especially if you go out there when there's nothing going on and sit in one of the seats, contemplating the vast, perfect emptiness. When the architectural history class at the University of Houston created a series of full-size drawings of a number of classical buildings, the Astrodome was the obvious—perhaps the only—place in the city to hang them, thus bringing into the Dome the "architecture" it otherwise lacks.

If the monumental work is able to transcend its function, it also invites speculation about what else it might have been. While the Dome was still being designed, Hofheinz hit on the idea of making the place double as the world's largest fallout shelter—perhaps fulfilling one of Barthes's criteria through a uselessness of intentions. Hofheinz's motives were more a matter of opportunism than anything else, an attempt to gather eight million federal dollars into his project through the even-then-vestigial Civil Defense program.

The idea prompted the digging of an oversized basement level before it was quashed, apparently by functionaries in the Kennedy Administration seeking to put LBJ in his place.[5] Judge Hofheinz, who built a luxury apartment for himself that included a barber and beauty shop, a medieval chapel, and a circus room behind the right-field wall, prompted University of Houston student David Bucek to create a design that relined the Dome as a mixed-use development for allergy sufferers, answering the question of what to do with the Dome when the fans stop coming to watch another season of the local also-rans.

THE NEXT 25?

The Dome presented itself on opening day in 1965 as an object of self-induced adoration, made manifold through expansive figures of speech. Twenty-five years have made it a more comfortable object. Perhaps still a renegade building, it nonetheless fits comfortably into the Houston scheme. Coming as close to being a symbolic, public place as Houston can manage, it draws the transportable center of the city southward.

Whether it's the Oilers or the Astros, the rodeo or the Rolling Stones, they're playing in the big urban room. Or the Guru Maharaj Ji, who once played the Dome and tried to raise its roof with collective medita-

Paul Hester, 1990.

Rodeo carnival at the Astrodome, 1990.

tion, without result. He put it in a more spiritual metaphor: "The Astrodome is like God. You have to experience them both first-hand."

Notes

1. Edgar W. Ray, *The Grand Huckster* (Memphis: Memphis State University Press, 1980). Ray's book is the most extensive study of the building of the Dome and was an invaluable source for this article.
2. Etienne-Louis Boullée, "Architecture, Essay on Art," in Helen Rosenau, *Boullée and Visionary Architecture* (London: Academy Press, 1967), 94.
3. Philip Bess, *City Baseball Magic: Plain Talk and Uncommon Sense About Cities and Baseball Parks* (Minneapolis: Knothole Press, 1999), 5. This little publication offers an incisive critique of the modern baseball stadium and a glowing eulogy for the traditional urban ballpark. In the final chapter the author proposes a new design for Armour Field, a new ballpark for the Chicago White Sox that seeks to re-create the intimacy and ambience of the early generation of urban ballparks.
4. Roland Barthes, *The Eiffel Tower and Other Mythologies* (New York: Hill and Wang, 1979).
5. Ray, *Grand Huckster*, 273.

2002 UPDATE

After delighting the sports world of the 1960s and exerting considerable influence over the evolution of stadium design, the Astrodome became the stadium nobody wanted. Forsaken by Astros owner Drayton McLane and by the National Football League, both of whom found it inadequate for the profitability of their respective sports, it has been displaced by two new purpose-built venues: Minute Maid Park in downtown Houston and Reliant Stadium next to the Astrodome. The new stadiums both feature retractable roofs.

The Astrodome figured prominently in Houston's recent bid to host the 2012 Olympics, for which it would have been made over into a climate-controlled, indoor location for track and field events. Without the Olympic bid, the Dome faces an unknown future, including the possibility that it might be torn down. For now it continues to eke out an existence hosting the occasional high school game and monster truck event. But its vast interior continues to inspire big ideas. Proposals for resurrecting the Dome have included fitting it with a glass roof to create an arboretum, using it for a history museum, a planetarium, an indoor zoo, a hotel, and even an indoor parking lot. *Bruce C. Webb*

The Astrodome has been the focus of several other *Cite* articles: David Kaplan, "Let it Rain," *Cite* 14 (summer 1986); Drexel Turner "Beamers: The Houston Conventions of 1928 and 1992," *Cite* 29 (fall 1992/winter 1993); Larry Albert, "Last Days of the Dome," *Cite* 55 (fall 2002); Brad Tyer, "How the Astrodome Killed Rock 'n' Roll," *Cite* 55 (fall 2002); and Bruce C. Webb, "Becoming Self-Reliant," *Cite* 55 (fall 2002).

Cite 44
SPRING
1999

Fair or Foul?

Jim Zook

Supporters of the Ballpark at Union Station claim it will hit a home run for downtown Houston. But some people caution it could turn out to be a foul ball.

Regardless of whether you get the close-up view from US-59, the skyline perspective from the inbound lanes of I-10, or merely a glimpse on the horizon from the South Loop, the emerging Ballpark at Union Station is a captivating sight. The steel span that will support the stadium's retractable roof bears the shape and scale of a humpback whale, surging skyward from the depths of the northeast corner of downtown. The concrete underbelly of the stadium is taking shape, a tangible sign that the first pitch will be thrown just a year from now. Amid the constant clang-clang-clang of progress, the army of construction workers and steady stream of onlookers seem to personify Kevin Costner's most famous cliché from the movie *Field of Dreams*— "If you build it, they will come."

For Houston's ballpark, though, Costner's line demands a critical addendum: "When the game's over, will they have reason to stay?" Business leaders sold the ballpark to the community as a sure ticket to economic revival for the east side of downtown—the exact same argument used 15 years earlier to justify building the neighboring George R. Brown Convention Center. Still, though the convention center had failed to deliver on its promise, supporters of the November 1996 stadium referendum insisted the $250 million ballpark would become a hub for a bustling commercial and residential district. "You are a part of something that will change Houston and Harris County," Astros owner Drayton McLane Jr. told a crowd of supporters on election night. McLane's comments marked a dramatic change of heart; only four months earlier he had told the *Houston Chronicle* that a move downtown "could be a big mistake for me."

Setting aside the Astros' prospects on the field, what will be the lasting image of the Ballpark at Union Station in the eyes of Houstonians? Will it be viewed as a major public asset that anchors the rebirth of one of Houston's oldest neighborhoods? Will it trigger growth that extends the loft projects and urban cityscape now emerging around Market Square? Or will it spawn development that ignores the context and replicates the cheap construction all too common in the suburbs? Worse, will it become a financial black hole that funnels millions into the pockets of McLane and his players but offers little added value to the city before and after games?

Any new stadium represents such a massive undertaking that it can be studied on several levels. For now and in the years to come, three issues will merit particular attention—its architectural contribution to the cityscape, its power as an engine for growth and development, and its value as a public asset. Since the picture has yet to be filled in on any of these issues, all of them are ripe for exploration.

One certainty about the Ballpark at Union Station is that it is already a hulking presence that stands to grow even larger. A telltale sign of a modern-day ballpark is the amount of land it consumes when compared to its predecessors, multi-use stadiums such as the Astrodome. The Ballpark at Union Station complex (including the station building) will cover just over 15 acres—59 percent more space than the 9.5-acre Astrodome structure. And when closed, the ballpark's retractable roof will loom 242 feet above the playing surface, 34 feet higher than the Astrodome roof.

Yet the Astrodome seats 12,000 more people for baseball. How can that be? One answer is that all the added amenities demanded from a modern ballpark— the luxury boxes, bigger clubhouses, larger press boxes, a kids' play area, escalators and elevators, the 262-seat Diamond Lounge behind home plate, retail areas, seated restaurants, and the structure that supports the retractable roof—devour a tremendous amount of space. In addition to covering more turf, these features drive up the overall cost of the ballpark considerably.

Part of the ballpark's mega-appearance stems from its location. Where the Astrodome's size is minimized by its position in an ocean of parking in a 260-acre complex, the ballpark's presence is magnified by the density of downtown and the stadium's proximity to the elevated freeway. That sense of bigness is an intentional aspect of the design, says Earl Santee, the ballpark's lead architect with the Kansas City–based firm HOK Sport. "The verticality of downtown Houston, there are some strong influences of that on the ballpark," Santee says. "How the building addresses Texas Avenue is important from an architectural and an

Hester + Hardaway, 1999.

Ballpark at Union Station, retractable roof under construction (HOK Sports Facilities Group, 1999).

urban design standpoint . . . The regional aspects include the use of granites, brick, things that are common to the context of the site. We hope that will make it a good neighbor."

The behemoth of stadium design, HOK Sport's portfolio includes more than 350 athletic facilities, including most of the Major League ballparks built over the last 10 years. The HOK look is captured in the firm's characterization of "ballparks" as different from "stadiums" on its web site—a distinction that hearkens to an era long before Astroturf, the designated hitter, and other modern encroachments that rile baseball purists.

Its ballparks make heavy use of brick, masonry, and neo-traditional design elements to create a nostalgic aesthetic while also serving the ravenous revenue needs of team owners by incorporating skyboxes and amenities for holders of "personal seat licenses" in prime sections of the stadium.

HOK'S WAY
HOK's initial foray into the neo-traditional style of ballpark — Chicago's new Comiskey Park, which opened in 1991 across the street from the site of the 80-year-old

Camden Yards, Baltimore (HOK Sports Facilities Group, 1992).

Coors Field, Denver (HOK Sports Facilities Group, 1995).

Comiskey Park on the city's South Side — was considered a disappointment. Fans and critics blasted the new facility because many seats (particularly in the upper deck) are farther removed from the playing field than they were in the old Comiskey Park, sacrificing much of the intimacy that endeared fans to the turn-of-the-century model. The numbers tell the story: hampered by a mediocre White Sox squad last season, Comiskey's attendance ranked 12th among 14 American League teams.

But in the wake of the Comiskey disaster HOK hit a home run with Baltimore's Camden Yards, which opened in 1992 to national acclaim and triggered the current vogue in retro ballparks. The style has proven wildly successful: last season, teams playing in HOK-designed stadiums in Baltimore and Cleveland boasted the top two attendance figures in the American League, while the top-drawing National League team was the Denver Rockies, playing in HOK-designed Coors Field.

Of course, unlike Chicago's Comiskey Park, the Baltimore and Denver ballparks are both located in popular downtown areas that offer restaurants, bars, and other attractions. That raises the question of whether the ballparks led to the success of their surrounding areas, or whether the success of the surrounding areas fed the success of the ballparks. More to the point, it raises the question of whether retro is the only way to go.

That's particularly pertinent in Houston, a city more known for looking to the future than to the past. Still, Santee maintains that the Ballpark at Union Station is not simply a retread of earlier HOK projects. "In the building that fans will experience, we tried to create an aura of Houston that existed when the station was there," he says. "We created a glass wall and a steel roof structure that has its own image, and it will stand there in reflection of the glass, steel, and the contemporary nature of downtown Houston. There is a contrast there that hopefully will satisfy all the purists."

The selection of HOK as the architects for the Ballpark at Union Station seems to have been motivated by the same thinking that inspired the *Houston Chronicle*'s former advertising slogan—"the biggest newspaper in Texas has to be the best." HOK's past success seems to be the sole criterion used to select the firm—which, courtesy of the Sports Authority's legislative exemption, was done without a public bid process—for one of the most expensive public works projects in the history of Harris County.

When McLane was first clamoring for a new facility, the Astros retained HOK to study possible renovations of the Astrodome, as well as to perform preliminary work for a stadium in northern Virginia, should the team relocate there. By the time the Harris County–Houston Sports Authority took control of the ballpark project in late 1997, McLane had paid more than $3 million in fees to HOK. The Sports Authority reimbursed McLane for those costs, and since McLane's demand for a new facility by the 2000 season made speed crucial, any thought of holding a design competition went out the window.

"In the final analysis, [HOK] was doing enough other stadiums and they had the experience," says Sports Authority Vice Chairman Billy Burge. "The feeling was that we wanted something similar to Camden or Coors with the Union Station façade, and HOK did both of those facilities."

Sports Authority spokesman Chris Begala stresses the economic soundness of the authority's contracts with HOK and the lead contractor, Houston-based Brown & Root. Begala says no other stadium deal in the country stipulates a guaranteed maximum price or a guaranteed completion date. In addition, the retractable roof carries a 10-year guarantee for its design, fabrication, installation, maintenance, and operation. "If it's not on time or under budget, other people will be on the hook rather than the taxpayers," Begala says.

While the contracts offer the public a degree of financial assurance, the sentiments about the stadium design are less inspiring. Regardless of the ultimate success of the Ballpark at Union Station, the failure to consider a range of design schemes is troubling and would never be considered for another public works project of similar importance. Too, the seemingly blind acceptance of the prevailing trend in stadium design shows Houston's leaders to be, in this case, followers. It's a dramatic change from the creation of the Astrodome, which, for all its faults, was a bold idea. The Ballpark at Union Station may turn out to be wildly popular, but it will never be seen as wildly original.

BALLPARK POLITICS

Still, hope runs high among downtown business leaders that the ballpark will pull the boomlet in residential and entertainment development around Market Square several blocks to the east. Competing visions of what constitutes appropriate development, though, have already created problems. And while there has been a spate of speculative real estate transactions in the blocks surrounding the ballpark, no evidence of commercial or residential development is yet visible in the area.

"My sense is that on the real estate development side, the action will come a little slower than most people think," says Bob Eury, president of the Houston Downtown Management District. "Smaller [developers] are going to lead the market. There are big fish out there looking, too, and the big fish may arrive at some point."

The experiences of other cities with new downtown ballparks offer some important lessons to anyone who thinks a ballpark is an economic cure-all for any neighborhood. Denver's Coors Field and Baltimore's Camden Yards gave a modest boost to growth in downtown neighborhoods that were already on the rise, whereas the Ballpark at Union Station sits across a gulf of largely undeveloped property six blocks east of Market Square. Though the Ballpark at Union Station will certainly pump some life into downtown's most desolate area, it could also easily underscore the relative isolation of the neighborhood if property owners decide parking lots make the most economic sense.

"The area has a historic character that we'd like to see preserved, and we'd like the infill development to be compatible with the existing buildings, on a scale and in proportion to those buildings," says Ron Pogue, canon missioner at Christ Church Cathedral and immediate past chairman of the Downtown Historic District. In the blocks immediately north and east of the site, a handful of vintage buildings offers great potential for the sort of lively, pedestrian-oriented entertainment and loft development that is driving growth around Market Square. The Eller Wagon Works building at Franklin and Commerce, the Purse & Co. furniture warehouse at Chenevert and Ruiz, and the old Maxwell House warehouse at Preston and St. Emmanuel are among the fabulous old buildings that offer the potential for authentic renewal.

Still, Pogue and others admit to a sense of uneasiness about the direction that growth may take around the ballpark. The real estate speculation makes it difficult to predict what mix of development will ultimately emerge. In the hope of influencing the nature of that development, the Houston Downtown Management District is seeking legislative approval to expand its boundaries to include everything inside the elevated freeway perimeter. The addition of the ballpark and the adjacent warehouse area north of the site to the management district could provide important services to property owners, while the assessment charged to businesses and property owners operating within the district could serve as a deterrent to cheap development.

Also the first phase of the city's $35 million Cotswold project, which is due to be completed in time for the ballpark's opening day, will add street and sidewalk enhancements—including vintage streetlights and di-agonal, on-street parking—along Texas Avenue from the Theater District to the ballpark. Meanwhile, the Downtown Historic District is writing a set of voluntary development guidelines to encourage development on a scale that encourages pedestrian traffic and fits within a warehouse district. The guidelines will include sections on renovation of existing buildings, design of new structures, and streetscape issues.

And yet, concerns about what may or may not emerge linger. One of the first questions that comes to mind involves Houston's paramount development concern—parking. Some fear the ballpark will become surrounded by parking garages, although market forces make this scenario unlikely. When the ballpark opens, Eury says, an estimated 15,000 parking spaces will exist within a nearby area equal to the size of the Astrodome grounds. Transit services can bring downtown workers from more remote sections. While this plan may seem radical in a city where valets make good money working in strip malls, it follows the lead of Denver and Baltimore, which have relied heavily on pre-existing downtown parking facilities.

A more likely impediment to development is exorbitantly high land prices, says Reggie Bowman, a downtown real estate broker who has negotiated several deals in the area in recent months. Bowman says some prime properties are being held captive by owners who are asking too much, which was a problem that hindered development in Midtown for many years. "The biggest thing that will affect things around the ballpark is whether investor expectations will exceed reality," Bowman says.

An uncertainty that lurks for property owners is the fear of condemnation raised by the recent dust-up over Houston's World Trade Center property. Sports Authority Chairman Jack Rains coveted the property, which sits cater-corner from Union Station at the corner of Texas and Crawford, for a park that would serve as a verdant gateway to the ballpark. However, when its owner, the Port Authority of Houston, put the property up for sale, the Sports Authority chose not to bid on it. After the building was purchased by a group of investors led by Rockets star Hakeem Olajuwon, Rains publicly hinted that he might invoke the Sports Authority's power of eminent domain to wrest control of the prime parcel. Eury, who credits Rains's vision of a park as "trying to do the right thing," says several property owners told him the condemnation threats created at least a short-term chilling effect on development in the area. Rains declined to answer questions on design and development issues around the ballpark, deferring to Santee and Burge.

The Houston World Trade Center dispute, which dragged on in the local media for several months before Mayor Lee Brown weighed in on the side of Olajuwon and the other investors, points to the problems caused by the absence of land use policies. High land prices will serve as a check on certain types of development, but no ordinance exists to prevent such out-of-context development as strip malls or the suburban-style, gated, auto-centric apartment complexes that are consuming large chunks of Midtown. Given that the area in question is a virtual blank slate, the massive public investment in the ballpark would seem to justify special considerations to encourage the kind of development that people seem to want in the area.

"There's no way to ensure that it's done well," says Barry Moore, a University of Houston architecture professor and an author of the historic district's guidelines. "Houston should put in place development guidelines to create a wonderful neighborhood where there isn't one, but I don't think we can do it. The only people who have a stake in it sell the dirt, make millions, and move to New Mexico.

DENVER'S EXPERIENCE

Does it have to be this way? Business leaders in another pro-developer city, Denver, credit limited land use controls around Coors Field as a contributing factor to the rebirth of a downtown neighborhood that is considered a national model. Coors Field sits on the boundary of Denver's Lower Downtown District, known among the locals as LoDo—a bustling collection of renovated warehouses that's home to more than 60 restaurants and nightclubs, 17 art galleries, and more than 1,300 housing units. But barely a decade ago, LoDo resembled the current, rundown condition of the northeast corner of downtown Houston.

The rebirth of LoDo began with the formation of the Lower Downtown District in 1988, three years before the decision was made to build Coors Field. The City of Denver reports that taxable sales in LoDo grew an average of 22 percent per year in the early nineties. Thus, a critical mass of commercial and residential space had taken hold in LoDo before Coors Field opened in 1995. Since then, growth has continued at a slower pace, and it has dispersed over a broader area.

"One of the misnomers about LoDo is that Coors Field made LoDo," says Bill Mosher, president of the Downtown Denver Partnership. Mosher credits an intensive and, at times, contentious series of public hearings on a host of issues—including parking and traffic, economic development, and the look and design of the stadium—with effectively integrating Coors Field into the surrounding neighborhood of low-rise warehouses.

The debate, which was fostered by a series of public hearings hosted by the Mayor's Task Force on Baseball, led Denver to take several unusual steps that were crucial to the project's success. Foremost among them was a moratorium on the creation of parking lots within two blocks of Coors Field. When the ballpark opened, Mosher says, fans grew accustomed to using the 26,000 parking spaces that existed within a 15-minute walk. Only 5,500 parking spaces were added to serve a stadium that holds just over 50,000 spectators.

"At first, we thought that [moratorium] was pretty

Ballpark at Union Station, now Minute Maid Park, under construction.

stupid," Mosher says. "[But] what it did was it took all the fuel out of an overheated market, and let everybody see what was happening. In fact, there was not much demand for parking. That was another thing that was good for the surrounding neighborhood. As a result, there's new housing, new retail, new business development going into that neighborhood."

Denver's experience offers some lessons to Houston, particularly in the aftermath of Rains's heavy-handed attempt to steer development according to his own vision. The type of development that downtown backers hope will emerge around the ballpark is still new to Houston, limited to a handful of projects around Market Square. And the lack of a publicly backed urban design plan for the ballpark area raises a level of uncertainty that may serve to deter investment.

Though Houston Planning Director Bob Litke points to the Cotswold project as evidence of the city's in-volvement, one official involved in the ballpark's development, who spoke on the condition of anonymity, questioned the extent of the benefits that Cotswold will provide. "Cotswold is happening because of [Mayor] Brown, and it is important to the streets around the ballpark," the official says. But, he adds, "Wouldn't it make sense to not just build sidewalks and parking, but to make sure that there's private investment along those streets as well?"

TEST OF TIME

The most remarkable element of the Ballpark at Union Station may come to be the speed with which it is built. Only 18 months after the Sports Authority came into being, construction of the ballpark has reached the halfway mark. The success in staying on schedule to meet the April 2000 deadline set by McLane reflects an impressive rallying of the troops by city leaders. Un-

Ballpark at Union Station, now Minute Maid Park, interior.

fortunately, it also underscores the degree to which owners of pro sports teams now hold their host cities hostage to their financial demands.

The rise of the ballpark is sure to lead to another loss for Houstonians that will be much talked about in the coming year. The Astrodome—the landmark that symbolizes Houston to the world—faces an uphill battle to survive. The contrasting histories of the Dome and the ballpark speak volumes about the times in which they emerged.

As the first-ever domed stadium and the "Eighth Wonder of the World," the Astrodome was a truly Texan creation. It marked the start of the transition of the city's image in the eyes of the nation from a cow town to Space City, even though Judge Roy Hofheinz and his business associates fired pistols at the groundbreaking. As it turned out, the Astrodome is a perfectly awful venue for watching baseball—too cavernous to be a hitter's park, too vast to feel intimate, too synthetic to engender the adoration of the fans. But it was ours.

If the Ballpark at Union Station is anything like Camden Yards, it will be a transformative experience for Astros fans. As a former resident of Washington, D.C., I made regular treks to Baltimore because simply visiting Camden Yards offered as much appeal as the games played there. The return of outdoor baseball to Houston will replace the sterility of the Astrodome with the sweaty, natural aura that makes baseball the national pastime. And yet, Houston will give up a defining piece of itself in the process. Whether the city can muster the vision to replace it with a new destination remains to be seen. Santee appreciates the challenge of replacing an icon. "Is [the Ballpark at Union Station] another eighth wonder of the world?" he asks. "I couldn't tell you. That's a test of time."

Cite 44
SPRING
1999

Deconstructing the Rice

Bruce C. Webb

Of the short stock of historically significant buildings left unclaimed in Houston's downtown at the advent of the current wave of inner-city revivalism, none was more compelling, or a bigger challenge, than the old Rice Hotel. Boarded up in 1977, the substantial building had resisted both demolition and renovation for more than 20 years. Standing vacant with its once-elegant interiors rotting and crumbling, it had become a faded memory of a bygone era as well as a symbol of the flagging fortunes of downtown's north end.

The Rice was the third in a series of three hotels to occupy the prominent site on the corner of Travis and Texas Avenues, where the capitol of the Republic of Texas once stood. The first, a conversion of the old wooden capitol building and cleverly called The Capitol Hotel, was demolished in 1881 and replaced by a second hotel that was bought by William Marsh Rice and renamed the Rice Hotel and, following his death, ceded to the Rice Institute. Jesse H. Jones bought the structure in 1911 and had it razed to make way for the present building, designed by St. Louis architects Mauran, Russell & Crowell. The classically detailed building with red brick facings and terra cotta architectural decorations was constructed in 1913 as twin 17-story tower wings in a C-shaped arrangement; a third tower wing was added by Houston architect Alfred C. Finn in 1925 to form the present E-shaped configuration.

More than any other building of its time, the Rice served as a marker for the aspirations of the emerging city. During its nearly 65 years of operation it sheltered many of the notables who visited the city, and its refined public rooms dignified Houston's social life and high-stakes political wheeling and dealing. But by the 1970s, the Rice had become an antiquated hotel, one badly in need of modernization both to meet Houston's new and more stringent fire codes and to compete with newer hotels such as 1972 Portman-look-alike Hyatt Regency downtown, with its soaring lobby, glass elevators, and revolving Spindletop cocktail lounge.

After passing through the hands of several owners, among them the Houston Endowment (the Jones family foundation), Rice University, and the Rittenhouse Capital Corporation, the failing hotel was sold to Carl Ince and Associates, who operated it for only about four months before closing it for good in 1977. Over the ensuing 20 years, the derelict building was the subject of a number of schemes that would have returned it to service, among them a 1977 proposal to reopen it as an apartment building with 20 percent of its proposed 338 apartments reserved as subsidized housing for low-income families—a plan surprisingly similar to the one put together in the mid-1990s by developer Randall Davis that finally led to the Rice's renovation. But before Davis, the deals somehow never got done. The aging building became more of a liability than an asset, both to its owners and to the city's plans for downtown redevelopment. Slipping deeper into the shadows of the prosperous-looking cluster of downtown office towers to the south, it became a haven for a collection of transients who found the generous awning that surrounds the building a commodious shelter from the elements.

DOWNTURN IN DOWNTOWN

Like many American cities, Houston's attitude about its downtown during the 1970s and 1980s was ambivalent at best. Many of the city's commercial attractions drifted away, lured out to the open spaces in the sub-urbs where the affluent population was settling. Left behind was an expanding cluster of corporate and speculative office towers intermixed with holding sites temporarily outfitted for on-grade parking. Foley's, the lone remaining downtown department store, cut back its operation to only six floors, smaller in square footage than its suburban store at Sharpstown Center. Sakowitz, its upscale competitor across the street, closed, leaving the prominent building to suffer an ignominious future first as a storage warehouse and later as a thinly disguised multilevel parking garage.

Most of the smaller retail shops that once lined the downtown streets also gave up, leaving behind empty storefronts and equally empty sidewalks. Visitors to

Rice Hotel, ca. 1917 (Mauran, Russell & Crowell, 1913).

Houston looking for the nightlife and shopping that conventioneers and tourists crave were usually directed away from the central city. They were frequently told as well to stay off the downtown streets at night.

The action was moving out of town, fueled by the kind of thinking summed up by shopping center magnate Edward DeBartolo in a 1973 article in the *New York Times*: "I wouldn't put a penny in downtown. It's bad. Face it, why should people come in? They don't want the hassle. They don't want the danger . . . So what do you do? Exactly what I'm doing. Stay out in the country. That is the new downtown."

A feeling of desperation about losing their centers altogether propelled cities into modern formats that traded historic identity for new symbols of corporate prosperity. The collaboration between developer capitalism and modern architecture promoted a species of urbanism based on the high-rise office tower, which gobbled up much of the scale and charm of older cities and converted them into nine-to-five workplaces. The more prosperous a city became, the more gobbling it did, and the fewer older buildings were left for anyone who cared.

But modernizing downtown was an incomplete project. By the time it reached the limits of its success, cities still harbored a shadowy ring of places with unabated historic flavor. Although marginalized and left to deteriorate, they still retained a character that couldn't be found in the ubiquitous outward-migrating sprawl, with its endless subdivisions, malls, and strips of fast food chains. Several high-profile downtown revitalization projects, most notably in Cleveland and Baltimore, brought considerable attention to the development potentials of inner-city projects. Both cities plotted strategies to catalyze downtown development by, among other things, constructing new retro baseball stadiums attached to the gritty, 19th-century urban tissue. Seeking to create a sense of place by reinvesting in their histories, these cities began to view the older sections of their downtowns as marketable commodities for attracting people back to the central city.

Unlike Cleveland and Baltimore, though, Houston wasn't built on near-in working-class urban neighborhoods and heavy industry that had bottomed out. As one of the cities that had led the way in creating an impressive modern skyline, Houston had few buildings and little in the way of contiguous block districts left to inspire revitalization. Back-tracking was a short trip and led to places such as the relentlessly dull and obtrusive hull of the Albert Thomas Convention Center, which became vacant when the new George R. Brown Convention Center was completed across town.

Sitting idle for many years, its three-block-long, blank concrete walls providing a dismal background view from the formal window of the Wortham Theater Center's lobby, the Albert Thomas was peddled as Houston's version of a potential Fanueil Hall, eliciting, among other proposals, project Luminiere, the high-tech product of a collaboration between developer Kenneth Schnitzer and visionary film impresario George Lucas. Brought back to life last year as Bayou Place, a 1990s-style pedestrian strip center, it added several restaurants, a concert venue, and a movie house to the downtown repertoire. And despite its still rather ordinary appearance, which decoration of its ungainly concrete hide and massive frame could not effectively disguise, Bayou Place has proven to be a successful addition to the theater district, affirming what many had contended: there was a viable market for nightlife downtown. It was just such a belief that helped set the stage for the resurrection of the Rice.

LIVING DOWNTOWN?

Before fixing his sights on the Rice Hotel, Randall Davis had tested the waters for downtown living with several smaller loft conversion projects, among them the Dakota Lofts, the Tribeca Lofts, and the Hogg Palace Lofts, all of which had met with considerable success. Rescuing an old building and returning it to usefulness is a complicated and risky business. The old building must be brought up to modern health and safety regulations, a task that can require everything from meeting new emergency exit requirements to abating asbestos and other hazardous materials. Often, the entire utility infrastructure — plumbing, heating and air conditioning, electricity — must be replaced, a major expense. Interior finishes, the fragile linings of buildings, suffer from mildew and moisture damage in the humid Houston climate once the air-conditioning is turned off. And carving out new, purpose-built functional spaces within an old structural system can be a challenge, particularly when changing from one kind of occupancy to another. Finally, there is the problem of meeting today's parking requirements. In a badly deteriorated building the size of the Rice, these difficulties proved sufficiently daunting to discourage a number of developers until Randall Davis became interested in the project.

Davis, who is wholeheartedly devoted to the loft concept, has the necessary chutzpah required for tackling difficult problems. Despite his predilection for building intrusive and outsized new apartment and condominium buildings with grotesque architectural decoration (the Gotham, the Metropolis), his treatment of the remodeling of older buildings is considerably more restrained. On his web page he has himself described in expansive terms: "The idea of loft living in downtown Houston has changed dramatically due to Randall Davis, a true urban pioneer. He is part of the downtown rebirth." The page goes on to note that Davis takes care to preserve the historic integrity of each of his loft projects so they can be "nominated to the National Register of Historic Places," which resulted in several awards, among them a Good Brick

Award from the Greater Houston Preservation Alliance.

TAX INCENTIVES

As an inducement to developers, governments, both local and federal, provide incentives for projects that undertake the challenge of preserving and restoring old buildings. Typical is the preservation program sponsored by the National Parks Service, which doles out tax credits to encourage preserving America's historic structures as a part of the nation's heritage. Local governments, too, can create incentive programs or deals, usually in the form of tax abatements, to encourage developers to further civic goals.

In many other American cities, where a project like the Rice would not be considered extraordinary, the use of these strategies is common. For example, over the last two years Philadelphia, stimulated by a 1997 city tax abatement program, abetted a dozen such projects using older buildings to add an additional 1,000 downtown apartments. A January 17, 1999, *New York Times* article reported that although most of these apartments were for standard leasing arrangements, others were being made over into extended-stay corporate apartments for relocating executives and long-term consultants.

Based on a law devised for lower Manhattan, the Philadelphia tax abatement program allows developers to avoid taxes based on the higher values accruing from redevelopment. Portland, Oregon, which has been viewed as something of an urban miracle, has promoted its vision of downtown by using both incentives and disincentives to mandate that buildings have display windows at street level, encourage downtown apartments, and put a cap on downtown parking spaces, thus reducing the impact of large tracts of downtown parking lots and, by encouraging people to use the light rail system, unburdening the vehicular arteries.

Crystal Ballroom, Rice Hotel, 1920s.

Crystal Ballroom, mid-1990s, after initial demolition.

Crystal Ballroom, 1998, following restoration.

Rice Hotel, lobby and mezzanine, 1920s, with Tiffany skylight.

Rice Hotel, lobby and mezzanine, 1998, with mural simulating original Tiffany skylight.

Compared to these programs, Houston's experience in using incentives to achieve planning objectives seems amateurish, particularly with regard to the deal put together for developing the Rice. Both the tax incentives worked out with the National Parks Service and the financing arrangement negotiated with the Houston Housing Finance Authority seemed like ad hoc arrangements developed on the run. Financing and incentives would continue to be a point of contention even as the project moved to completion.

RICE REDUX

The Rice is a near-perfect urban building type. Vertically zoned to accommodate both public and private uses, it fulfills an obligation to create an accommodating pedestrian zone at street level. It works the way buildings worked before the advent of modern high-rises created intensely privatized blocks that eschew visible commercial activities for the anonymity of high-style corporate lobbies and empty, setback plazas.

Davis approached his architects, PageSoutherlandPage, with a general plan to take advantage of some of the features of the building's original organizational framework by providing 25,000 square feet of shops and restaurants on the ground level and apartments from the second through the 14th levels, a plan that would have wiped out the public rooms on the mezzanine.

But during meetings with officials of the Texas State Historical

Commission it was suggested that Davis consider restoring the Crystal Ballroom on the mezzanine level, an idea that the developer took to heart after doing some informal market research that convinced him of the profit potentials of first-rate, leasable party rooms for receptions and meetings. The program was revised not only to incorporate restoration of the Crystal Ballroom, but also to include replication of the original two-story lobby, with its stained glass skylight and paintings, and the Empire Room on the mezzanine level.

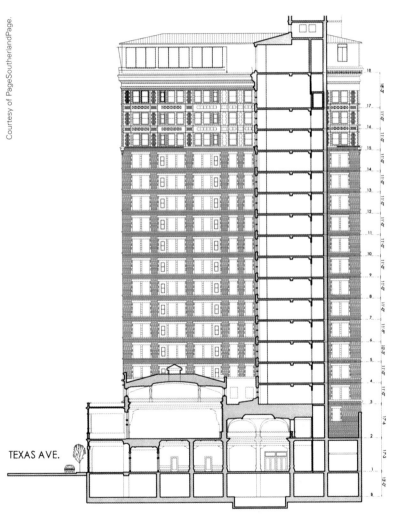

Courtesy of PageSoutherlandPage.

TEXAS AVE.

Rice Hotel, cutaway elevation.

Before: Upper-floor room stripped to bare walls.

After: Same room, post-renovation.

Restoring the lobby and party rooms was a significant urban gesture, giving the building a more or less public zone of showcase quality that serves as both an elegant entrance for tenants and a rich setting for galas, parties, and receptions. In the basement, the architects discovered an old mosaic swimming pool that had been covered over years ago, which Davis had them restore as the centerpiece of a new fitness center.

The decorative cast-iron canopies that surround the building, one of its best features, used to be a common identifying feature of the architecture in the hot, muggy Houston climate and should be a requirement for all new downtown construction if the city is at all serious about being pedestrian-friendly. The generous depth of the canopies, which extend almost to the curb, leaves plenty of room for sidewalk seating outside Sambuca or Mission Burrito. Atop the canopies, an equally generous balcony extends the public rooms of the mezzanine into a veranda overlooking the street.

With so much going for it, it's no wonder that the Rice has become the locus for numerous gala occasions since it was dedicated last fall. In the evening, tenants must frequently work their way through a party crowd in the disproportionately small lobby on the way to the elevators. Rising over this splendid social setting are an array of living units of various sizes and configurations from 500 to 1,500 square feet culminating in luxe two- and three-story penthouse apartments (two of them with their own private courtyards). Within the existing fire exit matrix, the plans for the apartment levels have been generally well conceived, particularly the connecting corridors and elevator lobbies on each floor, which are uncharacteristically generous in width and allowed to amble along the exterior walls, where they enjoy access to window views to the outside.

1,000 ROOMS = 312 APARTMENTS

The 312 rental units themselves show signs of the necessary shoehorning, which creates a considerable amount of marginally useful space as well as a scarcity of windows within. To relieve the claustrophobic feeling of windowless spaces and nominally conform to window requirements for residential construction, many of the floor plans have been treated as one more or less continuous space. In smaller units, windowless bedrooms have been formed into alcoves sometimes located along the procession from entrance to living room. In some of the larger units, this spatial continuity is extended to include a loft that overlooks the living space and borrows light from its exterior windows. In the "terrace lofts," which open onto the canopy veranda on the mezzanine, the single large front window leaves much of the unit in the dark.

By contrast, the bathrooms in these units are awkwardly outsized (Davis did market research with tenants in some of his previous loft conversions and found that bigger bathrooms were high on the wish list) and look like swingers' playgrounds, with showers resembling the gang showers found in a gymnasium.

Still, people attracted to the loft concept expect certain idiosyncrasies and are willing to give up some of the commodity one finds in a newer, purpose-built apartment. This loss of commodity is partially offset by the unique look and feel of individual units, a by-product of the fact that the new apartments are not at all coincidental with the way space was divided up in the Rice's 1,000 hotel rooms.

Since the Rice was constructed using a column and beam system with masonry infill units, the architects at PageSoutherlandPage were able to remove most of the interior partitions and then reconfigure the space into loft apartments. The perimeter walls were stripped back to expose infill tiles and column trusses, which were then left exposed in a manner resembling the older industrial buildings and warehouses where the loft idea was born.

Decorating the apartments through exposing construction materials that lay beneath the aging plaster and leaving behind the large, attractive windows with their beefy wooden frames intact gave each apartment a distinct character. In re-outfitting the building, new utilities were installed on the surface and left exposed—electrical conduits were affixed to the wall, and air-conditioning ducts and sprinkler systems were suspended from the ceiling—a treatment that is both

cost-effective and sympathetic with the loft idea. Interior designers Cynthia Stone and Pamela Kuhl-Libscombe were retained to create four different decor packages (the Lanier, the Jones, the Kennedy, and the Rice), which were matrixed with the various unit types. These decorative treatments are generally successful in supporting the loft theme. However, many of the new accoutrements seem manifestly cheaper and less substantial than the objects salvaged from the original building.

RESTORATION OR RENOVATION?

Late in the construction process, referees from the National Parks Service visited the Rice and decided that the treatment of the apartments was not in keeping with the original character of the building—a decision that could have cost the developers some $4.4 million in federal tax credits. The first point of contention was the rearrangement of the residential floors into a single loaded configuration by relocating the central corridor to the perimeter. The developer/architect team argued that the old corridors, which had been subject to numerous renovations, had little or no historic value, and what remained of it was badly deteriorated. With more than half the units already occupied, the National Parks Service settled on a compromise. The Rice's developers were allowed to keep the new configuration but required to cover the exposed materials in the public corridors, as well as any unoccupied units, with sheetrock to create an ersatz plaster wall look that more closely resembled the hotel's original wall finishes.

A particularly unfortunate result of the agreement was the loss of the hearty, steel-riveted column trusses that, when clad in sheetrock, cease to be markers of the tectonic framework of the building and appear instead as immaterial column boxes. This process of "rehistoricizing" the interior, which includes a provision requiring that units that were rented at the time the agreement was reached be given the same sheetrock treatment once they become vacant, will inexorably move the building from the specific to the general.

An equally tricky issue was the need to provide sufficient adjacent parking for the Rice's new residents. While downtown housing typically discourages car dependency and even car ownership, Houston's less-than-adequate mass transit, coupled with the attachment most Houstonians feel for their cars (particularly since the dearth of downtown shopping means that residents of the central city have to outmigrate for most consumer needs) led the developer to a formula of providing one parking space for each small apartment and two for the larger ones. No guest parking spaces are provided.

Few things are as incompatible with a restoration project as the addition of a sizable parking structure. While a share of the parking could be accommodated underground, economy required that such a structure be built at the rear of the Rice Hotel, where a 1958 annex once stood. A primary prescription for the eight-story structure was that it should screen the cars, which, after exploring a number of unacceptable solutions, the architects did by simply surrounding the lower levels with split concrete block and erecting a mesh screen on the structural frame above. The result is a disappointing disjuncture that disrupts the integrity of the historic block by giving it a front and back dichotomy. The garage is also uncomfortably close to the hotel, giving the units on the lower floors that face onto it a view into an 8-foot-wide gap that is as depressing as the light wells in turn-of-the-century tenements.

Despite its rough edges, the Rice has enjoyed spectacular occupancy rates, with only some 5 percent of the units still unleased as of March, an indication that developer Davis's lofts have captured a niche in the limited expectations of the pre-millennial zeitgeist.

The loft concept that Davis turned into a successful marketing theme has its roots in the warehouse districts of older cities, particularly New York, where an adventuresome soul, often an artist, could find a large chunk of unrefined living and working space at a reasonable price. The loft concept pushes architecture into the background, treating it as a rough container for a citified version of camping out. This kind of loft living has taken hold in a limited way in Houston's north end warehouse district, where a small colony of artists and kindred spirits have created a vigorous market for unclaimed industrial buildings. Davis's lofts are the designer-jeans version of this concept and come at a significantly higher price.

Many of the early tenants of the Rice are self-styled urban pioneers, eager to step aboard a high-profile adventure in downtown living. Along with similarly minded colonizers who will take up residency in the dozen or so other remodeling projects following in the Rice's wake, they are willing to forgo many of the amenities that market researchers have been building into the programs for conventional apartments in order to plug into the downtown theater district and the nascent network of restaurants and bars that is turning the north end of downtown into a closer-set version of Richmond Avenue.

But there is a difference between the pioneers and the colonizers of an idea, and the romance with adventure can be short-lived, a possibility that Davis anticipated when he designed a lease agreement for the Rice that reportedly disallows nearly every tenant complaint about ongoing annoyances and construction inconveniences in the project, problems that have been protracted by the required refinishing of the interior. The tenants themselves have begun to show signs of building a community by organizing a tenants' social group that sponsors meetings and social outings.

ENGAGING THE PUBLIC

On a visit to the Rice on a pleasantly balmy Saturday evening in late February, I found the building teeming with life on both its public levels. Streetside, Sambuca was nearly full with a crowd that looked more like

Revitalized sidewalk café under original cast-iron awning.

tourists from the suburbs than downtown dwellers. Upstairs on the veranda members of a more formally attired crowd in ball gowns and tuxedos were catching a breath and a smoke. A team of parking-lot attendants uniformed in blue T-shirts lined the curb in front of the main entrance. From a distance the Rice looked like an ocean liner preparing to depart on a party cruise.

Venturing inside, however, was not so easy; the place was booked for three different events, and no one without an invitation was allowed to enter. So I walked out into the darkness for a stroll around the Rice block, which has the look and feel of a specimen urban block, though much of it still awaits salvation.

There were other lighted spots. Cabo, across from the back of the Rice, was full, and off in the distance the blue and red lights of Bayou Place beckoned across the darkness. Other companion buildings, the multilevel parking structure across Texas Avenue and the Houston Chronicle Building, except for its pressroom window, were dark. But what caught my eye was a strange light show, a pattern of white dots configured like the holes in a rotary phone dial, projected onto the dark sides of buildings along Main Street, including the upper reaches of the back side of the Rice. It took me a while to find their source, which turned out to be a small, robotic tower mounted on a trailer that someone had set up in a parking lot on across from the Rice in a desperate attempt to light up a little more of the block, suburban style.

In the daylight the downtown enterprise is more apparent, with building activities and heroic construction scratching the sky around the new baseball park — sights that were all but unthinkable except to a handful of downtown romantics only a few years ago. Projects such as the Rice, which has delivered a resident population the size of a small neighborhood on half a city block, and the Ballpark at Union Station, which promises to deliver crowds of 35,000 (and their cars) on game day, have anchored the redevelopment. They have helped create a window of opportunity for downtown that won't come along again soon. Already, land prices in the area have skyrocketed, a precursor of more changes to follow. But as the heavy construction stops and the stock of old buildings available for adaptation dwindles, the district might lose much of its grittiness and perhaps too its ability to stir the imagination.

Seeking to take full possession of the project to renovate the Rice,

Hester + Hardaway, 1998.

Rice Hotel transformed into a loft apartment building (PageSoutherlandPage, 1998).

Randall Davis had a plaque affixed to a wall in the entry foyer that reads: "I went forward as confidently as I could in the direction of my dream to restore the Rice Hotel, standing vacant for 20 years, because how many times do you have the rare opportunity to accomplish something both important and meaningful in your life?"

The same kind of opportunity exists for Houston; it's found in the challenge of guiding and coordinating the continued development of the area to produce something both important and meaningful as a civic enterprise. Even in a poly-nucleated city such as Houston, one with many centers, each seeking to strike its own identity, downtown still retains a privileged status as the location of greatest diversity, concentration, and historic continuity. For its part, the city is proceeding with plans to shape the identity of downtown districts with a package of lighting standards, furnishings, and landscaping. Included in the plans is special articulation of Texas Avenue as a link between the new baseball stadium and the theater district, and the redevelopment of Preston into a link between the stadium and Buffalo Bayou at Sesquicentennial Park.

If the filling-in and rebuilding of the north end disappoints — as it will if what follows is conceived in the franchised terms of the suburbs and the strip — it would be a great loss, greater even than doing nothing but holding out the promise of something better yet to come.

Other *Cite* articles on this subject include: Margie C. Elliott and Charles D. Maynard Jr., "The Rice Hotel," *Cite* 29 (fall 1992 / winter 1993); and Dan Searight, "Urban Glue," *Cite* 42 (summer / fall 1998).

About the Authors

Joel Warren Barna ("Mother of All Freeways" and "Filling the Doughnut") was the first managing editor of *Cite* (1982–1984). He was editor of *Texas Architect* (1986–1995) and was a contributing editor to *Progressive Architecture*. His book *The See-Through Years: Creation and Destruction in Texas Architecture 1981–1991* (Rice University Press, 1992) was chosen the best architectural publication of 1992 by the *New York Times*.

Stephen Fox ("Big Park, Little Plans," "Planning in Houston," "Scraping the Sky," "Howard Barnstone," and "Framing the New") is a fellow of the Anchorage Foundation of Texas. He was a founding editor of *Cite* and continues to be its most prolific writer. His many publications on Houston architecture include *Houston Architectural Guide* (American Institute of Architects, Houston Chapter, 1990) and *Rice University: An Architectural Guide* (Princeton Architectural Press, 2001).

Diane Y. Ghirardo ("Wielding the HACHet") is a professor of architecture at the University of Southern California in Los Angeles, where she teaches architectural history and theory. Her publications include *Architecture after Modernism* (Thames and Hudson, 1996), *Out of Site: A Social Criticism of Architecture* (Bay Press, 1991), and *Building New Communities: New Deal America and Fascist Italy* (Princeton University Press, 1989).

Mark A. Hewitt ("Much Ledoux about Nothing?"), the principal of Mark Alan Hewitt Architects, was assistant professor of architecture at Rice University (1986–1989) before moving to the New York area, where he taught at Columbia University (1986–1989) and the New Jersey Institute of Technology (1990–1997). His books include *Gustav Stickley's Craftsman Farms: The Quest for an Arts and Crafts Utopia* (Syracuse University Press, 2001) and *The Architect and the American Country House 1980–1940* (Yale University Press, 1990).

Richard Ingersoll ("Academic Enclaves" and "Utopia Limited"), who now resides and writes in Montevarchi, Italy, taught at the Rice University School of Architecture from 1990 to 1996. During that time he also served as editor of *Design Book Review* and wrote regularly for *Casabella* and *Arquitectura Viva* as well as *Cite*. His books include *Le Corbusier: A Marriage of Contours* (Princeton Architectural Press, 1989) and, as co-editor, *Streets: Critical Perspectives on Public Space* (University of California Press, 1994).

John Kaliski ("The Wright Stuff") is principal of Urban Studio in Los Angeles and was professor of urban design theory at Southern California Institute of Architecture. From 1982 to 1985 he lived in Houston, where he was on the architecture faculty at the University of Houston.

David Kaplan ("Suburbia Deserta") lives and writes in Houston. He is currently a business reporter for the *Houston Chronicle*.

Phillip Lopate ("Pursuing the Unicorn") is an essayist, novelist, and poet whose books include *Being with Children*, *Bachelorhood*, *Against Joie de Vivre*, *The Rug Merchant*, *Portrait of My Body*, and *The Art of the Personal Essay*. He taught at the University of Houston from 1980 to 1988 and is currently a professor of English at Hofstra University in New York.

Peter Papademetriou ("Loose Fit") is a professor and graduate program director of the New Jersey School of Architecture at the New Jersey Institute of Technology and principal of Peter C. Papademetriou, Architect, in New York City. He served on the architecture faculty at Rice University for 20 years and was the first executive editor of the *Journal of Architectural Education*. While in Houston he authored *Transportation and Urban Development in Houston 1830–1980* (METRO, 1982) and *Houston: An Architectural Guide* (American Institute of Architects, Houston Chapter, 1972).

Barrie Scardino ("H$_2$Ouston"), a Houston resident from 1979 to 1998, is an architectural writer living in New York City. She was a founding editor of *Cite* in 1982 and from 1996 to 1998 was its managing editor. In addition to writing articles and reports on Texas architecture, she co-authored *Houston's Forgotten Heritage* (Rice University Press, 1991) and *Clayton's Galveston* (Texas A&M University Press, 2000).

William F. Stern ("Twombly Gallery" and "Floating City") is a principal with Stern and Bucek Architects in Houston and teaches design and architectural history at the Gerald D. Hines College of Architecture, University of Houston. He was a founding editor of *Cite* in 1982 and has frequently served as chairman of its editorial board.

Drexel Turner ("Neighborhood of Make-Believe") is a city planner who teaches at the Gerald D. Hines College of Architecture, University of Houston, and has been on the *Cite* editorial board since its founding. Turner is co-author of *Clayton's Galveston* (Texas A&M University Press, 2000).

Deborah Velders ("Houston's Indo-Chinatown") is head of exhibitions and public programs at the Menil Collection in Houston. She lived in the heart of Houston's Indo-Chinatown for two years.

Peter Waldman ("Recent Housing in Houston") is associate professor of architecture at the University of Virginia in Charlottesville. He taught at the Rice University School of Architecture from 1981 to 1992.

Bruce C. Webb ("Diamond in the Round," "Deconstructing the Rice," and "Evolving Boulevard") is professor of architecture and former dean of the Gerald D. Hines College of Architecture, University of Houston. He was a founding editor of *Cite* in 1982. Webb is co-editor of three volumes in the Casa series published by Texas A&M University Press: *Constancy and Change in Architecture* (1991), *Urban Forms, Suburban Dreams* (1993), and *The Culture of Silence* (1998).

Jim Zook ("Fair or Foul"), now living in Atlanta, Georgia, is a former reporter for the *Houston Chronicle* and the *Dallas Morning News*. His writing has appeared in *Metropolis*, *Metropolitan Home*, and the *Washington Post*.

Paul Hester, 1990.

Monument au Fantûme at 1100 Louisiana Street in downtown Houston (Jean Dubuffet, 1977).

Index